To my dear friend Edd

With hopes and wishes for the future — for us, our families and our friends. Carpe diem!

Faithfully,

J.

ADVANCES IN NEUROPSYCHIATRY AND PSYCHOPHARMACOLOGY
VOLUME 2

REFRACTORY DEPRESSION

ADVANCES IN NEUROPSYCHIATRY AND PSYCHOPHARMACOLOGY

EDITORIAL BOARD

Ross J. Baldessarini *(Boston, Massachusetts)*
Floyd E. Bloom *(La Jolla, California)*
Benjamin S. Bunney *(New Haven, Connecticut)*
William E. Bunney, Jr. *(Irvine, California)*
Graham D. Burrows *(Melbourne, Australia)*
William T. Carpenter, Jr. *(Baltimore, Maryland)*
Roland D. Ciaranello *(Stanford, California)*
C. Robert Cloninger *(St. Louis, Missouri)*
Alec Coppen *(Epsom, UK)*
Joseph T. Coyle *(Baltimore, Maryland)*
Jeffrey L. Cummings *(Los Angeles, California)*
Kenneth L. Davis *(Bronx, New York)*
Daniel X. Freedman *(Los Angeles, California)*
Jes Gerlach *(Roskilde, Denmark)*
Elliot S. Gershon *(Bethesda, Maryland)*
Frederick K. Goodwin *(Bethesda, Maryland)*
Hans Hippius *(Munich, FRG)*
Philip S. Holzman *(Cambridge, Massachusetts)*
Jerome H. Jaffe *(Baltimore, Maryland)*
David S. Jankowsky *(Chapel Hill, North Carolina)*
John M. Kane *(Glen Oaks, New York)*
Kenneth K. Kidd *(New Haven, Connecticut)*
David J. Kupfer *(Pittsburgh, Pennsylvania)*
Bernard Lerer *(Jerusalem, Israel)*
Herbert Y. Meltzer *(Cleveland, Ohio)*
Julian Mendlewicz *(Brussels, Belgium)*
Charles B. Nemeroff *(Durham, North Carolina)*
Steven M. Paul *(Bethesda, Maryland)*
Elaine K. Perry *(Newcastle Upon Tyne, UK)*
Michael E. Phelps *(Los Angeles, California)*
Robert M. Post *(Bethesda, Maryland)*
S. Charles Schulz *(Cleveland, Ohio)*
B. B. Sethi *(Lucknow, India)*
Solomon H. Snyder *(Baltimore, Maryland)*
Carol A. Tamminga *(Baltimore, Maryland)*
Daniel R. Weinberger *(Washington, DC)*
David de Wied *(Utrecht, The Netherlands)*
Itaru Yamashita *(Sapporo, Japan)*

ADVANCES IN NEUROPSYCHIATRY AND PSYCHOPHARMACOLOGY
VOLUME 2

REFRACTORY DEPRESSION

Editor

Jay D. Amsterdam, M.D.

Department of Psychiatry
Director, Depression Research Unit
University of Pennsylvania School of Medicine
Philadelphia, Pennsylvania

RAVEN PRESS NEW YORK

Raven Press, 1185 Avenue of the Americas, New York, New York 10036

© 1991 by Raven Press, Ltd. All rights reserved. This book is protected by copyright. No part of it may be reproduced, stored in a retrieval system, or transmitted, in any form or by any means, electronic, mechanical, photocopying, recording, or otherwise, without the prior written permission of the publisher.

Made in the United States of America

Library of Congress Cataloging-in-Publication Data
Refractory depression / editor, Jay D. Amsterdam.
    p.   cm.—(Advances in neuropsychiatry and psychopharmacology ; v. 2)
   Includes bibliographical references.
   Includes index.
   ISBN 0-88167-676-4
   1. Depression, Mental—Treatment—Complications and sequelae.
2. Psychotherapy—Failure. 3. Depression, Mental—Chemotherapy.
4. Antidepressants. I. Series.
   [DNLM: 1. Antidepressive Agents—therapeutic use. 2. Depressive Disorders—drug therapy. WM 171 R332]
RC537.R437   1990
616.85′27061—dc20
DNLM/DLC
for Library of Congress   90-9158
                                                                           CIP

   The material contained in this volume was submitted as previously unpublished material, except in the instances in which some of the illustrative material was derived.
   Great care has been taken to maintain the accuracy of the information contained in the volume. However, neither Raven Press nor the editors can be held responsible for errors or for any consequences arising from the use of the information contained herein.
   Materials appearing in this book prepared by individuals as part of their official duties as U.S. Government employees are not covered by the above-mentioned copyright.

9 8 7 6 5 4 3 2 1

Preface

Refractory depression is not a new problem. It characterizes the majority of patients with affective disorders and accounts for a substantial morbidity and a large proportion of suicide attempts and completed suicides. Although we have seen remarkable therapeutic advances in the treatment of affective disorders, patients with resistant depression continue to account for a disproportionate amount of physician treatment time.

In his introductory remarks to the 1973 symposium on therapy-resistant depression (organized by the World Psychiatric Association Section Committee on Pharmacopsychiatry in Basel, Switzerland), Dr. Fritz Freyhan stated:

> The modern treatment of mood disorders belongs to one of the most successful forms of psychiatric therapy. The rapid progression from virtually no treatment to ECT and then to pharmacotherapy during the past three decades may well be regarded as the triumph of clinical empiricism. But [there is a] growing awareness that we must reappraise the problems of therapeutic limitations and failures. It is understandable but hardly defensible that most publications dealing with treatment of depressions have devoted only a minimum of space to therapy-resistant depressions.[1]

Seventeen years later, therapy-resistant depression continues to confound our conventional neurochemical, psychopharmacological and psychodynamic theories and assumptions about affective disorders. As many as 30% of affectively ill patients fail to demonstrate a meaningful response to conventional pharmacological agents or ECT, and many more patients (if not the majority) fail to achieve a complete clinical recovery.

Unfortunately, the paucity of attention given to this ubiquitous syndrome by clinical researchers and the pharmaceutical industry has resulted in inconsistent definitions and unsystematic treatment approaches. In turn, this situation has led to a certain degree of diagnostic confusion and therapeutic nihilism on the part of clinicians and patients alike. In this context, a patient who describes himself or herself as feeling "better" (but not "normal") after drug or ECT therapy is often regarded as either a therapeutic success or in need of continued psychotherapy to treat the remaining psychological symptoms. However, these individuals might also be regarded as suffering from a form of partial therapy-resistant endogenous depression and may represent as many as 60% to 75% of the patients treated with medication or ECT. Moreover, many physicians are not prepared to manage the large numbers of patients who fail to respond to several conventional therapies, and the systematic use of alternative treatment algorithms is rarely applied.

Thus, while the term "refractory depression" may be helpful for identifying certain patient groups for research studies, the clinical applicability of this designation is less certain. For example, one might ask whether treatment-resistant endogenous depression per se really exists? Or is refractory depression merely a function of our limited diagnostic and therapeutic abilities? To what extent should treatment failure be used to classify a patient as "therapy resistant?" Moreover, should depressed patients who cannot tolerate

---

[1] Freyhan FA. Contribution to the definition of therapy-resistant depressions. *Pharmacopsychiatry* 1974;7:70–75.

adverse drug effects or who experience only partial response to treatment be viewed as any less therapy resistant than patients who have only a marginal improvement?

The need to address these compelling questions, as well as a desire to gain a more comprehensive understanding of those factors that contribute to the etiology and successful treatment of resistant depression, eventually led to the present volume.

This book represents the thoughts and current research work of more than 40 internationally renowned researchers in the field of therapy-resistant depression. The chapter topics range from issues of etiology, nosology, and classification to some of the most provocative new strategies for treating this difficult syndrome.

Thus, it is my hope and the hope of each contributor that the information presented in this volume will help our colleagues enhance their clinical knowledge and understanding of factors involved in therapy-resistant depression and use some of the new and unique diagnostic and treatment approaches for helping their patients with refractory depression.

Jay D. Amsterdam, M.D.
Philadelphia, Pennsylvania
June 1990

Acknowledgments

This book was partially supported by an educational grant-in-aid from Marion Merrell Dow Inc., The Jack Warsaw Fund for Research in Biological Psychiatry, and The Depression Research Unit of the University of Pennsylvania School of Medicine.

Contents

1. Methodological Considerations for the Study of Treatment-Resistant Depression 1
   Andrew A. Nierenberg, Paul E. Keck, Jr., Jacqueline Samson, Anthony J. Rothschild, and Alan F. Schatzberg

2. The Neurochemistry of Refractory Depression: A Molecular View on Therapy-Resistant Signal Transfer 13
   Fridolin Sulser

3. Current Hypotheses of the Mechanism of Antidepressant Treatments: Implications for the Treatment of Refractory Depression 23
   Dennis S. Charney, Pedro L. Delgado, Steven M. Southwick, John H. Krystal, Lawrence H. Price, and George R. Heninger

4. Potentiation of Dopamine in the Treatment of Refractory Depression ... 41
   Ossama T. Osman and William Z. Potter

5. Refractory Childhood Depressive Disorders from a Pharmacotherapeutic Perspective 53
   Norman E. Alessi

6. Regional Cerebral Blood Flow in Refractory Depression 65
   Shigeru Morinobu, Katsuo Sagawa, Shinobu Kawakatsu, Shiro Totsuka, Akio Komatani, and Koichi Yamaguchi

7. A Model for Refractory Depression: Cerebral Ventricular Size and CSF Transmitter Metabolite Concentrations in Refractory Depression 71
   H. Standish-Barry

8. Polysomnography in Refractory Depression 81
   Steven P. James, Larry Potter, Neil Berwish, and Jay D. Amsterdam

9. A Trial of ECT Is Essential Before a Diagnosis of Refractory Depression Is Made 87
   Max Fink

10. Selectivity of Antidepressants and Resistant Depression 93
    Stuart A. Montgomery

11. Fluoxetine Enhancement of Heterocyclic Antidepressants 105
    Jesse S. Rosenthal, Malcolm J. Kaswan, Camille Hemlock, and Arnold Winston

12.	Rapid Downregulation of Cerebral β-Adrenoceptors by Combined Treatment with Imipramine and Mianserin .... *René Klysner and Arne Geisler*	109
13.	Combined MAOI-TCA Treatment in Refractory Depression .... *Atul C. Pande, Margaret M. Calarco, and Leon J. Grunhaus*	115
14.	Use of High Dose Tranylcypromine in Resistant Depression .... *Jay D. Amsterdam*	123
15.	Treatment-Resistant Bipolar Affective Disorder: Phenomenological Characteristics, Pathophysiological Mechanisms, and Novel Therapies .... *Richard L. Hauger, Michael R. Irwin, Renee M. Dupont, and Demitri F. Papolos*	131
16.	Anticonvulsants as Adjuncts or Alternatives to Lithium in Refractory Bipolar Illness .... *Robert M. Post*	155
17.	A Review of Psychostimulants in Elderly Patients with Refractory Depression .... *David Gurevitch, Curtis A. Bagne, Eliezer Perl, and Manuel S. Dumlao*	167
18.	Lithium Augmentation for Refractory Depression in Old Age .... *C. L. E. Katona and E. J. L. Finch*	177
19.	Thyroid Hormone Potentiation of Antidepressants........................ *Russell T. Joffe and William Singer*	185
20.	Rapid Cycling Bipolar Disorder: Clinical Features, Treatment, and Etiology .... *Mark S. Bauer and Peter C. Whybrow*	191
21.	Estrogen and Refractory Depression .... *Barbara B. Sherwin*	209
22.	Reserpine Augmentation in Resistant Depression: A Review .... *Joseph Zohar, Zeev Kaplan, and Jay D. Amsterdam*	219
23.	Narcotherapy in Resistant Depressive Patients .... *Rudolf Karazman, Greta Koinig, Gerhard Langer, Georg Schönbeck, Julius Neumark, and Regina Dittrich*	223
24.	The Role of Stereotactic Cingulotomy in the Treatment of Intractable Depression .... *Anthony J. Bouckoms*	233
Subject Index...		243

Contributors

Norman E. Alessi, M.D.
Diagnostic and Research Unit
Childhood Affective Disorders Program
Child and Adolescent Psychiatric Hospital
University of Michigan Medical Center
Ann Arbor, MI 48109-1716

Jay D. Amsterdam, M.D.
Depression Research Unit
Department of Psychiatry
1 Gibson
Hospital of the University of Pennsylvania
Philadelphia, PA 19104

Curtis A. Bagne, Ph.D.
Lafayette Clinic
951 E. Lafayette
Detroit, MI 48207

Mark S. Bauer, M.D.
Affective Disorders Program
Department of Psychiatry
University of Pennsylvania
Philadelphia, PA 19104

Neil Berwish, M.D.
Depression Research Unit
Department of Psychiatry
1 Gibson
Hospital of the University of Pennsylvania
Philadelphia, PA 19104

Anthony J. Bouckoms, M.B.Ch.B.
Warren 6
Department of Psychiatry
Massachusetts General Hospital
Boston, MA 02114

Margaret M. Calarco, R.N., M.S.N., C.S.
Depression Program
Department of Psychiatry
University of Michigan Medical Center
Ann Arbor, MI 48109-0118

Dennis S. Charney, M.D.
Psychiatry Service
West Haven VA Medical Center
West Haven, CT 10516
Clinical Neuroscience Research Unit
Connecticut Mental Health Center
Department of Psychiatry
Yale University School of Medicine
34 Park Avenue
New Haven, CT 16508

Pedro L. Delgado, M.D.
Psychiatry Service
West Haven VA Medical Center
West Haven, CT 06516
Clinical Neuroscience Research Unit
Connecticut Mental Health Center
Department of Psychiatry
Yale University School of Medicine
34 Park Avenue
New Haven, CT 06508

Regina Dittrich, Ph.D.
Department of Psychiatry
University of Vienna
Währinger Gürtel 18-20
A 1090 Vienna
Austria

Manuel S. Dumlao, M.D.
Lafayette Clinic
951 E. Lafayette
Detroit, MI 48207

Renee M. Dupont, M.D.
Department of Psychiatry
University of California, San Diego; And
VA Medical Center
3350 La Jolla Village Drive
San Diego, CA 92161

E. J. L. Finch, M.B.
Unviersity College and Middlesex School of
    Medicine
Whittington Hospital
London, UK

Max Fink, M.D.
Department of Psychiatry and Behavioral
  Science
SUNY at Stony Brook
P.O. Box 457
St. James, NY 11780

Arne Geisler, M.D.
Department of Pharmacology
University of Copenhagen
Juliane Maries Vej 20
DK-2100 Copenhagen
Denmark

Leon J. Grunhaus, M.D.
Depression Program
Department of Psychiatry
University of Michigan Medical Center
Ann Arbor, MI 48109-0118

David Gurevitch, M.D., Ph.D.
Layfayette Clinic
951 E. Lafayette
Detroit, MI 48207

Richard L. Hauger, M.D.
Department of Psychiatry
University of California, San Diego; And
VA Medical Center
3350 La Jolla Village Drive
San Diego, CA 92161

Camille Hemlock, M.D.
Division of Clinical Psychopharmacology
Beth Israel Center
Mount Sinai School of Medicine
New York, NY 10029

George R. Heninger, M.D.
Psychiatry Service
West Haven VA Medical Center
West Haven, CT 06516
Clinical Neuroscience Research Unit
Connecticut Mental Health Center
Department of Psychiatry
Yale University School of Medicine
34 Park Avenue
New Haven, CT 16508

Michael R. Irwin, M.D.
Department of Psychiatry
University of California, San Diego; And
VA Medical Center
3350 La Jolla Village Drive
San Diego, CA 92161

Steven P. James, M.D.
Yorba Hills Medical Plaza
16960 East Chury Road
Yorba Hills, CA 92686

Russell T. Joffe, M.D.
Department of Psychiatry
Clark Institute of Psychiatry
University of Toronto
Ontario, Canada

Zeev Kaplan, M.D.
Beer Sheva Mental Health Center
Ben Gurion University
Beer Sheva, Israel

Rudolf Karazman, M.D.
Department of Psychiatry
University of Vienna
Währinger Gürtel 18-20
A 1090 Vienna
Austria

Malcom J. Kaswan, M.D.
Division of Clinical Psychopharmacology
Beth Israel Center
Mount Sinai School of Medicine
New York, NY

C. L. E. Katona, MRCPsych
University College and Middlesex School of
  Medicine
Whittington Hospital
London, UK

Shinobu Kawakatsu, M.D.
Department of Neuro-Psychiatry
Yamagata University School of Medicine
Iida-Nishi 2-2-2
Yamagata, Japan 990-23

Paul E. Keck, Jr., M.D.
Harvard Medical School
Affective Disorders Program
115 Mill Street
Belmont, MA 02178

René Klysner, M.D.
Department of Pharmacology
University of Copenhagen
Juliane Maries Vej 20
DK-2100 Copenhagen
Denmark

CONTRIBUTORS

Greta Koinig, M.D.
Department of Psychiatry
University of Vienna
Währinger Gürtel 18-20
A 1090 Vienna
Austria

Akio Komatani, M.D.
Department of Radiology
Yamagata University School of Medicine
Iida-Nishi 2-2-2
Yamagata, Japan 990-23

John H. Krystal, M.D.
Psychiatry Service
West Haven VA Medical Center
West Haven, CT 06516
Clinical Neuroscience Research Unit
Connecticut Mental Health Center
Department of Psychiatry
Yale University School of Medicine
34 Park Avenue
New Haven, CT 06508

Gerhard Langer, M.D.
Department of Psychiatry
University of Vienna
Währinger Gürtel 18-20
A 1090 Vienna
Austria

Stuart A. Montgomery, M.D.
St. Mary's Hospital Medical School
London, UK

Shigeru Morinobu, M.D.
Department of Neuro-Psychiatry
Yamagata University School of Medicine
Iida-Nishi 2-2-2
Yamagata, Japan 990-23

Julius Neumark, M.D.
Department of Psychiatry
University of Vienna
Währinger Gürtel 18-20
A 1090 Vienna
Austria

Andrew A. Nierenberg, M.D.
Harvard Medical School
McLean Hospital
Affective Disorders Program
115 Mill Street
Belmont, MA 02178

Ossama T. Osman, M.D.
Section on Clinical Pharmacology
National Institute of Mental Health
Building 10, Room 2D46
9000 Rockville Pike
Bethesda, MD 20892

Atul C. Pande, M.B.B.S., M.D. F.R.C.P.C.
Depression Program
Department of Psychiatry
University of Michigan Medical Center
Ann Arbor, MI 48109-0118

Demitri F. Papolos, M.D.
Department of Psychiatry
Albert Einstein College of Medicine
Montefiore Medical Center
111 East 210 Street
Bronx, NY 10467

Eliezer Perl, M.D.
The Talbieh Hospital
Jerusalem 9110
Israel

Robert M. Post, M.D.
Biological Psychiatry Branch
National Institute of Mental Health
Building 10, Room 3N212
9000 Rockville Pike
Bethesda, MD 20892

Larry Potter, B.A.
Depression Research Unit
Department of Psychiatry
1 Gibson
Hospital of the University of Pennsylvania
Philadelphia, PA 19104

William Z. Potter, M.D., Ph.D.
Section on Clinical Pharmacology
National Institute of Mental Health
Building 10, Room 2D46
9000 Rockville Pike
Bethesda, MD 20892

Lawrence H. Price, M.D.
Psychiatry Service
West Haven VA Medical Center
West Haven, CT 06516
Clinical Neuroscience Research Unit
Connecticut Mental Health Center
Department of Psychiatry
Yale University School of Medicine
34 Park Avenue
New Haven, CT 06508

Jesse S. Rosenthal, M.D.
Division of Clinical Psychopharmacology
Beth Israel Center
Mount Sinai School of Medicine
New York, NY 10029

Anthony J. Rothschild, M.D.
Harvard Medical School
McLean Hospital
Affective Disorders Program
115 Mill Street
Belmont, MA 02178

Katsuo Sagawa, M.D.
Department of Neuro-Psychiatry
Yamagata University School of Medicine
Iida-Nishi 2-2-2
Yamagata, Japan 990-23

Jacqueline Samson, Ph.D.
Harvard Medical School
McLean Hospital
Affective Disorders Program
115 Mill Street
Belmont, MA 02178

Alan F. Schatzberg, M.D.
Harvard Medical School
McLean Hospital
Affective Disorders Program
115 Mill Street
Belmont, MA 02178

George Schönbeck, M.D.
Department of Psychiatry
University of Vienna
Währinger Gürtel 18-20
A 1090 Vienna
Austria

Barbara B. Sherwin, Ph.D.
Departments of Psychology and Obstetrics and
 Gynecology
McGill University
1205 Docteur Penfield Avenue
Montreal, Quebec H3A 1B1
Canada

William Singer, M.D.
Department of Endocrinology
St. Michael's Hospital
The University of Toronto
Ontario
Canada

Steven M. Southwick, M.D.
Psychiatry Service
West Haven VA Medical Center
West Haven, CT 06516
Clinical Neuroscience Research Unit
Connecticut Mental Health Center
Department of Psychiatry
Yale University School of Medicine
34 Park Avenue
New Haven, CT 06508

H. Standish-Barry, MRCPsych
Consultant Psychiatrist
West Park Hospital
Horton Lane
Epsom, Surrey
KT22 7NG UK

Fridolin Sulser, M.D.
Departments of Psychiatry and Pharmacology
Vanderbilt University School of Medicine
Nashville, TN 37232

Shiro Totsuka, M.D.
Department of Neuro-Psychiatry
Yamagata University School of Medicine
Iida-Nishi 2-2-2
Yamagata, Japan 990-23

Peter C. Whybrow, M.D.
Affective Disorders Program
Department of Psychiatry
University of Pennsylvania
Philadelphia, PA 19104

Arnold Winston, M.D.
Division of Clinical Psychopharmacology
Beth Israel Center
Mount Sinai School of Medicine
New York, NY 10029

Koichi Yamaguchi, M.D.
Department of Radiology
Yamagata University School of Medicine
Iida-Nishi 2-2-2
Yamagata, Japan 990-23

Joseph Zohar, M.D.
Beer Sheva Mental Health Center
Ben Gurion University
Beer Sheva, Israel

ADVANCES IN NEUROPSYCHIATRY AND PSYCHOPHARMACOLOGY
VOLUME 2

REFRACTORY DEPRESSION

1

Methodological Considerations for the Study of Treatment-Resistant Depression

Andrew A. Nierenberg, Paul E. Keck, Jr., Jacqueline Samson, Anthony J. Rothschild, and Alan F. Schatzberg

This chapter analyzes methodological problems in the definition and evaluation of treatment approaches to resistant depression (TRD). Specifically, it discusses problems associated with the lack of standardized criteria for type of treatment, adequacy of medication dosage, and duration of treatment, the lack of a standardized method for obtaining treatment histories relevant to the determination of resistance to treatment, difficulties in assessing treatment outcome retrospectively, and the absence of any method to determine prognosis for TRD. We have proposed solutions for overcoming many of these methodological obstacles and present results from a preliminary study of predictors of TRD using a specialized database.

The study of possible predictors of poor response (resistance) to antidepressant medication has received limited attention, even though 10% to 30% of depressed patients fail to respond adequately to these agents (1,2). The lack of clarity concerning the causes of treatment-resistant depression is due, in part, to the lack of operational criteria for defining this condition (3,4). Most investigations of TRD have used ad hoc definitions of treatment resistance with unproven reliability or validity.

This approach has limited severely the generalizability of study results because different definitions of TRD have made it difficult to compare findings. Given these limitations, a more systematic approach to the study of TRD is needed.

A methodical approach must begin with an adequate definition of TRD. Since up to 60% of patients referred for an evaluation of resistance to treatment may have had inadequate trials of antidepressants (5,6), any standard definition of TRD should include criteria for adequacy of prior treatment trials (7,8). Moreover, for maximal integration of research and clinical data, a method for the collection of treatment data is required that is practical for clinicians and useful for researchers. Finally, a definition of treatment resistance should include a range of resistance levels because some patients are more refractory than others (9,10). A rating for the degree of treatment resistance can then be generated along with other relevant clinical variables to stratify cases and assess prognosis. With an acceptable definition of TRD and a method for stratifying cases, empirical studies of causes of resistance can then be performed.

METHODOLOGICAL ISSUES

The methodological issues relevant to TRD can be separated into five categories: definition of TRD, definition of adequate

Affective Disorders Program, Harvard Medical School, McLean Hospital, Belmont, MA 02178.

treatment trial, systematic acquisition of treatment history, assessment of prior therapies, and the formulation of a prognostic index. The following sections review the literature in each of these areas.

Definition of TRD

Freyhan despaired that he could not find a definition for therapy-resistant depression after a great deal of thought (11). In contrast, Ayd suggested that resistance to treatment was defined as either "relative" or "absolute" in nature (12). In this context, relative resistance was defined as failure to respond to one inadequate drug trial, and absolute resistance was defined as failure to respond to an adequate drug treatment regimen. Although a lack of response to an inadequate trial often arises clinically, it does not seem logical to consider a patient resistant if a reasonably adequate trial of treatment has not been given.

Fawcett and Kravitz proposed seven degrees of treatment resistance as a guide for clinicians to choose the next best therapeutic approach (9). Each level was based on duration of illness, type and dose of antidepressant or use of electroconvulsive therapy (ECT), and the use of augmentation procedures, such as the addition of triiodothyronine (T_3) or stimulant drugs. This nosology is difficult to use clinically because the criteria for each level are complex. Many patients meet one criterion but fail to meet another, with the result that the appropriate assigned level is unclear. Schatzberg et al. proposed three levels of treatment resistance (basic/minimal, secondary, and tertiary) based on the number and type of failed adequate treatment trials that would be expected to be effective for different subtypes of depression (melancholic, atypical, and psychotic) (10). For example, patients with psychotic depression would have to fail treatment with an adequate trial of either ECT or a combination of an antidepressant plus a neuroleptic drug to qualify for the minimal level of treatment resistance. This approach appears reasonable, but its prognostic value remains to be verified.

Other proposed definitions of treatment resistance (3,13) include (a) an episode of depression that does not respond to tricyclic antidepressants (TCA), ECT, or monoamine inhibitors (MOAI) (14), (b) an episode of major depression that fails to respond, or sustain a response, to a 4-week trial of therapeutic doses of an antidepressant drug of established efficacy (15), (c) documented failure to respond to either TCAs or MAOIs plus a duration of the episode for at least 2 years (16), and (d) failure to return to premorbid self, inability to leave an inpatient hospital without additional medication or ECT, or necessity for additional psychotropic medication within 1 week of discharge after treatment with either imipramine with plasma levels >200 ng/ml of imipramine plus desipramine or nortriptyline with plasma levels between 50 and 150 ng/ml for 4 weeks (1). Definitions that require a minimum number (e.g., three) and type of failed treatments may exclude patients who have TRD. For example, if a definition of resistance requires a patient to have failed a trial of either a MAOI or ECT, patients who refuse these treatments could not be considered resistant even if they had failed a TCA trial. This limited type of definition seems too restrictive. It is striking that none of these many proposed definitions of TRD have been tested for reliability, validity, or predictive value, nor has any been used by other investigators.

Until more information regarding the prognostic value of number and type of failed antidepressant treatments becomes available, we suggest defining TRD based on the model proposed by Schatzberg et al. (10). In this definition, subjects are considered to be treatment resistant if they have a poor response to any number of adequate antidepressant trials. The number of failed adequate trials of antidepressant treatments will define levels of treatment resistance.

Severity of resistance will range from failure of one antidepressant trial to failure of three or more. The rationale for this is that a range of resistance probably does exist (as reviewed earlier). How should adequacy be defined, however? How can treatment history and response be assessed retrospectively? These questions are addressed in the next sections.

Definition of Adequate Antidepressant Trial

Schatzberg et al. defined an adequate drug trial as reaching two thirds of the maximum recommended medication dose given for a minimum of 3 weeks (6). They did not provide supporting data for this definition. Quitkin concluded that the dose of an adequate trial should reach (a) 300 mg of imipramine daily or its equivalent or (b) a separate trial of up to 90 mg daily of phenelzine or its equivalent (17). Keller et al. documented low levels of treatment received by depressed patients and proposed composite ordinal levels of intensity of treatment for several types of affective disorders without specifying minimal criteria for an adequate trial (5,18,19). Goethe et al. studied the records of unipolar depressed inpatients to assess differences in adequately versus inadequately treated patients, noting an "absence of uniform criteria for adequacy" (8). To compensate for this deficiency, they proposed seven levels of treatment, the highest being 200 mg imipramine or equivalent given for ≥ 4 weeks. Although this scheme was useful to survey treatment adequacy, it did not focus specifically on treatment-resistant patients.

The difficulty of applying the criteria described to TRD is that many patients probably derive benefit from relatively low doses of antidepressants, with or without nominally therapeutic plasma drug levels. Unfortunately, few scientifically adequate studies exist that examine the proportion of patients responding to various dose ranges of TCAs versus placebo. Simpson et al. compared the efficacy of imipramine 150 mg versus 300 mg given daily for 4 weeks in a double-blind study of 51 inpatients with mixed depressive diagnoses (20). These investigators reported that 12 of the 51 patients failed to improve, without specifying the criteria for failure. Ten (33%) of the 29 patients taking 150 mg and 2 (9%) of the 22 patients taking 300 mg of imipramine failed to improve. If 33% of the low-dose group failed to improve, it may be assumed that 67% must have improved while taking only 150 mg of imipramine daily. Therefore, even though the authors reported that 300 mg of imipramine daily produced more improvement in individual items of the Hamilton and Zung depression scales, a substantial proportion of patients responded to 150 mg daily.

Preskorn recommended that adequate plasma levels of TCAs (imipramine or amitriptyline 150–300 ng/ml, desipramine 125–300 ng/ml, and nortriptyline 50–150 ng/ml) given for at least 4 weeks are the sine qua non of an adequate trial (21). His argument is cogent because of the wide variability in plasma levels after equivalent oral doses of TCAs. Nevertheless, this recommendation does not solve the problem of assessing retrospectively the adequacy of antidepressant treatment, either in the absence of plasma levels or for the majority of TCAs for which the definition of optimal plasma levels remains limited or inadequate.

Regarding the minimal duration of an adequate trial, Quitkin found that 27% (25/92) of depressed patients who start taking an antidepressant will fail to respond at 4 weeks but will respond after 6 weeks of treatment (17). Another way to view these data is to note that 40% (25/62) of patients who failed to respond after 4 weeks of a TCA will go on to respond by 6 weeks. Georgotas et al. found that improvement began in elderly depressives only after 4 weeks of treatment with either MAOIs or TCAs (22). Some symptoms of depression may take up to 7 weeks to respond (23), and almost half of 33, of an original group of

100, elderly depressed patients who failed to respond by 7 weeks did respond by 9 weeks (24). Nevertheless, the duration of most reported clinical trials has been less than 6 weeks (17), and in a significant part of the trial duration, insufficient doses may be given, since the amount of medication is started low and gradually adjusted upward.

The type of evidence reviewed here suggests the need for systematic criteria applied to TRD. We propose defining an adequate drug trial by using the dose and duration criteria (Table 1) based on recommendations for high levels of treatment (19) and the minimum duration of an adequate trial (17). Probable and definite adequate drug trials are defined according to dose and duration criteria to include a range of treatments used in general clinical practice.

If only definite adequate trials are used, too many patients with reasonably high levels of treatment would be classified as having inadequate trials. Augmentation of an ongoing antidepressant trial by addition of another drug should be considered as a separate probable trial. The rationale for this is that failure to respond to a 3-week trial of lithium augmentation does not seem clinically equivalent to failure to respond to a full trial of an MAOI or ECT. For example, if a depressed patient had a poor response to desipramine 300 mg daily for 6 weeks and then failed to respond to augmentation therapy with lithium carbonate for 3 additional weeks, that patient would be considered to have failed one and a half drug trials. A 6-week duration is proposed as the criterion for a definite adequate trial be-

TABLE 1. Criteria for adequacy of antidepressant trials

	Definite (1 point) All durations ≥6 weeks except fluoxetine, which is 8 weeks Daily dose	Probable (½ point) All durations ≥4 but <6 weeks except fluoxetine, which is 6 weeks Daily dose
Tricyclics		
Nortriptyline	≥100 mg or plasma levels between 50 and 150 ng/ml	75–99 mg
Maprotiline	≥200 mg	150–199 mg
Protriptyline	≥60 mg	40–59 mg
All others	≥250 mg	200–249 mg
MAO inhibitors		
Phenelzine	≥60 mg	45–59 mg
Isocarboxazide or tranylcypromine	≥40 mg	30–39 mg
Fluoxetine	≥40 mg	20–39 mg
Other agents		
Trazodone	≥300 mg	200–299 mg
Amoxapine	≥300 mg	200–299 mg
Alprazolam	≥4 mg	3.0–3.9 mg
Lithium	Plasma levels 0.7–1.1 meq/L	Plasma levels 0.4–0.69 meq/L
ECT	≥12 total, at least 6 bilateral	9–11 unilateral

Potentiating agents (added to an ongoing antidepressant trial). All durations are 2 weeks except lithium, which is 3 weeks. Only definite adequate criteria are listed, since there is too much uncertainty about probable adequate criteria.

Lithium	Plasma levels 0.7–1.1 mEq/L
Cytomel	25 μg
Synthroid	0.1 mg
D-Amphetamine	10 mg
Methylphenidate	15 mg
Pemoline	37.5 mg
L-Tryptophan	2 g

cause of Quitkin's recommendations (17). Few, if any, patients are given longer trials by most clinicians, especially during hospitalizations that are limited by insurance. We recognize that some of these criteria are open to debate, but we believe that any criteria would provoke controversy, and some standard has to be used to assess adequacy.

Systematic Acquisition of Treatment History

The longitudinal interval follow-up evaluation (LIFE) was developed and used by the NIMH collaborative study on the psychobiology of depression (25). This instrument provides an organized and comprehensive method for recording the retrospective and prospective course of depressive illness as well as the response to treatment. The main advantages of the LIFE assessment is that this instrument has been validated and appears to be especially useful for retrospective assessment of a patient's treatment history (26). The disadvantages are that its use requires special training and it is not readily applicable in a general clinical setting.

Roy-Byrne et al. developed a life chart method to graph the longitudinal course of affective illness and its treatment (27). They solved the problem of how to record previous episodes of affective illness by developing a three-tier system characterizing severity based on "the spirit of RDC [Research Diagnostic Criteria]". In this paradigm, mild depression is defined as subjective distress without impairment of functioning, moderate depression is defined as mood dysregulation consistent with RDC criteria together with signs of impaired social functioning, and severe depression is defined as an affective episode requiring hospitalization or causing incapacitation. Type of medication, dose, and duration of treatments are recorded above the graphic depiction of the course of illness. Portions of this life chart method may be applicable to TRD research.

An order to organize more systematically the raw data with which to assess treatment adequacy and treatment resistance, the McLean Hospital Antidepressant Treatment Record (McATR) (Fig. 1) was developed by the McLean Hospital Treatment Resistant Depression Research Group (A.A. Nierenberg, P.E. Keck, K.L. White, S. McElroy, S.T. Aaronson, and L. Tynes, unpublished observations). In contrast to the systems described previously, McATR can be used easily by clinicians as well as investigators to assess the dose and duration adequacy of antidepressant trials, estimate treatment response, and determine the primary reason treatment was stopped. If adverse effects outweigh therapeutic response, a patient can be considered to be intolerant rather than resistant. Interrater reliability was good among six investigators assessing 10 condensed clinical vignettes for number of failed adequate trials of antidepressants, with an intraclass correlation coefficient of 0.6 in a preliminary study (A.A. Nierenberg, P.E. Keck, K. White, S. McElroy, S.T. Aaronson, L. Tynes, and T. Grady, unpublished observations).

Assessment of Prior Therapies

Since most clinicians do not routinely use the Hamilton Depression Rating Scale (HDRS) (28) or patient-rated Symptom Checklist 90 (SCL-90) (29), as described by Keller and Lavori (7), no standard method exists at present for retrospectively assessing symptom severity or treatment outcome to antidepressant therapy. Previous approaches have included chart review and patient self-report. These methods, however, are limited by the absence of a consistent methodology for rating clinical response, with different clinicians using different definitions of response, missing information, and selective patient recall.

The method developed by Roy-Byrne et al. (27) to estimate retrospectively the global severity of affective symptoms could

PATIENT NAME _____ ID # _____ DATE _____

SOURCE
___ Interview
___ Patient records
___ Pharmacy
___ Family members
___ Physician/Treater

RESPONSE
−3 = Very much worse
−2 = Much worse
−1 = Minimally worse
 0 = No change
+1 = Minimally improved
+2 = Much improved
+3 = Very much improved
 9 = Unknown

PRIMARY REASON STOPPED
0 = Poor response
1 = Relapse (≤2 months)
2 = Recurrence (>2 months)
3 = Adverse event
4 = Mania
5 = Recovered
6 = Other (specify)
9 = Unknown

ADEQUATE TRIAL
0 = No
1 = Probable
2 = Definite
9 = Unknown

DEPRESSION STATE
0 = Euthymic
1 = Mild
2 = Moderate
3 = Severe

REFRACTORY SCORE
0 = Trial successful or inadequate
0.5 = Reason stopped is 0, 1, or 2 and probable trial
1 = Reason stopped is 0, 1, or 2 and definite trial

RELIABILITY
___ Poor
___ Adequate
___ Excellent

Drug name ECT type	Total daily dose (level)[a]	Start mm/dd/yr /stop date	Weeks on Rx	Max amt	Duration max amt	Dep state before/after	Response	Reason stopped	Adequate trial?	Ref Score (see guide)
_____	_____ (__)	__/__/__ __/__/__	_____	_____	_____	___/___	_____	_____	_____	_____
_____	_____ (__)	__/__/__ __/__/__	_____	_____	_____	___/___	_____	_____	_____	_____
_____	_____ (__)	__/__/__ __/__/__	_____	_____	_____	___/___	_____	_____	_____	_____
_____	_____ (__)	__/__/__ __/__/__	_____	_____	_____	___/___	_____	_____	_____	_____
_____	_____ (__)	__/__/__ __/__/__	_____	_____	_____	___/___	_____	_____	_____	_____
_____	_____ (__)	__/__/__ __/__/__	_____	_____	_____	___/___	_____	_____	_____	_____

[a]Include total no. of ECT.

Total refractory score: _____

Rater: _____   Front page _____
                                 + Next page _____

Drug name ECT type	Total daily dose (level)[a]	Start mm/dd/yr	Weeks on Rx /stop date	Max amt	Duration max amt	Dep state before/after	Response	Reason stopped	Adequate trial?	Ref Score (see guide)
_____	_____ (__)	_/_/_	_____	___	___	__/__	___	___	___	___
_____	_____ (__)	_/_/_	_____	___	___	__/__	___	___	___	___
_____	_____ (__)	_/_/_	_____	___	___	__/__	___	___	___	___
_____	_____ (__)	_/_/_	_____	___	___	__/__	___	___	___	___
_____	_____ (__)	_/_/_	_____	___	___	__/__	___	___	___	___

COMMENTS:

Refractory score: Back page _____

FIG. 1. McLean Hospital Antidepressant Treatment Record. (From A.A. Nierenberg, P.E. Keck, K. White, S. McElroy, S.T. Aaronson, and L. Tynes, 1988.)

be used to estimate treatment response in the absence of specific rating scales. Here, we propose that a determination of poor response be made by comparing retrospective estimates of illness severity (27) before and after treatment. Failure to reduce global severity by one category after treatment will define a poor response. A clinical global improvement score of minimally improved or less also can define poor response. If there is a relapse or recurrence while a patient reliably is taking medication, that antidepressant will be considered to have failed at the time of the reappearance of depression regardless of how long the patient has been symptom free. If HDRS scores are available, a poor response can be defined as a decrease in HDRS $\leq 40\%$, and response can be defined as a decrease $\geq 60\%$. The rationale for using these parameters, rather than the standard 50% decrease, is to eliminate the group of patients who might have only a partial response. Several investigators have reported their concerns that a 50% decrease in HDRS scores may overestimate response (30,31). If biological and psychosocial correlates of response and resistance are to be assessed, these two groups should be as clinically different as possible. In this way, possible causes of nonresponse are more likely to be detected.

Formulation of a Prognostic Index

A prognostic index for treatment outcome of psychotherapy in a group of diagnostically heterogeneous patients was developed by Auerbach et al. (32) and verified by Rounsaville et al. (33). These investigators analyzed the prognostic index using multivariable statistical model analyses without specifying the clinical implication of individual prognostic scores. Although predictors of response to antidepressant therapy have long been the subject of intensive research (30), no clinically useful prognostic index for pharmacotherapy of depression or TRD has yet been proposed.

Furthermore, none of the previously proposed definitions of TRD have been tested for prognostic value.

SUMMARY OF PROPOSED SOLUTIONS FOR METHODOLOGICAL PROBLEMS

Given all of the problems in studying TRD, we propose a methodology that accomplishes three goals: (a) developing a definition of treatment resistance, (b) constructing a framework for systematically collecting the data needed to determine the level of treatment resistance, and (c) developing criteria for defining treatment adequacy. In this regard, treatment resistance is defined as a poor response to any number of adequate antidepressant drug trials. Levels of extent of resistance are assessed by identifying the number of previously failed trials, and poor response is defined as failure to reduce global severity of illness by one category. Furthermore, patients intolerant to the side effects of medication are considered to be in a separate, intolerant category. Relevant data concerning the assessment of treatment resistance can thus be collected and organized within the framework of the McATR format. Thus, we have proposed a set of definite and probable adequacy criteria for antidepressant trials.

Preliminary Study

To test the adequacy of the system just described, we used data obtained from the McLean Hospital Depression Research Facility. We used this database because it contained both biochemical and psychosocial aspects of 100 drug-free patients with major depression. We reviewed all available hospital and research records with the McATR to assess retrospective and potential prospective treatment adequacy. If records were unavailable or incomplete, patients were excluded from the database.

All patients were drug free for at least

TABLE 2. Baseline characteristics (n = 20)

Mean age ± SD	34.8 ± 12.0 years
Gender	
Male	9
Female	11
HDRS[a] ± SD	21.5 ± 4.4
Diagnosis	
MD	14
Melancholic	1
Psychotic + melancholic	1
Psychotic	1
Bipolar I	1
Bipolar II	1
Treatment	
TCA alone	7
TCA + Li	1
TCA + AP	1
TCA + AP + Li	1
MAOI	1
MAOI + Li	1
MAOI + AP	1
Fluox	4
Fluox + AP	1
ECT	1
Carb	1

[a]HDRS, Hamilton Depression Scale; MD, major depression without melancholia or psychosis; Melancholic, major depression with melancholia without psychosis; Psychotic, major depression with psychosis without melancholia; TCA, tricyclic antidepressant; Li, lithium carbonate; AP, antipsychotic; MAOI, monamine oxidase inhibitor; Fluox, fluoxetine; ECT, electroconvulsive therapy; Carb, carbamazepine.

2 weeks and were given a standard 1.0 mg dexamethasone suppression test (34, 35). Predexamethasone and postdexamethasone plasma cortisol and catecholamine concentrations and a 24-hour urinary 3-methoxy-4-hydroxyphenylglycol (MHPG) concentration were measured. Patients were diagnosed with the structured interview instrument (SCID) (36). A global severity scale of personality disorder also was assessed, based on the SCID-2, and ranged from 1 (superior functioning) to 7 (grossly impaired). All patients were rated for HDRS score three times during the drug-free baseline period (Table 2).

Since this study used a naturalistic design and was not structured as a clinical trial, the HDRS was repeated 6 weeks after the baseline period regardless of the treatment received. If patients did not receive an adequate antidepressant trial because they could not tolerate the adverse effects of the drug, these patients were classified as intolerant rather than treatment resistant. Furthermore, this pilot study focuses only on those patients classified as treatment resistant to prior therapy. Of the total available sample of 39 patients, we found 20 who met stringent criteria for either treatment resistance or response to a 6-week prospective, adequate drug trial (Table 3) and had sufficient documentation to assess prior history of treatment adequacy and response.

Nineteen patients were excluded because either they had hospital records with insufficient information (n = 6) or they did not have adequate treatment within the fixed 6-week period (n = 13). Records usually were insufficient because of the lack of data about the duration of prior antidepressant drug trials.

Of the 20 patients with sufficient documentation, 14 were considered treatment resistant, and 6 were classified as re-

TABLE 3. Responders vs resistant patients to a prospective 6-week antidepressant trial

	n	Mean refractory level[a]	Age at onset	Post-dex cortisol 8 AM	Post-dex cortisol 4 PM	24-hour urinary MHPG	SCID-2
Resistant	14	1.1	25 ± 14	2.2	3.2	2356	4
Responders	6	1.0	24 ± 10	1.2	3.2	2091	4

[a]Mean refractory levels, number of failed adequate antidepressant trials prior to the prospective 6-week trial; Age at onset, estimate of when depressive symptoms needing medical attention first appeared; Post-dex cortisol, postdexamenthasone plasma cortisol; MHPG, 3-methoxy-4-hydroxyphenylglycol; SCID-2, global severity scale of personality disorder.

sponders within a 6-week therapeutic trial. There were no differences between the therapy-resistant and responsive patients in number of prior failed antidepressant trials, age of illness onset, gender, postdexamethasone plasma cortisol levels, 24-hour urinary MHPG concentration, or SCID-2 global severity scores. When patients were stratified by their degree of treatment resistance based on the number of failed drug trials, there were too few patients within each stratum for differences to approach statistical significance. Nevertheless, the difference in mean ($\pm$ SD) 24-hour urine MHPG concentration was significantly lower in the combined group of responders to the prospective trial plus patients who failed only that antidepressant trial when compared to those patients with two or more treatment failures to adequate trials of antidepressant trial medication (2,072 $\pm$ 736 vs 2,950 $\pm$ 1,083, respectively) ($t = 1.778$, $df = 17$, $p < 0.05$).

The importance of this preliminary study is in the methods applied. We found that routine clinical records contained insufficient data to determine the adequacy of medication dose or treatment duration. Generalizing the results of this study, there is a need to improve standard clinical record keeping of antidepressant treatment history, especially for patients who have a history of TRD. The McATR system is one such method that potentially could help clinicians and researchers in devising more systematic diagnostic and treatment approaches to TRD.

The heterogeneous group of depressed patients with sufficient records revealed that two or more failed adequate antidepressant trials were associated with higher 24-hour urinary MHPG levels. This finding is consistent with previous studies that showed that high urinary MHPG predicted nonresponse to imipramine (37–39). However, other studies using desipramine, maprotiline, and indalpine failed to replicate this interesting observation (40–42). The preliminary results for this naturalistic study are limited by diagnostic and treatment heterogeneity as well as a small sample size. The methods developed to assess TRD retrospectively should be applied to larger, diagnostically homogeneous groups that can be stratified for the number of treatment failures. Prospective, longitudinal studies also are needed to determine the prognostic value of failure to respond to the number and type of antidepressant treatments so that baseline, drug-free biological and psychosocial correlates of TRD can be assessed.

SUMMARY AND CONCLUSIONS

We reviewed methodological difficulties in defining TRD, proposed solutions to these problems, and presented the results of a preliminary study.

No standards exist for the research of TRD. Defining the spectrum of resistance is essential for generalizing clinical and preclinical findings. The McATR, along with the proposed criteria for defining adequacy of antidepressant treatments, could help standardize data collection by both clinicians and researchers and clarify the epidemiology and correlates of resistance. This may lead to more acceptance of research findings by the clinicians who treat the majority of these challenging patients (19).

ACKNOWLEDGMENTS

We gratefully acknowledge the Poitras Charitable Foundation and the Massachusetts Charitable Foundation for their generous support.

REFERENCES

1. Roose SP, Glasman AH, Walsh BT, Woodring S. Tricyclic responders: Phenomenology and treatment. *Am J Psychiatry* 1986;143:345–348.
2. Wagner SG, Klein DF. Drug therapy strategies for treatment-resistant depression. *Psychopharmacol Bull* 1988;24:69–74.

3. Feinberg SS, Halbreich U. The association between definition and reported prevalence of treatment-resistant depression. In: Halbreich U, Feinberg SS, eds. *Psychosocial aspects of nonresponse to antidepressant drugs.* Washington, DC: American Psychiatric Press, 1986;6–34.
4. Leonard BE. Biochemical aspects of therapy-resistant depression. *Br J Psychiatry* 1988;152:453–459.
5. Keller MB, Klerman GL, Lavori PW, Fawcett JA, Coryell W, Endicott JA. Treatment received by depressed patients. *JAMA* 1982;248:1848–1855.
6. Schatzberg AF, Cole JO, Cohen BM, Altesman RI, Sniffin CM. Survey of depressed patients who have failed to respond to treatment. In: Davis JM, Maas JW, eds. *The affective disorders.* Washington, DC: American Psychiatric Press, 1983;73–85.
7. Keller MB, Lavori PW. The adequacy of treating depression. *J Nerve Ment Dis* 1988;176:471–474.
8. Goethe JW, Szarek BL, Cook WL. A comparison of adequately vs inadequately treated depressed patients. *J Nerve Ment Dis* 1988;176:465–470.
9. Fawcett J, Kravitz HM. Treatment refractory depression. In: Schatzberg AF, ed. *Common treatment problems in depression.* Washington, DC: APA Press, 1985;2–27.
10. Schatzberg AF, Cole JO, Elliott GR. Recent views on treatment-resistant depression. In: Halbreich U, Feinberg SS, eds. *Psychosocial aspects of nonresponse to antidepressant drugs.* Washington, DC: American Psychiatric Press, 1986;95–109.
11. Freyhan FA. Contributions to the definition of therapy-resistant depressions. *Pharmacopsychiatry* 1974;7:70–75.
12. Ayd FJ. Treatment-resistant depression. *Int Drug Ther Newsletter* 1983;18:25–27.
13. Prien RF. Somatic treatment of unipolar depressive disorder. In: Francis AJ, Hales RE, eds. *Review of psychiatry,* vol. 7. Washington, DC: American Psychiatric Press, 1988;213–234.
14. Shaw DM. The practical management of affective disorders. *Br J Psychiatry* 1977;130:432–451.
15. Goodman WK, Charney DS. Biological approaches to the treatment of refractory depression. *Yale Psychiatric Q* 1984;summer:5–23.
16. Feigner JP, Herbstein J, Damlouju N. Combined MAOI, TCA, and direct stimulant therapy of treatment resistant depression. *J Clin Psychiatry* 1985;46:206–209.
17. Quitkin FM. The importance of dosing in prescribing antidepressants. *Br J Psychiatry* 1985;147:593–597.
18. Keller MB, Lavori PW, Klerman GL, et al. Low levels and lack of predictors of somatotherapy and psychotherapy received by depressed patients. *Arch Gen Psychiatry* 1986;43:458–466.
19. Keller MB. Undertreatment of major depression. *Psychopharmacol Bull* 1988;24:75–80.
20. Simpson GM, Lee JH, Cuculic Z, Kellner R. Two dosages of imipramine in hospitalized endogenous and neurotic depressives. *Arch Gen Psychiatry* 1976;33:1093–1102.
21. Preskorn SH. Treatment of tricyclic-resistant depression: The role of tricyclic antidepressant plasma level monitoring. In: Extein IL, ed. *Treatment of tricyclic-resistant depression.* Washington, DC: American Psychiatric Press, 1989;3–25.
22. Georgotas A, McCue RE, Hapworth W, et al. Comparative efficacy and safety of MAOIs versus TCAs in treating depressed elderly. *Biol Psychiatry* 1986;21:1115–1166.
23. Georgotas A, McCue RE, Friedman E, Cooper TB. The response of depressive symptoms to nortriptyline, phenelzine, and placebo. *Br J Psychiatry* 1987;151:102–106.
24. Georgotas A, McCue RE, Cooper TB. Factors affecting the delay of antidepressant effect in responders to nortriptyline and phenelzine. *Psychiatry Res* 1989;28:1–9.
25. Keller MB. The longitudinal interval follow-up evaluation: A comprehensive method for assessing outcome in prospective longitudinal studies. *Arch Gen Psychiatry* 1987;44:540–548.
26. Keller MB, Lavori PW, McDonald-Scott P, et al. The reliability of retrospective treatment reports. *Psychiatry Res* 1983;9:81–88.
27. Roy-Byrne P, Post RM, Uhde TW, Porcu TP, David D. The longitudinal course of recurrent affective illness: Life chart data from research patients at NIMH. *Acta Psychiatr Scand* 1985;71(Suppl 317):3–33.
28. Hamilton M. A rating scale for depression. *J Neurol Neurosurg Psychiatry* 1960;23:56–62.
29. Derogatis LR, Lipman RS, Covi L. SCL-90: An outpatient psychiatric rating scale—Preliminary report. *Psychopharmacol Bull* 1973;9:13–25.
30. Joyce PR, Paykel ES. Predictors of drug response in depression. *Arch Gen Psychiatry* 1989;46:89–99.
31. Zimmerman M, Coryell W, Pfohl B. The treatment validity of DSM-III melancholic subtyping. *Psychiatry Res* 1985;16:37–43.
32. Auerbach AH, Luborsky L, Johnson M. Clinician's predictions of outcome of psychotherapy: A trial of a prognostic index. *Am J Psychiatry* 1972;128:64–69.
33. Rounsaville BJ, Weissman MM, Prusoff BA. Psychotherapy of depressed outpatients: Patients and process variables of outcome. *Br J Psychiatry* 1981;138:67–74.
34. Carroll BJ, Feinberg M, Greden JF, et al. A specific laboratory test for the diagnosis of melancholia. Standardization, validation, and clinical utility. *Arch Gen Psychiatry* 1981;38:15–22.
35. Arana GW, Baldessarini RJ, Ornsteen M. The dexamethasone suppression test for diagnosis and prognosis in psychiatry. *Arch Gen Psychiatry* 1985;42:1193–204.
36. Spitzer RL, Williams JBW, Gibbon M, First MB. Structured clinical interview for DSM-III-R. Biometrics Research Department, 1988.
37. Schatzberg AF, Orsulak PJ, Rosenbaum AH, et al. Toward a biochemical classification of depressive disorders. IV. Pretreatment urinary

MHPG levels as predictors of antidepressant response to imipramine. *Comp Psychopharmacol* 1980;4:441–445.
38. Beckmann H, Goodwin FK. Antidepressant response to tricyclics and urinary MHPG in unipolar patients. *Arch Gen Psychiatry* 1975;32:17–21.
39. Cobbin DM, Requin-Blow B, Williams LR, Williams WO. Urinary MHPG levels and tricyclic antidepressant drug selection. *Arch Gen Psychiatry* 1979;36:1111–1115.
40. Veith RC, Bielski RJ, Bloom V, Fawcett JA, Narasimhachari N, Friedel RO. Urinary MHPG excretion and treatment with desipramine or amitriptyline: Prediction of response, effect of treatment and methodological hazards. *J Clin Psychopharmacol* 1983;3:18–27.
41. Muscettola G, Potter WZ, Pickar D, Goodwin FK. Urinary 3-methoxy-4-hydroxyphenylglycol and major affective disorders. *Arch Gen Psychiatry* 1984;41:337–342.
42. Loo H, Benkelfat C, Vanelle JM, et al. Urinary 3-methoxy, 4-hydroxyphenylthylene glycol and therapeutic response to maprotiline and indalpine in major depression. *J Neural Transm* 1986;66:47–58.

2

The Neurochemistry of Refractory Depression: A Molecular View on Therapy-Resistant Signal Transfer

Fridolin Sulser

The emergence of psychotropic drugs in the late 1950s and early 1960s (chlorpromazine, reserpine, MAO inhibitors, imipramine) and studies on their mode of action contributed greatly to our understanding of neuronal function. Whereas the early studies on the mode of action of reserpine and antidepressant drugs focused on acute presynaptic events, elucidating the mechanisms of synthesis, storage, release, metabolism, and reuptake of biogenic amines, discoveries made in the mid-1970s switched the research emphasis to the regulation of receptor systems and adaptive regulatory mechanisms of signal transfer (1). The elucidation of the sequence of events by which extracellular signals generate physiological responses represents one of the primary recent research goals that promise to generate answers on the mode of action of psychotropic drugs on a fundamental molecular level and, in doing so, should generate testable hypotheses on the role of impaired signal transfer in the pathophysiology of affective disorders. It is the aim of this chapter to review briefly recent advances concerning the mode of action of antidepressant treatments and to discuss molecular events in signal transduction that are presumed to be relevant to our understanding of the neurochemistry of refractory depression.

THE SEROTONIN–NOREPINEPHRINE–GLUCOCORTICOID LINK SYSTEM AS A TARGET OF ANTIDEPRESSANT TREATMENTS

A wealth of psychopharmacological studies as well as the morphological organization of central monoamine systems (2) have suggested a functional linkage of noradrenergic and serotonergic neurons. Studies with antidepressants, administered on a clinically relevant time basis, have generated additional strong support for such an aminergic link. Chronic administration of antidepressants, including electroconvulsive therapy (ECT), causes a desensitization of the norepinephrine (NE) β-adrenoceptor-coupled adenylate cyclase system (3), linked in most cases to a downregulation of the β-adrenoceptor density (4). The delayed desensitization of the β-adrenoceptor system in brain seems to be a biochemical action that is shared by most if not all clinically effective antidepressant treatments (Table 1). Adaptive changes in serotonin$_2$ (5HT$_2$) receptors linked to phosphatidylinositol hydrolysis also have been reported following chronic treatment with antidepressants (5), although downregulation of 5HT$_2$ receptors is not common to all antidepressant treatments. For example, ECT, one of the most

Departments of Psychiatry and Pharmacology, Vanderbilt University School of Medicine, Nashville, TN 37232.

TABLE 1. *Antidepressant treatments that cause subsensitivity of the NE-sensitive adenylate cyclase and/or downregulate the number of β-adrenoceptors*

1. Drugs that block uptake of NE
   Desipramine, Nortriptyline, Maprotiline, Oxaprotiline
2. Drugs that block more selectively uptake of 5HT
   Zimelidine, Fluvoxamin, Sertraline, Fluoxetine
3. Drugs that block uptake of NE and 5HT
   Imipramine, Amitriptyline, Chlorimipramine, Triflucarbine (γ-carboline derivative)
4. Drugs that block MAO
   Pargyline, Nialamid, Tranylcypromine; Clorgyline and Moclobemide (MAOA)
5. Drugs that do not block uptake of either NE or 5HT
   Iprindole, Mianserin, Clenbuterol; Rolipram, Progabide, Fengabine (GABA B); Bupropion; Trazodone
6. Nondrug treatments
   Electroconvulsive treatment (ECT), REM sleep deprivation

Computed from the literature as of 5/25/90.

efficacious treatments of depression, is upregulating not downregulating the density of $5HT_2$ receptors (6). Unlike the remarkable pharmacological specificity observed in the β-adrenoceptor system, $5HT_2$ receptors are downregulated by drugs with no clinical antidepressant activity (7). Studies on the mechanism of the antidepressant-induced desensitization of the central β-adrenoceptor-linked adenylate cyclase system have shown that NE and 5HT are corequired for the downregulation of β-adrenoceptors (8–17). An impairment of the synaptic availability of 5HT did not, however, alter the responsiveness of the adenylate cyclase to NE (10,16), although it caused a marked decrease in agonist affinity of β-adrenoceptors (1).

An examination of agonist competition binding curves by nonlinear regression analysis revealed (a) that the reduction in the density of β-adrenoceptors by antidepressants, e.g., desipramine (DMI) is confined to the β-adrenoceptor population with high agonist affinity (Table 2) and (b) that this important β-adrenoceptor population is reduced by DMI to the same level in cortical membrane preparations from animals with reduced serotonergic activity as in preparations from normal animals. The impairment of serotonergic activity by lesioning with 5,7-dihydroxytryptamine (5,7-DHT) or inhibition of the synthesis of 5HT kg p-chlorophenylalanine markedly increased β-adrenoceptors with low micromolar agonist affinity and thus masked the DMI-induced decrease in the density of these receptors (as determined by Scatchard analysis of saturation isotherms). Since the β-adrenoceptors with high agonist affinity are linked to adenylate cyclase, these data can explain the reported discrepancies between receptor number and receptor responsiveness. The significance of subjecting agonist competition binding curves to nonlinear regression analysis is illustrated further in recent studies on the dual aminergic regulation of central β-adrenoceptors. As can be seen in Table 3, reserpine upregulates β-adrenoceptors with both high nanomolar (R_H) and low micromolar (R_L) affinity for NE. DMI, a predominantly noradrenergic antidepressant, abolished the reserpine-induced increase in the number of R_H but did not alter the increased number of R_L. In contrast, the selective 5HT uptake blocker fluoxetine abolished the reserpine-induced increase in the number of β-adrenoceptors with low affinity for isoproterenol or NE (R_L) but did not influence the DMI-sensitive R_H population. None of the drugs altered the dissociation constants K_H or K_L. These results demonstrate the selectivity of the two drugs in regulating the two receptor populations, one (R_H) being a β-adrenoceptor linked to adenylate cyclase and the other (R_L) being sensitive to 5HT.

Recent results have strengthened the view that the R_L sites with low agonist affinity for isoproterenol represent $5HT_{1B}$ receptors that are induced following a reduction of serotonergic neuronal function (20). The observations that these inducible $5HT_{1B}$ sites are regulatable by 5HT in vitro and by 5-hydroxytryptophan and the 5HT uptake inhibitor fluoxetine in vivo (19) suggest that

TABLE 2. *a. Effect of desipramine on cortical β-adrenoceptors: Nonlinear regression analysis of competition binding curves[a]*

Treatment	Dissociation constants (nM) K_H	K_L	β-adrenoceptor concentration (fmol/mg protein) R_H	R_L
Sham-saline	45 ± 5 (6)	39,800 ± 8,200 (6)	86 ± 4 (6) (75%)	29 ± 2 (6) (25%)
Sham-DMI	51 ± 4 (5)	44,800 ± 10,600 (5)	57 ± 4* (5) (73%)	21 ± 2 (5) (27%)

Rats were given desipramine (DMI) (15 mg/kg IP/day) for 1 week. The animals were killed 24 hours after the last injection. Competition binding curves were constructed using cortical membrane preparations and analyzed by nonlinear regression analysis using the program LIGAND (two-site model). R_H and R_L define β-adrenoceptor populations with high and low agonist affinity conformations respectively. K_H and K_L designate the corresponding dissociation constants. Values are means ± SEM; numbers in parentheses indicate the number of animals.
*$p < .001$.

TABLE 2. *b. Consequences of 5,7-DHT-induced lesions on cortical β-adrenoceptors and their downregulation by desipramine: Nonlinear regression analysis of competition binding curves*

Treatment	Dissociation constants (nM) K_H	K_L	β-adrenoceptor concentration (fmol/mg protein) R_H	R_L
5,7-DHT-saline	61 ± 12 (7)	21,600 ± 2,300 (7)	90 ± 9 (7) (53%)	80 ± 3* (7) (47%)
5,7-DHT-DMI	51 ± 7 (6)	21,900 ± 4,800 (6)	51 ± 6** (6) (41%)	74 ± 5*** (6) (59%)

Serotonergic neurons were lesioned by intraventricular injection of 5,7-dihydroxytryptamine (5,7-DHT). Ten days after lesioning, the animals were given desipramine (DMI) (15 mg/kg IP/day) for 1 week. The animals were killed 24 hours after the last injection. For definitions of abbreviations see legend to Table 2a. Values are means ± SEM; numbers in parentheses indicate the number of animals.
[a]Reprinted from ref 18.
*$p<.001$ (5,7-DHT vs sham-saline).
**$p<.005$ (5,7-DHT-DMI vs 5,7-DHT-saline).
***$p<.001$ (5,7-DHT-DMI vs sham-DMI in Table 4a).

TABLE 3. *Selective regulation of R_H and R_L of β-adrenoceptors in the reserpinized animal[a]*

	[³H]-Dihydroalprenolol binding fmol/mg protein ± SEM R_H	R_L
A. Saline (control)	73 ± 3 (9)	31 ± 3 (9)
Reserpine	113 ± 4 (8)[b]	48 ± 2 (8)[b]
Reserpine + DMI	72 ± 8 (9)	50 ± 3 (9)[c]
B. Saline (control)	112 ± 5 (6)	30 ± 1 (6)
Reserpine	147 ± 5 (6)[b]	42 ± 2 (6)[b]
Reserpine + DMI	94 ± 5 (7)	39 ± 1 (7)[c]
Reserpine + fluoxetine	146 ± 6 (7)[d]	33 ± 1 (7)

Rats were given reserpine (1 mg/kg IP) every third day for 14 days, at which time DMI (10 mg/kg IP BID) or fluoxetine (10 mg/kg IP BID) was administered for 4 days. All animals were killed 16 hours after the last dose, and agonist competition binding curves were constructed using cortical membrane preparations and subjected to nonlinear regression analysis. The dissociation constants K_H and K_L varied between 430 and 532 nM (K_H) and 390 and 499 μM (K_L) if NE was used as the displacing agonist and 40 and 50 nM (K_H) and 27 and 50 μM (K_L) if isoproterenol was used as the displacing agonist. The numbers in parentheses indicate the number of animals.
[a]Reprinted from ref 19.
[b]$p<.001$ (reserpine vs saline control).
[c]$p<.001$ (reserpine + DMI vs saline control).
[d]$p<.002$ (reserpine + fluoxetine vs saline control).

these sites are physiologically relevant receptors. The molecular basis of the substantial loss of β-adrenoceptors displaying high agonist affinity following antidepressants and of the substantial increase in the R_L population (5HT$_{1B}$ sites) following impairment of serotonergic function remains to be elucidated. The new findings derived from nonlinear regression analysis of agonist competition binding curves demand a conceptual revision of the 5HT–NE link; i.e., the two aminergic signal transduction pathways are more likely to converge at a level beyond the receptors and second messengers, perhaps at the level of transcriptional activation.

Glucocorticoids represent the third physiologically important endogenous compounds involved in the regulation of the sensitivity of the NE-stimulated adenylate cyclase in brain (21–24). Adrenalectomy enhances in brain the sensitivity to NE but not to isoproterenol, and this sensitivity is normalized by corticosterone replacement. This action is not associated with a change in the density of β-adrenoceptors or the activities of adenylate cyclase or phosphodiesterase (22) but seems to be mediated via the $α_1$-adrenergic component of the noradrenergic receptor system (25–27). The regulation by glucocorticoids represents a significant third link affecting the net noradrenergic information flow via the second messenger, cyclic AMP (cAMP). Glucocorticoid receptors have been identified immunocytochemically in the nuclei of NE, 5HT, and epinephrine-containing cell bodies (28), and studies on the distribution of glucocorticoid receptor mRNA have shown that the relative distribution of glucocorticoid receptor protein in different brain nuclei reflects differences in glucocorticoid receptor mRNA levels (29). Since glucocorticoid receptors are DNA binding proteins and influence the rate of transcription of various genes (30), glucocorticoids may affect the diffusely projecting stress responsive monoamine systems in brain by modifying transcription of pivotal neuronal and/or glial proteins.

BIOCHEMICAL EFFECTOR SYSTEMS OF THE SEROTONIN–NOREPINEPHRINE–GLUCOCORTICOID RECEPTORS

To understand the cascade of signal transduction via 5HT–NE–glucocorticoid receptor systems under normal physiological conditions, it is necessary to know about the sequence of events occurring upon receptor occupancy by the endogenous agonists, NE, 5HT, and glucocorticoids, respectively. Whereas the occupancy of β-adrenoceptors by NE has been known for some time to be linked in a stimulatory way via guanine nucleotide regulatory proteins (G_S) to adenylate cyclase, the situation with regard to 5HT is much more complex due to the diversity of 5HT receptors. 5HT$_{1A}$ and 5HT$_{1B}$ receptors appear to be linked via G proteins (G_S or G_I) in a stimulatory and inhibitory way, respectively, to adenylate cyclase, whereas 5HT$_2$ and 5HT$_{1C}$ receptors are coupled via G_S to phospholipase C, generating two second messengers, diacylglyercol and inositol triphosphate (IP$_3$), which mobilizes calcium as a third messenger (31). 5HT$_3$ receptors belong to the ligand-gated ion channel superfamily. The pharmacology of 5HT receptors in the central nervous system has been competently reviewed (32,33).

Receptor-mediated cAMP formation causes an activation of the cAMP-dependent kinase (A kinase), leading to phosphorylation of pivotal proteins. Stimulation of the receptors linked to phospholipase C leads to activation of the protein kinase C via diacylglycerol and of the calcium–calmodulin-stimulated kinase by calcium, mobilized by IP$_3$. Emerging evidence suggests that protein kinase C is involved in the process of desensitization, both homologous and heterologous, thus suggesting a possible mechanism for the observed corequirements of 5HT and NE for antidepressant-induced downregulation of β-adrenoceptors. Moreover, diacylglycerol is a substrate for diacylglycerol kinase, which catalyzes the formation of arachidonic acid. In addition to being a second messenger in its own right, arachidonic acid is metabolized by cyclooxygenase or lipoxygenase to prostaglandins and leukotrienes, respectively. These eicosanoids also have properties of second messengers (34). The activation of protein kinases by second messengers formed on receptor activation seems to be a common feature, thus suggesting that protein kinase-mediated protein phosphorylations represent the final common pathway of signal transduction (35,36). The cascade of signal transduction—consisting of receptor occupancy by the agonist, coupling to effector systems via guanine nucleotide regulatory proteins, formation of second messengers with the subsequent activation of protein kinases, leading to phosphorylation of pivotal proteins—functions as a highly effective kinetic amplification mechanism. Thus, small changes in the number of receptors or the formation of second messengers can cause a marked amplification if the net effect on signal transduction is examined (37). It remains a great challenge to identify brain phosphoproteins that reflect changes in the sensitivity of 5HT and NE receptor systems and, importantly, to elucidate the function of these phosphoproteins, some of which may act as DNA binding proteins and thus modify genomic expression.

In contrast to aminergic receptors that are embedded in the cell membrane, glucocorticoid receptors are intracellular proteins belonging to the nuclear transacting receptor family (38). Receptors of this family are characterized by three functional domains: a ligand binding domain, a DNA binding domain, and a transcriptional modulation domain. The DNA binding domain is the most highly conserved region among steroid receptor proteins (45–90% amino acid homology), followed by the hormone binding domain, with a 15 to 55% amino acid homology. Binding of the glucocorticoid receptor complex to glucocorticoid regulatory sequences causes upregulation or downregulation of the transcription of a large number of genes containing glucocorticoid regulatory elements upstream of the promoter. It is of interest that the genes for β-adrenoceptors and also the gene for CRF contain such glucocorticoid-responsive elements in their promoter region (39,40). It is thus tempting to speculate that glucocorticoids affect the diffusely projecting stress-responsive, 5HT-linked, and antidepressant-sensitive β-adrenoceptor system in brain via enhancement or repression of genes at the transcriptional level. Studies by Sabol et al. at the NIH using cell cultures, support such a contention. Thus, the abundance of preproenkephalin mRNA in cultured rat C_6 glioma cells is enhanced by NE, blocked by propranolol, and synergistically regulated by glucocorticoids (41,42). A stimulation of β-adrenoceptors has been shown also to increase the mRNA for β-NGF (nerve growth factor) in C_6-2B astrocytoma cells, and this action is also blocked by propranolol (43). Recently, it was demonstrated that glucocorticoids regulate the expression of the β-subunit of G proteins in rat fat cells at the mRNA level (44). This regulation may provide the basis for the modulation of transmembrane signaling by glucocorticoids, e.g., the supersensitivity of the β-adrenoceptor system in adrenalectomized rats and its reversal by substitution with glucocorticoids (22).

How the information is transferred from the receptor to the genes and whether or not results obtained in tissue culture and in peripheral tissues can be extrapolated to the central nervous system remain to be elucidated. However, in addition to the known role of glucocorticoid receptors as ligand-dependent transcription factors, some protooncogene products are of intense current interest, since they may form missing components of signal transduction pathways (45,46). For example, recent data suggest that the *cfos* protooncogene may be involved in events mediating the physiological regulation of preproenkephalin gene expression (47) or that *cfos* may function as a nuclear switch to convert short-term receptor-mediated stimulation to long-term adaptive changes via modification of transcription (48). Protooncogenes that encode proteins important in signal transduction have been reviewed (45). Their gene products include receptors, growth factors, subunits of G proteins, membrane-associated tyrosine kinases, cytoplasmic A kinase and C kinase, and nuclear DNA binding proteins. These remarkable developments in our understanding of the cascade of signal transduction—from the receptor via G proteins to effector system and to the transcriptional machinery via DNA binding proteins—make it tempting to speculate that the antidepressant-sensitive, 5HT-linked, and glucocorticoid-responsive β-adrenoceptor system in brain may be involved in a much more general way in stimulus-transcription coupling and in the regulation of brain-specific gene expression. Hypothetical models for the convergence of protein kinase A (activated by the second messenger cAMP) and protein kinase C (activated by the second messengers diacylglycerol and arachidonic acid) pathways at the level of transcriptional activation have been proposed (49).

THE SEROTONIN–NOREPINEPHRINE–GLUCOCORTICOID LINK SYSTEM AS AN AMPLIFICATION–ADAPTATION SYSTEM AND A MOLECULAR VIEW OF THERAPY-RESISTANT SIGNAL TRANSFER AS A BASIS OF THERAPY-RESISTANT DEPRESSION

Considering the briefly reviewed neuroanatomical, neurochemical, neuropharmacological, molecular biological, and clinical aspects of the interrelated 5HT–NE receptor systems in brain, we previously have formulated the serotonin–norepinephrine link hypothesis of affective disorders (50). Since neuropharmacological and molecular biological studies point to a pivotal role of glucocorticoids in the modulation of transmembrane signaling, one must now include glucocorticoid receptor systems as physiologically important regulatory elements. Consequently, one is tempted to formulate the serotonin–norepinephrine–glucocorticoid receptor link hypothesis of affective disorders. As previously suggested (50)

> This multicomponent beta adrenoceptor system in brain functions as an integrative amplification/adaptation system of a wide variety of vital physiological functions including mood, sleep, arousal, pain, neuroendocrine and central autonomic regulation. Under normal physiological conditions, the system seems to function as a protective adaptive system against excessive oscillations in sensory input. Conversely, an impairment in the regulation of the serotonin/norepinephrine glucocorticoid receptor-effector system—occurring at any one of the multiple steps involved—is hypothesized to result in maladaptation leading, for example, to the precipitation of depressive illness. Successful antidepressant treatment (pharmacotherapy and ECT) will then depend on a successful facilitation of this adaptation.

This hypothesis is of heuristic value and testable. Indeed, Stone and Platt (51) have provided animal data suggesting a causal relationship between subsensitivity of noradrenergic receptor systems and the development of adaptation to stress. They have hypothesized that the well-known deamplification of central β-adrenoceptor systems by antidepressant treatments causes an increased resistance to emotional stress.

Figure 1 depicts in a simplified schematic manner the serotonin–norepinephrine–glucocorticoid cascade of signal transduction. Since the overall physiological responses are hypothesized to result from gene transcription in topographically defined areas in the brain (e.g., reticular activating system, limbic structures, thalamic nuclei, cortical layers), drugs can influence the information flow at various levels of the cascade-presynaptic events (change in the availability of NE and/or 5HT), membrane events (Fig. 1A,B,C), cytosolic amplifier systems (Fig. 1D) and transcriptional

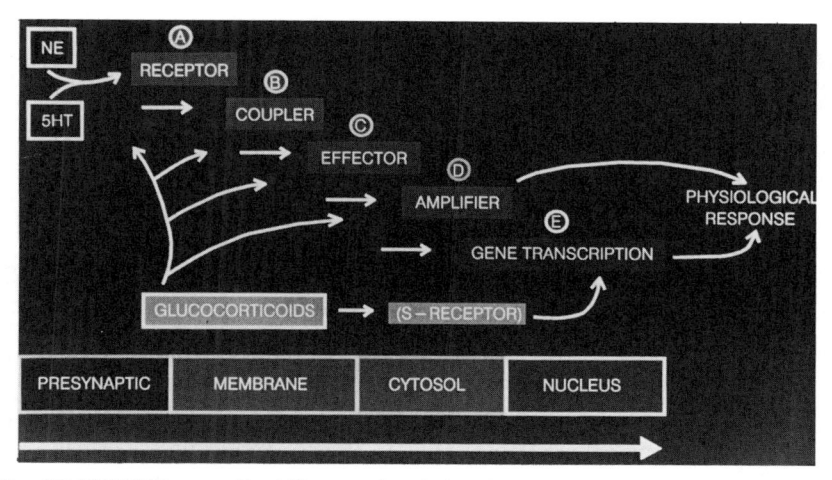

FIG. 1. The "5HT/NE/Glucocorticoid" cascade of signal transduction: targets for antidepressants.

nuclear events (Fig. 1E). Therapeutic resistance to currently available drugs that affect the cascade via presynaptic or receptor modification could simply reflect our inability to correct an impairment of the cascade at steps beyond the receptors (refractory depression). Current research on the convergence of signal transduction at the level of transcriptional activation will rigorously test this heuristic hypothesis and should provide a basis for the development of novel and more efficacious antidepressant treatments.

ACKNOWLEDGMENTS

Research from this laboratory has been supported by USPHS grant MH-29228 and by the Tennessee Department of Mental Health and Mental Retardation. I thank Mrs. Lynne Lindsey for the expert typing of the manuscript.

REFERENCES

1. Sulser F, Conn PJ, Zawad JS, Sanders-Bush E. Molecular aspects of altered transmembrane regulation of the noradrenaline signal by antidepressants. In: Schou JS, Geisler A, Norm S, eds. Alfred Benzon Symposium 22, *Drug receptors and dynamic processes in cells*. Copenhagen: Munksgaard, 1986;364–379.
2. Dahlstrom A, Fuxe K. Evidence for the existence of monoamine-containing neurons in the central nervous system. I. Demonstration of monoamines in the cell bodies of brain stem neurons. *Acta Physiol Scand* 1964;62(Suppl 232):1–55.
3. Vetulani J, Sulser F. Action of various antidepressant treatment reduces reactivity of noradrenergic cyclic AMP generating system in limbic forebrain. *Nature* 1975;257:495–496.
4. Banerjee SP, Kung LS, Riggi SJ, Chanda SK. Development of beta adrenergic receptor subsensitivity by antidepressants. *Nature* 1977; 268:455–456.
5. Sulser F, Sanders-Bush E. From neurochemical to molecular pharmacology of antidepressants. In: Costa E, ed. *Tribute to B.B. Brodie*. New York: Raven Press, 1989;289–302.
6. Kellar KJ, Bergstrom DA. Electroconvulsive shock: Effects on biochemical correlates of neurotransmitter receptors in rat brain. *Neuropharmacology* 1983;22:401–406.
7. McKenna DJ, Nazaraki AJ, Himeno A, Ladvedra JM. Chronic treatment with (±)-DOT, a psychotomimetic 5HT$_2$ agonist, down-regulates 5HT$_2$ receptors in rat brain. *Neuropsychopharmacology* 1989;2:81–87.
8. Schweitzer JW, Schwartz R, Friedhoff AJ. Intact presynaptic terminals required for beta-adrenergic receptor regulation by desipramine. *J Neurochem* 1979;33:377–379.
9. Janowsky AJ, Steranka LR, Gillespie DD, Sulser F. Role of neuronal signal input in the downregulation of central noradrenergic receptor function by antidepressant drugs. *J Neurochem* 1982;39:290–292.

10. Janowsky A, Okada F, Manier D, Applegate CD, Sulser F. Role of serotonergic input in the regulation of the beta adrenergic receptor coupled adenylate cyclase system. *Science* 1982; 218:900–901.
11. Stockmeier CA, Martino AM, Kellar KJ. A strong influence of serotonin axons on beta adrenergic receptors in rat brain. *Science* 1985; 230:323–325.
12. Manier DH, Gillespie DD, Sanders-Bush E, Sulser F. The serotonin/noradrenaline link in brain: I. The role of noradrenaline and serotonin in the regulation of density and function of beta adrenoceptors and its alteration by desipramine. *Naunyn Schmiedebergs Arch Pharmacol* 1987; 335:109–114.
13. Brunello N, Barbaccia ML, Chuang DM, Costa E. Down-regulation of beta adrenergic receptors following repeated injections of desmethylimipramine: Permissive role of serotonergic axons. *Neuropharmacology* 1982;21:1145–1149.
14. Brunello N, Volterra A, Cagiano R, Ianieri GC, Cuomo V, Racagni G. Biochemical and behavioral changes in rats after prolonged treatment with desipramine: Interaction with *p*-chlorophenylalanine. *Naunyn Schmiedebergs Arch Pharmacol* 1985;331:20–22.
15. Dumbrille-Ross A, Tang SW. Noradrenergic and serotonergic input necessary for imipramine induced changes in beta but not S_2 receptor densities. *Psychiatry Res* 1983;9:207–215.
16. Manier DH, Gillespie DD, Sulser F. A pivotal role for serotonin in the down-regulation of beta adrenoceptors by antidepressants: Reversibility of the action of *p*-chlorophenylalanine (PCPA) by 5-hydroxytryptophan. *Experientia* 1984;40: 1223–1226.
17. Nimgaonkar VL, Goodwin GM, Davies CL, Green AR. Down-regulation of beta adrenoceptors in rat cortex by repeated administration of desipramine, electroconvulsive shock and clenbuterol requires 5HT neurones but not 5HT. *Neuropharmacology* 1985;24:279–283.
18. Manier DH, Gillespie DD, Sulser F. 5,7-Dihydroxytryptamine induced lesions of serotonergic neurons and desipramine induced down-regulation of cortical beta adrenoceptors: A re-evaluation. *Biochem Pharmacol* 1987;36:3308–3310.
19. Manier DH, Gillespie DD, Sulser F. Dual aminergic regulation of central beta adrenoceptors: Effect of atypical antidepressants and 5-hydroxytryptophan. *Neuropsychopharmacology* 1989;2:89–95.
20. Gillespie DD, Manier DH, Sulser F. Characterization of the 5HT sensitive dihydroalprenolol binding sites with low affinity for isoproterenol. *Neuropsychopharmacology* 1989;2:265–271.
21. Mobley PL, Sulser F. Adrenal corticoids regulate sensitivity of noradrenaline receptor coupled adenylate cyclase in brain. *Nature* 1980; 286:608–609.
22. Mobley PL, Manier DH, Sulser F. Norepinephrine sensitive adenylate cyclase system in rat brain: Role of adrenal corticosteroids. *J Pharmacol Exp Ther* 1983;226:71–77.

23. Roberts VJ, Singhal RL, Roberts DCS. Corticosterone prevents the increase in noradrenaline stimulated adenylcyclase activity in rat hippocampus following adrenalectomy or metopirone. *Eur J Pharmacol* 1984;103:235–240.
24. Harrelson AL, Rosterre W, McEwen BS. Adrenocortical steroids modify neurotransmitter stimulated cyclic AMP accumulation in the hippocampus and limbic brain of the rat. *J Neurochem* 1987;48:1648–1655.
25. Duman RS, Strada SJ, Enna SJ. Effect of imipramine and adrenocorticotropin administration on the rat brain norepinephrine coupled cyclic nucleotide generating system: Alterations in alpha and beta adrenergic components. *J Pharmacol Exp Ther* 1985;234:409–414.
26. Stone EA, Platt JE, Herrera AS. Effect of repeated restraint stress, desmethylimipramine or adrenocorticotropin on the alpha and beta adrenergic components of the cyclic AMP response to norepinephrine in rat brain slices. *J Pharmacol Exp Ther* 1986;237:702–707.
27. Stone EA, McEwen BS, Herrera AS, Carr KD. Regulation of alpha and beta components of noradrenergic cyclic AMP response in cortical slices. *Eur J Pharmacol* 1987;141:347–356.
28. Harfstrand A, Fuxe K, Cintra A, et al. Demonstration of glucocorticoid receptor immunoreactivity in monoamine neurons of the rat brain. *Proc Natl Acad Sci USA* 1986;83:9779–9783.
29. Sousa RJ, Tannery NH, Lafer EM. In situ hybridization mapping of glucocorticoid receptor messenger ribonucleic acid in rat brain. *Mol Endocrinol* 1989;3:481–494.
30. Ringold GM. Steroid hormone regulation of gene expression. *Annu Rev Pharmacol Toxicol* 1985; 25:529–566.
31. Berridge MJ. Inositol trisphosphate and diacylglycerol: Two interacting second messengers. *Annu Rev Biochem* 1987;56:159–193.
32. Conn PJ, Sanders-Bush E. Central serotonin receptors: Effector systems, physiological roles and regulation. *Psychopharmacology* 1987;92: 267–277.
33. Peroutka SJ. Serotonin receptor subtypes. *ISI Atlas Pharmacol* 1988;1–4.
34. Piomelli D, Volterra A, Dale N, et al. Lipoxygenase metabolites of arachidonic acid as second messengers for presynaptic inhibition of Aplysia sensory cells. *Nature* 1987;328:38–43.
35. Nestler EJ, Greengard P. Protein phosphorylation in brain. *Nature* 1983;305:583–588.
36. Nestler EJ, Walaas ST, Greengard P. Neuronal phosphoproteins: Physiological and clinical implications. *Science* 1984;225:1357–1364.
37. Walsh DA. The modulation of skeletal muscle glycogenolysis as a model of cyclic AMP action. In: Schmitt FO, Schneider DM, Crothess DM, eds. *Functional linkage in biomolecular systems*. New York: Raven Press, 1975;206–209.
38. Green S, Chambon P. A superfamily of potentially oncogenic hormone receptors. *Nature* 1986;324:615–617.
39. Burnstein KL, Cidlowski JA. Regulation of gene

expression by glucocorticoids. *Annu Rev Physiol* 1989;51:683–699.
40. Roche PJ, Crawford RJ, Fernley RT, Tregean GW, Coghan JP. Nucleotide sequence of the gene coding for bovine corticotropin-releasing factor and regulation of its mRNA levels by glucocorticoids. *Gene* 1988;71:421–431.
41. Yoshikawa K, Sabol St. Expression of the enkephalin precursor gene in C_6 rat glioma cells: Regulation by beta adrenergic agonists and glucocorticoids. *Mol Brain Res* 1986;1:75–83.
42. Yoshikawa K, Sabol St. Glucocorticoids and cyclic AMP synergistically regulate the abundance of pre-proenkephalin mRNA in neuroblastoma glioma hybrid cells. *Biochem Biophys Res Commun* 1986;139:1–10.
43. Dal Toso R, Bernardi MADe, Costa E, Mochetti I. Beta-adrenergic receptor regulation of NGF-mRNA in rat C_6-2B glioma cells. *Neuropharmacology* 1987;26:1783–1786.
44. Ros M, Watkins DC, Rapiejko PJ, Malbon CC. Glucocorticoids modulate mRNA levels for G-protein beta subunit. *Biochem J* 1989;260:271–275.
45. Hanley MR. Protooncogenes in the nervous system. *Neuron* 1988;1:175–182.
46. Herrlich P, Ponta H. Nuclear oncogenes convert extracellular stimuli into changes in the genetic program. *TIG* 1989;5:112–116.
47. White JD, Gall ChM. Differential regulation of neuropeptide and protooncogene mRNA content in the hippocampus following recurrent seizures. *Mol Brain Res* 1987;3:21–29.
48. Morgan JI, Cohen DR, Hempstead JL, Curran T. Mapping patterns of c-fos expression in the central nervous system after seizure. *Science* 1987;237:192–197.
49. Hoeffler JP, Deutsch PJ, Lin J, Habenes LF. Cyclic adenosine monophosphate and phorbol esters-responsive signal transduction pathways converge at the level of transcriptional activation by the interactions of DNA-binding proteins. *Mol Endocrinol* 1989;3:868–880.
50. Sulser F, Sanders-Bush E. The serotonin–norepinephrine link hypothesis of affective disorders: Receptor–receptor interactions in brain. In: Ehrlich YH, Lenox RH, Kornecki E, Berry WO, eds. *Molecular basis of neuronal responsiveness.* New York: Plenum Press, 1987;439–502.
51. Stone EA, Platt JE. Brain adrenergic receptors and resistance to stress. *Brain Res* 1982;237:405–414.

3

Current Hypotheses of the Mechanism of Antidepressant Treatments: Implications for the Treatment of Refractory Depression

Dennis S. Charney, Pedro L. Delgado, Steven M. Southwick, John H. Krystal, Lawrence H. Price, and George R. Heninger

An improved understanding of the possible neurobiological mechanisms of action of antidepressant treatments (ADT) should be of considerable value to both researchers and clinicians as they attempt to devise novel therapeutic approaches to the treatment of the refractory depressed patient. This chapter initially reviews data relevant to current theories on the mechanism of action of antidepressant treatment, then discusses the data in relation to treatment strategies for refractory depression.

CATECHOLAMINE AND INDOLEAMINE DEFICIENCY HYPOTHESES OF ANTIDEPRESSANT ACTION

The original catecholamine hypothesis postulated that a deficit in central nervous system norepinephrine (NE) was responsible for clinical depression and that the therapeutic mechanism of action of antidepressant treatments was related to an ability to increase brain NE function by NE reuptake or monoamine oxidase (MAO) inhibition (1,2). However, this theory of antidepressant action has been challenged based on several observations. The hypothesis in its simplest form has not been validated by studies of monoamine levels and monoamine metabolite levels in plasma, urine, and CSF in depressed patients (3). In addition, some drugs that are potent NE reuptake blockers, such as cocaine and amphetamine, were shown to be ineffective antidepressants. Conversely, effective antidepressants, such as iprindole and mianserin, did not block uptake of NE or breakdown of MAO inhibition. Furthermore, pharmacokinetic studies failed to find a dose–response relationship between clinical improvement and NE blockade. Instead, effective antidepressants varied markedly in their ability to affect NE reuptake. The catecholamine hypothesis also failed to account for the temporal discrepancy between the onset of NE reuptake inhibition and clinical improvement. The former occurred within hours, whereas the latter occurred at least 7 to 14 days after the initiation of drug treatment.

A second competing pharmacological hypothesis of depression, the indoleamine hypothesis, was developed at approximately the same time and stated that a functional deficit in serotonin (5HT) produced depressive symptoms, and antidepressants worked

---

Psychiatry Service, West Haven VA Medical Center, West Haven, CT 06516, and Clinical Neuroscience Research Unit, Connecticut Mental Health Center, and Department of Psychiatry, Yale University School of Medicine, New Haven, CT 06508.

by increasing 5HT activity through 5HT reuptake inhibition or MAO inhibition (4). This theory has been challenged on similar grounds as the NE hypothesis of antidepressant action, particularly in relation to the temporal disparity between the delay required for clinical effects and the rapid onset of 5HT reuptake inhibition.

In recent years, with the development of more sophisticated neurobiological methodologies, investigators have increased their understanding of the multiple effects of antidepressants on neurotransmitter systems. This has resulted in a number of receptor sensitivity hypotheses, which suggest that the ability of long-term antidepressant drugs to reduce β- or α_2-adrenergic receptor sensitivity or to enhance the responses of serotonergic or α_1-adrenergic receptor stimulation may be related to the therapeutic mechanism of action of antidepressant treatments (3,5). To develop a foundation from which to consider these hypotheses, certain important elements of neurotransmitter metabolism and neuroreceptor regulation of neuronal activity are presented.

Neurotransmitter Metabolism Is Regulated at Multiple Levels

A schematic diagram of neurotransmitter metabolism and function is illustrated in Fig. 1. The metabolism of the monoamine neurotransmitter serotonin has been used as an example, since the importance of the serotonergic regulation of mood and the mechanism of antidepressant drugs are of considerable research interest. However, similar diagrams could be drawn for other monoamines, such as dopamine and NE. It is evident that effective function of monoamine systems is dependent on the sequential and interdependent activity of many

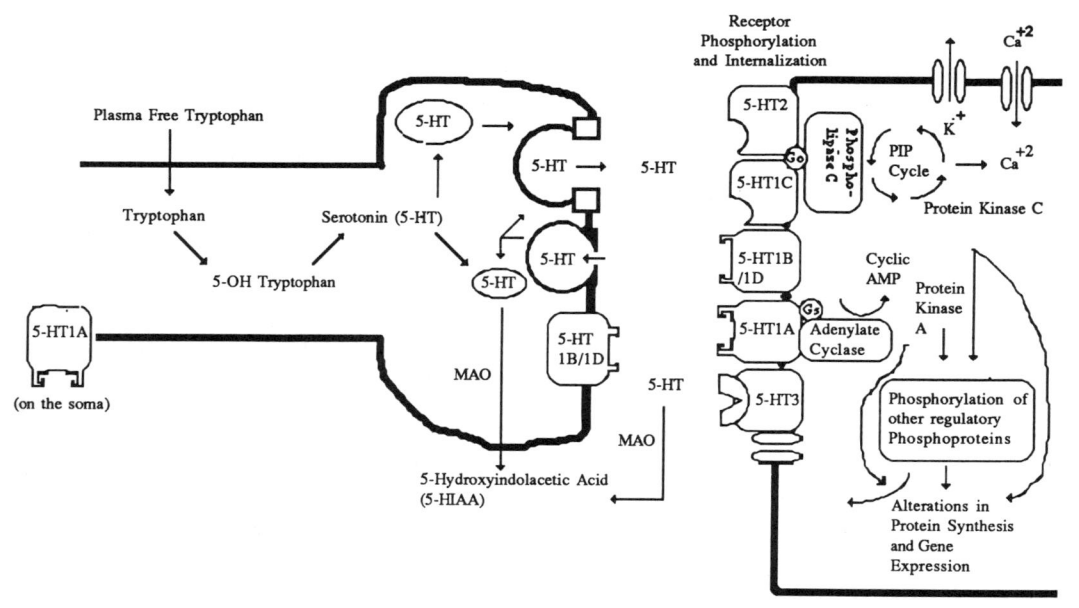

FIG. 1. Schematic representation of serotonergic neuronal mechanisms. Presynaptic factors: plasma tryptophan level, tryptophan uptake, serotonin synthesis, serotonin storage, serotonin release, serotonin reuptake, serotonin degredation, regulatory autoreceptors. Postsynaptic factors: transmitter binding, receptor-G protein coupling, second messenger generating systems, phosphorylation of regulatory phosphoproteins, calcium release, regulation of ion channels, regulation of receptor number and function, regulation of protein synthesis and gene expression.

subsystems. Thus, there are a number of possible sites for impairment of function in monoamine systems that could lead to illness. Consequently, these locations represent possible sites for pharmacological treatments to reverse the effects of specific abnormalities and produce therapeutic responses. For 5HT, there are data supporting the importance of drugs influencing the function of the system at many of the levels listed (Table 1).

Monoamine Receptors and Neuronal Regulation

Recent advances in basic neuroscience have identified presynaptic receptor mech-

TABLE 1. *Multiple sites of 5HT system at which drugs have been shown to alter depressive symptoms*

Presynaptic function	Directional change in function	Intervention	Therapeutic effect
1. Precursor availability	↓	Reduction in plasma tryptophan by tryptophan-free amino acid drink.	Two thirds of maintained antidepressant-remitted patients experience a relapse
	↑	Oral tryptophan supplementation of antidepressants in refractory depressed patients	Tryptophan augmentation of MAOI treatments can be therapeutic; not helpful in TCA-maintained patients
2. Neurotransmitter synthesis	↓	Parachlorophenylalanine (PCPA) inhibition of hydroxylation of tryptophan to 5-hydroxytryptophan	Antidepressant-maintained remitted patients relapse
	↑	Tetrahydrobiopterin, natural cofactor of tryptophan hydroxylase and tyrosine hydroxylase	May have antidepressant properties
3. Neurotransmitter storage	↓	Reserpine releases monoamines from storage sites.	Produces depression in some patients
4. Neurotransmitter release	↑	Fenfluramine and 3,4-methylenedioxy-methamphetamine MDMA (Ecstacy) increase in serotonin release	May produce increased sense of well-being; antidepressant effects not demonstrated
5. 5HT autoreceptor function	↓ Acute ↑ Chronic	$5HT_{1A}$ receptor agonists acutely decrease 5HT neuronal activity; may increase function with chronic treatment	$5HT_{1A}$ agonists (e.g., buspirone) have no effect acutely; may have antidepressant properties with chronic treatment
6. Neurotransmitter reuptake	↑	Serotonin reuptake inhibitor drugs	Very effective antidepressants
7. Neurotransmitter metabolism	↑	Monoamine oxidase inhibitor drugs	Very effective antidepressants
Postsynaptic function 1. Neurotransmitter binding	↓	$5HT_2$ receptor antagonists	Preliminary data suggest efficacy of $5HT_2$ antagonists, such as ritanserin, in dysthymic patients
	As above	$5HT_{1A}$ receptor agonists	Preliminary data suggest $5HT_{1A}$ agonists, such as gepirone, are effective antidepressants
2. 2nd messenger systems	↑	Phosphodiesterase inhibitors (PI)	Roliptam, a PI, is an effective antidepressant

anisms that are capable of independent regulation of cell firing and transmitter release. When occupied by the transmitter, these receptors generally reduce the rate of cell firing and transmitter release (6). For example, in the noradrenergic system, presynaptic α_2-adrenergic receptors are called autoreceptors because when stimulated by NE in the synaptic cleft, they inhibit the firing of noradrenergic neurons. In the 5HT system, the $5HT_{1A}$ receptor functions as an autoreceptor when located presynaptically, in an analogous fashion to the α_2-adrenergic receptor.

Antidepressant drugs can alter the function of presynaptic receptors and thereby produce important functional changes in neurotransmitter systems. There is a decrease in turnover of monoamines following acute administration of compounds that inhibit uptake of monoamines, particularly NE or 5HT. The apparent paradoxical decrease in monoamine and monoamine metabolite levels following reuptake blocking compounds can be understood when the role of the presynaptic receptors is taken into account (5). Long-term exposure of these autoreceptors to elevated levels of their endogenous neurotransmitter can alter their functional responsiveness. For example, long-term administration of NE and 5HT reuptake inhibitor drugs produce a desensitization of the α_2 and $5HT_{1A}$ receptors, respectively (7,8).

Less information is available on the regulatory properties of postsynaptic monoamine receptors. β_1, β_2, and α_1-adrenergic receptors are postsynaptic, whereas α_2-adrenergic receptors are both presynaptic and postsynaptic. The 5HT receptor subtypes of relevance to antidepressant action are the $5HT_1$ and $5HT_2$ receptors. The $5HT_1$ receptor has been subdivided further into at least four subtypes, $5HT_{1A}$, $5HT_{1B}$, $5HT_{1C}$, and $5HT_{1D}$ (9). Preclinical studies indicate that chronic antidepressant treatments resulting in long-term exposure of receptors to altered neurotransmitter concentrations modify a series of intracellular mechanisms involved in the regulation of receptor sensitivity (10).

Beyond the Receptor: Second and Third Messenger Systems

The interaction of neurotransmitters and receptors causes a conformational change that promotes complexing to transmembrane G proteins. When stimulated, the G proteins link to the intracellular enzyme, adenylate cyclase, which then converts ATP to cAMP, also referred to as a second messenger. A cascade of biochemical events follows, ending with the phosphorylation and activation of target enzymes. Another second messenger system, the phosphatylinositol system, is linked to the breakdown of phospholipids. In this system, stimulation of G proteins leads to activation of phospholipase C rather than adenylate cyclase. Both cAMP and phosphoinositide second messenger systems involve transmembrane activation of enzymes and are important mediators of signal transduction (10).

RECEPTOR SENSITIVITY HYPOTHESES OF ANTIDEPRESSANT ACTION

Each of the major receptor sensitivity hypotheses is discussed briefly based on findings from preclinical and clinical investigations. Clinical studies of the neurobiological effects of antidepressant drugs and therapeutic approaches based on receptor sensitivity hypotheses of antidepressant efficacy also are reviewed to assess the validity of the different hypotheses.

Enhancement of Serotonin Neurotransmission Hypothesis

It has long been hypothesized that the mechanism of action of some antidepressants is related to changes in 5HT neuronal function. This originally was thought to occur via inhibition of 5HT reuptake. Several research groups have developed a 5HT hypothesis suggesting that antidepressant efficacy involves alterations in 5HT receptor sensitivity during chronic drug administration, producing enhanced 5HT neurotransmission (3,5,11).

Preclinical Studies

Receptor Binding

Recent investigations involving radioligands, such as spiperone and ritanserin, that label $5HT_2$ receptors have shown that these receptors are decreased in density by many, but not all, antidepressant drugs (Table 2). For many of these drugs, the reduction in $5HT_2$ density appears to require long-term administration. However, mianserin can initiate this effect after only a few doses. Since mianserin requires chronic administration for therapeutic effect, there appears to be a dissociation between mianserin's ability to reduce $5HT_2$ receptors and its clinical efficacy. In contrast, ECT increases $5HT_2$ receptor density, effects that are opposite to those caused by antidepressant drugs (12). The imipramine binding receptor is intimately involved in the 5HT reuptake site, and this receptor has been found to be reduced in numbers on the platelets of depressed patients (13). However, there does not appear to be a consistent effect of ADTs on imipramine binding sites in the brains of laboratory animals or on the platelets of depressed patients (13–15).

Electrophysiological Studies

Single unit electrophysiological investigations have shown consistently that chronic antidepressant administration enhances serotonergic neurotransmission in various brain regions by either autoreceptor desensitization or postsynaptic receptor supersensitivity (3,5). Chronic treatment with specific 5HT reuptake inhibitors and MAOIs increase serotonergic transmission by inducing a desensitization of the 5HT autoreceptor without altering postsynaptic 5HT sensitivity, whereas tricyclic antide-

TABLE 2. *The effects of chronic antidepressant administration on serotonin receptor function*

Antidepressant category	Receptor binding $5HT_1$	$5HT_2$	TMI	Neurophysiological sensitivity 5HT autoreceptor	5HT postsynaptic	Behavioral sensitivity $5HT_1$	$5HT_{1A}$ Autoreceptor	$5HT_2$
NE reuptake inhibitors	0 ↓[a]	↓	↓ 0	0	↑	↓	↓	↑ 0
Mixed NE and 5HT reuptake inhibitors	0	↓	↓ 0	0	↑	↓	↓	↑ ↓ 0
5HT reuptake inhibitors	0	↑ 0	↑	↓	0	↓	↓	↓ 0
MAOI	↓	↓	↑ 0	↓	0	↓	↓	↓
Typical antidepressants								
Tiazodone	0	↓	—	—	—	—	—	0 ↑
Bupropion	0	0	—	—	—	—	—	—
Mianserin	0	↓	0	—	↑	—	↓	0 ↓
Nomifensine	—	—	—	—	—	—	—	—
Maprotiline	—	0	—	—	—	—	—	—
ECT	0	↑	↓ 0	—	↑	↓ ↑	↓	↓

[a] ↑, increase; ↓, decrease; 0, no change; —, not tested; averaged over different brain regions and different drugs; mixed results are indicated by more than one symbol.

pressants and iprindole induce postsynaptic 5HT receptor supersensitivity without altering autoreceptor function (16–20). The explanation for this may be that tricyclic drugs are demethylated rapidly into their secondary metabolites, which are weak 5HT uptake inhibitors. These observations suggest that sustained blockade of 5HT reuptake is required for desensitization of the autoreceptor.

Behavioral Studies

Investigations of serotonin-mediated behavior do not reveal uniform effects of antidepressant drugs on 5HT function (3,5). A major limitation of these studies is their inability to assess brain regions that are likely to be involved in antidepressant drug action. For example, the 5HT-induced head twitch response in animals, which is associated with $5HT_2$ receptors, does not involve 5HT receptors located in the frontal cortex (21).

Clinical Investigations

Many clinical studies designed to evaluate monoamine receptor function using pharmacological probes have evaluated serotonergic function (Table 3). For example, a series of studies examined the effect of various antidepressant agents on the ability of IV tryptophan to increase prolactin secretion. Evidence has accumulated indicating that the prolactin response to tryptophan can be used as a reflection of $5HT_1$ receptor function. It has been observed in depressed patients that many antidepressants, including (in rank order of potency) fluvoxamine, amitriptyline, tranylcypromine, desipramine, and lithium, significantly increase the prolactin response to tryptophan (22–25).

However, the potentiation of the tryptophan induced prolactin response is not universal among antidepressant drugs, and trazodone, mianserin, and bupropion do not appear to enhance the tryptophan-induced increase in prolactin (26). The inability of

TABLE 3. Clinical investigations of antidepressant effects on serotonin receptor function in depressed patients[a]

Antidepressant category	Tryptophan → ↑ PRL[b]	Fenfluramine → ↑ PRL	$5HT_2$ → ↑ CORT	IMI binding
NE reuptake inhibitors	↑[c]	—	↓	0
Mixed NE and 5HT reuptake inhibitors	↑	↑	↓	0
5HT reuptake inhibitors	↑	—	—	↑
MAOI	↑	—	↑	—
Typical antidepressants				
Trazodone	0	—	—	—
Bupropion	0	—	—	—
Mianserin	—	—	—	—
Nomifensine	—	—	—	—
Maprotiline	—	—	—	0
ECT	—	—	—	0

[a] Unless otherwise noted, the specific technique used to evaluate monoamine receptor subtypes are described in the text.
[b] PRL, prolactin; CORT, cortisol; IMI, imipramine.
[c] ↑, increase; ↓, decrease; 0, no change; —, not tested; averaged over different brain regions and different drugs.

trazodone and mianserin to increase the prolactin response to tryptophan probably relates to the postsynaptic 5HT antagonist properties of these drugs.

Fenfluramine, a drug that releases 5HT and prevents 5HT reuptake, also increases prolactin (27). The prolactin response to fenfluramine has been found to be decreased in some depressed patients and increased by TCA and ECT treatment (27–29).

Another paradigm used to evaluate 5HT function is the cortisol increase following 5-hydroxytryptophan (5-HTP) administration. Depressed patients receiving imipramine, desipramine, or nortriptyline exhibited a decreased cortisol response to 5-HTP in comparison to the drug-free condition. These findings clearly contrast with the enhancement of 5HT function identified by the tryptophan infusion test. This may be because of the possibility that 5-HTP-induced increases in cortisol are related to effects on the $5HT_2$ receptors, whereas tryptophan neuroendocrine actions appear to be via $5HT_1$ receptor stimulation. In addition, 5-HTP may have peripheral effects at the level of the adrenal gland and actions on catecholamine as well as indoleamine function (30–32).

Therapeutic Studies

The addition of lithium, which increases 5HT synaptic release, to ongoing antidepressant administration in patients who were either refractory or only partially responsive to treatment is based on the hypothesis that an enhancement of 5HT function is critical to therapeutic efficacy. The original open study by deMontigny et al. (33) and a subsequent double-blind placebo controlled study by Heninger et al. (34) have now been replicated by others (35–46). Lithium augmentation of antidepressant treatment has been beneficial in 169 of 243 patients (70%) described in the literature, including TCAs, tetracyclic antidepressants, MAOIs, and carbamazepine (47).

Lithium augmentation is now a routine clinical treatment.

The initial studies by Shopsin et al. demonstrating that parachlorophenylalanine (PCPA), which decreases 5HT synthesis, induces a recurrence of depressive symptoms in recovered depressed patients receiving antidepressant treatment provided important support of a critical role for 5HT in antidepressant action (48,49). Our research group recently replicated these findings by using a novel method for acutely depleting plasma tryptophan by a 24-hour, 160 mg/day, low TRP diet, followed the next morning by a tryptophan free amino acid drink (TFD). This paradigm results in a reduction in plasma tryptophan of over 90% 5 hours after the TFD. Ongoing investigations indicate that over 60% of remitted patients maintained on antidepressants relapse 2 to 7 hours after the TFD, with a gradual return over 24 hours to the remitted state with normal tryptophan intake (50). Preliminary observations suggest that patients remitted on drugs with strong 5HT-enhancing effects (e.g., fluvoxamine) are more vulnerable to the effects of the TFD than are patients remitted on NE reuptake inhibitors (e.g., desipramine) (Table 4).

Summary

Neurophysiological studies have indicated consistently that a spectrum of antidepressant drugs increases serotonergic neurotransmission. The increase in 5HT neurotransmission observed in neurophysiological studies has not been associated with an increase in the density of 5HT receptors. In contrast, $5HT_2$ receptor density is reduced by most antidepressant treatments, with ECT a major exception. The apparent contradictory findings of the neurophysiological and binding studies may be due to the assessment of different 5HT receptor subtypes by the two methods and the reciprocal functional interactions between $5HT_1$ and $5HT_2$ receptors.

TABLE 4. *Therapeutic studies relevant to serotonin enhancement hypotheses of antidepressant action*

Therapeutic approach	Results and implications
Serotonin depletion reverses antidepressant action	Consistent with the serotonin neurotransmission potentiation hypothesis of antidepressant action, PCPA, a tryptophan hydroxylase inhibitor, which reduces serotonin synthesis and acute depletion of plasma tryptophan by a tryptophan-free amino acid drink, reverses the therapeutic effects of antidepressants
Lithium augmentation of antidepressant action	In numerous investigations, lithium has been demonstrated to augment the therapeutic effects of a spectrum of antidepressant drugs in treatment refractory depressed patients; this treatment was developed and based on the serotonin neurotransmission potentiation hypothesis of antidepressant action

Clinical investigations have shown that most, but not all, types of antidepressants enhance 5HT neurotransmission. Important exceptions are bupropion, trazodone, and mianserin. From a clinical perspective, a major difficulty with the 5HT hypothesis as currently proposed (i.e., enhancement of function) is that it is overly simplistic. It is clear from infusion studies of 5HT precursors (tryptophan) and receptor agonists (MCPP) and therapeutic augmentation of antidepressants with 5HT-enhancing agents (fenfluramine) that there is not a linear relationship between increased 5HT neurotransmission and improvement in depressed mood. A more complex relationship between antidepressant-induced changes in 5HT function and therapeutic response is likely to exist.

However, the ability of lithium to potentiate antidepressant efficacy in treatment-refractory patients and the rapid reversal of antidepressant responses with rapid reductions in 5HT function by PCPA or a 90% reduction in plasma tryptophan by a TFD are supportive of an important role for antidepressant-induced alterations in 5HT function in the mechanism of action of antidepressants.

Noradrenergic Mechanisms of Antidepressant Treatments

The original catecholamine hypothesis of depression (1,2) postulated an absolute or relative deficiency in noradrenergic function. However, a considerable amount of work has failed to confirm the hypothesis (3,5). Although there is some evidence that depressed bipolar patients do excrete lower levels of catecholamine metabolites, other diagnostic categories of depressed patients demonstrate equal or even greater amounts of NE metabolites than do normal subjects (51). Furthermore, since specific 5HT uptake inhibitors and other antidepressants that do not affect noradrenergic function are equally effective antidepressants, the effects on NE reuptake system do not appear to be necessary for the antidepressant action of these drugs.

Recent noradrenergic hypotheses of antidepressant mechanisms have focused on alterations in α and β noradrenergic receptors. The β-receptor downregulation hypothesis proposes that the net effect of chronic antidepressant administration is a reduction of neurotransmission through β-adrenergic receptors in the central nervous system (52). Since the α_2-adrenergic receptor, when located presynaptically, inhibits noradrenergic neuronal activity, the α_2-receptor hypothesis proposes that net noradrenergic function is increased by chronic antidepressant administration (53). The α_1-receptor hypothesis suggests that the mechanism of action of antidepressants may be related to an ability of antidepressants to increase the function of postsynaptic α_1-adrenergic receptors (54,55).

TABLE 5. *The effects of chronic antidepressant administration on noradrenergic receptor function[a]*

Antidepressant category	NE/isoproterenol-mediated cAMP	α_2-Agonist-mediated cAMP	Receptor binding β	Receptor binding α_2	Receptor binding α_1	Neurophysiological sensitivity β	Neurophysiological sensitivity α_2	Neurophysiological sensitivity α_1	Behavioral sensitivity Presynaptic β	Behavioral sensitivity Presynaptic α_2	Behavioral sensitivity α_1
NE reuptake inhibitors	↓[b]	—	↓	0↓↑	0↑	↓0	↓	↑	↓	↓	↑0
Mixed NE and 5HT reuptake inhibitors	↓	↓	↓	0↓↑	0↑	↓0	↓0	↑	↓	↓0	↑0
5HT reuptake inhibitors	↓0	↓	0↓[c]	0	0↑	0	↓	—	—	—	↑0
MAOI	↓	—	↓	↓	0↑	↓	—	—	—	↓	↑0
Typical antidepressants											
Trazodone	—	↓	↓	—	—	—	—	—	—	—	—
Bupropion	0↓[d]	—	0↓[d]	0	↑	—	—	—	—	—	—
Mianserin	0↓[d]	↓	0↓[e]	0↑	↑	—	0	—	—	0	↓↑
Nomifensine	0	—	0	—	—	—	—	—	—	—	—
Maprotiline	0	—	0↓[e]	—	—	↓	—	—	—	—	—
ECT	↓	—	↓	↓0	↑	0	—	—	↓	↓	↑0

[a] The specific techniques used to evaluate noradrenergic receptor subtypes are described in the text.
[b] ↑, increase; ↓, decrease; 0, no change; —, not tested; averaged over different brain regions and different drugs; mixed results are indicated by more than one symbol.
[c] Effect observed only in specific brain regions.
[d] High doses were required to obtain effect.
[e] Effect observed 6 hours but 24 hours after final dose.

Preclinical Studies

In Table 5 are listed the effects of chronic antidepressant treatment on noradrenergic receptor function based on biochemical, binding neurophysiological, and behavioral studies. It can be seen that long-term administration with most antidepressant treatments so far tested markedly and reliably reduces β-receptor binding and β-adrenergic agonist-stimulated cAMP accumulation (56–59). A major exception is the antidepressant, bupropion. Findings consistent with the biochemical changes have been observed in several investigations of the physiological and behavioral responsiveness to β-receptor agonists. Thus, in terms of a common mechanism of action, most of the antidepressants studied produce diminished responsiveness in the β-adrenergic system in at least some brain areas.

The changes in the α_1-receptor system are more variable but tend to follow a general pattern of increased physiological responsiveness and increased behavioral responsiveness (60–63). This contrasts with the variable but generally decreased receptor binding, neurophysiological responsiveness, and behavioral responsiveness to agonists of the α_2-system (64). Thus, the pattern of upregulating the α_1-system and downregulating the α_2-system suggest that since the inhibitory presynaptic α_2-receptors are less sensitive and the postsynaptic α_1-receptors are more sensitive, an overall increase in postsynaptic α_1-noradrenergic function may occur with at least some antidepressants.

Clinical Studies

In Table 6, a summary of observed abnormalities in noradrenergic receptor sys-

TABLE 6. Clinical investigations of antidepressant effects on noradrenergic receptor function in depressed patients[a]

Antidepressant category	α_2 platelet binding	α_2 pre	α_2 post	α_2 iris dilation	β melatonin levels	Amphetamine → ↑ cortisol
5HT reuptake inhibitors	0[b]	↓	0	↓	↑	0
Mixed NE and 5HT reuptake inhibitors	↓ (clon)	↓	0	—	—	0
5HT reuptake inhibitors	—	—	—	—	—	—
MAOI	0	↓	0	↑	↑	—
Typical antidepressants						
Trazodone	—	0	—	—	—	—
Bupropion	—	—	—	—	—	—
Mianserin	—	0	—	0	—	—
Nomifensine	—	—	—	—	—	—
Maprotiline	—	—	—	—	—	—
ECT	0	—	—	—	—	0

[a] The specific techniques used to evaluate monoamine receptor subtypes are described in the text.
[b] ↑, increase; ↓, decrease; 0, no change; —, not tested; averaged over different brain regions and different drugs.

tem function in depressed patients is presented. A number of investigations have been conducted in patients using the α_2-agonist clonidine and the α_2-antagonist, yohimbine. Clonidine reduces plasma 3-methoxy-4-hydroxyphenylglycol (MHPG), cortisol, and blood pressure and increases sedation and growth hormone secretion in patients. However, only a blunting of the clonidine-induced growth hormone increase and an increase in the drop in cortisol have been observed consistently in depressed patients (65). Drugs with considerable noradrenergic reuptake inhibition (desipramine and amitriptyline) and the MAOIs produce decreased responsiveness in many of the indices of the α_2-adrenergic system responsiveness (66,67). However, similar changes were not observed following long-term treatment with trazodone or mianserin (68,69). Of interest is the lack of antidepressant effects on the blunted growth hormone response to clonidine during depression, and this might suggest a biochemical trait marker for depression (70). Depressed patients have shown an increased cortisol and blood pressure response to the α_2-antagonist yohimbine, although the plasma MHPG response was normal (71).

The responsiveness of the α_1-system has been more difficult to assess clinically. When the α_1-receptor agonist phenylephrine is placed in the eye, there is dilation of the iris. This effect is increased by MAOIs but decreased by TCAs (72–74). Amphetamine-induced NE release stimulates α_1-receptors, producing increased cortisol levels. This response is blunted in depressed patients, but there is no effect of ECT or TCA on this response (75,76).

The downregulation of the β-adrenergic receptor system by most antidepressants makes its assessment in patients of vital importance. In this regard, the secretion of melatonin is dependent on stimulation of the β-adrenergic receptor in specific neurons leading to the pineal gland, where melatonin is synthesized. Melatonin is a light-dependent hormone, and when lights are turned on during the night, the nocturnal rise in melatonin is abolished. Furthermore, the normal nighttime rise in melatonin is blunted in depressed patients, and desipramine treatment appears to increase it. This finding is opposite to that which would be predicted in depression from laboratory animal studies because a decrease in β-adrenergic receptor sensitivity would produce a blunting of the effects of light on nighttime melatonin (77,78).

Therapeutic Studies

The role of β-adrenergic receptor downregulation in the therapeutic actions of antidepressants has been evaluated indirectly by determining if a desipramine–yohimbine combination would result in more rapid antidepressant efficacy than desipramine alone. This study was based on the observation that combined desipramine–yohimbine administration treatment in laboratory rats results in a reduction in β-adrenergic receptor function and density within 4 days of drug administration, compared to the 2 to 3 weeks usually required by antidepressants alone. However, the desipramine–yohimbine combination was not effective in depressed patients who subsequently had therapeutic responses to lithium–antidepressant combinations (79).

Another approach to evaluate the clinical validity of the β-adrenergic receptor hypothesis of depression is to determine the effects of drugs with specific effects on β-adrenergic receptors. In this regard, the β-blocker propranolol would be expected to improve depressive symptoms based on this hypothesis. Instead, propranolol may induce depression in some vulnerable individuals (80). Furthermore, the β-receptor downregulation hypothesis of antidepressant action predicts that treatment that antagonize the antidepressant-induced decrease in β-adrenergic receptor density should prevent antidepressant responses. High doses of triiodothyronine (T_3) increase β-adrenergic receptor density in cerebral cortex and hypothalamus and block the decrease in β-adrenergic receptor downregulation produced by imipramine and desipramine (81). Yet, clinical investigations indicate that T_3 augments antidepressant effects, the opposite of what would be expected (82) (Table 7).

Summary

Although not all antidepressants reduce β-adrenergic receptor function and density, the β-adrenergic receptor downregulation hypothesis of antidepressant action continues to be a viable hypothesis and requires further testing. However, the relative paucity of preclinical behavioral models and

TABLE 7. *Therapeutic studies relevant to β-receptor sensitivity hypotheses of antidepressant action*

Therapeutic approach	Results and implications
Desipramine–yohimbine combination treatment of depression	Since this combination produced a rapid downregulation of β-adrenergic receptors in laboratory rats, it was predicted it would have rapid antidepressant effects; however, the combination was not effective in depressed patients who subsequently responded to other antidepressant combinations
Triiodothyronine augmentation of antidepressant action	Clinical investigations have demonstrated that triiodothyronine administration augments antidepressant effects; however, contrary to the β-adrenergic downregulation hypothesis of antidepressant action, in laboratory rats triiodothyronine blocks the decrease in β-adrenergic receptor downregulation produced by antidepressants
Propranolol use in cardiovascular disease	Contrary to the β-adrenergic downregulation hypothesis of antidepressant action, propranolol, when used for cardiovascular disease, has been shown to produce depression in vulnerable individuals

clinical paradigms capable of assessing β-receptor functions that are relevant to antidepressant actions has limited conclusions regarding the therapeutic relevance of β-receptor downregulation. To date, the clinical studies that have been conducted do not support the β-adrenergic receptor downregulation hypothesis.

Preclinical and clinical investigations have demonstrated that the ability to reduce α_2-receptor sensitivity is a property shared only by select antidepressants with strong NE uptake inhibition or MAOI properties. These data indicate that α_2-receptor downregulation probably does not represent a common therapeutic mechanism of action of antidepressant treatments. Studies designed to differentiate the functional properties of presynaptic and postsynaptic α_2-receptors and the relative effects of antidepressants on these receptors will be of value. In addition, it is possible that certain depressive subtypes (e.g., bipolar disorder) will have therapeutic responses to α_2-receptor antagonists. Such studies are in progress with the α_2-receptor antagonist idazoxan (83).

The role of α_1-adrenergic receptors in the mechanism of action of antidepressant treatment remains to be classified. More work is needed to define the function of these receptors in brain and better understand the relationship between the neurophysiological and receptor binding studies. Improved clinical methods are required to evaluate appropriately α_1-receptor function in human subjects. Therapeutic studies designed to test the validity of the α_1-receptor hypothesis of antidepressant action also are indicated.

OTHER NEUROTRANSMITTER RECEPTOR HYPOTHESES OF ANTIDEPRESSANT ACTION

GABA$_B$ Receptor Upregulation

Chronic but not acute administration of some antidepressants may increase ^{3}H-GABA binding to GABA$_B$-receptors in the frontal cortex (84). A possible consequence of the upregulation of GABA$_B$ recognition sites is an enhancement of monoaminergic neurotransmission. GABA$_B$ sites occur on noradrenergic terminals in the rat cerebral cortex. Baclofen, a GABA$_B$ agonist, enhances NE-stimulated cAMP production, and this effect is potentiated by long-term imipramine treatment. Five days of combined baclofen–imipramine administration results in significant decreases in β-adrenergic receptor density and NE-stimulated cAMP accumulation, effects not induced by either drug alone. The findings suggest that GABA$_B$ agonists, either alone or in combination with antidepressants, may be useful antidepressant treatments (85).

Enhancement of Dopamine Neurotransmission

Antidepressant drugs do not have consistent effects on dopamine D$_2$-receptor density in the limbic system (86). However, there is evidence that acute administration of some antidepressants decreases dopamine D$_1$-receptor binding as reflected by changes in ^{3}H-SCH 23390 binding in the striatum and limbic forebrain (87).

The behavioral paradigms used to evaluate postsynaptic dopamine function include amphetamine- and apomorphine-induced increases in locomotor hyperactivity and stereotypy. Various antidepressant drugs enhance amphetamine- or apomorphine-induced changes in locomotor activity, but not all antidepressants are active in these models. In general, amphetamine- or apomorphine-induced stereotypy is not altered consistently by antidepressant treatments. Biochemical and behavioral studies also indicate that long-term antidepressant administration does not consistently alter dopamine autoreceptor function (86,88–90).

Clinical studies demonstrate that apomorphine-stimulated growth hormone release is not affected reliably by repeated ECT and is decreased by long-term amitryptyline treatment. However, the validity of this model of dopamine function has been questioned. Apomorphine-induced prolactin inhibition was observed to be increased by repeated ECT in two of three investigations. Bromocriptine-induced prolactin inhibition has been found to be increased by chronic amitriptyline treatment (86).

Clinical efficacy studies using dopamine precursors or drugs that increase dopamine release indicate that simply increasing the availability of synaptic dopamine is not an effective antidepressant treatment for the majority of depressed patients. However, the dopamine agonist piribedil may have antidepressant properties, particularly in patients with low pretreatment CSF HVA (91). Nomifensine, which potently antagonizes dopamine neuronal reuptake, has been demonstrated to have robust antidepressant properties (92). There are considerable anecdotal data that nomifensine is effective for some depressed patients refractory to conventional treatments. Unfortunately, nomifensine is no longer generally available because of hematological side effects. Therefore, an effort should be made to develop and evaluate the effects of other potent dopamine reuptake inhibitors in depressed patients.

Downregulation of Cholinergic Function

At clinical doses, some TCAs are as potent cholinergic receptor blockers as classic anticholinergic drugs. However, the rank order of their potency as anticholinergics and as antidepressant drugs differs (93). Despite the evidence for a role of cholinergic mechanisms in the development of depressed mood, an evaluation of the anticholinergic effects of antidepressants demonstrates that if anticholinergic action is important, it is, at best, an enhancing one rather than the underlying primary therapeutic action. This issue could be addressed more definitively by placebo-controlled investigations of the antidepressant efficacy of centrally acting selective anticholinergic drugs.

IS THERE A COMMON MECHANISM FOR ANTIDEPRESSANT ACTION?

One of the purposes of this review is to determine whether a specific alteration in neuronal receptor sensitivity during long-term antidepressant treatment may account for the therapeutic mechanism of most antidepressant drugs. Unfortunately, to date, preclinical paradigms of receptor function have not revealed an alteration of receptor function that is consistent across the spectrum of therapeutic agents. Clinical investigations have failed to determine unequivocally which of the neurobiological actions of antidepressant treatment are necessary or sufficient for antidepressant efficacy.

However, it can be concluded that the effects of long-term antidepressant treatment on enhanced 5HT function appear relevant to their therapeutic activity. Similarly, the reduction in 5HT availability by PCPA or by a TFD produces depressive relapse in remitted depressed patients. These observations suggest that the integrity of the 5HT neuronal system may be necessary for maintenance of the remission induced by at least some antidepressant drugs.

The 5HT neuronal enhancement hypothesis has led to a new, effective treatment approach for resistant depression. The original studies of lithium augmentation were based on a clearly defined preclinical hypothesis of psychotropic drug mechanism (i.e., potentiation of 5HT function). Although the demonstrated efficacy of lithium augmentation was consistent with the preclinical prediction, direct clinical demonstration of the mechanism of this action is lacking at present. The observations of Price et al. (46) indicate that the rapid antidepressant effect of lithium augmentation (less than 7 days) is less common than originally suggested and that up to 3 weeks of lithium administration may be required to obtain therapeutic responses. This suggests that the acute effect of lithium of increasing presynaptic 5HT release may not be the primary therapeutic mechanism and that the actions of lithium on the regulation of 5HT neurotransmission must be considered. Lithium may work by stabilizing homeostatic systems that may be dysregulated in affective disorder patients (94–96). This may explain why the addition of 5HT precursors, tryptophan and 5-HTP, and fenfluramine to antidepressant regimens in treatment-refractory patients has been therapeutically disappointing.

BIOLOGICAL HETEROGENEITY OF DEPRESSIVE ILLNESS AND THE TREATMENT OF REFRACTORY DEPRESSION

A major advance in the treatment of depression will occur with the development of biological markers capable of subtyping different forms of depressive illness. Rational treatment strategies could then be devised for the treatment of refractory patients. For example, patients whose depression is related to reduced 5HT function may respond preferentially to 5HT reuptake inhibitors, such as fluoxetine and fluvoxamine, alone or in combination with lithium (97). It has been speculated that MAOIs may be a better alternative to TCAs in treating depressed patients with decreased 5HT activity (98). In this regard, there is clinical support for the effectiveness of MAOI–tryptophan and MAOI–lithium combinations in the treatment of refractory depressed patients (99).

A subgroup of patients may be depressed because of a reduction in noradrenergic neuronal activity. There is some evidence suggesting that bipolar depression is characterized by decreased noradrenergic function. It would be of interest to determine if α_2-receptor antagonists, such as yohimbine and idazoxan, which cause large increases in noradrenergic neuronal activity, are effective in this biologically defined subgroup.

Similarly, it is probable that some depressed patients will benefit from an enhancement of dopamine function. This is supported by the observations that the dopamine reuptake inhibitor nomifensine was particularly effective in selected patients. The beneficial effects of antidepressant–stimulant combinations in some refractory depressed patients may relate to an augmentation of dopamine function (100).

There are specific effective treatments for treatment-refractory depressed patients that cannot be related to specific neurotransmitter mechanisms. The addition of T_3 to TCAs and MAOIs has been shown to be clinically useful (82,101). A number of different mechanisms have been proposed to explain this action. Most authors suggest that T_3 augments noradrenergic function by increasing NE synthesis and β and α_1-noradrenergic receptor sensitivity. Some have argued that certain depressed patients may suffer from a subclinical hypothyroid state accompanied by normal routine thyroid indices.

Bupropion is an atypical antidepressant that is structurally unique and is not a monoamine reuptake inhibitor that alters receptor sensitivity (102). Its mechanism of action is not known, yet there is some evidence that bupropion may be effective in patients in whom other treatments have failed. Identification of the therapeutic mechanism of action of bupropion may result in a new class of antidepressant drugs.

There is an extensive body of evidence that supports an important role for ECT in the treatment of refractory depression, particularly for patients with psychotic symptoms. However, the mechanism of ECT's superior antidepressant efficacy remains obscure despite preclinical studies that identify numerous effects of ECT on brain neurotransmitter function. This is, in part, because very few clinical neurobiological investigations of ECT have been conducted.

DISCUSSION

It is generally believed that monoamine systems are involved either as primary steps in the pathogenesis of depression or at least as secondary reflections of abnormalities in other parts of the brain. Most effective antidepressants produce changes in monoamine receptor system function, although the essential and critical dimensions of these changes that apply in the clinical situation have not yet been fully identified. The probable involvement of multiple monoamine transmitter systems in the mechanism of action of antidepressants and the complex presynaptic and postsynaptic regulation of involvement of each monoamine system function have suggested several generic approaches to the treatment of refractory depression.

Treatment augmentation strategies use knowledge of the multiple levels of biochemical events that occur at both the presynaptic and postsynaptic levels within a neurotransmitter system in order to maximize the influence of antidepressants on neurotransmission. For example, the combination of a precursor and a blocker of metabolic enzymes, such as the addition of tryptophan to MAOIs treatment, is a useful therapeutic strategy based on knowledge of the function of the 5HT system. In addition, the use of lithium, which increases 5HT release, in combination with antidepressants, which sensitize postsynaptic 5HT receptors, was based on similar knowledge. It is likely that with improved understanding of the effects of antidepressant drug action beyond receptor recognition sites, more specific methods for augmenting an ongoing treatment and improving neurotransmission will be developed.

REFERENCES

1. Bunney WE Jr, Davis JM. Norepinephrine in depressive reactions: A review. *Arch Gen Psychiatry* 1965;13:483–494.
2. Schildkraut JJ. The catecholamine hypothesis of affective disorders: A review of supporting evidence. *Am J Psychiatry* 1965;122:509–522.
3. Charney DS, Menkes DB, Heninger GR. Receptor sensitivity and the mechanism of action of antidepressant treatment. *Arch Gen Psychiatry* 1981;38:1160–1180.
4. Lapin IP, Oxenkrug GF. Intensification of the central serotonergic processes as a possible determinant of the thymoleptic effect. *Lancet* 1969;1:132–136.
5. Heninger GR, Charney DS. Mechanisms of action of antidepressant treatments: Implications for the etiology and treatment of depressive disorders. In: Meltzer HY, ed. *Psychopharmacology, The third generation of progress.* New York: Raven Press, 1986;535–544.
6. Cooper JR, Bloom FE, Roth RH. *The biochemical basis of neuropharmacology,* 5th ed. New York: Oxford University Press, 1986.
7. Scuvee-Moreau JJ, Svensson TH. Sensitivity in vivo of central α_2- and opiate receptors after chronic treatment with various antidepressants. *J Neural Trans* 1982;54:51–63.
8. deMontigny C, Blier P, Chaput Y. Electrophysiologically identified serotonin receptors in the rat CNS: Effect of antidepressant treatment. *Neuropharmacology* 1984;23:1511–1520.
9. Peroutka SJ. 5-Hydroxytryptophan receptor subtypes: Molecular, biochemical and physiological characterizations. *Trends Neurosci* 1988;11:496–500.
10. Baraban JM, Worley PF, Snyder SH. Second messenger systems and psychoactive drug action: Focus on the phosphoinositide system and lithium. *Am J Psychiatry* 1989;146:1251–1260.
11. deMontigny C, Aghajanian GK. Tricyclic antidepressants: Long-term treatment increases responsivity of rat forebrain neurons to serotonin. *Science* 1978;202:1303–1306.
12. Green AR, Heal OJ, Goodwin GM. The effects of electroconvulsive therapy and antidepressant drugs on monoamine receptors in rodent brain. In: Porter R, Bock G, Clark S, eds. *Antidepressant and receptor function.* New York: John Wiley & Sons, 1986;246–259.
13. Langer SZ, Galzin AM, Lee CR, Schoemaker H. Antidepressants—Binding sites in brain and platelets. In: Porter R, Bock G, Clark S, eds. *Antidepressants and receptor function.* New York: John Wiley & Sons, 1986;3–17.
14. Asberg M, Wagner A. Biochemical effects of antidepressant treatment—Studies of monoamine metabolites in cerebrospinal fluid and platelet ^{3}H-imipramine binding. In: Porter R, Bock G, Clark S, eds. *Antidepressants and receptor function.* New York: John Wiley & Sons, 1986;57–76.
15. Wagner A, Aberg-Wistedt A, Asberg M, Bertilsson L, Montero D, Martensson B. Platelet ^{3}H-imipramine binding in depression: Short and long-term effects of antidepressant drugs, ECT, and lithium. *Arch Gen Psychiatry* 1987;44:870–877.
16. Blier P, deMontigny C. Electrophysiological in-

vestigations on the effect of repeated zimelidine administration on serotonergic neurotransmission in the rat. *Soc Neurosci* 1983;3:1270–1278.
17. Blier P, deMontigny C, Tardif D. Effects of the two antidepressant drugs mianserin and indalpine on the serotoninergic system: Single-cell studies in the rat. *Psychopharmacology* 1984;84:242–249.
18. Blier P, deMontigny C. Serotoninergic but not noradrenergic neurons in rat central nervous system adapt to long-term treatment with monoamine oxidase inhibitors. *Neuroscience* 1985;16:949–955.
19. Blier P, deMontigny C, Azzaro AJ. Modification of serotonergic and noradrenergic neurotransmissions by repeated administration of monoamine oxidase inhibitors: Electrophysiological studies in the rat central nervous system. *J Pharmacol Exp Ther* 1986;237:987–994.
20. Chaput Y, deMontigny C, Blier P. Effects of a selective 5-HT reuptake blocker, citalopram, on the sensitivity of 5-HT autoreceptors: Electrophysiological study in the rat brain. *Naunyn Schmiedebergs Arch Pharmacol* 1986;333:342–348.
21. Lucki I, Minugh-Purvis N. Serotonin-induced head shaking behavior in rats does not involve receptors located in the frontal cortex. *Brain Res* 1987;420:403–406.
22. Charney DS, Heninger GR, Sternberg DE. Serotonin function and mechanism of action of antidepressant treatment: Effects of amitriptyline and desipramine. *Arch Gen Psychiatry* 1984;41:359–364.
23. Price LH, Charney DS, Delgado PL, Heninger GR. Lithium treatment and serotonergic function. *Arch Gen Psychiatry* 1989;46:13–19.
24. Price LH, Charney DS, Heninger GR. Effects of tranylcypromine treatment on neuroendocrine, behavioral and autonomic response to tryptophan in depressed patients. *Life Sci* 1985;37:809–818.
25. Price LH, Charney DS, Delgado PL, Anderson GM, Heninger GR. Effects of desipramine and fluvoxamine treatment on the prolactin response to tryptophan. *Arch Gen Psychiatry* 1989;46:625–631.
26. Price LH, Charney DS, Heninger GR. Effects of trazodone treatment on serotonergic function in depressed patients. *Psychiatry Res* 1988;24:165–175.
27. Muhlbauer HD, Muller-Oerlinghausen B. Fenfluramine stimulation of serum cortisol in patients with major affective disorders and healthy controls: Further evidence for a central serotonergic action of lithium in man. *J Neural Trans* 1985;61:81–94.
28. Shapira B, Reiss A, Kaiser N, Kindler S, Lerer BJ. Effect of imipramine treatment on the prolactin response to fenfluramine and placebo challenge in depressed patients. *J Aff Dis* 1989;16:1–4.
29. Shapira B, Kindler S, Gropp C, Lichtenberg P, Lerer B. ECT enhances prolactin response to fenfluramine challenge. *Abstracts VIII World Congress of Psychiatry*, p 195.
30. Meltzer HY, Lowy M, Robertson A, Goodnick P, Perline R. Effect of 5-hydroxytryptophan on serum cortisol levels in major affective disorders. *Arch Gen Psychiatry* 1984;41:391–397.
31. Van de Kar LD, Karteszi M, Bethea CL, Ganong WF. Serotonergic stimulation of prolactin and corticosterone secretion is mediated by different pathways from the mediobasal hypothalamus. *Neuroendocrinology* 1985;41:380–384.
32. Fuxe K, Butcher LL, Engel J. D,L-5-Hydroxytryptophan-induced changes in central monoamine neurons after peripheral decarboxylase inhibition. *J Pharm Pharmacol* 1971;23:420–424.
33. deMontigny C, Grunberg F, Mayer A, Deschenes JP. Lithium induces rapid relief of depression in tricyclic antidepressant drug nonresponders. *Br J Psychiatry* 1981;138:252–256.
34. Heninger GR, Charney DS, Sternberg DE. Lithium carbonate augmentation of antidepressant treatment: An effective prescription for treatment-refractory depression. *Arch Gen Psychiatry* 1983;40:1335–1342.
35. deMontigny C, Cournoyer G, Morissette R, Langlois R, Caille G. Lithium carbonate addition in tricyclic antidepressant-resistant depression: Correlations with the neurobiologic actions of tricyclic antidepressant drugs and lithium ion on the serotonin system. *Arch Gen Psychiatry* 1983;40:1327–1334.
36. Nelson JC, Byck R. Rapid response to lithium in phenelzine non-responders. *Am J Psychiatry* 1982;141:85–86.
37. Price LH, Conwell Y, Nelson JC. Lithium augmentation of combined neuroleptic–tricyclic treatment in delusional depression. *Am J Psychiatry* 1983;140:318–322.
38. Birkhimer LJ, Alderman AA, Schmitt CE, Ednie KJ. Combined trazodone–lithium therapy for refractory depression. *Am J Psychiatry* 1983;140:1382–1383.
39. Joyce PR, Hewland HR, Jones AV. Rapid response to lithium in treatment-resistant depression. *Br J Psychiatry* 1983;142:204–205.
40. Louie AK, Meltzer HY. Lithium potentiation of antidepressant treatment. *J Clin Psychopharmacol* 1984;4:316–321.
41. deMontigny C, Elie R, Caillé C. Rapid response to the addition of lithium in iprindole-resistant unipolar depression: A pilot study. *Am J Psychiatry* 1984;142:220–223.
42. Schrader GD, Levien HEM. Response to sequential administration of clomipramine and lithium carbonate in treatment-resistant depression. *Br J Psychiatry* 1985;147:573–575.
43. Roy A, Pickar D. Lithium potentiation of imipramine in treatment-resistant depression. *Br J Psychiatry* 1985;147:582–583.
44. Nelson JC, Mazure CM. Lithium augmentation in psychotic depression refractory to combined drug treatment. *Am J Psychiatry* 1986;143:363–366.
45. Kushnir SL. Lithium–antidepressant combina-

tions in the treatment of depressed, physically ill geriatric patients. *Am J Psychiatry* 1986; 143:378–379.
46. Price LH, Charney DS, Heninger GR. Variability of response to lithium augmentation in refractory depression. *Am J Psychiatry* 1986; 143:1387–1392.
47. Kramlinger KG, Post RM. The addition of lithium to carbamazepine: Antidepressant efficacy in treatment-resistant depression. *Arch Gen Psychiatry* 1989;46:794–800.
48. Shopsin B, Friedman E, Gershon S. Parachlorophenylalanine reversal of tranylcypromine effects in depressed patients. *Arch Gen Psychiatry* 1976;33:811–819.
49. Shopsin B, Friedman E, Goldstein M, Gershon S. The uses of synthesis inhibitors in determining a role for biogenic amines during imipramine treatment in depressed patients. *Psychopharmacol Commun* 1975;1:239–249.
50. Delgado PL, Charney DS, Price LH, et al. Behavioral effects of acute tryptophan depletion in depressed and obsessive compulsive disorder (OCD) patients. *Arch Gen Psychiatry* (in press).
51. Bowden CL, Koslow S, Maas JW, et al. Changes in urinary catecholamines and their metabolites in depressed patients treated with amitriptyline or imipramine. *J Psychiat Res* 1987;21:111–128.
52. Sulser F, Vetulani J, Mobley PL. Mode of action of antidepressant drugs. *Biochem Pharmacol* 1978;27:257–261.
53. Finberg JP. Antidepressant drugs and downregulation of presynaptic receptors. *Biochem Pharm* 1987;36:3557–3562.
54. Menkes DB, Kehne JH, Gallager DW, Aghajanian GK, Davis M. Functional supersensitivity of CNS A_1-adrenoceptors following chronic antidepressant treatment. *Life Sci* 1983;33:181–188.
55. Lipinski JF, Cohen BM, Zubenko GS, Waternaux CM. Adrenoceptors and the pharmacology of affective illness: A unifying theory. *Life Sci* 1987;40:1947–1963.
56. Costa E, Ravizza ML, Barbaccia ML. Evaluation of current theories on the mode of action of antidepressants. In: Bartholini G, Lloyd KG, Morselli PL, eds. *Mode of action of antidepressants.* New York: Raven Press, 1986;9–21.
57. Duman RS, Strada SJ, Enna SJ. Effect of imipramine and adrenocorticotropin administration on the rat brain norepinephrine-coupled cyclic nucleotide generating system. Alteration in alpha and beta adrenergic components. *J Pharmacol Exp Ther* 1985;234:409–414.
58. Garcia G, Smokeum RWJ, Stephenson JD, et al. Effect of some atypical antidepressants on beta adrenoceptor binding and adenylate cyclase activity in the rat forebrain. *Eur J Pharmacol* 1985;108:1–7.
59. Hyttel J, Overo KF, Arnt J. Biochemical effects and drug levels in rats after long-term treatment with the specific 5-HT uptake inhibitor, citalopram. *Psychopharmacology* 1984; 83:20–27.
60. Menkes DB, Kehne JH, Gallager DW, et al. Functional supersensitivity of CNS alpha$_1$ adrenoceptors following chronic antidepressant treatment. *Life Sci* 1983;33:181–188.
61. Hong KW, Rhim BY, Lee WS. Enhancement of central and peripheral alpha$_1$ adrenoceptor sensitivity and reduction of alpha$_2$ adrenoceptor sensitivity following chronic imipramine treatment in rats. *Eur J Pharmacol* 1986;120:275–283.
62. Maj J, Rogoz Z, Skuza G, et al. Repeated treatment with antidepressant drugs potentiates the locomotor response to (+)-amphetamine. *J Pharm Pharmacol* 1984;36:127–130.
63. Maj J, Klimek V, Nowak G. Antidepressant drugs given repeatedly increase binding to alpha$_1$ adrenoceptors in the rat cortex. *Eur J Pharmacol* 1985;119:113–116.
64. Cohen RM, Aulakh CS, Campbell IC, et al. Functional subsensitivity of alpha$_2$ adrenoceptors accompanies reductions in yohimbine binding after clorgyline treatment. *Eur J Pharmacol* 1982;81:145–148.
65. Siever LJ, Uhde TW, Silberman EK, et al. The growth hormone response to clonidine as a probe of noradrenergic receptor responsiveness in affective disorder patients and controls. *Psychiatry Res* 1982;6:171–183.
66. Charney DS, Heninger GR, Sternberg DE, et al. Presynaptic adrenergic receptor sensitivity in depression: The effect of long-term desipramine treatment. *Arch Gen Psychiatry* 1981;38: 1334–1340.
67. Charney DS, Heninger GR, Sternberg DE. Alpha$_2$ adrenergic receptor sensitivity and the mechanism of action of antidepressant therapy: The effect of long-term amitriptyline treatment. *Br J Psychiatry* 1983;142:265–275.
68. Charney DS, Heninger GR, Sternberg DE. The effect of mianserin on alpha$_2$ adrenergic receptor function in depressed patients. *Br J Psychiatry* 1984;144:407–416.
69. Price LH, Charney DS, Heninger GR. Effects of trazodone treatment on alpha$_2$ adrenoceptor function in depressed patients. *Psychopharmacology* 1986;89:38–44.
70. Charney DS, Heninger GR, Sternberg DE. Failure of chronic antidepressant treatment to alter growth hormone response to clonidine. *Psychiatry Res* 1982;7:135–138.
71. Heninger GR, Charney DS, Price LH. Alpha$_2$ adrenergic receptor sensitivity in depression: The plasma MHPG, behavioral, and cardiovascular responses to yohimbine. *Arch Gen Psychiatry* 1988;45:165–175.
72. Checkley SA, Corn TH, Glass IB, Thompson C, Franey C, Arendt J. Neuroendocrine and other studies of the mechanism of antidepressant action of desipramine. In: Porter R, Bock G, Clark S, eds. *Antidepressants and receptor function.* New York: John Wiley & Sons, 1986;126–142.
73. Shur E, Checkley SA. Pupil studies in de-

pressed patients: An investigation of the mechanism of action in desipramine. *Br J Psychiatry* 1982;140:181–184.
74. Shur E, Checkley SA, Delgado I. Failure of mianserin to affect autonomic function in the pupils of depressed patients. *Acta Psychiatr Scand* 1983;67:50–55.
75. Checkley SA. Corticosteroid and growth hormone responses to methylamphetamine in depressive illness. *Psychol Med* 1979;9:107–115.
76. Sachar EJ, Asnis G, Nathan S. Dextro amphetamine and cortisol in depression: Morning plasma cortisol levels suppressed. *Arch Gen Psychiatry* 1980;37:755–757.
77. Cowen PJ, Green AR, Grahame-Smith DG, et al. Plasma melatonin during desmethylimipramine treatment—Evidence for changes in noradrenergic transmission. *Br J Clin Pharmacol* 1985;19:799–805.
78. Murphy DL, Tamarkin L, Sunderland T, et al. Human plasma melatonin is elevated during treatment with the monoamine oxidase inhibitors clorgyline and transycypromine but not deprenyl. *Psychiatry Res* 1986;17:119–127.
79. Charney DS, Price LH, Heninger GR. Desipramine–yohimbine combination treatment of refractory depression: Implications for the β-adrenergic receptor hypothesis of antidepressant action. *Arch Gen Psychiatry* 1986;43:1155–1161.
80. Avorn J, Everitt DE, Weiss S. Increased antidepressant use in patients prescribed β-blockers. *JAMA* 1986;255:357–360.
81. Mason GA, Bondy SC, Nemeroff CB, Walker CH, Prange AJ Jr. The effects of thyroid state on beta-adrenergic and serotonergic receptors in rat brain. *Psychoneuroendocrinology* 1987;12:261–270.
82. Goodwin FK, Prange AJ, Post RM, Muscettola G, Lipton MA. Potentiation of antidepressant effect by triiodothyronine in tricyclic nonresponders. *Am J Psychiatry* 1982;139:34–38.
83. Osman OT, Rudorfer MV, Potter WZ. Idazoxan, a selective alpha$_2$ antagonist and effective sustained antidepressant in two bipolar depressed patients. *Arch Gen Psychiatry* 1989;46:958–959.
84. Lloyd KG, Thuret F, Pilc A. Upregulation of γ-aminobutyric acid GABA$_B$ binding sites in rat frontal cortex: A common action of repeated administration of different classes of antidepressants and electroshock. *J Pharmacol Exp Ther* 1985;235:191–199.
85. Enna SJ, Karbon EW, Duman RS. GABA$_B$ agonists and imipramine-induced modifications in rat brain β-adrenergic receptor binding and function. In: Bartholini G, Lloyd G, Morselli PL, eds. *GABA and mood disorders.* New York: Raven Press, 1986;23–31.
86. Willner P. Dopamine and depression: A review of recent evidence. III. The effects of antidepressant treatments. *Brain Res Rev* 1983;6:237–246.
87. Klimek V, Nielsen M. Chronic treatment with antidepressants decreases the number of ^{3}H-SCH 23390 binding sites in the rat striatum and limbic system. *Eur J Pharmacol* 1987;139:163–169.
88. Chiodo LA, Antelman SM. Repeated tricyclics induce a progressive dopamine autoreceptor subsensitivity independent of daily drug treatment. *Nature* 1980;287:451–454.
89. Mac Neill DA, Gower M. Do antidepressants induce dopamine autoreceptor subsensitivity? *Nature (Lond)* 1982;298:302–303.
90. Diggory GL, Buckett WR. Chronic antidepressant administration fails to attenuate apomorphine-induced decreases in rat striatal dopamine metabolites. *Eur J Pharmacol* 1984;105:257–263.
91. Post RM, Gerner RH, Carman JS, et al. Effects of dopamine agonist piribedil in depressed patients. *Arch Gen Psychiatry* 1978;35:609–615.
92. Brogden RN, Heel RC, Speight TM, Avery GS. Nomifensine: A review of its pharmacological properties and therapeutic efficacy in depressive illness. *Drugs* 1979;18:1–24.
93. Richelson E. The newer antidepressants: Structures, pharmacodynamics, and proposed mechanisms of action. *Psychopharmacol Bull* 1984;20:213–223.
94. Rudorfer MV, Karoum F, Ross RJ, Potter WZ, Linnoila M. Differences in lithium effects in depressed and healthy subjects. *Clin Pharmacol Ther* 1985;37:66–71.
95. Siever LJ, Davis KL. Overview: Toward a dysregulation hypothesis of depression. *Am J Psychiatry* 1985;142:1017–1031.
96. Price LH, Charney DS, Delgado PL, Heninger GR. Lithium treatment and serotoninergic function: Neuroendocrine and behavioral responses to intravenous tryptophan in affective disorder. *Arch Gen Psychiatry* 1989;46:13–19.
97. Delgado PL, Price LH, Charney DS, Heninger GR. Efficacy of fluvoxamine in treatment-refractory depression. *J Affect Dis* 1988;15:55–60.
98. Aulakh CS, Cohen RM, Dauphin MM, McLellan CA, Murphy DL. Role of serotonergic input in the down-regulation of β-adrenoceptors following long-term clorgyline treatment. *Eur J Pharmacol* 1988;156:63–70.
99. Price LH, Charney DS, Heninger GR. Efficacy of lithium–tranylcypromine treatment in refractory depression. *Am J Psychiatry* 1985;142:619–623.
100. Wharton RN, Perel JM, Dayton PG. A potential clinical use for methylphenidate (Ritalin) with tricyclic antidepressants. *Am J Psychiatry* 1971;127:619–623.
101. Joffe RT. Triiodothyronine potentiation of the antidepressant effect of phenelzine. *J Clin Psychiatry* 1988;49:409–410.
102. Ferris RM, Beaman OJ. Bupropion: A new antidepressant drug the mechanism of action of which is not associated with downregulation of postsynaptic beta adrenergic, serotonergic (5-HT$_2$), alpha$_2$ adrenergic, imipramine, and dopaminergic receptors in brain. *Neuropharmacology* 1983;22:1257–1267.

4

Potentiation of Dopamine in the Treatment of Refractory Depression

Ossama T. Osman and William Z. Potter

The biochemical changes related to affective syndromes have been investigated extensively in biological psychiatry research (1,2). The biogenic amine hypotheses implicate different central monoamine neurotransmitters, including norepinephrine, serotonin, and dopamine systems (1,3–5). The norepinephrine and serotonin systems have been most widely implicated in the mode of action of antidepressant treatments (1,6). On the other hand, the occasional considerations of dopamine system involvement in depression are overshadowed by the many studies of dopamine in relationship to the mode of action of antipsychotic drugs (7,8). It is still postulated that the blockade of dopamine receptors in some way contributes to the antipsychotic efficacy of drugs (9). It is much less clear, however, that stimulation of the dopamine system necessarily leads to psychosis. The most potently psychotomimetic compounds, such as LSD, appear to function more as serotonin agonists. Rather than starting with the notion of specific neurotransmitter links to nosological entities or circumscribed roles in either the antidepressant or antipsychotic action of drugs, we return to empirical clinical observations. We argue that many of the clinical treatments that are used in practice to manage depressions not responding to standard approaches, i.e., refractory depressions, involve stimulation of dopamine function.

The pharmacotherapeutic strategies that most likely involve transient or sustained increases of dopamine function (Table 1) include the psychostimulants, cocaine, amphetamine, and methylphenidate, the latter two of which are added by clinicians to other regimens. Alone, none of these agents appears to be a good antidepressant following chronic administration. This point is important, since it suggests that in depression, whether refractory or not, sustained antidepressant effects may involve effects on more than one system, a point to which we shall return. Antidepressant drugs that involve at least some enhancement of dopamine include nomifensine, probably bupropion, and monoamine oxidase inhibitors (MAOIs), whether alone or in combination with standard tricyclic antidepressants (TCAs). Interestingly, the direct dopamine agonists, piribedil and bromocriptine, have been clinically disappointing.

The role of these direct dopamine agonists (Table 2) in the treatment of depression has been reviewed elsewhere (10,11). Although reported in less than three patients, the relatively selective postsynaptic dopamine agonist, piribedil, appeared to have antidepressant properties (12,13). Dysphoric effects that emerged over time (13) seem to have discouraged further research with this compound. More recently, the dopamine agonist, bromocriptine, has

---

Section on Clinical Pharmacology, National Institute of Mental Health, Bethesda, MD 20892

TABLE 1. *Pharmacological bridge for dopamine neurotransmitter effects vs behavioral response*

Drug	Output	Effect
Cocaine	(DA, NE)[a]	Euphoria/rush
Dextroamphetamine	(DA, NE)	Activation
Nomifensine	(DA, NE)	Antidepressant (for refractory patients)
Bupropion	(DA, ? NE)	Antidepressant (for refractory patients)
MAOI + TCA	(DA, NE, 5HT)	Antidepressant (for refractory patients)
Bromocriptine	(DA)	Antidepressant (for refractory patients)

[a] DA, dopamine; NE, norepinephrine.

been reported to have antidepressant effects, especially in bipolar patients who sometimes develop manic symptoms (14). As pointed out by Jimerson and Post (10), dose may be very important in determining whether dopamine agonists have a predominant postsynaptic stimulatory effect or a mixed effect secondary to inhibition of neuronal firing by activation of dopamine autoreceptors (15). It is difficult to conclude from the limited reports whether direct dopamine agonists per se constitute a potentially useful class of drugs for depression.

Similarly, to the extent that the psychostimulants act by releasing dopamine, it may be that they suffer from the same limitations as direct agonists. This leaves the more indirect acting drugs, such as partial dopamine uptake inhibitors or MAOIs, which presumably enhance intrasynaptic dopamine by increasing the amount released per impulse (16). These latter actions more gradually shift the balance and permit various intact presynaptic (and perhaps postsynaptic) homeostatic mechanisms to grade the increase in active dopamine. Particularly in the case of MAOIs, it is now clear in both rat and human that some dopamine-mediated functions are enhanced. For instance, type A MAO appears to play the primary role in regulating synaptic dopamine at D_1 and D_2 receptors in rat striatum (16). The MAO type B inhibitor, deprenyl, both reduces the dopamine metabolite homovanillic acid (HVA) in human cerebrospinal fluid (CSF) (17) and shows great promise in parkinsonism (18). It may be that MAO type A inhibitors would also be efficacious if the peripheral blood pressure increases resulting from combination with L-DOPA could be avoided. In any event, clorgyline, a type A MAOI, also reduces concentrations of HVA in CSF, suggesting an effect on dopamine function or turnover in depressed patients (19). In clinical practice, those MAOIs that are used can be presumed to affect both types A and B MAO, especially at the high doses employed in refractory depression (see Youdim et al., ref. 20, for a review of consequences of types A and B MAO inhibition). Moreover, at least in some depressed patients, measures of HVA in CSF support an abnormality of dopamine function.

Recently, it has become apparent that the reference treatment for refractory depression, electroconvulsive therapy (ECT) (see Chapter 9), may itself work partly through effects on dopamine function and increase HVA in the CSF of patients (21). As summarized in a recent review by Lerer (22), perturbation of more than one monoamine neurotransmitter likely plays a role in the antidepressant effects of ECT.

Multiple models are used in animals to study this question, including pharmacological challenges and lesioning of monoaminergic pathways (23). For example, the functional activity of the central dopamine

TABLE 2. *Direct dopamine agonists*

Drug	Clinical effects
Piribedil	Dysphoric over time
Bromocriptine	Can induce mania

system is assessed using dopamine agonists, e.g., apomorphine and quinpirole, releasing agents, e.g., amphetamine, the precursor L-DOPA, and indirect enhancers, such as MAOIs (22,24).

ECS alters dopamine receptor sensitivity, as shown by a number of measures. It enhances rats' ability to discriminate amphetamine (25), an effect that is dopamine mediated in the central nervous system (26,27). ECS induces supersensitivity to apomorphine as reflected in increased behavioral stereotypy. These changes, however, are not accompanied by alterations in the D_2 dopamine receptors as measured by ^{3}H-spiperone (28).

More recently, our laboratory found a selective increase of D_1 receptors in the substantia nigra (29) using quantitative autoradiography with iodinated SCH-23390 as a ligand. In complementary studies, Newman and Lerer (30) have shown enhancement of D_1-stimulated cAMP in the caudate after chronic ECS but not in the absence of D_2-stimulated inhibition of cAMP. These findings are in contrast to the reported enhancement of D_2 (quinpirole)-stimulated locomotor hyperactivity by a variety of antidepressant drugs (31). The effects of ECS on D_1 receptor function in rats also should be considered in light of the recent double-blind demonstrations of parkinsonism in humans (32) (for review, see 33).

By contrast, the noradrenergic effects of ECT include both downregulation of β_1-adrenergic receptors (34) and reduced adenylate cyclase (35). These effects are, of course, similar to those of antidepressant drugs. It is of interest to note that, unlike other antidepressants, ECT produces upregulation of serotonin $5HT_2$ receptors, at least in a narrowly defined area of prefrontal cortex (36). An intact noradrenergic function appears necessary for the ECT effects on enhancing dopamine and serotonin functions. Depletion of NE, by 6-hydroxydopamine lesioning of the locus coeruleus and dorsal and ventral noradrenergic bundles, did not alter behavioral responses to serotonergic (quipazine) and dopaminergic (apomorphine) agents but abolished the ECT-induced enhancement of these responses (37). Damage of central NE neurons by peripheral injection of the novel neurotoxin DSP-4 (N-[2-chloroethyl]-ethyl-2-bromo-benzylamine) produced similar effects (38).

In humans, ECT may increase the dopamine receptors' responsiveness, as suggested by post-ECT enhancement of apomorphine-induced suppression of prolactin in depressed patients (39). As mentioned at

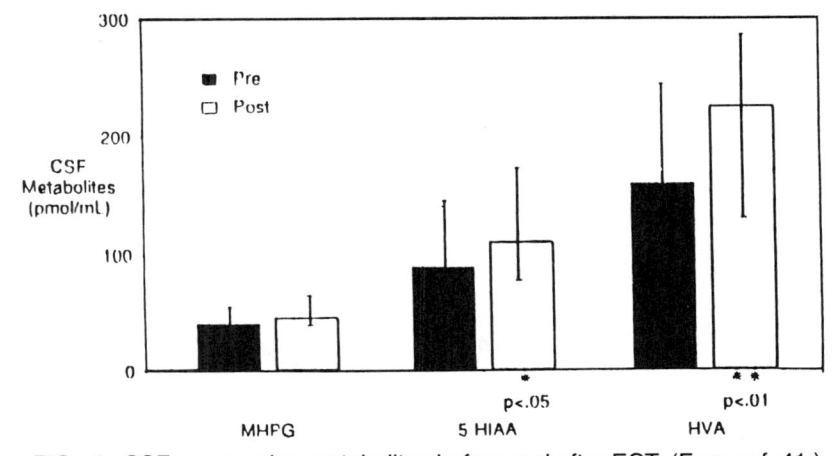

FIG. 1. CSF monoamine metabolites before and after ECT. (From ref. 41.)

TABLE 3. *Biochemical effects of ECT in humans*

CSF	MHPG	0
	5-HIAA	↑
	HVA	↑
Plasma	Norepinephrine	↓
	MHPG	0
	HVA	0
Urine	Norepinephrine	0
	MHPG	0
	VMA	0
	HVA	0

0 = unchanged.

the outset, biochemical effects of ECT include marked elevation in concentrations of HVA and 5-HIAA in ECT-responsive depressed patients, suggesting increases of both dopamine and serotonin turnover (Fig. 1). These findings are particularly striking, since a significant reduction of NE and serotonin turnover is observed after most antidepressant pharmacotherapies, including MAOIs and TCAs (40). Moreover, repeated ECT treatments do not reduce NE turnover (41). Biochemical studies on human CSF are summarized in Table 3.

This brings us to a consideration of studies relevant to dopamine turnover in untreated depression.

CEREBROSPINAL FLUID CONCENTRATIONS OF HOMOVANILLIC ACID

CSF concentrations of the neurotransmitter metabolite, HVA, reflect the activity of the brain dopamine system (42), especially that of the nigro striatal pathway adjacent to the lateral ventricles (43). The most consistent CSF finding in groups of depressed patients is an average reduction of HVA (44) (Table 4). For instance, in a study by Åsberg et al. (45) using a large number of subjects, it was found that unmedicated patients with melancholia ($n=83$) had approximately a 19% lower concentration of HVA than had healthy volunteer controls ($n=66$), which is consistent with some degree of central dopamine dysregulation.

Another line of evidence suggesting dopaminergic dysregulation arises from a consideration of genetic factors that clearly are involved in predisposition to psychotic illnesses, e.g., bipolar depressive illness and schizophrenia (46). The biochemical abnormalities correlated with these predispositions are not yet established. It appears, however, that family history of psychiatric morbidity is accompanied by greater variabilities in central neurotransmitter metabolite concentrations (47). In a study of a group of healthy subjects free of personal history of psychosis, 32 had no family history of psychiatric problems and 28 had a family history of psychiatric morbidity. Greater variabilities in CSF HVA concentrations were found in the second group. Subjects in the second group who had low HVA concentrations tended to have family members with depression. On the other hand, subjects with schizophrenic relatives had significantly higher HVA concentrations (47).

There is also evidence for a decreased rate of CSF HVA accumulation in subgroups of depressed patients: in those with bipolar versus unipolar depression, in those

TABLE 4. *CSF studies in depression: Patients vs controls*

	Through 1980 ($n=352$)	Karolinska 1984 ($n=83$)	NIMH Collaborative ($n=92$)
Depression vs normal			
HVA	↓	↓	↓
5HIAA	↓	↓	0
MHPG	0	0	0

0 = unchanged.

with marked psychomotor retardation versus agitation, and in those who are nonpsychotic versus those with hallucinations (for a review, see ref. 48).

Despite these biochemical lines of evidence implicating dopamine either in the action of certain treatments or in the pathophysiology of depression, most depressed patients (70–80%) are reported to improve on standard TCAs. Over a decade ago, Randrup and Braestrap (5) did suggest that the modest but consistent dopamine uptake-inhibiting potency of TCAs (IC$_{50}$ in the 5–10 μM range) might be important. On the other hand, the most selective TCA that they investigated in terms of NE uptake inhibition, desipramine (IC$_{50}$ of 0.0015 μM), is the compound shown to achieve a greater than 80% efficacy rate in more seriously depressed patients (49). Moreover, neither we nor others have been able to show effects of TCAs on concentrations of HVA in CSF.

This brings us to a consideration of the possibility that effects on multiple monoamine systems may be required in some patients. Put simply, drugs working primarily on the NE or 5HT system may work in most depressions, but in difficult cases, it may be necessary to add a dopaminergic compound. Probably the most consistent preclinical finding (in rodents) with antidepressants is some form of brain noradrenergic β-receptor downregulation following chronic administration. The next most frequent finding is alteration of serotonin receptors or function. Antidepressants are not reported to appreciably affect dopamine receptors (50,51), at least in striatum. The mesolimbic system, however, has a more important role in mediating the reward process, a function that is impaired in depression (52). Chronic administration of the TCA desipramine induces supersensitivity of postsynaptic dopamine receptors in this region (53).

As for effects on presynaptic dopamine receptors, antidepressants, such as imipramine, amitriptyline, and iprindole, produce a time-dependent and progressive subsensitization of dopamine autoreceptors (54). Thus, it may be that even antidepressants that act primarily on the NE or 5HT systems also affect some components of dopamine function. It is this notion to which we now briefly turn.

FUNCTIONAL AND BIOCHEMICAL EVIDENCE FOR NOREPINEPHRINE–DOPAMINE INTERACTIONS

Antelman and Chiodo (54) hypothesized that functional facilitation in the dopamine system occurs as a result of stressful stimuli to compensate for diminished intensity of noradrenergic activity and to maintain normal functioning. On the other hand, selective damage or interference with the central dopamine system may result in a significant dysfunction in noradrenergic-mediated stereotyped behaviors.

The evidence for interactions between NE and dopamine is accumulating, especially with regard to maintenance of behavioral reward, a parameter in animals that may model a response that is significantly impaired in depression (48). The dopaminergic mesolimbic system is of particular importance in mediating this reward behavior. O'Donohue et al. (55) studied the effects of noradrenergic ventral bundle transection on both NE and dopamine concentration and turnover in the mesolimbic system of rats. Unilateral ventral bundle transection increased dopamine in the A-10 region (mesolimbic dopamine cell bodies) and decreased dopamine in the nucleus accumbens, olfactory tubercle, and interstitial nucleus of the striae terminalis (mesolimbic terminal areas). Other studies have demonstrated that the mesolimbic dopamine cell bodies and their projections are necessary for the production of the so-called reward effect produced by i.v. self-administration of amphetamines (55,56). To put this in clinical perspective, depressed parkinsonian patients show a lack of response to i.v. methylphenidate as compared to controls without CNS or psychiatric disease, nondepressed parkinsonians, or typical depressed patients without parkinsonism (57). Such findings suggest a complex interplay between the ability to experience reward, intact dopaminergic and noradrenergic systems, and functional (depression) or pathologic (parkinsonism) disruption of these systems.

Moving beyond the concept of reward mechanisms, Oades (58) has suggested a more general model for NE–dopamine interactions based on an integration of electrophysiological and behavioral studies. The notion of NE as a modulator that subserves the function of enhancing signal/noise ratios in targeted brain areas is combined with the notion of dopamine as involved in the switching between channels of activity to different brain regions (58). In this model, smoothly working brain function would depend on both systems being intact. We would add to the model the concept that the modulatory function of the NE system can have as its target components of the dopamine system without invoking a role of dopamine in switching inputs to the NE system. Support for NE modulation of dopamine function is based on new studies that point to α_2-adrenergic receptor-mediated tonic control of the regularity (pattern) with which dopaminergic cells in the A_{10} region fire (59). Thus, drugs acting primarily on the NE system could affect the regularity of dopamine cell firing. Chronic but not acute administration of at least two classes of noradrenergic drugs, uptake inhibitors and α_2-antagonists, potentiate the locomotor effects of the D_2 agonist quinpirole (31). This finding is consistent with a modulation of dopamine receptor function that might result from sustained alteration of the firing pattern of dopamine neurons. These speculations hark back to the findings of Chiodo and Antelman (60), who demonstrated that chronic TCAs produced a progressive attenuation of apomorphine's ability to inhibit dopamine neuronal firing. As noted before, these investigators were the original proponents of an interacting dopamine–NE model in manic-depressive illness.

If we translate this information to a more general perspective on the treatment of depression, it would suggest that even if some modulation of dopamine function is involved in antidepressant efficacy (48), it might be achieved by drugs acting initially on NE. In patients refractory to standard TCAs, it may be necessary to alter dopamine function more directly. Thus, addition of amphetamine or methylphenidate to a TCA, the combination of TCAs and MAOIs, or use of putative dopamine inhibitors, such as bupropion (Table 1), may be required. Such explanations, however, cannot be sufficient because at least one other neurotransmitter, serotonin, is implicated in the mechanism of action of antidepressant treatments. Thus, a brief consideration of interactions between serotonin and dopamine is presented.

SEROTONIN AND DOPAMINE INTERACTIONS

There has been considerable interest in whether interactions between serotonergic and noradrenergic systems are necessary for antidepressant effects. Early (13) and more recent (61) studies have pointed to normally functioning serotonin in humans as necessary to sustain antidepressant responses. Furthermore, data supporting interactions between serotonin and dopamine in depression appear at least as strong as those supporting a serotonin–norepinephrine link (for review, see ref. 62).

In earlier studies, 5,7-dihydroxytryptamine (5,7-DHT) treatment, which destroys serotonin neurons, was reported to modify the response of rat frontoparietal neurons to iontophoretic application of both dopamine and NE. This was interpreted as consistent with presynaptic serotonin receptors modulating the release of the catecholamines from their nerve terminals (63).

Subsequent work has supported the potential for serotonergic modulation of NE release, although whether this represents a functional in vivo role of endogenous serotonergic tone is not clear (64). The availability of compounds directed toward subtypes of serotonin receptors has led to clearer distinctions between the types of effects on NE and dopamine. For instance, serotonin does not affect dopamine via $5HT_{1A}$ receptors (65) whereas $5HT_{1A}$ (and $5HT_{1B}$) receptor stimulation may affect NE by modifying locus coeruleus firing, at least in slice preparations (66). It should be noted in this regard that the $5HT_{1A}$ and $5HT_{1B}$-mediated effects probably are through presynaptic terminals of the glutamatergic or GABAergic neurons that impinge on the locus coeruleus (66).

Thus, the 5HT–NE link may be more indirect than the 5HT–dopamine link, which appears to be mediated at least in part through $5HT_2$ receptors located on dendrites of dopamine cells in the zona compacta of the substantia nigra (67). Nonetheless, as cautioned by Svensson's group (67), the relatively low density of $5HT_2$ receptors so far described in the substantia nigra (68) suggests consideration of other sites of action. What is not in question, however, is the evidence for direct synaptic contact of serotonergic terminals onto dopamine cells (69,70) or the repeated demonstration in vivo of biochemical and behavioral (71) as well as electrophysiological (72) modification of dopamine function by serotonin.

If we turn to relevant clinical research, we are limited to neuroendocrine response data and measures of the dopamine (HVA) and serotonin (5HIAA) metabolites in CSF. In brief, one can argue that serotonin agonist-mediated release of prolactin may be more through effects of serotonin on dopamine in the median eminence (73,74) than through putative prolactin-releasing factors (75). Interestingly, some of the evidence for a role of serotonin in depression rests on blunted prolactin responses to the indoleamine precursor, L-tryptophan, as well as the reuptake inhibitor, clomipramine (76,77). Whether such probes really test serotonergic function has been questioned (78). It could be that blunted prolactin reflects abnormalities at the level of the dopamine neuron rather than at serotonergic receptors or terminals. Furthermore, the biochemical changes produced by chronic administration of 5HT uptake inhibitors suggest that they affect dopamine turnover in the human central nervous system. The point to be made is that one cannot clearly separate serotonergic from dopaminergic abnormalities in humans given our current investigative approaches.

In human CSF, the most replicated biochemical finding is of a high correlation between the concentrations of HVA and 5HIAA, a finding that cannot be explained away simply by a common transport mechanism (62). As discussed elsewhere, modeling of the CSF monoamine metabolite values in the context of external factors, such as age, weight, and sex, is compatible with a unidirectional influence of serotonin on dopamine (62). When values from the literature are plotted as a frequency distribution of the regression of HVA on 5HIAA (Fig. 2), a single peak emerges in healthy volunteers, and an extra lower peak is found in a depressed population (79). Another way of expressing the relationship in each individual is to construct a ratio of CSF HVA/5HIAA that is found to be low in depression (80).

We also have studied the effects of drugs on the CSF HVA/5HIAA ratio in patients treated for depression. Serotonin uptake inhibitors, such as zimelidine, produce a marked increase in the ratio substantially beyond what can be explained by the decrease in 5HIAA. In contrast, the NE uptake inhibitor, desipramine, which significantly reduced 5HIAA in CSF, did not alter the HVA/5HIAA ratio (81). A tentative interpretation is that the effects of serotonin uptake inhibitors in humans may be, at least in part, through dopamine. The absence of a sedative effect of such drugs (de-

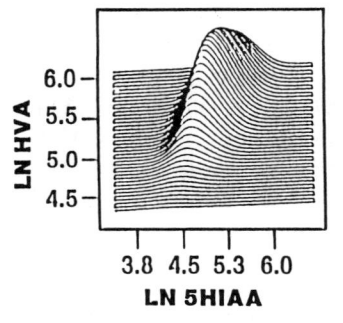

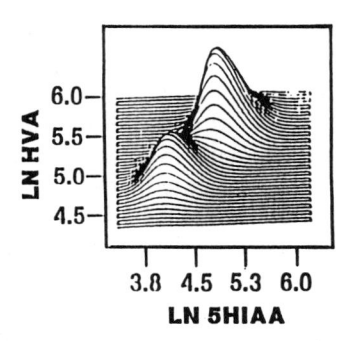

FIG. 2. Bivariate distribution of natural log transformed (LN) concentrations of 5-hydroxyindoleacetic acid (5-HIAA) and homovanillic acid (HVA) in cerebrospinal fluid from control (**left**) and depressed (**right**) populations. (According to ref. 79 using data from ref. 45.)

spite the putative hypnotic use of L-tryptophan) would be compatible with a more dopaminergic mechanism. On the other hand, neither the acute nor the chronic effects of these drugs mimic dopamine agonists. They are not euphorogenic in volunteers, and they may be less likely to produce mania (82), although administration of fluoxetine has been associated with manic episodes (83). The clinical consequences of any 5HT–dopamine interaction, therefore, need to be more fully elucidated. The point being made here is that dopamine systems may be involved in the action of serotonergic drugs.

INTERRELATIONSHIPS OF DOPAMINE, NOREPINEPHRINE, AND SEROTONIN

Given the preceding discussion, it is logical to question whether depressions involve various degrees of imbalance among multiple neurotransmitter systems. As a corollary, antidepressant effects might be achieved through initial effects on one or more neurotransmitters, setting off a cascade of biochemical events that after a couple of weeks establishes a new balance or set point of and between the systems. On this model, the likelihood of achieving a response following failure of an initial drug (e.g., a selective NE uptake inhibitor) might be greatest with the addition rather than substitution of a drug affecting another neurotransmitter system. Hence, the addition of a dopaminergic agent or use of high doses of MAOIs would be appropriate in refractory depression.

Antidepressant response might, therefore, be dependent on relatively intact relationships among neurotransmitters. Our group has attempted to look at this question by comparing the intercorrelations between the CSF concentrations of the three major monoamine metabolites—HVA, 5HIAA, and MHPG for NE—in patients who fail to respond to standard pharmacotherapies versus those who do respond (84). As shown in Fig. 3, the intercorrelations between the metabolites observed in responders are relatively high (and almost identical to those reported in healthy volunteers), whereas those in nonresponders are diminishingly low. This brings us back to the permissive notion of Prange et al. (85), whereby intact neurotransmitter systems are necessary to achieve antidepressant effects. In future studies, it will be of interest to see if combination therapies or high-dose MAOIs produce therapeutic response and normalization of neurotransmitter metabolite relationships in groups of patients identified as refractory.

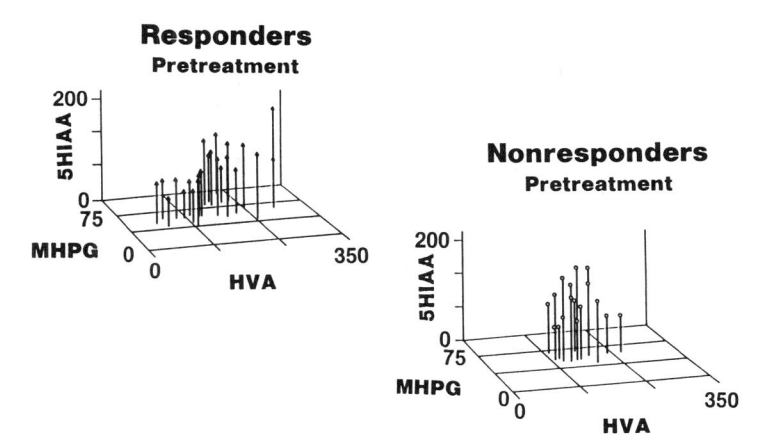

FIG. 3. Three-dimensional scatterplots of metabolite concentrations before treatment in responders and nonresponders. Perfect positive correlation among all three metabolites would produce a line from front lower left toward rear upper right in each plot. 5-HIAA, 5-hydroxyindoleacetic acid; MHPG, 3-methoxy-4-hydroxyphenylethyleneglycol; HVA, homovanillic acid. (From ref. 84.)

CONCLUSION

In this chapter, we have presented a case for alteration of dopamine as a means of achieving response in refractory depression. Four lines of evidence have been emphasized in the preceding discussion that support a role for dopamine.

1. Anhedonic states respond to dopamine agonists.
2. Low HVA in CSF is found consistently in a proportion of depressed patients.
3. ECT selectively affects dopaminergic measures.
4. There appears to be a clinically relevant linkage of noradrenergic, serotonergic, and dopaminergic systems.

These observations also suggest that, in developing new treatments, attention be given to less specific compounds, e.g., those combining, for instance, both dopamine and serotonin or NE uptake inhibition.

REFERENCES

1. Potter WZ. Psychotherapeutic drugs and biogenic amines: Current concepts and therapeutic implications. *Drugs* 1984;28:127–143.
2. Bunney WE, Davis JM. Norepinephrine in depressive reactions. *Arch Gen Psychiatry* 1965; 13:483–494.
3. Potter WZ, Calil HM, Extein I, Gold PW, Wehr TA, Goodwin FK. Specific norepinephrine and serotonin uptake inhibition in man: A crossover study with pharmacokinetic, neuroendocrine and biochemical parameters. *Acta Psychiatr Scand* 1981;290(Suppl):152–165.
4. Ashcroft GW, Eccleston D, Murray LG, et al. Modified amine aetiology of affective illness. *Lancet* 1972;2:573–577.
5. Randrup A, Braestrup C. Uptake inhibition of biogenic amines by newer antidepressant drugs: Relevance to the dopamine hypothesis of depression. *Psychopharmacology* 1977;53:309–314.
6. Heninger GR, Charney DS. Mechanism of action of antidepressant treatments: Implications for the etiology and treatment of depressive disorders. In: Meltzer HY, ed. *Psychopharmacology: The third generation of progress*, New York: Raven Press, 1987;535–544.
7. Meltzer HY, Stahl S. The dopamine hypothesis of schizophrenia: A review. *Schizophr Bull* 1976;2:19–76.
8. Crow TJ. Positive and negative schizophrenia symptoms and the role of dopamine. *Br J Psychiatry* 1981;139:251–254.

9. Snyder SH, Banerjee SP, Yamamura HI, Greenberg D. Drugs, neurotransmitters and schizophrenia. *Science* 1974;184:1243–1253.
10. Jimerson DC, Post RM. Psychomotor stimulants and dopamine agonists in depression. In: Post RM, Ballenger JC, eds. *The neurobiology of mood disorders.* Baltimore: Williams & Wilkins, 1984;619–628.
11. Jimerson DC. Role of dopamine mechanisms in the affective disorders. In: Meltzer HY, ed. *Psychopharmacology: The third generation of progress,* New York: Raven Press, 1987;505–510.
12. Post RM, Gerner RH, Carman JS, et al. Effects of a dopamine agonist piribedil in depressed patients. *Arch Gen Psychiatry* 1978;35:609–615.
13. Shopsin B, Gershon S. Dopamine receptor stimulation in the treatment of depression in piribedil. *Neuropsychobiology* 1978;4:1–14.
14. Silverstone T. Response to bromocriptine distinguishes bipolar from unipolar depression [Letter]. *Lancet* 1984;1:903–904.
15. Walters JR, Bunney BS, Roth RH. Piribedil and apomorphine: Pre- and post-synaptic effects on dopamine synthesis and neuronal activity. In: Calne DB, Chase TN, Barbeau A, eds. *Advances in neurology.* New York: Raven Press, 1975;273–284.
16. Liccione J, Azzaro AJ. Different roles for type A and type B monoamine oxidase in regulating synaptic dopamine at D-1 and D-2 receptors associated with adenosine-3', 5'-cyclic monophosphate (cyclic AMP) formation. *Arch Pharm* 1988;337:151–158.
17. Sunderland T, Tariot PN, Cohen RM, et al. Dose-dependent effects of deprenyl on CSF monoamine metabolites in patients with Alzheimer's disease. *Psychopharmacology* 1987; 91:293–296.
18. Tetrud JW, Langston JW. The effect of deprenyl (selegiline) on the natural history of Parkinson's disease. *Science* 1989;245:519–522.
19. Potter WZ, Scheinin M, Golden RN, et al. Selective antidepressants and cerebrospinal fluid. *Arch Gen Psychiatry* 1985;42:1171–1177.
20. Youdim MBH, Finberg JPM, Tipton KF. Monoamine oxidase. In: Trendelenburg U, Weiner N, eds. *Catecholamines 1,* vol 90/1. New York: Springer-Verlag, 1988;119–192.
21. Rudorfer MV, Risby ED, Hsiao JK, Linnoila M, Potter WZ. Disparate biochemical actions of electroconvulsive therapy and antidepressant drugs. *Convulsive Ther* 1988;4:133–140.
22. Lerer B. Neurochemical and other neurobiological consequences of ECT: Implications for the pathogenesis and treatment of affective disorders. In: Meltzer HY, ed. *Psychopharmacology: The third generation of progress,* New York: Raven Press, 1987;577–588.
23. Grahame-Smith DG, Green AR, Costain DW. Mechanism of the antidepressant action of electroconvulsive therapy. *Lancet* 1978;1:254–257.
24. Green AR, Youdim MBH, Grahame-Smith DG. Quipazine: Its effects on rat brain 5-hydroxytryptamine metabolism, monoamine oxidase activity and behavior. *Neuropharmacology* 1976; 15:173–179.
25. White DK, Barrett RJ. The effects of electroconvulsive shock on the discriminative stimulus properties of D-amphetamine and apomorphine: Evidence for dopamine receptor alteration subsequent to ECS. *Psychopharmacology* 1981;73: 211–214.
26. Ho BT, Huang J. Role of dopamine in D-amphetamine-induced discrimination responding. *Pharmacol Biochem Behav* 1975;3:108–115.
27. Silverman PB, Ho BT. Characterization of discrimination response control by psychomotor stimulants. In: Lal H, ed. *Neurobiological mechanisms of adaptation.* New York: Plenum Press, 1977;107–117.
28. Globus M, Lerer B, Hamburger R, Belmaker RH. Chronic electroconvulsive shock and chronic haloperidol administration are not additive in effects on dopamine receptors. *Neuropharmacology* 1981;20:1125–1128.
29. Fochtmann LJ, Aiso M, Cruciani R, Potter WZ. Chronic electroconvulsive shock increases D_1 receptor binding in rat substantia nigra. *Eur J Pharmacol* 1989;167:305–306.
30. Newman ME, Lerer B. Effects of chronic electroconvulsive shock on D_1 and D_2 dopamine receptor-mediated activity of adenylate cyclase in homogenates of striatum and limbic forebrain of rat. *Neuropharmacology* 1989;28:787–790.
31. Maj J, Rogoz Z, Sukuza G, et al. Antidepressants given repeatedly increase the behavioural effect of dopamine D_2 agonist. *J Neural Transm* 1989;78:1–8.
32. Andersen K, Balldin J, Gottfries CG, et al. A double-blind evaluation of electroconvulsive therapy in Parkinson's disease with "on-off" phenomena. *Acta Neurol Scand* 1987;76:191–199.
33. Fochtmann L. A mechanism for the efficacy of ECT in Parkinson's disease. *Convulsive Ther* 1988;4:321–327.
34. Pandey GN, Heinz WJ, Brown BD, David JM. Electroconvulsive shock therapy decreases β-adrenergic receptor sensitivity in rat brain. *Nature* 1979;280:234–235.
35. Vetulani J, Stawarz RJ, Sulser F. Adaptive mechanisms of the noradrenergic cyclic AMP generating systems in the limbic forebrain of the rat: Adaptations to persistent changes in the availability of norepinephrine. *J Neurochem* 1976;27:661–666.
36. Stockmeier CA, Keller KJ. In vivo regulation of the serotonin-2 receptor in rat brain. *Life Sci* 1986;38:117–127.
37. Green AR, Deakin JFW. Brain noradrenaline depletion prevents ECS-induced enhancement of serotonin- and dopamine-mediated behavior. *Nature* 1980;285:232–233.
38. Heal DL, Davies CL, Goodwin GM. DSP-4 lesioning prevents the enhancement of dopamine and 5-hydroxytryptamine mediated behavioural changes by repeated electroconvulsive shock. *Eur J Pharmacol* 1985;115:117–121.

39. Balldin J, Granerus AK, Lindstedt G, Modigh K, Walinder J. Neuroendocrine evidence for increased responsiveness of dopamine receptors in humans following electroconvulsive therapy. *Psychopharmacology* 1982;76:371–376.
40. Potter WZ, Rudorfer MV, Linnoila M. Effects of antidepressants on norepinephrine and its metabolites in cerebrospinal fluid, plasma, and urine. In: *Progress in catecholamine research, Part C: Clinical aspects*. New York: Alan R Liss, Inc, 1988;301–306.
41. Rudorfer MV, Risby ED, Hsiao JK, Linnoila M, Potter WZ. Disparate biochemical actions of electroconvulsive therapy and antidepressant drugs. *Convulsive Ther* 1988;4:133–140.
42. Wood JH. Sites of origin and cerebrospinal fluid concentration gradients: Neurotransmitters, their precursors and metabolites and cyclic nucleotides. In: Wood JH, ed. *Neurobiology of cerebrospinal fluid*. New York: Plenum Press, 1980; 53–59.
43. Sourkes TL. On the origin of homovanillic acid (HVA) in the cerebrospinal fluid. *J Neural Transm* 1973;34:153–157.
44. Potter WZ, Rudorfer MV, Goodwin FK. Biological findings in bipolar disorders. In: Hales RE, Frances AJ, eds. *American Psychiatric Association annual review: vol 6*. Washington, DC: American Psychiatric Press, 1987;32–60.
45. Asberg M, Bertilsson L, Martensson B, Scilia-Tomba GP, Thoren P, Traskman-Bendz L. CSF monoamine metabolites in melancholia. *Acta Psychiatr Scand* 1984;69:201–219.
46. Mendlewicz J, Linkowski P, Brauman H. Growth hormone and prolactin response to levodopa in affective illness. *Lancet* 1977;1:652–653.
47. Sedvall G, Fryo B, Gullberg B, Nyback H, Wiesel F, Wode-Helgodt B. Relationships in healthy volunteers between concentration of monoamine metabolites in cerebrospinal fluid and family history of psychiatric morbidity. *Br J Psychiatry* 1980;136:366–374.
48. Willner F. Dopamine and depression: A review of recent evidence. III. The effect of antidepressant treatment. *Brain Res Rev* 1983;6:237–246.
49. Stewart JW, Quitkin FM, Liebowitz MR. Efficacy of desipramine in depressed outpatients. *Arch Gen Psychiatry* 1983;40:202–207.
50. Tang SW, Seeman P, Kwan S. Differential effect of chronic desipramine and amitriptyline treatment on rat brain adrenergic and serotonergic receptors. *Psychiatry Res* 1981;4:129–138.
51. Peroutka SJ, Snyder SH. Multiple serotonin receptors: Differential binding of [^{3}H]-5-hydroxytryptamine, [^{3}H]-lysergic acid diethylamide and [^{3}H]spiroperidol. *Mol Pharmacol* 1979;16:687–699.
52. Sugrue MF. Chronic antidepressant therapy and associated changes in central monoaminergic receptor functioning. *Pharmacol Ther* 1983;21:1–33.
53. Fibiger HC, Phillips AG. Increased intracranial self-stimulation in rats after long-term administration of desipramine. *Science* 1981;214:683–685.
54. Antelman SM, Chiodo LA. Dopamine autoreceptor subsensitivity: A mechanism common to the treatment of depression and the induction of amphetamine psychosis? *Biol Psychiatry* 1981; 16:717–727.
55. O'Donohue TL, Crowley WR, Jacobowitz DM. Biochemical mapping of the noradrenergic ventral bundle projection sites: Evidence for a noradrenergic–dopaminergic interaction. *Brain Res* 1979;172:87–100.
56. Lyness WH, Friedle NM, Moore KE. Destruction of dopaminergic nerve terminals in nucleus accumbens: Effect on D-amphetamine self-administration. *Pharmacol Biochem Behav* 1979;11:553–556.
57. Cantello R, Auguggia M, Gilli M, et al. Major depression in Parkinson's disease and the mood response to intravenous methylphenidate: Possible role of the "hedonic" dopamine synapse. *J Neurol Neurosurg Psychiatry* 1989;52:724–731.
58. Oades RD. The role of noradrenaline in tuning and dopamine in switching between signals in the CNS. *Neurosci Biobehav Rev* 1985;9:261–282.
59. Grenhoff J, Svensson TH. Clonidine modulates dopamine cell firing in rat ventral tegmental area. *Eur J Pharmacol* 1989;165:11–18.
60. Chiodo LA, Antelman SM. Repeated tricyclic antidepressants induce a progressive "switch" in the electrophysiological response of dopamine neurons to autoreceptor stimulation. *Eur J Pharmacol* 1980;66:255–256.
61. Delgado PL, Charney DS, Price LH, Aghajanian GK, Landis H, Heninger GR. Serotonin function and the mechanism of antidepressant action: Reversal of antidepressant-induced remission by rapid depletion of plasma tryptophan. *Arch Gen Psychiatry* 1990;47:411–418.
62. Agren H, Mefford IN, Rudorfer MV, Linnoila M, Potter WZ. Interacting neurotransmitter systems. A non-experimental approach to the 5HIAA-HVA correlation in human CSF. *J Psychiatr Res* 1986;20:175–193.
63. Ferron A, Descarries L, Reader TA. Altered neuronal responsiveness to biogenic amines in rat cerebral cortex after serotonin denervation or depletion. *Brain Res* 1982;231:93–108.
64. Feuerstein TJ, Hertting G. Serotonin (5-HT) enhances hippocampal noradrenaline (NA) release: Evidence for facilitatory 5-HT receptors within the CNS. *Naunyn Schmiedebergs Arch Pharmacol* 1986;333:191–197.
65. Hamon M, Fattaccini CM, Adrien J, Gallissot MC, Martin P, Gozlan H. Alterations of central serotonin and dopamine turnover in rats treated with ipsapirone and other 5-hydroxytryptamine$_{1A}$ agonists with potential anxiolytic properties. *J Pharmacol Exp Ther* 1988;246:745–752.
66. Bobker DH, Williams JT. Serotonin agonists inhibit synaptic potentials in the rat locus coeruleus in vitro via 5-hydroxytryptamine$_{1A}$ and 5-hydroxytryptamine$_{1B}$ receptors. *J Pharmacol Exp Ther* 1989;250:37–43.

67. Ugedo L, Grenhoff J, Svensson TH. Ritanserin, a 5-HT$_2$ receptor antagonist, activates midbrain dopamine neurons by blocking serotonergic inhibition. *Psychopharmacology* 1989;98:45–50.
68. Pazos A, Cortes R, Palacios JM. Quantitative autoradiographic mapping of serotonin-2 receptors. *Brain Res* 1985;346:231–249.
69. Hervé D, Pickel VM, Joh TH, Beaudet A. Serotonin axon terminals in the ventral tegmental area of the rat: Fine structure and synaptic input to dopaminergic neurons. *Brain Res* 1987;435:71–83.
70. Nedergaard S, Bolam JP, Greenfield SA. Facilitation of a dendritic calcium conductance by 5-hydroxytryptamine in the substantia nigra. *Nature* 1988;333:174–177.
71. Fuenmayor LD, Bermudez M. Effect of the cerebral tryptaminergic system on the turnover of dopamine in the striatum of the rat. *J Neurochem* 1985;44:670–674.
72. Aghajanian GK. The modulatory role of serotonin at multiple receptors in brain. In: Jacobs BL, Gelperin A, eds. *Serotonin neurotransmission and behavior.* Boston: MIT Press, 1981;156–185.
73. Pillotte NS, Porter JC. Dopamine in hypophyseal portal plasma and prolactin in systemic plasma of rats treated with 5HT. *Endocrinology* 1981;108:2137–2142.
74. Demarest KT, Moore KE, Riegle GD. Acute restraint stress decreases dopamine synthesis and turnover in the median eminence: A model for the study of the inhibitory neuronal influences of tubero-infundibular dopaminergic neurons. *Neuroendocrinology* 1985;41:437–444.
75. Clemens JA, Roush ME, Fuller RW. Evidence that serotonin neurons stimulate secretion of prolactin releasing factors. *Life Sci* 1978;22:2209–2214.
76. Heninger GR, Charney DS, Sternberg DE. Serotonergic function in depression: Prolactin response to intravenous tryptophan in depressed patients and healthy subjects. *Arch Gen Psychiatry* 1984;41:398–402.
77. Golden RN, Hsiao JK, Lane E, et al. Abnormal neuroendocrine responsivity to acute intravenous clomipramine challenge in depressed patients. *Psychiatry Res* 1990;31:39–47.
78. Van Praag HM. Serotonin disturbances in psychiatric disorders: Functional versus nosological interpretation. *Adv Biol Psychiatry* 1988;17:52–57.
79. Gibbons RD, Davis JM. Consistent evidence for a biological subtype of depression characterized by low CSF monoamine levels. *Acta Psychiatr Scand* 1986;74:8–12.
80. Ågren H, Terenius L. Hallucinations in patients with major depression: Interactions between CSF monoaminergic and endorphinergic indices. *J Affective Disord* 1985;9:25–34.
81. Risby ED, Hsiao JK, Sunderland T, Ågren H, Rudorfer MV, Potter WZ. The effects of antidepressants on the cerebrospinal fluid homovanillic acid/5-hydroxyindoleacetic acid ratio. *Clin Pharmacol Ther* 1987;42:547–554.
82. Extein I, Potter WZ, Wehr TA, Goodwin FK. Rapid mood cycles following a "noradrenergic" but not a "serotonergic" antidepressant. *Am J Psychiatry* 1979;136:1602–1603.
83. Lebegue B. Mania precipitated by fluoxetine. [Letter to the Editor]. *Am J Psychiatry* 1987;144:1620.
84. Hsiao JK, Ågren H, Bartko JJ, Rudorfer MV, Linnoila M, Potter WZ. Monoamine neurotransmitter interactions and the prediction of antidepressant response. *Arch Gen Psychiatry* 1987;44:1078–1083.
85. Prange AJ, Wilson IC, Lynn CL, Alltop LB, Stikeleather RA. L-Tryptophan in mania, contributions to a permissive hypothesis of affective disorders. *Arch Gen Psychiatry* 1974;30:56–62.

5

Refractory Childhood Depressive Disorders from a Pharmacotherapeutic Perspective

Norman E. Alessi

Childhood depressive disorders represent relatively new diagnostic entities within child psychiatry, their identification as a major mental health risk occurring during the last 20 years (1–4). Their identification has resulted in a wide and varied literature (5–10). It is within this context that the question is raised, "Can children have refractory depressive disorders?"

If we extrapolate from adult studies, one would expect to find not only children who have chronic or recurrent depressive illnesses but also children who are refractory to treatment (11–15). In the numerous studies, there is no mention of those children who fail to respond or who are refractory to treatment. Does this mean that children with refractory depressive disorders do not exist, or does this reflect the state of the development of this area? If such children do exist, how would we define them, and how would we treat them? A review of the adult literature does not help in defining refractory depressive disorders in children (16,17).

In this chapter, previous pharmacotherapeutic studies of childhood depression are reviewed to discern information as it relates to refractory childhood depressive disorders. Several cases reflective of a naturalistic pharmacotherapeutic approach are presented, demonstrating the use of several antidepressants and the use of treatment-augmenting strategies. A proposed decision tree for the selection of psychopharmacological agents in the treatment of depressed children is presented.

PHARMACOTHERAPY OF CHILDHOOD DEPRESSIVE DISORDERS: REVIEW OF THE LITERATURE

Table 1 contains a review of the studies reporting the use of antidepressants in the treatment of children with depressive disorders (1,16–26). The antidepressants include amitriptyline, imipramine, maprotiline, mianserin, nortriptyline, and phenelzine. Antidepressants are noted to be effective to some degree in all studies. There are conflicting results, however, in those using a double-blind design. Some report medications as no more effective than placebo, whereas others report them to be more effective than placebo if plasma levels for the antidepressants are within a therapeutic range (1,21,23,26). The conclusion often drawn from these studies is that childhood depression is no more responsive to antidepressants than to placebos. Therefore, the use of medications in the treatment of childhood depression is questioned (9,27,28).

From the perspective of wanting to understand the concept of refractory childhood depression, there is little mention of

Diagnostic and Research Unit, Childhood Affective Disorders Program, Child and Adolescent Psychiatric Hospital, University of Michigan Medical Center, Ann Arbor, MI 48109-0292.

TABLE 1. *Psychopharmacological treatment of depressed children*

Study	No. of patients	Age range (years)	Medication	Dosage (day)	Improved Medication	Improved Placebo	Not improved (%)
Lucas et al. (18)	10	10–17	Amitriptyline	30–75 mg	6/10	—	40
Frommer (1)	32	9–15	Phenelzine	30–45 mg	19/32	11/32	41
Puig-Antich et al. (19)	8	6–12	Imipramine	5 mg/kg	6/8	—	25
Minuti and Gallo (20)	20	4–15	Maprotiline	32 mg	12/20	—	40
Petti and Law (21)	6	6–12	Imipramine	5 mg/kg	2/3	0/3	66
Preskorn et al. (22)	20	7–12	Imipramine	5 mg/kg	12/20	—	40
Kashani et al. (23)	9	9–12	Amitriptyline	1.5 mg/kg	3/3	1/2	20
Dugas et al. (24)	80	8–19	Mianserin	1 mg/kg	51/80	—	36
Geller et al. (25)	22	6–12	Nortriptyline	20–50 mg/kg	14/22	—	36
Puig-Antich et al. (26)	38	7–12	Imipramine	5 mg/kg	9/16	15/22	63

children within these studies who did not respond to either placebo or antidepressants. Although of little consequence for the purpose of these studies, these nonresponders constitute a sizable group, anywhere from 20% to 66% of the children. These children did not respond to the pharmacotherapeutic agent, whether a medication or a placebo. Could these nonresponders be classified as refractory?

There are two perspectives that can be taken in regard to children who did not respond. Is the lack of response due to inadequate treatment, or were these children refractory to treatment? Inadequate treatment may be due to a number of factors—poor compliance, inadequate dose, misdiagnosis or a lack of consideration of all diagnoses, population sampling bias, or the lack of adequate treatment trials.

Compliance and Dosage

All studies were conducted so as to guarantee compliance. This is particularly evident in those cases where plasma levels were reported. Although the issue of dose is important, only two studies report on the effect of increasing the dosage of medication used for children not responsive to the dose used in the study (1,25). In these cases, the therapeutic response was facilitated by increasing the dosage of the medication.

Comorbidity

What diagnostic variables may have contributed to the lack of a clear therapeutic response in these cases? Were the populations diagnostically homogeneous? The ideal homogeneous population would include only those children with major depressive disorders. Exclusion diagnoses would include psychosis, attention deficit hyperactivity disorder, anxiety disorder, oppositional defiant disorder, conduct disorder, and dysthymia. Some studies attempt to deal with these issues, either by excluding children with other specific diagnoses or by at least mentioning the presence of these other diagnoses, even if they were not considered in the data analysis or the results (26). Did the presence of comorbid conditions influence the response of subjects to medications, possibly reducing the therapeutic response?

If the ideal study were conducted excluding children with comorbid conditions, would it be representative of children with depressive disorders? Several studies of depressed children have demonstrated the extent of comorbid conditions within this population (29–33). As evidenced by studies in the adult literature, depressed patients with comorbid conditions demand alternative therapeutic consideration (34). One would assume the same would be true for children with depressive disorders. For example, the most likely clinical population that would demand the consideration of medications in addition to antidepressants are depressed children with psychosis. Yet the use of neuroleptics is reported in only one study (35). This is particularly surprising given the noted incidence of 48% of depressed children having psychotic symptoms (36). According to the reports of comorbid conditions in depressed children, it would appear that their presence is an inescapable element that demands our attention in the management of depressed children and in the conceptualization of future studies.

Sampling Bias

Does the fact that a majority of these children are outpatients bias the sample toward less severely depressed children? Do less severely depressed children respond more readily to a placebo than do more severely depressed children? Although of critical significance and germane to this discussion, there is no information concerning treatment studies that would be of assistance in understanding this issue. Yet an important question to ask before seriously considering this point is whether hospitalized depressed children are more seriously depressed than are outpatient depressed children. In a recent review of these pharmacotherapeutic studies, it was suggested that a depressed child's hospitalization did not mean necessarily that it was based on the severity of the child's depression but instead could be a reflection of the home environment (9). This observation was not substantiated and should be viewed with skepticism until proven. A more likely interpretation is that depressed children who require hospitalization have more severe and difficult management problems that reflect a composite of the severity of the child's psychopathology, the severity of depression, and the severity of associated comorbid conditions. The other component of the composite would include parental psychopathology and family dysfunction.

Therefore, a simple dismissal of the true complexity of this issue appears unwarranted.

Adequate Treatment Trials

Were these children given adequate treatment trials? Do these studies portray adequate treatment trials? A more fundamental question is "What is an adequate treatment trial?" This is the pivotal question in discerning whether a case is or is not refractory. If these medication studies are accepted as adequate treatment trials, from 20% to 66% of these children have refractory depressive disorders. On the other hand, if these are not regarded as adequate trials, what would be?

Unfortunately, given the concerns about dosage, diagnostic homogeneity, sampling bias, and whether the studies constitute adequate treatment trials, little can be said for those subjects who did not respond except that there may be among this group children who were refractory.

PSYCHOPHARMACOLOGICAL TREATMENT OF PSYCHIATRICALLY HOSPITALIZED DEPRESSED CHILDREN: NATURALISTIC CLINICAL TRIALS

We have chosen to take a naturalistic approach in the treatment of depressed children. This approach has the advantage of allowing patients to be approached on an individual basis but has the major disadvantage of being difficult to replicate. There are few reports looking at a naturalistic approach to the treatment of children with depressive disorders using pharmacological agents.

Overview

Of 76 consecutive admissions to the Diagnostic and Research Unit (DRU), 25 children had discharge diagnoses of depressive disorders (7 major depressive disorder and 18 dysthymia). The children were 10.3 ± 1.9 years old (mean ± standard deviation), with a range from 5 to 13 years. There were 20 boys and 5 girls. Each child was interviewed by a senior staff psychiatrist and a resident in child psychiatry, and diagnostic decisions were based on DSM-III-R criteria using information from clinical interviews and medical and psychiatric history. Structured and semistructured diagnostic interviews were not chosen because many children were unable to comply with the structure necessary to complete the interview, and others had significant speech and language disturbances. Charts of these children were later reviewed for the ascertainment of medication dosages and blood levels. Clinical response was based on clinical observations of the changes in depression symptomatology. The levels of clinical response were: poor—little to no reduction in symptoms prior to discharge; fair—positive response discernible, yet difficulties continued in several areas; good—most or all symptoms resolved at discharge.

Figure 1 shows the breakdown of the therapeutic responses to pharmacotherapy. In summary, 5 (20%) patients spontaneously remitted within 2 weeks and did not require the use of medication during the hospitalization. Nine patients had a clinical response to either imipramine or desipramine, and 8 were treated with other medications depending on clinical needs. Three patients failed to demonstrate clinical response to medications. The spontaneously remitted group proved to be significantly younger (8.2 ± 2.6 years) than either the imipramine–desipramine group (11.1 ± 1.13 years), or the polypharmacy group (10.6 ± 1.3 years) (Student's t-test, $p < 0.05$). The age of the two therapeutic groups did not differ.

Of the 9 (36%) children taking imipramine or desipramine, 8 received imipramine at a mean (±Sd) dosage of 152.8 ± 38.4 mg, with a mean plasma level (imipramine plus desipramine) of 186.2 ± 54.5 ng/ml.

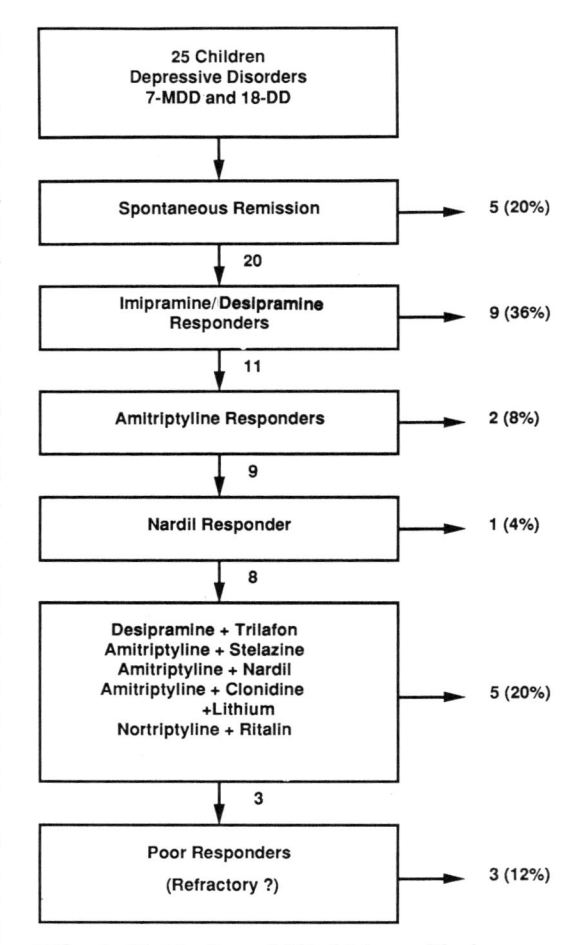

FIG. 1. Distribution of 25 children with depressive disorders by pharmacotherapeutic response. D, dysthymia; MDD, major depressive disorder.

Five children had a good response, and 4 had a fair response. The remaining 11 children were tried on a variety of medications, with 8 (32%) considered to have either a good or fair response and 3 (12%) to have a poor response. Therefore, among this group of 25 depressed children, 3 (12%) were considered refractory to treatment.

Table 2 provides information about those patients who required either additional or alternative medications.

TABLE 2. *Depressed children treated with medication other than imipramine or desipramine*

Case number	Age (years)	Sex	Depression diagnosis	Comorbid conditions DSM-III-R	Medication	Response
11	11	M	Dysthymia	CD[a]	Ami 150 mg + Stelazine 6 mg	Good
12	11	M	Major depressive disorder	CD, ADHD	Ami 150 mg	Good
13	9	M	Dysthymia	CD, ADHD	Nor 50 mg + Ritalin 5 mg	Fair
14	12	M	Dysthymia	CD	Des 150 mg + Trilafon 4 mg	Good
15	11	M	Major depressive disorder	CD, ADHD	Ami 25 mg + Nardil 45 mg	Good
16	13	M	Major depressive disorder		Nardil 45 mg	Fair
17	11	M	Dysthymia	ODD, ADHD	Ami 150 mg	Fair
18	10	M	Dysthymia	CD, ADHD	Ami 125 mg, Clon 0.125 mg qd, lithium 300 mg tid	Good

[a] ADHD, attention deficit hyperactivity disorder; CD, conduct disorder; ODD, oppositional defiant disorder; Ami, amitryptiline; Clon, clonidine; Des, desipramine; Imi, imipramine; Nor, nortriptyline.

Case Examples

Three individual case reviews are presented to better understand the strategies used, the response rate, and the time frame for clinical response (Fig. 2). Weekly Children's Depression Rating Scale (CDRS) scores were collected to document the course of the depressive illness during the hospitalization (8). The data for these cases were collected after the previously discussed 25 cases were seen and are not represented in Table 2.

Case 1. Bob, 11-year-old boy with dysthymia and major depressive disorder

Bob was referred because of suicidal ideas, including taking an overdose and shooting himself. Additional symptoms included intense nondirected anger and marked dysphoria. He was described as happy until 3 years before his admission. Following a parental divorce, he became sad, angry, and aggressive, destroying a number of his belongings. After his father left the state, he decompensated. Subsequently, suicidal ideas developed. At admission, he appeared tired, depressed, and angry. In addition to depression, he was anhedonic, had sleep difficulties, early and middle insomnia, decreased appetite, somatic complaints, and marked decrease in school performance. His CDRS score was 75. Laboratory workup, including laboratory screening, CT scan, and dexamethasone suppression test, was normal. He was diagnosed as having dysthymia with a major depressive episode.

Because of the aggression and agitation, which persisted during the initial 2 weeks of hospitalization, he was begun on amitriptyline, and his dosage was increased to 75 mg, with a blood level (amitriptyline plus nortriptyline) of 140 ng/ml (therapeutic range 120–250 ng/ml). There were few side effects, except dryness of mouth and constipation. Both were tolerated well. His CDRS score at the time of discharge was 28.

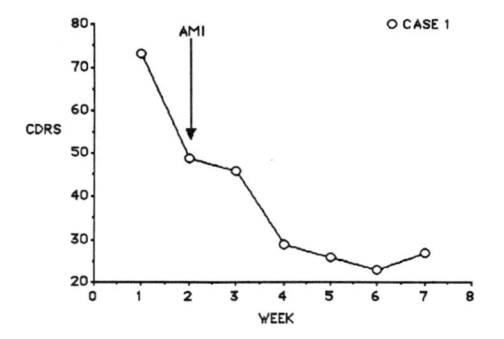

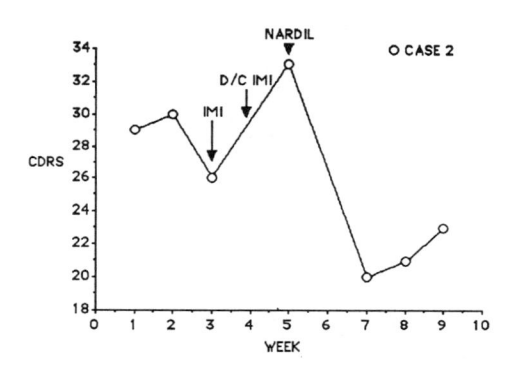

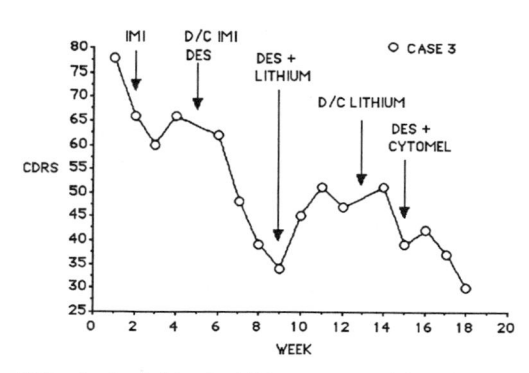

FIG. 2. Individual children treated for depressive disorders. AMI, amitriptyline; DES, desipramine; IMI, imipramine; Lithium, lithium carbonate.

Case 2. Nick, 9-year-old boy with major depressive disorder and oppositional defiant disorder

Nick was a 9-year-old boy with a 2-year history of behavioral difficulties characterized as aggression toward peers and family, threats of running away, and oppositional behavior. He was described as moody, often unhappy. There were suicidal threats for the last 12 months, and he had a poor appetite without weight loss. During the initial contact, Nick was irritable and depressed, with marked psychomotor retardation. There was no evidence of suicidal ideation, delusions, or hallucinations. Dexamethasone suppression test, CT scan, and routine laboratory work were normal. His CDRS score was 29 at the time of admission, and he was diagnosed as having a major depressive disorder with an associated oppositional defiant disorder.

Nick was begun on imipramine (50 mg/day), but because of cardiovascular side effects, tachycardia, and marked orthostatic hypotension, it was decided that he be placed on an MAOI, phenelzine (Nardil) (15 mg/day). This decision was made because of the severity of the cardiovascular difficulties that he experienced on a low dose of imipramine and concern that desipramine would elicit a similar response.

His clinical response to the phenelzine was described as "dramatic." Within 2 weeks, he became increasingly animated, less irritable, and more outgoing. His depression, which had been particularly bad in the morning, showed a marked improvement. The drop of 7 points in the CDRS does not appear to reflect the degree of improvement that occurred in his global functioning. The dietary restrictions did not pose a serious problem because the patient accepted the medication as being particularly helpful to him. At the time of discharge, his depressive disorder was in remission, and his oppositional defiant disorder had improved markedly, with an absence of aggression and provocative behavior.

Case 3. Mary, 10-year-old girl with major depressive disorder, agoraphobia with associated panic symptoms, and oppositional defiant disorder

Mary was a 10-year-old girl with a 2-month history of deterioration of her functioning, characterized by sleep disturbance, hypersomnia, middle and late insomnia, decreased appetite without weight loss, social withdrawal, fears of leaving home and appearing in public places, significant anxiety upon going to school and refusal to attend school in the last 6 weeks, lack of enjoyment of almost all activities, and a marked decline in her school performance, from being an A student to failing all classes.

On admission, Mary was described as markedly withdrawn with profound psychomotor retardation. Her hygiene, daily living skills, and ability to care for herself were profoundly impaired. There was a latency of minutes between questions and responses, with questions often going unanswered. She denied homicidal and suicidal thoughts and agreed on the information provided by her parents. The dexamethasone suppression test demonstrated a lack of suppression, with the postdexamethasone 8 AM cortisol value at 12.7 µg/dl. A CT scan was negative, as were other admission laboratory tests, including thyroid function tests. Her admission CDRS score was 77. She was diagnosed as having a major depressive disorder, agoraphobia with associated panic symptoms, and an oppositional defiant disorder.

She was begun on imipramine, but because of cardiovascular side effects, she was switched to desipramine. The dosage was increased to 225 mg/day. During the time that she was taking the desipramine, her CDRS score dropped 30 points to a score of 35. Because of continued and marked dysfunction during the morning, lithium carbonate was added and increased to a total daily dose of 900 mg/day in an attempt to augment the therapeutic effect of the desipramine. Mary did not improve on the lithium, and it was discontinued. Because of continued concerns about her functioning, with CDRS scores continuing in the 40s, she was placed on liothyronine sodium (Cytomel) (50 µg/day). With the addition of the liothyronine, she improved further. At discharge, her CDRS score was 28. The total CDRS score had been reduced over 60% from the admission score. The 28 represented a continuation of some depressive symptoms, which were not responsive to the medications.

Discussion of Cases

A comparison of the cases demonstrates their differences (Fig. 3) in severity of illness. Obviously, all cases were severe enough to warrant hospitalization. In cases 1 and 3, the primary reason was depression, whereas in case 2, it was severe behavioral dysfunction due to an unidentified depressive disorder. CDRS scores for cases 1 and 3 were quite similar, with CDRS total scores in the 70s. This was in contrast to case 2, where the admission CDRS score was in the 30s. The response patterns of the three children differed. A review demonstrates that case 1 had a rapid response to the medication, with a fall in CDRS scores from 75 to 28 in 6 weeks following the initiation of amitriptyline. This is in contrast to the response of case 3, where numerous interventions were tried and hospitalization lasted 18 weeks. Both are in further con-

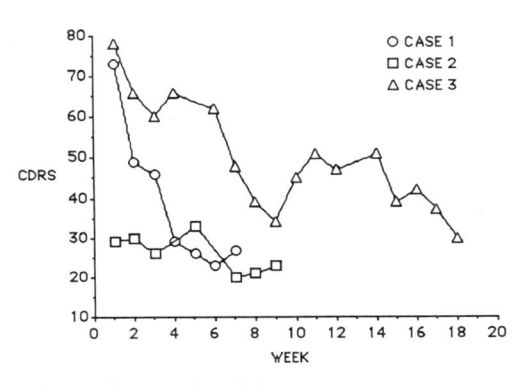

FIG. 3. Composite of three cases.

trast to case 2, where clinical improvement was of major significance but not on a level with that observed with either case 1 or case 3.

All cases represent severe depressive disorders that demonstrated good clinical responses, yet cases where there continued to be depressive symptoms. This was most notable in case 3. Could these cases be classified as refractory depressive disorders? Certainly, if the current knowledge as reflected by the earlier cited pharmacotherapeutic studies were used, one would have to say yes. Yet with different trials, even the most difficult case showed marked improvement. One could ask "Were not these patients still depressed enough to be considered refractory?" especially if a therapeutic response is considered to be not just a marked improvement but an alleviation of symptoms. If such criteria are used, these cases, although improved, would have to be classified as refractory.

PSYCHOPHARMACOLOGICAL SELECTION IN THE TREATMENT OF DEPRESSED CHILDREN: A PROPOSED MODEL

Before a depressed child can be diagnosed as refractory to treatment, all attempts must be made to treat the depression as aggressively as possible. How aggressively? There are no guidelines defining adequate treatment or what constitutes aggressive treatment. However, in an attempt to develop guidelines that could be used in the treatment of depressed children, the following decision tree has been developed. The basic rationale behind its development was (a) develop a model that reflects our current knowledge of depressive disorders in childhood, including the presence of comorbid disorders, (b) review the adult literature and determine the strategies that have been used to treat refractory depressive disorders and use them, if possible, in the development of a strategy to treat depressed children, (c) develop strategies that have an impact on the depression and the associated comorbid condition, (d) when possible, use a medication that will affect the depression and the comorbid condition, and (e) assume that children with dysthymia should be treated similarly (17, 29–33,37–43).

The result of experience in treating these children and in the application of this rationale is presented in Fig. 4. The flow chart begins with the identification of a depressed child with either a major depressive disorder or dysthymia. The first medication chosen is imipramine. If there is an inadequate response, it is necessary to determine whether the diagnosis is correct or if a comorbid condition exists. If the diagnosis is correct, several options are indicated (44). If the child has been determined to have a comorbid condition, different psychopharmacological agents may be chosen. Given the limited reporting on treatment of these children, the selection of potential agents reflects either past use in adults, our experience with the agent(s), or its proposed use based on theoretical considerations. These interventions are indicated with question marks. Undoubtedly, there will be cases that are refractory to all proposed interventions. This particular decision tree allows a clinician the opportunity to better organize interventions in a systematic manner, especially in complex cases where there are numerous diagnoses present.

Care should be taken in the aggressive pharmacotherapeutic treatment of depressed children. The proposed guidelines provided must be undertaken with great caution. Obviously, the use of these medications, especially several of the combinations, requires close monitoring and should be carried out only in a hospital setting. Further, it is absolutely necessary that parents be informed of each medication intervention, its potential benefit, and its potential liabilities. This becomes particularly important when augmentation is indicated or a combination is used in a treatment-

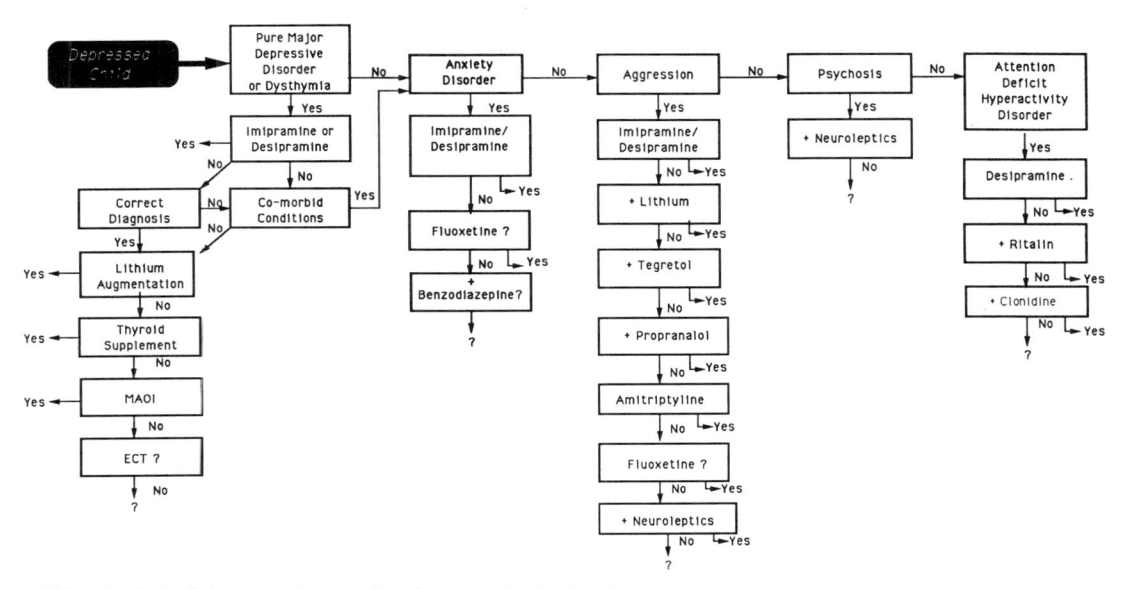

FIG. 4. A decision tree for psychopharmacological selection in the treatment of depressed children: a proposed model. ECT, electroconvulsive therapy; MAOI, monoamine oxidase inhibitors.

resistant depression for which there is no existing literature. The adverse effects of using these medications should always be weighed against the disruptive effects of the untreated illness.

SUMMARY

Refractory depressive disorders do exist in children. The primary obstacle in identifying this condition in children is the lack of clear guidelines that would guarantee comprehensive treatment. Neither pharmacological nor psychological studies have dealt adequately with this issue despite the rate of over 60% of depressed children being unresponsive to antidepressants. Therefore, the first step in the development of a method to identify children with refractory depression is the development of comprehensive therapeutic planning that would guarantee systematic use of pharmacotherapeutic agents in the treatment of these children.

A number of factors need to be considered when conceptualizing the use of pharmacological agents in the treatment of these children, as demonstrated in the naturalistic case presentations. These include the level of the child's premorbid functioning, identification of comorbid conditions, the severity of the depressive disorder, the duration of the depressive condition, and the degree of response to various pharmacotherapeutic agents. If the child remains unresponsive to the appropriate antidepressants, augmenting agents, and other pharmacological interventions, only then should the child be considered to have a refractory condition.

ACKNOWLEDGMENTS

I would like to thank John Wittekindt, M.D., and the child residents and members of the Diagnostic and Research Unit who provided direct care in the management of these cases, Daniel Devries, M.D., and Sue Eisner, R.N., for their participation in the collection and processing of the data, and

Annunciata Porterfield, Mary Schultz, and Jeffrey Dobek for their assistance in the preparation of the manuscript.

REFERENCES

1. Frommer E. Treatment of childhood depression with antidepressant drugs. *Br Med J* 1967;1:729–732.
2. Poznanski E, Zrull J. Childhood depression: Clinical characteristics of overtly depressed children. *Arch Gen Psychiatry* 1970;23:8–15.
3. Ling W, Oftedjak G, Weinberg W. Depressive illness in childhood presenting as a severe headache. *Am J Dis Child* 1970;120:122–124.
4. Weinberg W, Rutman J, Sullivan L, Penick E, Dietz S. Depression in children referred to an educational diagnostic center: Diagnosis and treatment. *Behav Pediatr* 1973;83:1065–1072.
5. Puig-Antich J, Blau S, Marx N, et al. Prepubertal major depressive disorder: A pilot study. *J Am Acad Child Psychiatry* 1978;17:695–707.
6. Chambers WJ, Puig-Antich J, Hirsch M, et al. The assessment of affective disorders in children and adolescents by semi-structured interview: Test–retest reliability of the Schedule for Affective Disorders and Schizophrenia for school age children, present episode version. *Arch Gen Psychiatry* 1985;42:695–702.
7. Costello EJ, Angold A. Scales to assess child and adolescent depression: Checklists, screens, and nets. *J Am Acad Child Adolesc Psychiatry* 1988;27:726–737.
8. Poznanski E, Cook S, Carroll B. A depression rating scale for children. *Pediatrics* 1979;64:442–450.
9. Ambrosini PJ. Pharmacotherapy in child and adolescent major depressive disorder. In: Meltzer HY, ed. *Psychopharmacology: the third generation of progress.* New York: Raven Press, 1987;1247–1254.
10. Puig-Antich J. Psychobiological markers: Effects of age and puberty. In: Rutter M, Izard CE, Read PB, eds. *Depression in young people.* New York: Guilford Press, 1986;341–381.
11. Kovacs M, Feinberg T, Crouse-Novak M, Paulauskas S, Pollack M, Finkelstein R. Depressive disorders in childhood: I. A longitudinal prospective study of characteristics and recovery. *Arch Gen Psychiatry* 1984;41:229–237.
12. Kovacs M, Feinberg T, Crouse-Novak M, Paulauskas S, Pollack M, Finkelstein R. Depressive disorders in childhood: II. A longitudinal study of the risk factors for a subsequent major depression. *Arch Gen Psychiatry* 1984;41:643–649.
13. Asarnow JR, Goldstein MJ, Carlson GA, Perdue S, Bates S, Keller J. Childhood onset depressive disorders: A follow-up study of rates of rehospitalization and out-of-home placement among child psychiatric patients. *J Affective Disord* 1988;15:245–253.
14. Poznanski E. Childhood depression: The outcome. *Acta Paedopsychiatr* 1980/1981;46:297–304.
15. Eastgate J, Gilmour L. Long-term outcome of depressed children: A follow-up study. *Dev Med Child Neurol* 1984;26:68–72.
16. Stern SL, Mendels J. Drug combinations in the treatment of refractory depression: A review. *J Clin Psychiatry* 1981;42:368–373.
17. Fawcett J, Kravitz H. Treatment refractory depression. In: Schatzberg AF, ed. *Common treatment problems in depression.* Washington DC: American Psychiatric Press, 1985;2–20.
18. Lucas AR, Lockett HJ, Grimm F. Amitriptyline in childhood depression. *Dis Nerv System* 1965;26:105–110.
19. Puig-Antich J, Perel J, Lupatkin W, et al. Plasma levels of imipramine and desmethylimipramine and clinical response in prepubertal major depressive disorder. *J Am Acad Child Psychiatry* 1979;18:616–626.
20. Minuti E, Gallo V. Use of antidepressants in childhood: Results of maprotiline (Ludiomil) treatment in 20 cases. In: Costa E, ed. *Typical and atypical antidepressants: Clinical practice.* New York: Raven Press, 1982;223–227.
21. Petti T, Law W. Imipramine treatment of depressed children: A double-blind pilot study. *J Clin Psychopharmacol* 1982;2:107–110.
22. Preskorn J, Weller E, Weller R. Depression in children: Relationship between plasma imipramine levels and response. *J Clin Psychiatry* 1982;43:450–453.
23. Kashani J, Shekim WO, Reid J. Amitriptyline in children with major depressive disorder: A double-blind crossover pilot study. *J Am Acad Child Psychiatry* 1984;23:347–351.
24. Dugas M, Mouren MC, Halfon O, Moron P. Treatment of childhood and adolescent depression with mianserin. *Acta Psychiatr Scand* 1985;72(suppl 320):48–53.
25. Geller B, Cooper TB, Chestnut EC, Anker JA, Schluchter MD. Preliminary data on the relationship between nortriptyline plasma level and response in depressed children. *Am J Psychiatry* 1986;143:1283–1286.
26. Puig-Antich J, Perel JM, Lupatkin W, et al. Imipramine in prepubertal major depressive disorders. *Arch Gen Psychiatry* 1987;44:81–89.
27. Campbell M, Spencer EK. Psychopharmacology in child and adolescent psychiatry: A review of the past five years. *J Am Acad Child Adolesc Psychiatry* 1988;27:269–279.
28. Weller RA, Weller E. Tricyclic antidepressants in prepubertal depressed children: Review of the literature. *Hillside J Clin Psychiatry* 1986;8:46–55.
29. Alessi NE, Magen J. Comorbidity of other psychiatric disturbances in depressed, psychiatrically hospitalized children. *Am J Psychiatry* 1988;145:1582–1584.
30. Mitchell J, McCauley E, Burke PM, Moss SJ. Phenomenology of depression in children and adolescents. *J Am Acad Child Adolesc Psychiatry* 1988;27:12–20.

31. Bernstein G, Garfinkel B. School phobia: The overlap of affective and anxiety disorders. *J Am Acad Child Psychiatry* 1986;25:235–241.
32. Biederman J, Munir K, Knee D, et al. High rate of affective disorders in probands with attention deficit disorder and in their relatives: A controlled family study. *Am J Psychiatry* 1987;144:330–333.
33. Alessi NE, Magen J. Panic disorder in psychiatrically hospitalized children. *Am J Psychiatry* 1988;145:1450–1452.
34. Grunhaus L. Clinical and psychobiological characteristics of simultaneous panic disorder and major depression. *Am J Psychiatry* 1988;145:1214–1221.
35. Freeman LN, Poznanski EO, Grossman JA, Buchsbaum YY, Banegas ME. Psychotic and depressed children: A new entity. *J Am Acad Child Psychiatry* 1985;24:95–102.
36. Chambers WJ, Puig-Antich J, Hirsch M, et al. Psychotic symptoms in prepubertal major depressive disorders. *Arch Gen Psychiatry* 1982;39:921–927.
37. Wharton RN, Perel JM, Dayton PG, Malitz S. A potential clinical use for methylphenidate with tricyclic antidepressants. *Am J Psychiatry* 1971;122:1619–1624.
38. Drimmer EJ, Gitlin MJ, Gwirtsman HE. Desimipramine and methylphenidate combination treatment for depression: Case report. *Am J Psychiatry* 1983;140:2241–2242.
39. Liebowitz MR, Quitkin FM, Stewart JW, et al. Phenelzine vs imipramine in atypical depression. *Arch Gen Psychiatry* 1984;41:669–677.
40. Prange AJ, Loosen PT, Wilson IC, Lipton MA. The therapeutic use of hormones of the thyroid axis in depression. In: Post RM, Ballenger JC, eds. *Neurobiology of mood disorders*. Baltimore/New York: Williams & Wilkins, 1984;311–322.
41. Feighner JP, Herbstein J, Damlouji N. Combined MAOI, TCA, and direct stimulant therapy of treatment-resistant depression. *J Clin Psychiatry* 1985;46:206–209.
42. Fine S, Moreth M, Haley G, Marriage K. Affective disorders in children and adolescents: The dysthymic disorder dilemma. *Can J Psychiatry* 1985;30:173–177.
43. Alessi NE, Wittekindt J. Childhood aggressive behavior. *Pediatr Ann* 1989;18:94–101.
44. Black DW, Wilcox JA, Stewart M. The use of ECT in children: Case report. *J Clin Psychiatry* 1985;46:98–99.

6
Regional Cerebral Blood Flow in Refractory Depression

Shigeru Morinobu,[1] Katsuo Sagawa,[1] Shinobu Kawakatsu,[1] Shiro Totsuka,[1] Akio Komatani,[2] and Koichi Yamaguchi[2]

The treatment of depression has been improved dramatically since the introduction of the first tricyclic antidepressant (TCA) imipramine, discovered by R. Kuhn in 1957 (1). Although many new antidepressants have been developed that have improved the overall outcome in the treatment of depression, the number of patients with refractory or therapy-resistant depression has been increasing in Japan. Therefore, the development of new treatment approaches for refractory depression becomes an increasingly important problem.

The factors that contribute to refractory depression are multiple and complex. Some investigators have reported that cerebral blood flow, oxygen consumption, and glucose metabolism are reduced in patients with depression and that these parameters may return to normal values after successful treatment. Thus, they have postulated the presence of certain central nervous circulatory and metabolic disturbances related to depressive illness. Therefore, we have measured regional cerebral blood flow (rCBF) using the Xe-133 inhalation technique (HEADTOME, ring type single photon emission computed tomography, SPECT, Shimadzu, Japan) in a group of patients with refractory depression in order to elucidate the possible abnormality of brain function in relation to cerebral circulation in refractory depression.

MATERIALS AND METHODS

Patients

A total of 19 patients participated in the study (Table 1). Fifteen patients with mean ($\pm$ SD) age of 47.9 $\pm$ 8.0 years met criteria for unipolar depression according to the ICD-9 and the DSM-III. The duration of illness from its onset was 4.9 $\pm$ 4.0 years. Four patients with a mean age of 41.0 $\pm$ 2.8 years met similar criteria for bipolar depression and had a mean illness duration of 7.4 $\pm$ 3.9 years. All patients satisfied our hospital's definition of refractory depression as follows.

1. The length of episodes of prolonged or recurrent depression was at least 1 year.
2. The depressive state proved resistant to appropriate treatment regimens.

All patients received adequate doses of tetracyclic antidepressants or TCAs for treatment of depression, and severity of illness was rated by the Hamilton Depression Rating Scale (HDRS) (2). Fourteen age-matched normal volunteers (age 41.7 $\pm$ 9.7 years) also were evaluated under similar experimental conditions to serve as a control group. The aim and procedures of the study

---

[1]Department of Neuro-Psychiatry and [2]Department of Radiology, Yamagata University, School of Medicine, Yamagata, Japan.

TABLE 1. *Subject characteristics*

Diagnosis	n	Age (years)	Mean HDRS score
Normal subjects	14	41.7 ± 9.7	—
Bipolar depression	4	41.0 ± 4.0	10.5 ± 3.7
Unipolar depression	15	47.9 ± 8.0	11.8 ± 5.9

were explained to all subjects, and all gave consent.

rCBF Measurement

Regional cerebral blood flow was measured tomographically in two planes situated 35 mm and 70 mm above the orbitomeatal plane with the Xe-133 inhalation technique (HEADTOME: ring type SPECT). After an explanation of the procedure, the patients were placed in the supine position and kept their eyes closed while the measurements were being made. The Xe-133 was then administered by rebreathing through a mouthpiece for 1 minute. During this period and the following 5 minutes of Xe-133 washout, a series of six consecutive Xe-133 distribution maps of the brain were made at 1 minute intervals (3).

We used the correction of the rCBF value for the end-tidal CO_2 concentration to enhance the accuracy of the rCBF value because there is a significant correlation between end-tidal CO_2 concentrations and $Paco_2$ concentrations during mouthpiece respiration of Xe-133 ($r = 0.93$) (4). We measured the end-tidal CO_2 concentration in normal subjects to determine the mean end-tidal CO_2 concentration and the relation between rCBF values and end-tidal CO_2 concentrations prior to the present study. In a preceding study, it was found that the mean end-tidal CO_2 concentration was 5.8% and that the mean CBF increased 14% for each 1% increase in the end-tidal CO_2 concentration (5). Therefore, we used the correction of rCBF data by normalizing the end-tidal CO_2 concentration around 5.8% corresponding to 41 mm Hg $Paco_2$.

Accordingly, the rCBF value was corrected by the following formula.

$$\text{Corrected CBF} = \text{CBF} - [(\%CO_2 - 5.8) \times 0.14] \times \text{CBF}$$

Detailed descriptions of the measurement system and the correction system are presented elsewhere (4,6).

Statistical Analysis

The values presented represent the mean ± SD. For statistical analysis, the rCBF values of two groups of patients and normal subjects were compared by using a one-way analysis of variance (ANOVA). The difference among the mean values was considered to be significant when a p value was < 0.05.

RESULTS

Examples of typical patterns of rCBF of a 52-year-old male patient with prolonged unipolar depression are shown in Fig. 1.

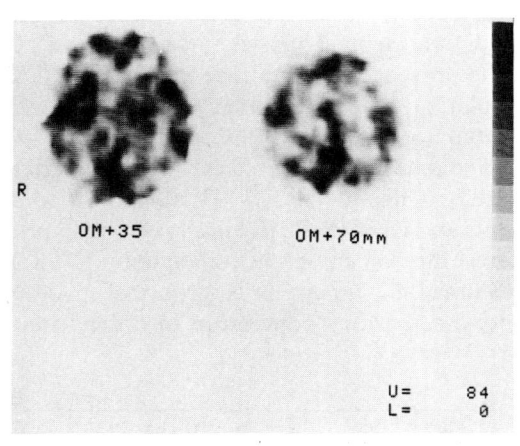

FIG. 1. Typical SPECT images in patient with prolonged unipolar depression. OM, orbitomeatol plane.

TABLE 2. *Mean hemispheric blood flow values*

Brain region	Normal subjects	Bipolar depression	Unipolar depression
Right hemisphere			
(OM + 35 mm)	50.5 ± 5.2[a]	54.0 ± 7.1	46.5 ± 8.3
(OM + 70 mm)	49.9 ± 4.8	53.3 ± 5.9	45.2 ± 6.9
Left hemisphere			
(OM + 35 mm)	50.6 ± 5.2	54.8 ± 6.5	46.0 ± 7.8
(OM + 70 mm)	48.6 ± 5.2	50.5 ± 3.9	43.7 ± 7.6

[a]Mean ± SD CBF value in ml/100 g/min.
*$p < 0.05$.

Reductions in the left superior frontal blood flow and the bilateral parietal blood flow are seen.

In the analysis of the clinical evaluation, the HDRS score of patients with unipolar depression was 11.8 ± 5.9. The HDRS score of patients with bipolar depression was 10.5 ± 3.7 (Table 1). There was no significant difference in the mean HDRS scores between patients with unipolar depression and those with bipolar depression.

Table 2 shows the mean bilateral hemispheric CBF values (OM + 35 mm, OM + 70 mm) for patients with unipolar depression, for those with bipolar depression, and for normal subjects. There were no significant differences in mean bilateral hemispheric CBF values (OM + 35 mm) among these three groups. No significant differences were seen in mean left hemispheric CBF values (OM + 70 mm) among these three groups. However, mean right hemispheric CBF values (OM + 70 mm) in patients with unipolar depression were significantly lower than those in patients with bipolar depression.

In the regional analysis, there were no significant differences in rCBF values of the right hemisphere among the unipolar depression, bipolar depression, and normal

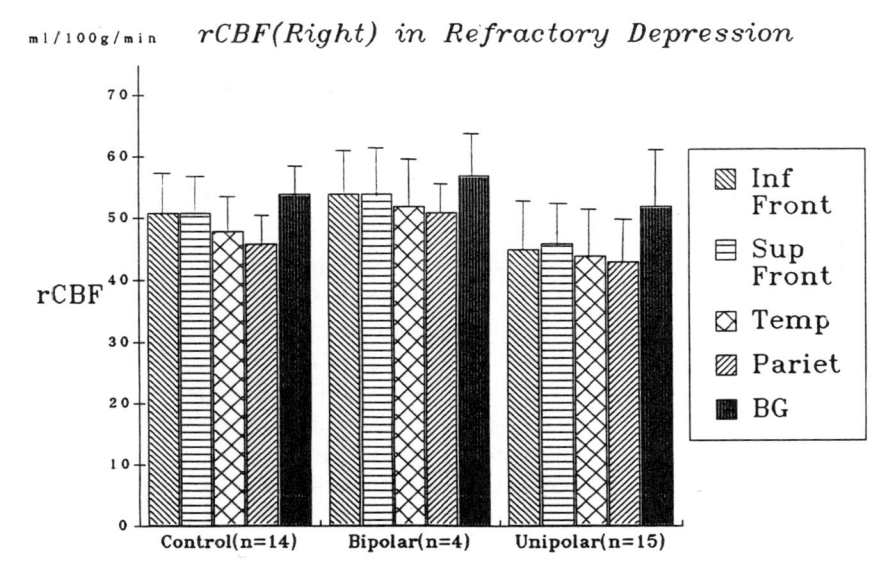

FIG. 2. Regional cerebral blood flow values for the right hemisphere in patients with depression and in normal subjects.

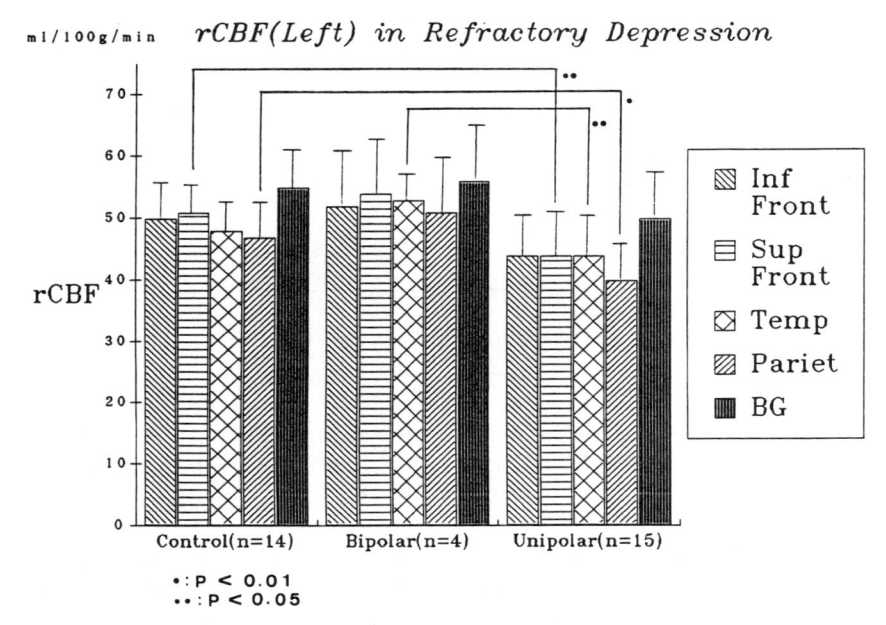

FIG. 3. Regional cerebral blood flow values for the left hemisphere in patients with depression and in normal subjects.

groups (Fig. 2). On the other hand, the left parietal and superior frontal blood flow values in unipolar depression were significantly lower than those in normal subjects (Fig. 3). The temporal blood flow value in unipolar depression was significantly lower than that in bipolar depression (Fig. 3).

There were no significant correlations between the HDRS scores and the bilateral hemispheric blood flow values or bilateral rCBF values in patients with unipolar depression. No significant correlations were found between the duration of illness and the bilateral hemispheric blood flow values or the bilateral rCBF values in patients with unipolar depression.

DISCUSSION

In the present study, we focused on unipolar depressed patients in considering the relation between diminished rCBF values and refractory depression because only four patients with bipolar depression were evaluated.

Our findings suggest that patients with refractory unipolar depression have significantly lower left superior frontal and left parietal blood flow values than do normal subjects. Although lower CBF values in depressed patients were reported by Mathew et al. (7,8), Gustafson et al. (9), Warren et al. (10), and Sackeim et al. (11), the data from the present study could not confirm those previous findings. For example, Mathew et al. (7,8) reported that depressed patients had significantly lower left and right hemispheric blood flow values as compared to normal subjects. In contrast, our study did not demonstrate significant differences in hemispheric blood flow values between depressed patients and normal subjects.

Gur et al. (12), Goldstein et al. (13), and Silfverskiold and Risberg (14) reported that there were no significant differences in rCBF values between depressed patients and normal subjects.

It is possible that the apparent conflict in the reported results is due to the influence of such factors as $Paco_2$ levels, neuroleptics, and the severity of depression on CBF values. In the present study, we measured the end-tidal CO_2 concentration and used the corrected blood flow values. However, the patients who participated in the study also received antidepressants and other neuroleptic drugs. It is possible, therefore, that the lower CBF values found in the present study might result from neuroleptics administered.

The severity of the illness is another important factor to consider when estimating CBF values. Mathew et al. (7,8) reported a significant negative correlation between the rCBF values and the HDRS scores. We could not confirm these negative correlations in the present study, possibly because our mean HDRS scores were lower than those reported in Mathew's studies (7,8).

We found decreased left superior frontal and left parietal blood flow values in patients with refractory unipolar depression, although the severity of the depression was modest according to the HDRS. These findings imply that hypoactivity of the left superior frontal and parietal cortex may play an important role in the pathogenesis of refractory depression.

There are some investigations that have suggested a role for left hemispheric hypoactivity in depression. Baxter et al. (15), using positron emission tomography, demonstrated that major depression was associated with left dorsal anterolateral prefrontal (DAP) cortex hypoactivity. The superior frontal cortex used in the present study is very similar to the DAP cortex in Baxter's study. Furthermore, it has been suggested that there are significant positive correlations between glucose metabolites and CBF in normal subjects (16). Hence, our study may support the results of Baxter's earlier investigation.

Some investigators suggest that a significant relationship exists between the strokes in the left hemisphere and the features of major depression (17,18). The study with language-related dichotic listening tests indicates that left hemispheric function may be associated with the pathogenesis of some affective disorders (19).

In conclusion, prolonged hypoactivity of the left superior frontal and the left parietal cortex or the failure of these cortices to recover from the hypoactive state may play an important role in the pathogenesis of refractory depression.

ACKNOWLEDGMENTS

We thank Mitsuyasu Yazaki, M.D., Toshihide Nadaoka, M.D., Yoshiaki Higashitani, M.D., Arata Oiji, M.D., Yukiko Morioka, M.D., Isoo Shibuya, M.D., and Tomiko Kawanami, M.D., for interviewing the patients.

REFERENCES

1. Kuhn R. Uber die Behandlung depressiver Zustande mit einem Iminodibenzyl derivat (Q22355). *Schweiz Med Wochenschr* 1957;87: 1135.
2. Hamilton M. A rating scale for depression. *J Neurol Neurosurg Psychiatry* 1960;23:56–62.
3. Kawakatsu S, Shinohara M, Morinobu S, et al. Regional cerebral blood flow in senile dementia of Alzheimer type and multi-infarct dementia. *Jpn J Gerontopsychiatry* 1987;4:790–797 (in Japanese).
4. Komatani A, Yamaguchi K. Measurement of cerebral blood flow using a Xe = 133 inhalation SPECT. *Adv Neural Sci* 1990;34:744–752 (in Japanese).
5. Sagawa K, Kawakatsu S, Shibuya I, et al. Correlation of regional cerebral blood flow with performance on neuropsychological tests in schizophrenic patients. *Schizophr Res* 1990;3:241–246.
6. Komatani A, Yamaguchi K, Sugai Y, et al. Assessment of demented patients by dynamic SPECT of inhaled xenon-133. *J Nucl Med* 1988;29:1621–1626.
7. Mathew RJ, Meyer JS, Francis DJ, Semchuk KM, Mortel K, Claghorn JL. Cerebral blood flow in depression. *Lancet* 1980;1:308.
8. Mathew RJ, Meyer JS, Francis DJ, Semchuk KM, Mortel K, Claghorn JL. Cerebral blood flow in depression. *Am J Psychiatry* 1980;137: 1449–1450.
9. Gustafson L, Risberg J, Silfverskiold P. Regional cerebral blood flow in organic dementia and affective disorders. *Adv Biol Psychiatry* 1981;6:109–116.
10. Warren LR, Butler RW, Katholi CR, McFarland CE, Crews EL, Halsey JH Jr. Focal changes in cerebral blood flow produced by monetary incentive during a mental mathematics task in normal and depressed subjects. *Brain Cogn* 1984; 3:71–85.

11. Sackeim HA, Prohovnik I, Apter S, et al. Regional cerebral blood flow in affective disorders: Baseline and effects of treatment. In: Takahashi R, Flor-Henry P, Gruzelier J, Niwa S, eds. *Cerebral dynamics, laterality, and psychopathology*. New York: Elsevier, 1987.
12. Gur RE, Skolnick BE, Gur RC, et al. Brain function in psychiatric disorders. 2. Regional cerebral blood flow in medicated unipolar depression. *Arch Gen Psychiatry* 1984;41:695–699.
13. Goldstein PC, Brown GG, Welch KMA, Marcus A, Ewing JR, Rosenbaum G. Age-related decline of rCBF in schizophrenia and major affective disorder. *J Cereb Blood Flow Metab* 1985;5(suppl 1):203–204.
14. Silfverskiold P, Risberg J. Regional cerebral blood flow in depression and mania. *Arch Gen Psychiatry* 1989;46:253–259.
15. Baxter LR, Schwartz JM, Phelps ME, et al. Reduction of prefrontal cortex glucose metabolism common to three types of depression. *Arch Gen Psychiatry* 1989;46:243–250.
16. Phelps ME, Mazziotta JC, Schelbert HR. *Positron emission tomography and autoradiography*. New York: Raven Press, 1986.
17. Robinson RG, Kubos KL, Starr LB, Rao K, Price TR. Mood disorders in stroke patients: Importance of location of lesion. *Brain* 1984;107:81–93.
18. Robinson RG, Lipsey JR, Bolla-Wilson K, et al. Mood disorders in left-handed stroke patients. *Am J Psychiatry* 1985;142:1424–1429.
19. Wexler BE, Mason JW, Giller EL. Possible subtypes of affective disorder suggested by differences in cerebral laterality and testosterone. *Arch Gen Psychiatry* 1989;46:429–433.

7

A Model for Refractory Depression: Cerebral Ventricular Size and CSF Transmitter Metabolite Concentrations in Refractory Depression

H. Standish-Barry

The scope of refractory depression is difficult to assess due to differences in the definition of treatment resistance or nonresponsiveness (1).

In 1972, Robins and Guze reviewed some 20 outcome studies of affective disorder and concluded that the illness took a chronic course in between 1% and 28% of patients (2). This very wide variation may be attributable to the different patient populations studied, the lack of uniformity in the diagnostic criteria for depressive illness, differing assessment methods, differing length of follow-up, and different definitions of chronicity. A review by Bebbington (3) also examined these issues.

Most authors tended to describe a depressive illness when there was persistance of symptoms beyond a given treatment length (4–7). Another important factor in describing chronic depression was impaired social functioning (8). Social impairment may result from the persistence of depressive symptoms that are, in themselves, mild (3), or social maladjustment may precede the onset of other depressive symptoms (9). If social impairment is used as a criterion for defining chronic depression, one will, therefore, find a higher level of chronicity reported. However, there seems to be little agreement on the definition of social dysfunction.

DEFINITIONS OF CHRONIC DEPRESSION

It is important that definitions of chronic depression should be agreed on and simple to use if existing studies are to be compared with each other and future studies planned. The simplest definition to date was proposed by Cassano et al. (9), who defined chronicity as the persistence of affective symptoms for a specified time, that is, 2 or more years. Using this definition, studies show that chronic depression evolves in some 12 to 15% of cases (10,11). Keller (12) found that about 20% of a patient sample suffering from a major depressive illness had not recovered within 2 years, and the recovery rate slowed with time. Some 64% had recovered within 6 months, and 74% had recovered within 12 months. However, only 79% of the sample had recovered within 2 years. A follow-up study of a group of elderly depressed patients (13) showed a 19% rate of chronic psychosis, and a study by Murphy (14) showed a poor outcome in 48% of elderly depressed patients at 1-year

---

West Park Hospital, Horton Lane, Epsom, Surrey, KT22 7NG, UK.

follow-up. In a study of female outpatient depressives (15) there was a prevalence of chronicity in 12%.

Most classifications define chronic minor and intermittent depression and chronicity as a function of personality. In 1980, the DSM-III replaced neurotic depression with dysthymic disorder. However, this perpetuated the idea that it is minor illness arising from an underlying personality disorder. Chronic major depression, it must be emphasized, often has been reported in patients whose premorbid personalities were normal. Akiskal et al. (16) suggested that patients whose chronicity of depression dates from early life (characterological depressives) should be distinguished from late onset chronic depressives, whose illness can be viewed as nonrecovery from one or more major episodes of depression. These authors divided chronic depression into chronic primary, chronic secondary, and characterological depressions. A subtype with major depressive episodes superimposed on a chronic minor depression has been described as double depression (17).

Chronic primary major depression is usually of late onset and represents an unresolved major depressive episode with no evidence of existing chronic minor disorder. It may be either unipolar or bipolar. Chronic secondary major depression can be viewed as an unremitting major depression arising secondary to physical ill health or nonaffective psychiatric disorder. Characterological or minor depression has an ill-defined onset in adulthood and appears to be interwoven with personality type. It occurs in a heterogeneous group of patients. In double depression, major depressive episodes are superimposed on an underlying chronic minor disorder. On recovering from the major episode, the patient returns to his or her premorbid dysthymic baseline. Progress of the minor depression is poor, and the major depressive episodes frequently recur.

Chronic primary major depression accounts for approximately 30% of all chronic depressive illness (9). Chronic secondary and characterological disorders have a worse prognosis than chronic primary depressions but the outcome for all groups tends to be unimpressive.

Older patients tend to be more at risk of developing chronicity in primary major depression than younger patients. The female/male ratio is similar to that of depressive disorders in general, but, after prolonged follow-up, women have been found to be more likely to develop a chronic depression than men (18). In the community in general, chronic depressive illness is 5 times more common in working class than in middle class females (19), although this has not been confirmed in inpatient or outpatient studies. The most important predictor of chronicity is the previous length of the illness episode. Every systematic study of chronicity has shown that the longer the illness episode persists before treatment or study entry, the more likely the illness is to become chronic. Incomplete recovery at the time of discharge predicts symptomatic chronicity (20).

TREATMENT STUDIES

Many chronic depressive states seem to result from treatment failure. It has been estimated that between 30% and 80% of refractory depressives have been given subtherapeutic doses of tricyclics or MAOIs (21). In one study, 50% of chronic depressives did not receive any treatment, although almost all had had previous depressive episodes that responded to antidepressant therapy. The longer a depressive illness persists, the less likely a patient is to receive adequate treatment (22), and the longer an episode lasts before treatment, the less likely it is to respond to tricyclics (21). Inadequate treatment at the onset of illness predicts more frequent chronicity and more often in females (23).

Evidence from several treatment studies supports the hypothesis that serotonergic function is altered in depressive illness. Parachlorophenylalanine, a drug causing decreased 5HT synthesis, has been shown to produce a recurrence of depressive symptoms in patients who had recovered on treatment with tranylcypromine (24). A number of reports suggest that accumulation of the 5HT metabolite 5HIAA after administration of probenicid is decreased in the CSF of depressed patients. Other studies have shown that addition of the 5HT precursor tryptophan can potentiate both an MAOI and the 5HT reuptake blocking antidepressant clomipramine (25, 26).

Further evidence for the role of abnormal 5HT function in depression has been provided by possible abnormalities in platelet ^{3}H-imipramine binding (27,28), a reduction of 5HT uptake in the platelets of depressed patients (29), lower CSF 5HIAA levels in suicide victims (30), and a significant relationship between lumbar and ventricular tryptophan and 5HIAA concentrations (31). Additional animal (32) and human data (33–35) suggest that plasma free tryptophan may be low in depression.

There are findings that tryptophan, in plasma and lumbar CSF, is reduced in patients with depressive disorders (36–38), and that 5HIAA is low in the lumbar CSF of depressed patients (30,36,39–42). Shaw et al. (43,44) found evidence that the concentration of tryptophan in the cells, its movement from extracellular to intracellular space, and its turnover in the body all are reduced in depression.

Banki et al. (45) report that severely depressed patients with relatively high lumbar CSF concentrations of HVA had significantly higher scores for anxiety, insomnia, and agitation and significantly lower scores for fatigability and retardation than a group with relatively low values. Post et al. (46,47) reported that a dopamine agonist, piribedil, and a dopamine antagonist, pimozide, were beneficial in depression and mania, respectively. Ventricular HVA and 5HIAA concentrations are likely to be more useful than lumbar CSF values in providing indices of turnover of their parent amines in at least the periventricular parts of the brain. Clearly reliable normal values are unobtainable. In neurological patients with restricted CSF flow, abnormally high HVA and 5HIAA concentrations often are found (48).

ORGANIC BRAIN DYSFUNCTION

The relationship of possible organic brain dysfunction, as measured by ventricular enlargement, in affective disorders to transmitter metabolite concentrations in ventricular fluid is a very complex one and may throw some light on the biochemical background to refractory depression. Standish-Barry et al. (49) reported that patients suffering from severe affective illness showed ventricular enlargement as measured by pneumoencephalographs and CT scans. Pearlson et al. (50,51) also have described cerebral atrophy, as assessed by ventricular enlargement and sulcal atrophy on CT scans in younger patients with bipolar illnesses. Jacoby and Levy (52) reported ventricular enlargement on CT scans in a group of elderly patients with late onset affective disorder. A number of other authors have reported similar findings. Standish-Barry et al. (49) postulated that enlargement of the cerebral ventricles would be associated with alterations of monoamine metabolite levels as a concomitant of affective disorder. In this context, 15 patients (6 male and 9 female) admitted to the Geoffrey Knight Psychosurgical Unit for stereotactic subcaudate tractotomy were studied. All patients were suffering from refractory depression and were selected for operation according to the criteria of Bridges et al. (53,54) and formed part of a larger group on whom Standish-Barry et al. (49) reported findings suggesting cerebral ventricular enlargement.

All patients were free from physical illness, had no evidence of organic cerebral abnormalities or dementia, and were drug free for 2 weeks before the procedure. The mean (± SD) age was 42.4 (± 11.9) years, with a range of 28 to 60 years. All patients had an RDC diagnosis of major depressive disorder (55). Stereotactic subcaudate tractotomy (56,57) was performed under general anesthesia, with burr holes made immediately above the frontonasal air sinuses on each side and air injected into the anterior horn of the lateral ventricles through a cannula after removal of CSF. In this way, the anterior horns are visualized to facilitate calculations for the stereotactic placement of the small radioactive yttrium rods, which produce the lesions in the ventromedial quadrants of the frontal lobes. Anteroposterior and lateral radiographs were taken in a standard way to monitor the siting of rods.

A CT scan was performed preoperatively, and pneumoencephalograhpy was performed during the operation. From the pneumoencephalographs, the Evans ratio (distance between the lateral extremities of the tips of the frontal horns of the lateral ventricles to the maximum internal diameter of the skull) was measured (58). By CT scan, the maximum ventricular area was measured. The area of the ventricle was traced three times, and the average of these readings was recorded. The internal area of the skull was measured in the same manner. A ratio of ventricular/internal skull area was made (VSR capsules), which gives a useful measure of ventricular size and has been shown to correlate well with computer-derived ventricular volume (59).

Before induction of anesthesia, 15 ml samples of blood were collected into heparinized tubes, and the plasma was flushed with 5% CO_2 capsules and stored at $-20°C$. The ventricular CSF displaced during pneumoencephalography was collected (after discarding the first 1–2 ml), centrifuged, and stored at $-20°C$. Plasma total tryptophan was measured as described by Bloxam and Warren (60), and free (nonalbumin-bound) tryptophan was determined by the method of Bloxam et al. (61). Plasma nonesterified fatty acids (NEFA) were determined by the method of Curzon and Kantanameni (62). 5HIAA was determined in CSF by the method of Korf and Valkenburgh-Kikkemal (63), except that CO_2 initially was passed through the CSF for a few seconds to prevent destruction of any traces of hemoglobin. HVA was determined in CSF by a modification of the method of Curzon et al. (31). Tryptophan and tyrosine were determined in CSF by the methods of Bloxam and Warren (60) and Waalkes and Udenfried (64), respectively.

RESULTS

The mean ±50 Evans ratio for the 15 patients was 29.9 or ± 2.1 (range 26–32), and this was significantly greater than that (26.0) reported by Synek et al. (65) in 15 normal subjects ($r=5.07, p<0.001$). The mean ventricular skull ratio (VSR) for the entire sample was 12.0 ± 2 (range 8.6–16.5), and this measure increased with age, the increase being statistically significant ($r=0.49; p<0.05$). The mean plasma total tryptophan concentration was 7.7 ± 1.4 µg/ml (range 4.58 µg/ml–9.79 µg/ml). The mean plasma free tryptophan concentration was 2.8 ± 0.59 µg/ml (range 1.74 µg/ml–4.03 µg/ml).

There were no gender differences in amine metabolite concentrations. The two prominent findings in the study were (a) plasma free tryptophan was reduced in patients with enlarged ventricles (as demonstrated by an increased Evans ratio), with a significant correlation between plasma free tryptophan and Evans ratio ($r = 0.46$, Pc 0.05), and (b) there was a significant positive relationship between ventricular CSF 5HIAA and the Evans ratio ($r = +0.55$, Pc 0.01) and a positive correlation between ventricular CSF 5HIAA and age ($r = 0.55$, Pc 0.01). This latter finding of enlargement of the ventricles with an increased CSF

5HIAA level suggests the presence of increased 5HT turnover. No relationship was found between ventricular size and CSF HVA.

The findings indicate that there is a group of severely depressed patients who have enlarged cerebral ventricles associated with raised CSF 5HIAA levels and lower plasma free tryptophan levels. This suggests the possibility that turnover of 5HT is increased, which may tend to deplete free plasma tryptophan, whereas the more usual explanation is that reduced plasma free tryptophan results in a reduction of 5HT neurotransmission. There is evidence that the rate of 5HT synthesis is dependent on the brain tryptophan concentration, which in turn is dependent on the plasma tryptophan concentration (66). Since most tryptophan (about 80%) is bound to plasma albumin, only about 20% is in a free form (67,68).

The Evans ratio tended to increase with age, but the correlation was not statistically significant. The Evans ratio also was greater than the mean 27 for a series of normal subjects (69) and the mean 23 described by Evans (58). The VSR varied considerably, and there are many difficulties in interpreting differences in VSR measurements, which have been discussed extensively by a number of authors (70–72).

Potkin et al. (73) found that a group of schizophrenic patients with enlarged ventricles had significantly lower lumbar CSF 5HIAA concentrations and that ventricular size correlated inversely with 5HIAA concentrations. In contrast, De Lisi et al. (74) found higher whole blood 5HT concentrations in schizophrenic patients with enlarged ventricles on CT scans. It is interesting to note that 9 of the patients studied by these workers were included in the study by Potkin et al. (73), in which 24 schizophrenic patients were examined. Potkin et al. suggest that there may be an inverse relationship between CSF 5HIAA concentration and blood 5HT to account for these differences, although the mechanism responsible for this is not clear. Nyback et al. (75) described a significant negative relationship between size of the lateral ventricles and lumbar CSF 5HIAA and HVA levels in schizophrenic patients. These findings confirm those of Potkin et al. However, in contrast, Zhang and Yucun (76) and Rimon et al. (77) found no differences in CSF 5HIAA between schizophrenic patients with and without ventricular enlargement on pneumoencephalography.

There has been considerable discussion as to whether the total plasma tryptophan or the free plasma tryptophan concentration influences brain tryptophan (78,79). Green (80) concluded that free tryptophan played a major role in controlling brain 5HT metabolism. However, the matter is further complicated by the finding that only a very small proportion of tryptophan (2%) enters the brain, since the rest is metabolized in the periphery (81). It has been suggested that increased activity of the enzyme tryptophan pyrrolase, which acts peripherally, would give rise to a greater metabolic rate in this pathway, with a consequent decrease in the amount of tryptophan available to the brain (82). The activity of tryptophan pyrrolase is increased by administration of tryptophan itself or of the steroids hydrocortisone and corticosterone (83). Such changes could be of great importance in depression (84–86), where one frequently finds altered corticosteroid metabolism, as shown by the dexamethasone suppression test. It has been shown that administration of hydrocortisone to rats increased tryptophan pyrrolase activity and decreased plasma tryptophan, with the probable consequence of decreasing brain tryptophan and 5HT concentrations (87,88).

Nine elderly depressed patients with enlarged cerebral ventricles, as defined by a neuroradiologist, had lower mean Hounsfield units (indicated reduced brain tissue density) than a group of depressed patients with normal ventricles (89). It is possible that this reduction in tissue density, associated with ventricular enlargement, might create a loss of 5HT and dopamine-containing neurons, thus causing alterations in the levels of their metabolites in the ventricular CSF, as well as altered neurophysiological responsiveness. Cawley et al. (90) have postulated that cerebral aging might have a facilitating role for depression in later life, from suggestions in a study of barbiturate tolerance and psychological functioning in elderly depressed patients. Hendrickson et al. (91) found a significant delay in the auditory evoked response of a group of elderly depressives, compared to matched controls, which lends support to this suggestion. This delay did not return to the control level after treatment.

Holder et al. (92) studied the relationship between brain neurophysiological activity and transmitted amine concentrations in ventricular CSF. These authors used pattern visual evoked potentials (PVEP) to measure brain neurophysiological activity, finding a positive correlation between ventricular HVA concentration and PVEP latency, and also between ventricular 5HIAA concentration and PVEP amplitude, which indicated a positive association between the physiological responsiveness of the brain to visual stimulation and release of the parent transmitter amine to receptors. These research workers further suggested that visual evoked cortical potentials could be influenced by 5HT or dopamine-containing neurons in regions involved in the transmission of visual impulses, situated near the ventricles (93–95). One could postulate that any reduction in brain tissue density might also predispose to alterations in evoked responses in depressed patients, as described by Hendrickson et al. (91). One also could expect that loss of 5HT and dopamine neurons in periventricular areas might result in a fall rather than a rise in metabolite levels, in association with ventricular enlargement. The apparent increase in CSF 5HIAA levels in the Standish-Barry study in association with ventricular enlargement could be explained by a compensatory increase in amine production by the remaining 5HT and dopamine neurons to main a homeostatic system.

Thus, one logically could extend this postulate to form a hypothesis for the failing treatment response in refractory depression to suggest that, in this condition, there is a failure of the homeostatic mechanism responsible for brain cellular loss, leading to ventricular enlargement and to an alteration in the 5HT metabolism, giving rise to the changes outlined.

REFERENCES

1. Scott J. Chronic depression. *Br J Psychiatry* 1988;153:287–297.
2. Robins E, Guze S. Classification of affective disorders: The primary secondary, the endogenous-reactive and the neurotic psychotic dichtomies. In: Williams TA, Katz MM, Shield JA, eds. *Recent advances of psychobiology of the depressive illnesses.* Washington, DC: U.S. Printing Office, 1972.
3. Bebbington PE. The course and prognosis of affective disorders. In: Wing JK, Wing L, eds. *Handbook of psychiatry 3: Psychoses of uncertain aetiology.* Cambridge: Cambridge University Press, 1982.
4. Wertheim FI. A group of benign chronic psychoses: Prolonged manic excitements. *Am J Psychiatry* 1929;86:17–78.
5. Lundquist G. Prognosis and course of manic-depressive psychoses: A follow-up study of 319 first admissions. *Acta Scand Psychiatr Neurol Suppl* 1945;35:1–96.
6. Braftos O, Haig JO. The course of manic depressive psychosis: A follow-up investigation of 215 patients. *Acta Scand Psychiatr* 1968;44:89–112.
7. Weissman MM, Kasl SV, Klerman GL. Follow-up of depressed women after maintenance treatment. *Am J Psychiatry* 1976;133:757–760.
8. Paykel ES, Weissman MM. Social adjustment and depression: A control study. A longitudinal study. *Arch Gen Psychiatry* 1973;28:659–663.
9. Cassano GB, Maggini C, Akiskal H. Short-term subchronic and chronic sequelae of affective disorders. *Psychiatr Clin North Am* 1983;6:555–568.
10. Kraepelin F. *Manic depressive insanity and paranoia.* 2nd ed. Edinburgh: E S Livingstone, 1921.
11. Murphy GE, Woodruff RA, Herjanic M, Super G. Variability of the clinical course of primary affective disorders. *Arch Gen Psychiatry* 1974;30:757–761.
12. Keller MB. Chronic and recurrent affective disorder incidence, course and influencing factors. In: Kemali D, Racagni G, eds. *Chronic treatment in neuropsychiatry.* New York: Raven Press, 1985.

13. Post F. The management and nature of depressive illnesses in late life: A follow-through study. *Br J Psychiatry* 1972;121:393–404.
14. Murphy E. The prognosis of depression in old age. *Br J Psychiatry* 1983;142:111–119.
15. Weissman MM, Klerman GL. The chronic depressive in the community: Unrecognized and poorly treated. *Comp Psychiatry* 1977;18:523–532.
16. Akiskal HS, King D, Rosenthal T, Robinson D, Scott-Strauss A. Chronic depressions—Part I. Clinical and familial characteristics in 137 probands. *J Affective Disord* 1981;3:297–315.
17. Keller MB, Shapiro RW. Double depression: Super imposition of acute depressive episodes on chronic depressive disorders. *Am J Psychiatry* 1982;139:438–444.
18. Winokur G, Morrison D. The Iowa 500: Follow-up of 225 depressives. *Br J Psychiatry* 1973;123:543–548.
19. Brown GW, Harris T. *Social origins of depression: A study of psychiatric disorders in women*. London: Tavistock Publications, 1978.
20. Toone BK, Ron M. A study of predictive factors in depressive disorders of poor outcome. *Br J Psychiatry* 1977;131:587–591.
21. Quitkin FM. The importance of dosage in prescribing antidepressants. *Br J Psychiatry* 1985;147:593–597.
22. Johnston DAW. A study of the use of antidepressant medication in general practice. *Br J Psychiatry* 1947;125:186–192.
23. Berti Ceroni GB, Pezzoli A, Neri C. Chronicity in major depression: A naturalistic prospective study. *J Affective Disord* 1984;7:123–132.
24. Shopsin B, Friedman E, Gershon S. Parachlorophenylalanine reversal of tranylcypromine effects in depressed patients. *Arch Gen Psychiatry* 1974;33:811–819.
25. Glassman A, Platman SR. Potentiation of a monoamine oxidase inhibitor by tryptophan. *J Psychiatr Res* 1969;7:83–88.
26. Walinder J, Skott A, Carlson A, Nagy A, Roos BE. Potentiation of the antidepressant action of clomipramine by tryptophan. *Arch Gen Psychiatry* 1976;33:1384–1389.
27. Briley MS, Langer SZ, Raisman R, Sechter D, Zarifian E. Tritiated imipramine binding sites are decreased in platelets of untreated depressed patients. *Science* 1980;209:303–305.
28. Paul SM, Rehavi M, Skolnich P, Ballenger JB, Goodwin FK. Depressed patients have decreased binding in tritiated imipramine to platelet serotonin "transporter." *Arch Gen Psychiatry* 1981;38:1315–1317.
29. Tuonisto J, Tukainen E. Decreased uptake of 5-hydroxytryptamine in blood platelets from depressed patients. *Nature* 1976;263:596–598.
30. Asberg MH, Traskman L, Thoren P. 5HIAA in the cerebrospinal fluid. A biochemical suicide predictor. *Arch Gen Psychiatry* 1976;33:1193–1197.
31. Kantamaneni BD, Van Boxel P, Gillman PK, Bartlett JR, Bridges PK. Substances related to 5-hydroxytryptamine in plasma and in lumbar and ventricular fluids of psychiatric patients. *Acta Psychiatr Scand* 1980;Suppl 280:3–19.
32. Bloxman DL, Curzon G. A study of prepared determinants of brain tryptophan concentration in rats after portacaval anastomosis or sham operation. *J Neurochem* 1978;31:1255–1263.
33. Young SN, Lal S, Feldmuller F, et al. Parallel variation of ventricular CSF tryptophan and free serum tryptophan in man. *J Neurol Neurosurg Psychiatry* 1976;39:61–65.
34. Sullivan PA, Murnaghan O, Callaghan N, Kantamaneni BO, Curzon G. Cerebral transmitter precursors and metabolites in advanced renal disease. *J Neurol Neurosurg Psychiatry* 1978;41:581–588.
35. Gillman PK, Bartlett JR, Bridges PK, Kantamaneni BD, Curzon G. Relationship between tryptophan concentrations in human plasma cerebrospinal fluid and cerebral cortex following tryptophan infusion. *Neuropharmacology* 1980;19:1241–1242.
36. Coppen A, Eccleston DG, Peet M. Total and free tryptophan concentrations in the plasma of depressive patients. *Lancet* 1973;2:60–63.
37. Sepping P, Kantamaneni BD, Curzon G. Precursors and metabolites of 5-hydroxytryptamine and dopamine in the ventricular cerebrospinal fluid of psychiatry patients. *Psychol Med* 1976;6:399–405.
38. Riley GJ, Shaw OM. Total and non-bound tryptophan in unipolar disease. *Lancet* 1976;2:1249.
39. Ashcroft GW, Crawford TBB, Eccleston D, et al. 5-Hydroxyindole compounds in the cerebrospinal fluid of patients with psychiatric or neurological diseases. *Lancet* 1966;2:1049–1052.
40. Ashcroft GW, Blackburn JM, Eccleston D, et al. Changes on recovery in the concentrations of tryptophan and the biogenic amine metabolites in the cerebro-spinal of patients with affective illness. *Psychol Med* 1973;3:319–325.
41. Prange AJ, Whybrow PC, Noguera R. Abnormalities of indoleamines in affective disorders. *Arch Gen Psychiatry* 1972;26:474–478.
42. Van Praag HM, Korf J. Serotonin metabolism in depression: Clinical application of the probenecid test. *Int Pharmacopsychiatry* 1974;9:35–51.
43. Shaw PM, Johnson AL, Tidmarsh SF, MacSweeney DA, Hewland HR, Woolcock NE. Multi compartmental analysis of amino acids. I. Preliminary data on concentrations, fluxes, flow constants of tryptophan in affective illness. *Psychol Med* 1974;5:205–213.
44. Shaw PM. Unipolar affective illness. *Lancet* 1976;2:363.
45. Banki CM, Molnar G, Voinik M. Cerebrospinal fluid amine metabolites, tryptophan and clinical parameters in depression. *J Affective Dis* 1981;3:91–99.
46. Post RM, Gerner RH, Carmon JS, et al. Effects of a dopamine agonist pirbedil in depressive patients: Relationship of pretreatment HVA to antidepressant response. *Arch Gen Psychiatry* 1978;35:609–615.
47. Jimerson DC, Bunney WE, Goodwin FK. Dopamine and mania: Behavioural and biochemical

effects of the dopamine receptor blocker pimozide. *Psychopharmacology* 1980;67:297–305.
48. West KA, Edwinson L, Nielson KG, Roos BE. Concentration of acid monoamine metabolites in ventricular CSF of patients with posterior fossa tumours. In: Broch M, Dietz H, eds. *Intracranial pressure*. Berlin: Springer, 1972.
49. Standish-Barry HMAS, Bouras N, Bridges PK, Bartlett JR. Pneumoencephalographic and computerised axial tomography scan changes in affective disorder. *Br J Psychiatry* 1982;141:614–617.
50. Pearlson GO, Veroff AE. Computerised tomographic scan changes in manic-depressive illness. *Lancet* 1981;2:470.
51. Garbacz DJ, Tompkins RH, Ahn HS, Gutterman DF, Veroff AE. Clinical correlates of lateral ventricular enlargement in bipolar affective disorder. *Am J Psychiatry* 1984;141:253–256.
52. Jacoby J, Levy R. Computed tomography in the elderly. *Br J Psychiatry* 1980;136:249–260.
53. Bridges PK, Bartlett J. Psycho-surgery: Yesterday and today. *Br J Psychiatry* 1977;131:249–260.
54. Gillman PK, Standish-Barry H. Selecting patients for psycho-surgery. In: Perris C, Struuve G, Jameson B, eds. *Biological psychiatry*. Amsterdam: Elsevier North-Holland Biomedical Press, 1981.
55. Spitzer RC, Endicott J, Robins E. *Research Diagnostic Criteria (RDC) for a selected group of functional disorders*. 3rd ed. New York: New York Psychiatric Institute, 1977.
56. Knight G. Stereotactic tractomy in the surgical treatment of mental illness. *J Neurol Neurosurg Psychiatry* 1965;28:304–310.
57. Goktepe EO, Young LB, Bridges PK. A further review of the results of stereotactic subcaudate tractotomy. *Br J Psychiatry* 1975;126:270–280.
58. Evans WA. An encephalographic ratio for estimating ventricular enlargement and cerebral atrophy. *Arch Neurol* 1942;47:931–937.
59. Penn RO, Belanger MG, Yasnoff WA. Ventricular volume in man computed from CAT scans. *Ann Neurol* 1978;3:216–223.
60. Penn RO, Warren WH. Error in the determination of tryptophan by the method of Oak and Dewey. A revised procedure. *Anal Biochem* 1974;60:621–625.
61. Penn RO, Hutson PH, Curzon G. A simple apparatus for the ultrafiltration of small volumes: Application to the measurement. *Anal Biochem* 1977;83:130–142.
62. Penn RO, Kantamaneni BD. Fluorimetric determination of plasma unesterified fatty acid. *Clin Chem* 1977;76:289–292.
63. Korf J, Valkenburgh-Sikkema T. Fluorimetric determination of 5-hydroxyindoleacetic acid in human urine and cerebro-spinal fluid. *Clin Chim Acta* 1969;26:301–306.
64. Waalkes TP, Udenfried S. A fluorimetric method for the estimation of tyrosine in plasma and tissues. *J Lab Clin Med* 1957;50:733–736.
65. Synek V, Reuben JR, DuBoulay GH. Comparing Evans Index and computerised axial tomography in assessing relationship of ventricular size to brain size. *Neurology* 1976;26:232–233.
66. Synek V, Seurkes TL. Tryptophan in the central nervous system: Regulation and significance. *Adv Neurochem* 1977;2:133.
67. McMenamy RH, Oncley JL. The specific binding of L-tryptophan to serum albumin. *J Biol Chem* 1958;233:1436.
68. Moir ATB. Interactions in the cerebral metabolism of the biogenic amines: Effect of the intravenous infusion of L-tryptophan on the tryptophan and tyrosine in brain and body fluid. *Br J Psychiatry* 1971;43:724.
69. Gawler J, Du Boulay GH, Bull JOW, Marshall J. Computerised tomography (the EMI scanner): A comparison with pneumoencephalography and ventriculography. *J Neurol Neurosurg Psychiatry* 1976;39:203–211.
70. Jernigan TL, Zatz LM, Moses JH Jr, Berger PA. Computed tomography in schizophrenics and normal volunteers. *Arch Gen Psychiatry* 1982;39:765.
71. Weinberger DR, De Lisi LE, Perman GP, Targum S, Wyatt RJ. Computed tomography in schizophreniform disorder and other acute psychiatric disorders. *Arch Gen Psychiatry* 1982;39:778.
72. Luchins DJ. Computerised tomography in schizophrenia. *Arch Gen Psychiatry* 1982;39:859–860.
73. Potkin SG, Weinberger DR, Linnoila M, Wyatt RJ. 5-Hydroxyindoleacetic acid in schizophrenic patients with enlarged cerebral ventricles. *Am J Psychiatry* 1983;140:21–25.
74. De Lisi LE, Neckers LM, Weinberger DL, et al. Increased whole blood serotonin concentrations in chronic schizophrenic patients. *Arch Gen Psychiatry* 1981;38:647–650.
75. Nyback H, Weisel FA, Hindmarsh T, Sedvall G. Cerebroventricular volume and cerebrospinal fluid monoamine metabolites in schizophrenic patients and in healthy volunteers. *Psychiatry Res* 1983;9:301–308.
76. Zhang W, Yucun S. 5-Hydroxytryptamine metabolism in schizophrenics. *Chin Med J [Eng]* 1979;92:817–884.
77. Rimon R, Roos BE, Kampman R, et al. Monoamine metabolite levels in cerebrospinal fluid and brain atrophy in lobotomized schizophrenic patients. *Ann Clin Res* 1979;11:25–29.
78. Wurtman RJ, Fernstrom JD. Control of neurotransmitter synthesis by precursor availability and nutritional state. *Biochem Pharmacol* 1976;25:1691.
79. Wurtman RJ, Knott PJ. Fatty acids and the disposition of tryptophan. *Ciba Foundation Symp* 1974;22:217.
80. Wurtman RJ. The effects of dietary tryptophan and its peripheral metabolism on brain 5-hydroxytryptamine synthesis and function. *Essays Neurochem Neuropharmacol* 1978;3:71.
81. Hagen PB, Cohen LH. Biosynthesis of indolealkylamines: Physiological release and transport of 5-hydrosytryptamine. In: Erspamer V, ed. *Handbook of experimental pharmacology, vol. 19*. Berlin: Springer-Verlag, 1966;182.

82. Hagen PB, Costain DW. The biochemistry of depression. In: Paybel ES, Coppen A, eds. *Psychopharmacology of affective disorders.* Oxford: Oxford University Press, 1979.
83. Knox WE, Auerback VH. The hormonal control of tryptophan peroxide in the rat. *J Biol Chem* 1955;214:307.
84. Mandell AJ. Some determinants of indole excretion in man. *Recent Adv Biol Psychiatry* 1963;5:137.
85. Curzon G. The biochemistry of depression. In: Cumings JN, Kremer M, eds. *Biochemical aspects of neurological disorders.* 2nd series. Oxford: Blackwell, 1965;257.
86. Curzon G. Tryptophan pyrrolase—A biochemical factor in depressive illness? *Br J Psychiatry* 1969;115:1367.
87. Green AR, Curzon G. Decrease of 5-hydroxytryptamine in the brain provoked by hydrocortisone and its presentation by allopurinol. *Nature* 1968;220:1095.
88. Curzon G, Grahame-Smith DG. 5-Hydroxytryptamine and other indoles in the central nervous system. In: Iversen LL, Iversen SD, Snyder SH, eds. *Handbook of psychopharmacology, vol 3.* New York: Plenum, 1975.
89. Jacoby RO, Dolan RJ, Levy R, Baldy R. Quantitative computed tomography in elderly depressed patients. *Br J Psychiatry* 1983;143:124–127.
90. Cawley RH, Post P, Whitehead A. Barbiturate tolerance and psychological functioning in elderly depressed patients. *Psychol Med* 1973;3:39–52.
91. Hendricksen E, Levy R, Post F. Averaged evoked responses in relation to cognitive and affective state of elderly psychiatric patients. *Br J Psychiatry* 1979;134:494–501.
92. Holder GE, Bartlett JR, Bridges PK, Kantameneni BD, Curzon G. Correlations between transmitter metabolite concentrations in human ventricular cerebrospinal fluid and pattern evoked potentials. *Brain Res* 1980;188:582–586.
93. Ternaux JP, Hery F, Bouroin S, Adrien J, Glowinski J, Hamon M. The topographical distribution of serotonergic terminals in the neostriatum of the rat and caudate nucleus of the cat. *Brain Res* 1977;12:315–326.
94. Ungerstedt U. Stereotoxic mapping of the monoamine pathways in the rat brain. *Acta Physiol Scand* 1971;Suppl 397:1–48.
95. Bodis-Wellner I, Yahr MD. Measurements of visual evoked potentials in Parkinson's disease. *Brain* 1978;101:661–671.

8

Polysomnography in Refractory Depression

Steven P. James, Larry Potter, Neil Berwish, and Jay D. Amsterdam

Complaints of poor sleep occur frequently in depression. When antidepressant medication is prescribed for a mood disturbance, the degree of sedation or activation of the drug often is used incidentally to treat the sleep disorder. Attention is thus directed more toward the change in mood while viewing the disturbance in sleep as a secondary phenomenon.

Although this approach generally is effective in the treatment of depression, a large percentage of patients do not respond to this therapy. Ayd et al. (1) estimate that approximately 10 to 20% of patients do not respond to accepted pharmacological and psychological treatments. What constitutes appropriate treatment response, however, varies widely depending on the background and interest of the clinician, the selection of the patient population included in the survey, and the length of participation by the patient in the various trials. Evidence continues to accumulate demonstrating that many refractory patients are responsive to treatment when aggressive treatment is provided.

Many changes in sleep occur in endogenous depression (2), and previous studies have reported alterations of the sleep EEG in refractory depression (3,4). In some respects, these studies may represent an inexact measure of physiological disturbances in these patients with persistent mood complaints.

In this chapter, we summarize our findings of sleep disturbances in a group of patients with refractory depression. Rather than viewing the sleep EEG as indicating severity or etiology of depression, we have chosen to reevaluate our refractory depressed patients, with greater importance placed on their sleep complaint as possible causes or contributing factors for a treatment-resistant state.

MATERIALS AND METHODS

Ten patients (six males, four females) (mean ± SE age 38 ± 4 years) with treatment-resistant depression were referred from the Depression Research Unit (DRU) at the Hospital of the University of Pennsylvania to the sleep disorders center. All patients previously had been diagnosed by two separate observers as having major depression using RDC (5) and had been followed on the DRU for a minimum of 2 years. During this time, they were treated with a minimum of one drug from the tricyclic class and at least one MAOI. Lithium was prescribed in five of the patients and was combined with TCAs in three patients. Six patients had previously participated in clinical trials with investigational antidepressants, the majority of which were double-blind, placebo-controlled studies.

At the time of their polysomnographic evaluation, all patients were medication free for at least 2 months. Beginning the week before the scheduled sleep study, patients were asked to maintain their usual

---

Depression Research Unit, Department of Psychiatry, Hospital of the University of Pennsylvania, Philadelphia, PA 19104.

sleep–wake cycle and to complete a sleep diary for subsequent review. No attempt was made to restrict the amount of caffeine, alcohol, or nicotine used by the patient. Instead, the normal amounts and patterns of usage were recorded and used in the subsequent clinical evaluation.

Using the 17-item Hamilton Depression Rating Scale (HDRS) (6), all patients were assessed by a rater unaware of the status of the patient. When possible, the HDRS was administered on the day of the study, although in several cases, the evaluation occurred within 7 days of the study. An HDRS of 17.5 ± 3.1 (SE) was found. All patients reported that this degree of depression was a typical mood for them over the past several years.

Each patient was scheduled for 2 consecutive nights of sleep recording in the laboratory. On the first night, they would sleep in the laboratory by 9 PM to adapt to the placement of electrodes, strain gauges, and oximeter and to control for the first night effect of the procedure. The following evening, the patients were asked to arrive in the laboratory by 9 PM to begin preparation for the sleep recording. Patients were instructed to try to fall asleep at their normal time and to wake up whenever they chose. On awakening, they completed a daily sleep questionnaire (DSQ) and a 100 mm line scale representing sleepiness, energy, and anxiety (7). In addition, information regarding the patient's perception of latency to sleep, total sleep time, and quality of sleep was obtained.

Scorers unaware of the past history of the patient read the polysomnogram. Sleep was scored using the criteria of Rechtschaffen and Kales (8), and final diagnosis was based on the nosology of the American Sleep Disorders Association (9).

RESULTS

All 10 subjects completed the study, and no untoward events were observed. A review of each sleep diary revealed considerable differences in the selected time of sleep and wake. For example, several of the patients noted that they customarily fall asleep before 10 PM but then sleep fitfully until the following morning when they awake between 5 AM and 7 AM. Often these individuals complained of excessive sleepiness during the day, with considerable problems in attention span and concentration. In this group, complaints of sexual dysfunction were common, with difficulties in maintaining an erection being the most frequent problem in men. Morning headaches, myalgia, arthralgia, and other somatic complaints were noted.

Persistent complaints of insomnia also were found in the other patients. In general, persistent insomnia was associated with the depression over several years. One patient reported sleeping only 1 hour nightly during the 2 weeks that the diary was used. This subjective sense of poor sleep was reported as having persisted for several years before evaluation.

The DSQ (7), a scale that surveys the patient's perception of duration and quality of sleep in comparison to home conditions, was also used in this evaluation. Because most patients express concerns regarding their ability to sleep under laboratory conditions, these reservations are reflected by the DSQ the morning after the first laboratory night. Invariably in the present study, the patients felt their ability to fall asleep was impaired, with a lighter quality of sleep and frequent awakenings. After the second night of laboratory sleep (the recording night), six of the patients felt that their sleep was similar to their sleep at home, two reported slightly less, one believed no sleep at all had occurred, and one reported much improved quality and duration. The results of the analysis of the sleep staging are shown in Table 1. As a group, many of the changes reported in depression were absent.

Although the patients were permitted to turn off the lights and sleep whenever they

TABLE 1. *Sleep EEG in refractory depression*

Stage	Mean	±SE
Sleep latency (min)	32.1	12.5
REM[a] latency (min)	102.0	10.5
Total sleep time (min)	362.0	12.1
Total delta time (min)	17.5	3.5
Delta percent	4.8	1.0
Total REM time (min)	59	8.8
REM percent	16	4.0
REM density	1.5	0.3
Sleep efficiency (%)	78	6.2
WASO (min)	65	15.7

[a]REM, rapid eye movement, WASO, wakening after sleep onset.

chose after they were prepared for laboratory study, no patient elected to stay up past 12:30 AM. After lights off, the time to fall asleep was 32.1 minutes. We define sleep onset as the latency from lights off to the first epoch of three continuous minutes of sleep. The 32 minutes to sleep onset does not differ significantly from the sleep latency found in preadapted normal controls in our laboratory.

A commonly reported sleep marker in depression is rapid eye movement (REM) latency, and in this group, the onset of REM sleep occurred 102 minutes after they fell asleep. Definitions of what constitutes a short REM latency differ among laboratories, although most would agree that our finding of 102 minutes would be considered normal. Examination of other REM sleep variables known to be altered in depression were also assessed and found to be unremarkable. The disturbance of REM sleep during the night and the amount of vigorous eye movements (referred to as REM density) were both normal in these patients.

Despite the fact that these were normal sleep parameters, which if abnormal would frequently be associated with affective disorder, these patients still had a variety of disturbances in their sleep. For example, the total sleep time and sleep efficiency were reduced in these patients. As a group, they slept only 362 minutes out of 459 minutes in bed, yielding a sleep efficiency of only 78%. A reduction in the depth of sleep also was observed. Only 4.8% of the total sleeping time was found to be deep delta sleep, and the REM percent also was decreased to only 8.8% of the time asleep. The overall findings in the sleep architecture were that sleep was of a shallow type, adequate in duration but frequently disrupted. Little evidence was found of sleep changes more generally associated with affective disorders.

Evaluations of sleep complaints require considerable more analysis than sleep scoring. Additional objective measures, including the monitoring of nasal and oral airflow, assessment of thoracic and abdominal respiratory effort, continuous evaluation of oxygen saturation using an oximeter, and the recording of leg movements, are obtained. These objective laboratory measures are then reviewed along with the patients prior sleep pattern, adaptation to the laboratory environment, and the subjective estimate of the time required to fall asleep, the total length of time asleep, and the qualitative sense of alertness on awakening.

Using the laboratory and subjective reports and the criteria of the American Sleep Disorders Association, the sleep diagnosis of these patients is shown in Table 2. Four patients were diagnosed as having sleep apnea syndrome. Three of these patients were found to have obstructive sleep apnea, and the other had predominantly central type.

TABLE 2. *Sleep diagnosis*

Patient	Diagnosis
1	DIMS,[a] psychophysiological persistent
2	DIMS, sleep apnea syndrome obstructive
3	DOES, sleep apnea syndrome obstructive
4	DIMS, atypical polysomnographic features
5	DIMS, sleep-related myoclonus
6	DOES, sleep apnea syndrome obstructive
7	DIMS, subjective without objective findings
8	DOES, sleep-related myoclonus
9	Normal sleep study
10	DOES, sleep apnea syndrome, central

[a]DIMS, disorder of initiation or maintaining sleep; DOES, disorder of excessive sleepiness.

The Apnea Index (AI), which is determined by dividing the number of apnea and hypoapneas by the hours of sleep, ranged from 7.5 to 35. The majority of desaturations were to the mid-80%, but two patients desaturated into the 70% range on several occasions.

The three patients with obstructive apnea were treated with continuous positive airway pressure (CPAP), and the one patient with central events was prescribed protriptyline. CPAP pressure was determined by having the patient return for another night of study and applying positive pressure through the nasal mask until all apnea and hypoapneas were eliminated. The patient then returned home the following day and was periodically reviewed by the Sleep Disorders Center. After 1 month of CPAP treatment, the HDRS decreased from 20.5 to 12.1. The one patient prescribed protriptyline also improved and HDRS decreased from 17 to 12. Because of the small number of subjects, no statistical analyses were performed.

Two patients were discovered to have sleep-related myoclonus. In these patients, leg movements associated with brief arousals from sleep were found to occur 95 and 147 times during the night, respectively. Both were prescribed clonazepam, with a change in the HDRS from 17 to 14 after 1 month. Although both patients reported feeling more alert during the day after taking clonazepam at bedtime, their subjective sense of depression seemed to persist.

The most common types of insomnia seen in sleep laboratories are psychophysiological insomnia and subjective insomnia without objective findings. One patient reported that, to her surprise, her sleep was much improved in the laboratory, demonstrating the conditioned quality of the sleep complaint. After further review of the history, a diagnosis of psychophysiological insomnia was made, and the patient was advised on sleep hygiene methods. One month after studying this regimen, the patient reported improved sleep but little change in mood.

Another patient noted that he felt he had slept for less than 1 hour, although the total sleep time using EEG criteria was longer than 5 hours. The patient also misinterpreted the time required to fall asleep, believing he was awake for 3 hours when sleep had occurred after 20 minutes. This individual had been treated previously with continuous exposure to benzodiazepines but had noticed that the effect had diminished over the past few years. Efforts were made to restrict the patient's perception of sleep by restricting the time in bed and the use of relaxation techniques. No change in mood was observed 1 month after starting treatment, although the reliance on benzodiazepines was absent.

Increased spindling and frequent alpha intrusions in delta sleep were found in one patient with the diagnosis of atypical polysomnographic features. The clinical significance of this category is controversial and often is the result of medication. In this patient, no centrally acting agent had been prescribed for 4 months.

Only one patient was found to have a normal sleep study. This patient had no complaints of a sleep disorder and was the least depressed of the entire patient group.

DISCUSSION

This study confirms the observation that patients with refractory depression have a substantial number of sleep-related disturbances and suffer from several types of sleep disorders. From this finding, the importance of evaluating complaints of poor sleep becomes apparent in the overall management of treatment-resistant depression.

Many sleep disorders often occur as changes in daytime behaviors, and complaints of decreased mood and concentration are common. Sleep apnea syndrome is a syndrome in which mood disturbance, poor concentration, fatigue, impaired sexual desire and function, and disturbed nighttime sleep are prominent complaints (10). Respiration often is more impaired during REM sleep, and medications that suppress REM (e.g., antidepressants) may provide some relief of the behavioral changes. This partial response to antidepressants may mislead the clinician into assuming that depression is the primary complaint and may delay the required evaluation and treatment of the sleep disorder.

The occurrence of nocturnal myoclonus (11) is another example of how sleep disorders may complicate the treatment of affective disorders. Myoclonus may occur as a primary sleep disorder or secondary to another sleep disturbance. Difficulty in falling asleep at night, frequent awakenings, and daytime fatigue and depression often are found. Treatment of depression with antidepressants is known to cause increased myoclonic movements in sleep, with arousals. We found that our two patients with nocturnal myoclonus were unable to tolerate several trials of antidepressant medication. With prescription and increase in the dosage of tricyclics, these patients complained of increased agitation and insomnia. They were thus unable to continue on treatment that was potentially beneficial, and they remained depressed.

It was not unexpected that one patient had sleep complaints as a result of negative conditioning (persistent psychophysiological insomnia). Since depression and sleep disruption may persist for several months, patients may become conditioned not to sleep at night. After the depression has been successfully treated, sleep complaints may persist because the negatively conditioned behavior of insomnia continues. Many patients who have insomnia and no current mood disturbance often have past histories of depression. These patients apparently have become negatively conditioned to not sleep during a depressive episode, and their insomnia becomes a long-term complication of their affective disorder.

Our finding of persistent psychophysiological insomnia in one refractory patient and the incidence in our sleep disorders center highlights the importance in attending to sleep complaints when the patient is depressed. Emphasis on sleep hygiene, including regular sleep–wake times, no napping, avoiding alcohol and caffeine, and restricting nicotine, should be part of the daily management of depressed patients.

It is important to recognize that other untoward effects in addition to myoclonus or conditioned insomnia may complicate the treatment of depression. As noted earlier, four of our patients were found to have sleep apnea. Sleep apnea is often (but not invariably) associated with depression, and all four of these patients weighed greater than 125% of their ideal weight. All four patients reported weight gains (between 10 and 40 pounds) as a result of taking antidepressants. It is possible that the apnea in these patients is an untoward result of prior pharmacological treatment. Since sleep apnea results not only in behavioral changes but also in significant cardiovascular complications, patients with significant weight gain and persistence of depression require careful monitoring by their clinician.

An important outcome of this study is to heighten the clinician's concern for the cause of sleep disturbances in refractory depression. Although this is only a preliminary observation of sleep disorders in this population, it should stimulate the clinician to reevaluate in a different light those patients who do not improve. Only through appropriate diagnosis of the patient's complaint can effective treatments be prescribed.

REFERENCES

1. Ayd FJ. Treatment resistant depression. *Therapeutic strategies in affective disorders preassessed*. In: Ayd FJ, Taylor IJ, Taylor, eds. Baltimore: Ayd Medical Communication, 1983;115–125.
2. Gillin JC, Silaram N, Wehrt DW, et al. Sleep and affective illness. In: Post R, Ballenger J, eds.

Neurobiology of mood disorders. Baltimore: Williams & Wilkins, 1984;157–189.
3. Akiskal HS, Rosenthal TL, Haykal RF, Lemmi H, Rosenthal RH, Scott-Strauss A. Characterological depressions: Clinical and sleep EEG findings separating "subaffective dysthymias" from "character spectrum" disorders. *Arch Gen Psychiatry* 1980;37:777–783.
4. Kupfer DJ, Thase ME. The use of the sleep laboratory in the diagnosis of affective disorders. *Psychiatr Clin North Am* 1983;6:3–25.
5. Spitzer RL, Endicott J, Robbins E. Research Diagnostic Criteria: Rationale and reliability. *Arch Gen Psychiatry* 1978;35:773–782.
6. Hamilton M. Development of a rating scale for primary depression illness. *Br J Soc Clin Psychol* 1967;6:278–296.
7. Mendelson WB, Weingarthner H, Greenblatt DJ, Garnett D, Gillin JC. A clinical study of flurazepam. *Sleep* 1982;5:350–360.
8. Rechtschaffen A, Kales A. *A manual of standardized terminology, techniques and scoring systems for sleep stages of human subjects.* Los Angeles: Brain Information Service/Brain Research Institute, 1968;1–60.
9. Roffwarg HP, ed. *Sleep. Diagnostic classification of sleep and arousal disorders.* 2nd ed. 1979;1.
10. Guilleminault C, Cummiskey J, Dement WC. Sleep apnea syndrome: Recent advances. *Adv Intern Med* 1980;26:347–372.
11. Coleman RM. Periodic nocturnal myoclonus in disorders of sleep and wakefulness, Ph.D. thesis. Ann Arbor: Yeshiva University, 1979.

9
A Trial of ECT Is Essential Before a Diagnosis of Refractory Depression Is Made

Max Fink

Despite a wide range of drug treatments and psychotherapy, some depressed patients do not recover, and they are then viewed as therapy resistant. Determination of therapy resistance is difficult, since it is defined by the physician when a patient is unresponsive to what the physician believes to have been adequate treatments. Therapy resistance is sometimes described among ambulatory patients, but I reserve the term for patients who are so ill as to warrant hospitalization and who fail repeated treatment trials. This is not to argue that treatment resistance does not occur in ambulatory patients, but such patients are inherently less ill, and the variety of their symptoms and complaints is so broad as to make their classification using modern diagnostic criteria (such as DSM-III, DSM-III-R, or RDC) difficult. Further, there are important treatment options available mainly for hospitalized patients. It seems practical to reserve the term therapy resistance for those patients who have been given the maximum opportunities for relief. In such patients, consideration must be given to the use of convulsive therapy.

Diagnostic classification, even with the operationally defined criteria of DSM-III and DSM-III-R, is difficult. Severely depressed patients are surprisingly diverse, exhibiting melancholia with severe inanition or suicidal thoughts and acts or dementia or catatonia or psychosis. The presence of psychosis, for example, complicates the diagnosis, particularly in allocating patients to classes of major depression with psychosis, schizophrenia with affective symptoms, schizoaffective syndromes, bipolar disorder with psychosis, or atypical psychoses. The separation of these subtypes is important because we teach that these syndromes are separate disorders with separate pathophysiologies, separate genetic patterns, and differential response to treatment.

Our philosophy of treatment (and our skills) limits the choices we consider for our patients. In treating depressed patients, the first line is either psychotherapy or tricyclic antidepressant (TCA) drugs, or TCA drugs with some form of psychotherapy. Initially, doses are generally low, but at some point, if the response is inadequate, dosages are increased, occasionally monitored by blood levels. If this regimen fails or if the patient is unable to tolerate the medication and has now been under treatment for 3 or more weeks, the following options apply.

1. Lithium replaces the TCA, or the two are combined.

Department of Psychiatry and Behavioral Science, SUNY at Stony Brook, St. James, NY 11780.
This work was aided, in part by the International Association for Psychiatric Research, Inc., St. James, New York 11780 and presented at the first International Conference on Refractory Depression, Philadelphia, PA, October 6–7, 1988.

2. An antipsychotic replaces the TCA, or the two are combined.
3. An MAOI replaces the TCA.
4. A second generation drug, such as maprotilene or chloripramine, replaces the TCA or MAOI.
5. A third generation drug, such as fluoxetine, trazodone, alprazolam, or buspirone, replaces the TCA, MAOI, or second generation medication.

Such tactics occasionally are successful. If they are not and the patient has been under treatment for 8 or 12 weeks, he or she is considered therapy resistant. Polypharmacy becomes a feature—if one or two drugs are not effective, perhaps a slew will be more so. It is not unusual to receive referrals of patients treated with five or more drugs at once.

In academic circles the options are further increased by such experimental regimens as

1. A selective MAOI, such as clorgyline, pargyline, or deprenyl
2. T_3 enhancement of TCA
3. Amine precursors, such as L-tryptophan or 5HTP or L-tyrosine
4. Psychostimulants, such as D-amphetamine or methylphenidate
5. Infusions of high doses of antidepressants, such as chloripramine, or sleep deprivation, bright light therapy, estrogens, or opioids

In this hierarchy, ECT is rarely considered or, if so, is considered as a treatment of last resort. Therapists insist on numerous adequate courses of therapy to which a patient has failed to respond before a referral for ECT is made. Such a philosophy has been enshrined in both law and practice in California, for example. Convulsive therapy generally is not discussed in symposia sponsored by the pharmaceutical industry or in teaching courses on therapy-resistant depressions, so that its use is kept further from the minds of practitioners.

Although I can trace the roots of this philosophy, a philosophy that eschews ECT as a consideration except as a last-resort option and that argues for repeated trials with new and mainly unproven treatments, with untested drug combinations, and with polypharmacy, I cannot condone such practice in our teaching. Convulsive therapy is the most effective treatment for affective disorders, especially those associated with or accompanied by psychosis. Patients who have failed TCA therapy or combination drug therapy frequently benefit from treatment with ECT. In this regard, in several random assignment studies, ECT was found to be more effective than TCA drugs alone, TCA and antipsychotic drug in combination, or MAOI (1–4). Thus, ECT surely deserves attention as a treatment option much earlier in the management of many depressed patients, especially those who have failed to respond to reasonable dosage trials of psychoactive medications.

Indeed, a more reasonable program for the treatment of the hospitalized depressed patient is to recommend a TCA trial, either alone or with antipsychotic medications for those with psychosis. For those who fail to respond to a 3 to 5 week trial, ECT should be considered, especially among the severely ill. Or, if patients prefer, a second course with an MAOI or a TCA supplemented by lithium or other enhancer should be tried for an additional 4 to 6 weeks. Surely, ECT should be a consideration for those patients hospitalized for 8 weeks or longer who have failed to respond to two adequate therapy trials, a model not unlike the definition of therapy-resistant schizophrenia recommended for patients who may be considered for trials with clozapine.

The efficacy of ECT is well documented. Reviewed in response to the antipsychiatry movements of the 1970s, efficacy trials are summarized in the APA Task Force reports (2,3), texts by Fink (4), Abrams and Essman (5), Kalinowsky et al. (6), Abrams (1), and Kiloh et al. (7). More recently, in response to the recommendations of the NIH

Consensus Conference (8), the American Psychiatric Association reestablished its Task Force on Electroconvulsive Therapy in 1988. Their detailed recommendations are now published (3).

EFFICACY OF ECT IN DEPRESSIVE DISORDERS

Many studies meet the technical criteria of random assignment, independent ratings, adequate dosage schedules, and defined outcome criteria. In these, ECT is equal to the other antidepressant treatments with which it has been compared, and considering the usual practice of treating depressed patients first with drugs and referring them for ECT only after drug treatment failure, the high success rates for ECT are truly remarkable (1–4).

Psychotic Depression

The superior efficacy of ECT over tricyclic drugs is seen in the 1964 study by deCarolis et al., recently translated by Avery and Lubrano (9). Hospitalized depressed patients were treated with high doses of imipramine—from 200 mg/day to 350 mg/day for 25 days. If the trial of imipramine was unsuccessful after 30 days, ECT was started, for a course of eight to ten bilateral treatments. Of the 437 patients treated with imipramine, 244 improved (56%). Of the 190 imipramine treatment failures who were next treated with ECT, 137 improved (72%).

The success rate with imipramine was significantly poorer (40%) in the 181 patients with delusional depression. Of the 109 delusional depressed patients who failed to improve with imipramine and who next received ECT, 91 (83%) improved.

Avery and Lubrano (9) cite three additional studies (10–12) in which the success rate for antidepressants alone in delusional depressed patients varied from 15 to 53%, whereas that with nondelusional patients varied from 67 to 86%. The delusional depressed compel special consideration. They respond poorly to antidepressant drugs alone even when plasma levels of tricyclic drugs are monitored (13).

Some authors suggest that delusional depressed patients may be treated adequately by the combination of a TCA and an antipsychotic drug or by antipsychotic drugs alone. In a review of the efficacy of different therapies for delusional depression, Kroessler (14) reported an overall efficacy rate of 34% for TCAs alone, 51% for antipsychotic drugs alone, 77% for the combination of a TCA and an antipsychotic drug, and 82% with ECT. Patients who had failed one or more of the drug therapy regimens usually were included among those referred for ECT, making this efficacy rate all the more compelling.

Catatonia

Although catatonia often is labeled a form of schizophrenia, it is a syndrome that has a high prevalence among patients with severe bipolar affective disorder (15,16). Like delusional symptoms in depression, catatonic symptoms often respond poorly to antidepressant or antipsychotic drugs alone, but they are particularly responsive to ECT. To the extent that depressed patients also exhibit the syndrome of catatonia, they should not be considered therapy resistant until they have had a course of ECT.

There is also a secondary catatonia that is not easily recognized. Some patients seriously ill with lupus erythematosus, during severe infections such as typhoid fever, or the neuroleptic malignant syndrome exhibit altered consciousness with stupor or hyperactivity. Their feeding is affected, and they lose weight and become emaciated. Psychoactive drugs often are to no avail. In such cases, a course of ECT has been lifesaving (17–21). Here, too, the usual statement that the patient is therapy resistant should not be accepted without consideration of an ECT trial, even in the face of severe inanition and poor medical condition.

Relapsing Mania

Although mania usually is responsive to lithium and antipsychotic drugs, the relapse rates are high, and treatments soon become ineffective. It is in such patients that the anticonvulsant drugs carbamazepine and valproic acid have been recommended. For other patients, cycling into and out of mania and/or depression is so frequent as to form a special class of therapy-resistant patients, those with rapid cycling mania (22). In the early literature, the efficacy of ECT in relieving acute and severe mania is well documented (23–25). This experience was generally forgotten in the enthusiasm for psychopharmacology, but recent reports again find an efficacy that compels consideration. Milstein et al. (26) and Small et al. (27) assigned their manic patients to either ECT or lithium combined with antipsychotic drugs and found ECT as effective as the drug combination. Mukherjee et al. (28) specifically sought out manic patients who had not been controlled with haloperidol and lithium and reported that this therapy-resistant sample was responsive to ECT.

Suicide

Suicide is the principal complication and risk in treating patients with depressive disorders, and it is a central consideration in therapy-resistant patients. The age-corrected death rate among depressed patients is nearly three times that of the general population. Suicide accounts for 15% of all deaths in patients with mood disorders and 60% of all deaths in the year postdepression. Among depressed patients, the death rate due to cardiovascular disease and infection also is higher than that of an age-corrected population.

In studies of the relative efficacy of ECT and antidepressant drugs, ECT is clearly superior in preventing death by suicide. Avery and Winokur (29,30) reviewed the records of more than 600 hospitalized depressed patients and found ECT superior to drug therapies in global antidepressant effects but not in relapse rates. At 6-month follow-up, the drug groups had four to seven times more suicide attempts than the ECT group, and there was a lower overall mortality in the ECT-treated group. They reviewed similar studies reporting on more than 4,500 patients and concluded that ECT improves the survival rate in the natural course of depressive disorders. Although ECT is effective for the index illness, it may not prevent suicide during recurrences of a depressive disorder (31).

Schizophrenia

A subgroup of patients with schizophrenia also fail to respond to antipsychotic drug therapy and various drug combinations, and some come to ECT. Friedel reported that among psychotic patients who failed multiple courses of antipsychotic drugs, he had used a combination of ECT and antipsychotic drugs. To his surprise, nine of nine patients improved markedly with the combination. He asserted that although his patients carried diagnoses of schizophrenia, they had exhibited other symptoms, usually of an affective nature, so that he was willing to consider ECT as an option (32).

Following this lead, we reviewed our experience with schizophrenic patients who had been referred for ECT after other treatments had failed. Of eight psychotic patients treated with ECT and an antipsychotic drug, seven had been discharged as improved, five of them to their homes (33). What was more striking were the results after 6 and 12 months follow-up, with six patients living at home after 12 months.

Caveats

Although use of ECT will surely reduce the population of patients classified as therapy-resistant depressions, the indiscriminate use of ECT among all types of depressed patients would be a disservice to the treatment. Convulsive therapy is effective for well-defined populations but not for all who exhibit depressive symptoms. It has not been reported as effective for those with dysthymia or atypical depression in which the depressive symptoms are part of a syndrome of anxiety, neurosis, or hypochondriasis, nor where the depression is complicated by alcoholism and drug dependence.

The experience with ECT over a half-century has identified clues to ECT responders. Good outcome is associated with age over 40, severity of the depression, prominence of vegetative symptoms, presence of delusions, and absence of neurotic symptoms (1).

PRACTICAL CONSIDERATIONS IN ECT THERAPY

Much hesitation in the use of convulsive therapy results from a widespread lack of acquaintance and training in its administration. In the first decades of its use, seizures were unmodified by anesthesia, and the risks of fracture, pain, missed and tardive seizures, panic, and even death were high. In the 1950s, anesthesia for all treatments made ECT a distinctly different therapy. Oxygenation, unilateral electrode placements, threshold induction currents, brief-pulse stimuli, and monitoring of seizure duration increase efficacy, decrease risk, and enhance acceptance of treatments. These modifications in treatment were the subject of the APA Task Force report of 1978 (2) and of numerous texts and reviews at the time.

These modifications, however, increase the complexity of the treatments, and we lack a cadre of trained therapists with competence to deliver ECT safely and effectively. The American Psychiatric Association recommendations and rationale clearly recognize the role of ECT in recurrent illnesses and in continuing and maintenance therapies. With regard to therapy-resistant illnesses, the report argues persuasively that no patient should be considered therapy resistant or be subjected to experimental and complex polypharmacies before a reasonable trial of ECT has been undertaken (3).

CONCLUSION

ECT is an effective therapy for delusional, catatonic, and suicidal depressed patients, as well as those with relapsing mania and some types of schizophrenia. Those patients who are ill enough to warrant hospitalization and who do not respond to pharmacotherapy should not be considered therapy resistant until they have received an adequate course of ECT. This is particularly true for patients over the age of 40, with delusions, melancholia, catatonia, severe suicidal drive, or prominent affective symptoms.

The complexities of modern convulsive therapy surely inhibit its more general use, and increased attention to education and training is needed to increase the cadre of trained electrotherapists. The 1990 APA Task Force report on ECT should be considered the guide to present-day treatment, training, and privileging.

REFERENCES

1. Abrams R. *Electroconvulsive therapy*. New York: Oxford University Press, 1988.
2. American Psychiatric Association. *Electroconvulsive therapy*. Task Force Report 14. Washington, DC: American Psychiatric Association, 1978.
3. American Psychiatric Association. *The practice*

of ECT: Recommendations for treatment, training and privileging. Washington, DC: American Psychiatric Press, 1990.
4. Fink M. Convulsive therapy: Theory and practice. New York: Raven Press, 1979.
5. Abrams R, Essman W, eds. Electroconvulsive therapy: Biological foundations and clinical applications. New York: Spectrum Publications, 1982.
6. Kalinowsky LB, Hippius H, Klein HE. Biological treatments in psychiatry. New York: Grune & Stratton, 1982.
7. Kiloh LG, Smith JS, Johnson GF. Physical treatments in psychiatry. Melbourne: Blackwell Scientific, 1988.
8. Consensus Conference. Electroconvulsive therapy. JAMA 1985;254:103–108.
9. Avery D, Lubrano A. Depression treated with imipramine and ECT: The DeCarolis study reconsidered. Am J Psychiatry 1979;136:559–562.
10. Glassman A, Kantor S, Shostak M. Depressions, delusions and drug response. Am J Psychiatry 1975;132:716–719.
11. Hordern A, Holt N, Burt C, Gordon W. Amitriptyline in depressive states. Br J Psychiatry 1963;109:815–825.
12. Simpson G, Lee J, Cuculic Z, Kellner R. Two dosages of imipramine in hospitalized endogenous and neurotic depressives. Arch Gen Psychiatry 1970;33:1093–1102.
13. Kantor SJ, Glassman AH. Delusional depressions: Natural history and response to treatment. Br J Psychiatry 1977;131:351–360.
14. Kroessler D. Relative efficacy rates for therapies of delusional depression. Convulsive Ther 1985;1:173–182.
15. Abrams R, Taylor M. Catatonia. A prospective clinical study. Arch Gen Psychiatry 1976;33:579–584.
16. Taylor MA, Abrams R. Catatonia. Prevalence and importance in the manic phase of manic-depressive illness. Arch Gen Psychiatry 1977;34:1223–1225.
17. Addonizio G, Susman VL. ECT as a treatment alternative for patients with symptoms or neuroleptic malignant syndrome. J Clin Psychiatry 1987;48:102–105.
18. Breakey WR, Kala AK. Typhoid catatonia responsive to ECT. Br Med J 1977;2:357–359.
19. Fricchione GL, Kaufman LD, Gruber BL, Fink M. Electroconvulsive therapy and cyclophosphamide in combination for severe neuropsychiatric lupus with catatonia. Am J Med 1990;88:443–444.
20. Mac DS, Pardo MP. Systemic lupus erythematosus and catatonia: A case report. J Clin Psychiatry 1983;44:155–156.
21. Mann SC, Caroff SN, Bleier HR, Welz WKR, Kling MA, Hayashida M. Lethal catatonia. Am J Psychiatry 1986;143:1374–1381.
22. Berman E, Wolpert EA. Intractable manic-depressive psychosis with rapid cycling in an 18-year-old woman successfully treated with electroconvulsive therapy. JNMD 1987;175:236–239.
23. Kalinowsky LB, Hoch PH. Shock treatments and other somatic procedures in psychiatry. New York: Grune & Stratton, 1946.
24. Kalinowsky LB, Hoch PH. Somatic treatments in psychiatry. New York: Grune & Stratton, 1961.
25. Sargant W, Slater E. An introduction to physical methods of treatment in psychiatry. Baltimore: Williams & Wilkins, 1954 and 1964.
26. Milstein V, Small JG, Klapper MH, Small IF, Kellams JJ. Universus bilateral ECT in the treatment of mania. Convulsive Ther 1987;3:1–9.
27. Small JG, Klapper MH, Kellams JL, et al. Electroconvulsive treatment compared with lithium in the management of manic states. Arch Gen Psychiatry 1988;45:727–732.
28. Mukherjee S, Sackeim HA, Lee C, Prohovnik I, Warmflash V. ECT in treatment-resistant mania. In: Shagass C, et al., eds. Biological psychiatry 1985. New York: Elsevier, 1986:732–734.
29. Avery D, Winokur G. Mortality in depressed patients treated with electroconvulsive therapy and antidepressants. Arch Gen Psychiatry 1976;33:1029–1037.
30. Avery D, Winokur G. Suicide, attempted suicide, and relapse rates in depression: Occurrence after ECT and antidepressant therapy. Arch Gen Psychiatry 1978;35:749–753.
31. Milstein V, Small JG, Small I, Green GE. Does electroconvulsive therapy prevent suicide? Convulsive Ther 1986;2:3–6.
32. Friedel RO. The combined use of neuroleptics and ECT in drug-resistant schizophrenic patients. Psychopharm Bull 1986;22:928–931.
33. Gujavarty K, Greenberg L, Fink M. Electroconvulsive therapy and neuroleptic medication in therapy-resistant positive-symptom psychosis. Convulsive Ther 1987;3:111–120.

10
Selectivity of Antidepressants and Resistant Depression

Stuart A. Montgomery

In any group of depressed patients, however carefully they may have been selected for the appropriateness of antidepressant treatment and the likelihood of their response, some 30 to 40% unfortunately fail to respond to an adequate course of treatment. The reasons for this disappointingly high failure rate are not clear, nor do we have a reliable means of identifying, either clinically or biochemically, those patients who will not respond. A proportion of individuals fail to respond not only to the first but also to a second and even a third course of treatment. These patients who suffer from what is termed resistant depression, refractory to treatment, form a small but important group who are very difficult to manage.

A variety of approaches to the treatment of resistant depression has been adopted, ranging from established treatments, such as electroconvulsive therapy (ECT), to the use of aggressively high doses of standard antidepressants, combinations of antidepressants, adjuvant therapies, such as lithium, neuroleptics, T_3 augmentation, and unusual therapies, such as i.v. antidepressants. More recently, the use of antidepressants with selective effects on particular monoamines has been shown to have some advantages in nonresponsive depression. The efficacy of these proposed treatments in resistant depression has yet to be tested properly in appropriate groups of patients whose depression is truly refractory to prior therapy.

POOR RESPONSE AS FAILURE OF ADEQUATE TREATMENT

Much of what is called resistant depression may actually represent inadequately or inappropriately treated depression. A number of contributory causes of failure of treatment have to be taken into account to get the best out of any treatment. These include compliance with the medication regimen and motivational issues, pharmacokinetic and pharmacodynamic factors, the appropriateness of dosage, and the length of treatment. A poor response to a course of antidepressant treatment may result from the influence of any of these factors, which, if corrected, will improve the response rate. These contributory factors to failure of treatment are discussed separately from the resistant depression that fails to respond to a careful and adequate course of treatment that has taken account of these issues. There is, however, an overlap between these two groups, and it is sometimes difficult to be sure whether an individual actually has resistant depression or has been treated inadequately. Attention to the simple issues remains the first approach to failed antidepressant response.

St. Mary's Hospital Medical School, London, UK.

Compliance as a Cause of Failure of Treatment

Many patients fail to take the antidepressant as prescribed (1). A study of compliance in primary care reported that 68% of patients had defaulted on treatment by 28 days (2). More specifically, this study also found that 57% of nonresponders at 6 weeks had defaulted from their tricyclic medication.

Noncompliance is more likely to result when drugs are used that have unpleasant side effects. The marked anticholinergic and other side effects of the tricyclic antidepressants (TCA) often are cited by patients as the reason for stopping treatment. In contrast, the very long half-life of the active metabolite of fluoxetine, norfluoxetine, makes this compound a very suitable antidepressant for patients with compliance problems. In a study, once a week treatment with 60 mg fluoxetine was found to be as effective as daily amitriptyline administration (3).

Many patients are upset by the unexpected nature of the side effects, and time spent discussing untoward effects and their expected duration would assist compliance. To reduce side effects, it is probably better to use less toxic antidepressants rather than a low dose of a TCA. If a patient cannot tolerate the side effects of a low dose TCA, it is better to change immediately to a different class of antidepressant.

Adequate Length of Treatment

A common failure of conventional prescribing is to assess response at too early a point. Treatment should be maintained for at least 4 weeks before a response may be seen. A relatively constant feature of large placebo-controlled trials is that there normally is no significant difference between placebo and active antidepressant at 2 weeks. Any judgment of drug response before 4 weeks is likely to be premature and would be made more reliably after 6 weeks. The practice, therefore, of judging response at 2 weeks and changing the drug is probably counterproductive.

Failure To Continue Treatment After Apparent Response

Some patients may be mistakenly classified as having resistant depression because of the inadequate length of antidepressant treatment following apparent response of the acute episode. Many individuals who experience recurrent unipolar depressive episodes may be suffering from a failure to provide effective continuation treatment. In any group of depressed patients who respond to initial treatment, about 50% will relapse early if their antidepressant is discontinued shortly after recovery of their acute episode. Patients understandably will want to stop treatment the moment they feel better, and physicians who do not discourage this will find that a proportion will embark on a cycle of rapidly returning, inadequately treated depression that may take on the appearance of depression that is resistant to treatment.

Inappropriate Dose

Failure to respond often is associated with inappropriate dosing. Although most treatment failures are associated with too low a dose, a proportion of patients fail to respond because the dose of certain drugs is too high. TCAs often are prescribed in inappropriately low doses because of unpleasant anticholinergic side effects. The claim that low doses of TCAs are effective cannot be sustained on the evidence from placebo-controlled trials, in which low doses are associated with a higher than expected failure to respond. Patients may be classified as having resistant depression when they have failed to respond to low doses of several antidepressants, whereas they probably have not yet been treated adequately.

The opposite problem also is reported. The plasma levels of some drugs have to be kept within a narrow range to obtain the best therapeutic effect, and there is evidence of such an optimum therapeutic window with nortriptyline and possibly amitriptyline. In these cases, higher doses might be expected to result in a higher than expected failure rate. In this regard, Kragh-Sorensen et al. (4) demonstrated that high plasma levels of nortriptyline were associated with more nonresponders than were moderate plasma levels and that lowering the dose (and thereby the plasma levels) under double-blind conditions often produced a better response. These findings are supported by the work of other investigators (5–9). As a result, the standard dose of nortriptyline 100 mg actually may be too high for the majority of patients (6). Most investigators now concur that high plasma levels of nortriptyline are a potential clinical problem. It has been recommended that appropriate plasma levels are more reliably obtained by individual dosage adjustment using either achieved steady state plasma levels or the single 24-hour predictor tests (10).

The picture is not quite so clear cut with amitriptyline. The majority of studies that used fixed doses of amitryptyline have reported that high plasma concentrations of amitriptyline plus its demethylated metabolite, nortriptyline, are associated with a poorer response than when moderate plasma levels are achieved (11–15), and others have reported similar findings (16,17). The most careful studies have found that much of the nonresponse to amitriptyline may be attributed to the high concomitant plasma levels of nortriptyline, and this is consistent with the nortriptyline literature.

Studies that used a rising dose schedule of amitriptyline with increases in dose permitted during the study have reported more equivocal results. The reason for this observation is difficult to unravel, but the changes in dose undoubtedly play a part. Rising dose schedules for plasma level response studies add extra confounding variables that may complicate the findings. Likewise, it is difficult to ascertain whether a response relates to low and moderate doses given over the first few weeks or the high dose at the end of treatment. Conclusions about the plasma level–clinical response relationship are very difficult to make on the basis of studies using a rising dose design, and it is for this reason that fixed dose studies are now used to provide more valid answers.

DEBRISOQUINE TESTING

Some 5 to 10% of the normal population have been shown to have abnormally slow metabolism of drugs that are metabolized by hydroxylation (18). This characteristic appears to be genetically determined and may be detected by testing for slow clearance of debrisoquine. Individuals with slow clearance may develop levels that are substantially higher than in those with normal hepatic metabolism. Depressed patients with abnormally slow metabolism would be more likely to have a poor response to an antidepressant for which there is evidence of a plasma level therapeutic window with high levels or doses associated with poorer response. The presence of a substantial minority of patients with abnormally slow clearance suggests that drugs with a narrow therapeutic range, such as nortriptyline, should not be used without plasma level monitoring.

Higher plasma levels may be associated with an increased frequency of adverse drug reactions, such as convulsions (imipramine, clomipramine, maprotiline, dothiepin, buproprion, and possibly amitriptyline and nortriptyline) (19), cardiotoxicity (amitriptyline, dothiepin, maprotiline, nortriptyline) (20), and death by overdosage (amitriptyline, dothiepin, doxepin) (21,22). An added problem is that some antidepressants have a narrow therapeutic index, with dangerous side effects occurring close to therapeutic levels (dothiepin, imipramine, amitriptyline, buproprion). It is wise to avoid this type of drug in depressed patients who have not been debrisoquine tested or in whom plasma antidepressant levels have not been obtained.

SEROTONERGIC ANTIDEPRESSANT PLASMA LEVELS AND RESPONSE

The possibility of a poorer response with higher drug plasma concentrations is not limited to TCAs. For example, a small study by Montgomery et al. (23) showed that high levels of norzimelidine, the active metabolite of the serotonin (5HT) reuptake inhibitor zimelidine, were associated with a poorer response than moderate levels. This was subsequently replicated by Walinder et al. (24). This observation was supported by a preclinical study of platelet 5HT uptake, which showed that optimum response was associated with moderate 5HT uptake as opposed to maximal 5HT uptake (25).

Similar findings have been reported for norfluoxetine, with nonresponders to 6 weeks of treatment with a fixed dose of 60 mg fluoxetine daily developing higher plasma levels than responders (3) (Fig. 1). The apparently reduced therapeutic response associated with higher plasma levels of norfluoxetine may account for the finding in the fixed dose studies that lower doses of 20 mg and 40 mg daily were more effective than the 60 mg dose (26). It seems that with fluoxetine high doses and high plasma levels are not associated with best response. The higher doses of 60 to 80 mg are more effective than placebo and are not associated with serious adverse reactions. There is, however, a higher incidence of 5HT-related side effects, such as nausea, dizziness, sleep disturbance, and anxiety, at higher fluoxetine doses. Furthermore, the potential for drug interactions with lithium and MAOIs, which can be fatal, are greatly increased with high dose treatment with 5HT uptake inhibitors.

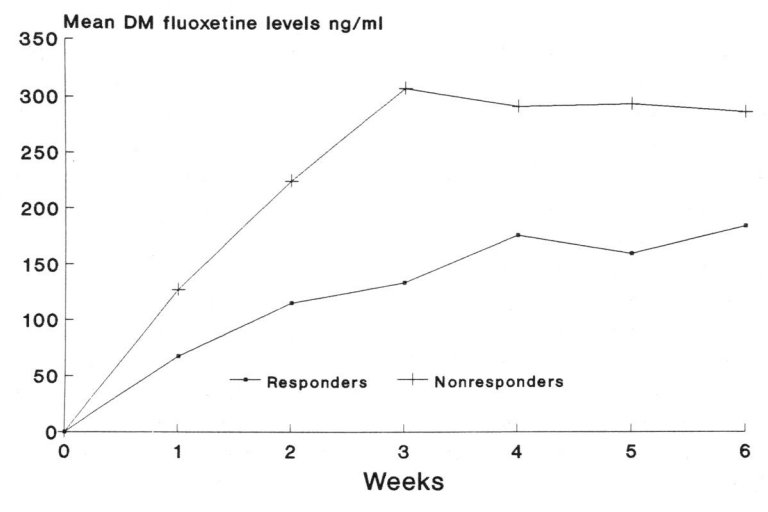

FIG. 1. Mean desmethyl fluoxetine levels of responders and nonresponders to 60 mg daily fluoxetine. Responders have significantly lower mean plasma levels of desmethyl fluoxetine ($p<0.05$) than nonresponders.

SHOULD THE DOSE OF AN ANTIDEPRESSANT BE RAISED IN NONRESPONDERS?

The apparently poorer response associated with higher plasma levels of some antidepressants brings into question the desirability of using higher doses for nonresponders. Traditionally, clinicians faced with a patient who did not respond to an antidepressant were likely to raise the dose of that drug. However, the assumption that this might improve the likelihood of response has not been a practice based on systematic pharmacological testing.

A recent large multicenter study on early nonresponders to fluoxetine provides an interesting test of this practice with a 5HT reuptake inhibitor drug (27). Nonresponders to treatment with 20 mg fluoxetine were assigned randomly to continue treatment under double-blind conditions with either a 20 mg or a 60 mg dose of fluoxetine. There was no difference in the final outcome in the two groups, suggesting that with 5HT uptake inhibitors, nonresponders in general will not benefit from a rise in dose. This study raises serious doubts about treatment with other antidepressants, especially since so many plasma level response studies indicate that a lowering of dose is pharmacologically a sounder practice.

SELECTIVE ANTIDEPRESSANTS IN NONRESPONDERS

Antidepressants are effective in only 60% of depressed patients, and it was hoped that the selective antidepressants would be able to improve the response rate. It was also hoped that these selective antidepressants might show some specificity for subtypes of depression. For example, based on the early amine hypothesis, it seemed possible that different types of depression might be associated with a disturbance of specific neurotransmitters and that they might, therefore, be amenable to treatment with drugs that selectively affect certain neurotransmitters. Thus a 5HT depression might respond better to 5HT-specific compounds and a noradrenergic depression to a noradrenergic active drug. However, a comparison of the response rates of the new selective antidepressants does not appear to substantiate this hypothesis. The response reported in the double-blind studies of selective antidepressants, such as maprotiline or nortriptyline, both fairly specific norepinephrine (NE) uptake inhibitors, appears to be identical to that of the nonselective antidepressants, such as amitriptyline or imipramine. Likewise, the 5HT uptake inhibitors, zimelidine and fluoxetine, appear to be associated with very similar response rates to the nonselective TCAs. These so-called selective antidepressants appeared in the clinic to be nonselective, and this would make selectivity of response in subgroups of patients less likely.

The selectivity theory has been tested and found largely wanting in more direct studies, which compared the effect of two antidepressants having a selective action on different neurotransmitters. The selective NE uptake inhibitors, e.g., maprotiline and desipramine, were found in double-blind comparisons to be associated with very similar response rates to the selective 5HT uptake inhibitor, zimelidine (28,29). It appeared that the selective antidepressants were rather effective general antidepressants and that any clinical selectivity was overwhelmed by the broad-spectrum antidepressant action. Treatment of nonresponders to one selective antidepressant with the alternate selective antidepressant was not associated with any selective extra response not accounted for by the extra 4-week treatment period (30).

Studies of monoamine metabolite levels in the CSF before treatment present a slightly more contradictory picture. Low levels of 5HIAA in a small number were reported by one group (31) to predict a better response to a 5HT uptake inhibitor. This could not however be confirmed in another study (28), which found that pretreatment CSF levels of 5HIAA did not predict response to a 5HT uptake inhibitor, nor did levels of MHPG predict response to a NE uptake inhibitor.

There seems, therefore, little evidence for the value of crossing a nonresponder from one selective antidepressant to another for DSM-III major depression. Any possible selective effect probably is overwhelmed by the nonselective antidepressant effect. Pharmacologically, the practice of changing drugs in the case of nonresponders appears to be an act of desperation tinged with optimism rather than a strategy supported by data.

SELECTIVITY IN RESISTANT DEPRESSION

Patients who do not respond to several treatment regimens may be different from those with nonresponse to a single treatment. Several studies have found an advantage for drugs acting on the 5HT system in resistant depression, and successful treatment has been reported with combinations of drugs that would maximize the effect on the 5HT system.

Treatment regimens, such as the Newcastle cocktail, which employed a combination of phenelzine, lithium, and tryptophan, were designed originally to have an adjuvant effect on the 5HT system, and the early open reports were favorable (32). Likewise, the open reports of Hale et al. (33) that lithium and tryptophan plus clomipramine had beneficial effects in resistant depression support this approach. Tryptophan in combination with amitriptyline appeared to have a better effect than low doses of amitriptyline alone, which also may reflect an extra effect on the 5HT system (34).

LITHIUM AUGMENTATION IN RESISTANT DEPRESSION

The double-blind studies investigating the use of lithium augmentation in resistant depression are a better test of the hypothesis. De Montigny et al. (35) reported that early nonresponders at 3 weeks benefited from a combination of TCAs plus lithium rather than lithium alone. Henninger et al. (36), looking at early nonresponders, found that a TCA plus lithium produced a better response than the TCA alone. Further support is provided by the study of Garbutt et al. (37), with similar findings. These studies are open to certain criticisms, since the patients studied did not have truly resistant depressions, and more careful criteria were needed in the selection of patients before generalizing the resistant depression.

Relatively low plasma levels of lithium (0.4 mEq/L) seemed to be sufficient to potentiate antidepressants. These low plasma levels of lithium have been shown in behavioral models to affect neurotransmission in the 5HT system (38), whereas much higher levels seemed necessary to affect the cAMP system. Lithium augmentation treatment would seem, therefore, to work by augmenting the 5HT system.

DANGERS OF COMBINATION TREATMENT WITH 5HT REUPTAKE INHIBITORS

The common mechanism of action of these treatments is thought to be via the induction of an extra responsivity of the 5HT system. So powerful is this serotonergic effect that several cases of a serotonin crisis have been reported with these combinations. The Committee on Safety of Medicines in the UK has received a worrying number of reports of movement disorders, hyperpyrexia, and one death associated with a combination of 5HT uptake inhibitors with lithium and tryptophan (39). Four deaths have been reported in the US following a combination of MAOIs and fluoxetine, and several in the UK are attributed to a combination of MAOIs and clomipramine. Movement disorders have been reported with combinations of fluoxetine and L-tryptophan in a very small open study, although the doses of fluoxetine were unacceptably high at three to four times the recommended dose (40).

Nevertheless, the evidence of efficacy does suggest some selective role for 5HT-specific treatments in nonresponders or resistant depression. Now that more specific and potent 5HT uptake inhibitors are available, it may be possible to achieve the desired increase in serotonergic effect without resorting to dangerous combinations. It may be sufficient to raise the dose of a selective 5HT uptake inhibitor to achieve an extra effect on 5HT, and it is probably wiser to use these drugs alone in resistant depression.

5HT REUPTAKE INHIBITORS AND RESISTANT DEPRESSION

There has been a paucity of studies that have specifically evaluated patients with resistant depression using selective 5HT reuptake inhibitors. Early work with the less selective but potent 5HT uptake inhibitor, clomipramine, suggested that this drug might be useful in resistant depression (41). More recently, there have been positive reports of the selective advantage of paroxetine in resistant depression from open observation (42) and from a partially controlled study (43), although the latter is misleading, since the population studied was apparently a group of early nonresponders in primary care rather than resistant depression.

To be sure that proposed treatments are effective in resistant depression, they must be assessed in appropriate patients who fulfill well-defined criteria of nonresponse. Various criteria have been considered in defining resistant depression, but a criterion of a minimum duration of 6 months depression with two documented adequate treatment courses would seem to be a reasonable position to take. It is hoped that in tests of the role of the newer selective 5HT uptake inhibitors in depression, adequate entry criteria will be adopted.

RESISTANT DEPRESSION MAY REFLECT DIFFERENT KINDS OF DEPRESSION

It is accepted that depression is a heterogeneous illness, and there is increasing evidence of different response to treatment in different subgroups of patients. The delayed response in some and the apparently poor response in others may well account for some of the patients included under the description of resistant depression. Some of these subgroups may have a differential response to specific treatments, and identification of these subgroups would help in the management of nonresponse.

Delusional Depression

The relatively poor response often seen in delusional depression raises the question whether delusional depression may form a separate subgroup with a different pharmacological response. Reports that delusional depression responded poorly to TCAs (44,45) were reinforced by reports that TCAs may be associated with precipitation or exacerbation of psychotic symptoms. The question of whether these delusions represent an increase in the severity of the depression or this represents a separate disorder has not yet been settled.

Neuroleptic Augmentation of TCAs in Delusional Depression

There is, of course, adequate evidence from placebo-controlled studies of the efficacy of antidepressants in severe depression and rather less evidence for the efficacy of neuroleptics used alone. There is better evidence for the efficacy as antidepressants of some neuroleptics in depression of moderate severity or, in an ill-defined group of anxious or neurotic depression (46–49). The numbers included in these studies were small, and this fact plus other methodological problems limit the conclusions that can be drawn.

Attempts to improve response by adding neuroleptics to TCAs in depressives with delusions were successful (50–52). Perphenazine added to amitriptyline is reported to be better than either treatment alone. Although more controlled studies are needed, preferably including a placebo control, there is evidence to suggest that neuroleptics are effective in adjuvant therapy.

Selectivity of ECT in Delusional Depression

ECT is effective in depression, but because of the legal and social restrictions on its availability, this treatment often is reserved for cases of resistant depression. There is compelling evidence that ECT is particularly effective in resistant depression and probably has a selective advantage over TCA treatment in delusional depression. In those early studies of predictors of response in depression where ECT was widely used, delusions were found to predict a good response (53), and delusions were included both in the Newcastle Diagnostic Scale and in the scale to predict response (54). Controlled studies of ECT have reported particular efficacy in depression with delusions (55–57).

ECT was shown to selectively alter dopamine receptor sensitivity in rats, whereas TCAs did not (58). This finding, coupled with a similar effect on dopamine receptors of neuroleptics, suggests that one difference between conventional depression and delusional depression may be sought in differences of dopamine receptor function.

Obsessional Depression

Recent studies of obsessive compulsive disorder (OCD) report a selective effect for 5HT uptake inhibitors compared with placebo or non-5HT-selective antidepressants. The response in this group of patients appears different from that seen in other psychiatric disorders. The placebo response appears minimal, whereas a significant response to clomipramine may be seen early in treatment, even in small studies (59–61). There is an early slow and sustained response that becomes more significant with time. This pattern of response is seen whether the patients suffer from significant concomitant depression or not, and there are suggestions that OCD should be regarded as a separate illness. It now appears that the major depression that is secondary to OCD is probably integral to the obsessional illness rather than separate. Unlike conventional major depression, the depression associated with OCD does not appear to respond to drugs acting on the norepinephrine system but responds selectively to 5HT uptake inhibitors. It seems possible that a proportion of patients with resistant depression may be unidentified obsessional, or at least their depression is linked with obsessional illness.

The evidence that OCD responds selectively to 5HT drugs is firmly based and marks OCD as a quite separate disorder from others in the anxiety–depression spectrum. There is some evidence, less firmly based, that panic disorder may have similar selective response properties (62). The only other disorders in psychiatry that relate to 5HT specifically are migraine and bulimia nervosa, and depression associated with those conditions may have a selective response to 5HT uptake inhibitors.

Recurrent Brief Depression

Classification of depressive illness has been considerably affected by the finding

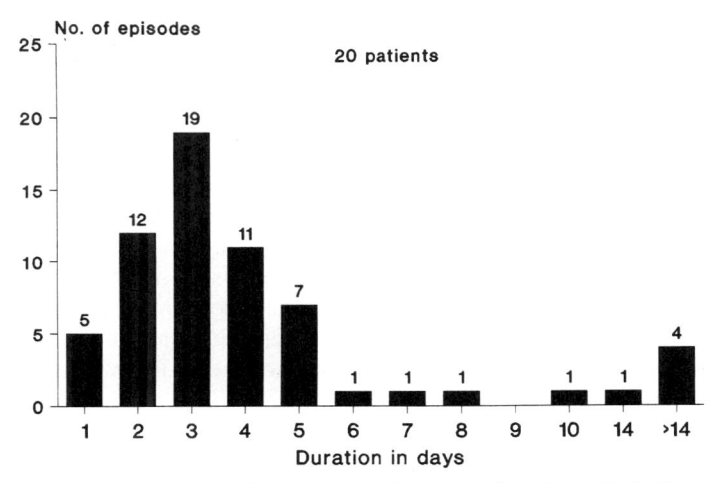

FIG. 2. Duration of brief depressive episodes. From Ref. 65.

that between 5% and 8% of the general population suffer from recurrent depression lasting only a few days (63). In our studies of patients with personality disorders, almost all have episodes of recurrent brief depression lasting about 3 days but recurring irregularly some 18 days later. These depressions are quite severe, with mean scores on the MADRS of around 30, which is of moderate severity. These depressions have very similar symptoms to major depression and satisfy DSM-III criteria without the necessary duration of 2 weeks (64,65) (Fig. 2).

Recurrent brief depression does not appear to respond well to TCAs or to drugs acting on the NE system, although there are reports of possible response with low dose neuroleptics (66), MAOIs (67), and lithium. Straightforward simple recurrent brief depression should not be confused with resistant depression but probably often is, although it is more likely to be confused with dysthymia.

In 20% of individuals with recurrent brief depression, a history of major depression is found. In these cases of combined depression, the combined illness appears more profound and has a greater risk of suicide than either illness alone. Although formal studies have not been done, some consider these long-term recurrent combined depressions to be relatively resistant to conventional TCAs. They may contribute to the apparent resistant depression group.

Dysthymia

The DSM-III diagnostic criteria for dysthymia (i.e., mild depressive symptoms on most days for at least a 2-year period) suggest the possibility of resistant depression. Retrospective assessment of symptoms over a 2-year period is most unreliable, and it is likely that many individuals diagnosed with dysthymia may actually have a more severe depression.

In the epidemiological studies of Angst et al. (63), the diagnosis of dysthymia overlapped with that of major depression in 50% of patients and with recurrent brief depression in 30%. In other words, in 80% of patients, the dysthymia was seen to satisfy DSM-III criteria for major depression with or without the 2 week duration. Dysthymia as a mild chronic depression category on its own is sufficiently rare that many of the attributed features probably belong to other, more serious depressions.

Double depressions, which are major

depression superimposed on a chronic depressive disorder, were seen to have a poorer outcome at 2 years than major depression alone (68,69), suggesting that this group of patients with double depression may be resistant to conventional antidepressant treatment.

CONCLUSION

Much of what is called resistant depression may simply reflect failure of adequate treatment because of noncompliance, inappropriate dosage, or an abbreviated treatment period. The more carefully defined resistant depression, which fails to respond to two or three adequate treatment courses under careful supervision, may include some patients with an uncorrected underlying organic disorder (such as hypothyroidism or carcinoma) who are misdiagnosed as primary depression. Others, however, may have resistant depression because of a genetic predisposition to develop inappropriate plasma levels of antidepressants.

Some treatment-resistant patients may have a form of depression that has not been recognized as requiring selective antidepressant treatment. The group of patients who suffer from resistant depression is likely to be considerably reduced if these subgroups, such as obsessional depressives, are recognized and given appropriate treatment. Those patients who suffer from combined depressions, with major depression superimposed on recurrent brief depression, apparently are more seriously ill, have a higher suicide attempt rate, and show some resistance to conventional TCAs. This group may well respond to a different pharmacological approach, but as yet there have been no prospective double-blind controlled studies.

The most consistent findings of treatment approaches to resistant depression point to the augmentation of effect on the serotonergic system. The use of combinations of drugs to achieve this is not without danger because of the risk of serious drug interactions, and the use of potent and selective 5HT uptake inhibitors on their own may be sufficient and safer.

Confidence in the treatment strategies of resistant depression is compromised by a general failure to undertake studies on well-defined resistant depression using the kind of placebo-controlled group comparative studies necessary to make a proper judgment of the efficacy of specific treatments.

REFERENCES

1. Blackwell B. Treatment adherence. *Br J Psychiatry* 1976;129:513–531.
2. Johnson DAW. Depression: Treatment compliance in general practice. *Acta Psychiatr Scand* 1981;63(Suppl 290):447–453.
3. Montgomery SA, James D, de Ruiter M, et al. Weekly oral fluoxetine treatment of major depressive disorder, a controlled trial. Presented at 15th CINP Puerto Rico, 1986.
4. Kragh-Sorensen P, Eggert-Hansen C, Baastrup PC, Hvidberg EV. Self-inhibiting action of nortriptyline's antidepressant effect at high plasma levels. *Psychopharmacologia* 1976;45:305–316.
5. Asberg M, Cronholm B, Sjoqvist F, Tuck D. Relationship between plasma level and therapeutic effect of nortriptyline. *Br Med J* 1971;3:331–334.
6. Montgomery S, Braithwaite RA, Crammer J. Routine plasma nortriptyline levels in the treatment of depression. *Br Med J* 1977;3:166–167.
7. Montgomery S, Braithwaite RR, Dawling S, McAuley R. High plasma nortriptyline levels in the treatment of depression. *Clin Pharmacol Ther* 1976;23:309–314.
8. Ziegler VE, Clayton PJ, Taylor JR, Co BT, Biggs JT. Nortriptyline plasma levels and therapeutic response. *Clin Pharmacol Ther* 1976;20:458–463.
9. Ziegler VE, Clayton PJ, Biggs JT. A comparison of amitriptyline and nortriptyline with plasma levels. *Arch Gen Psychiatry* 1977;34:607.
10. Montgomery SA, McAuley R, Montgomery DB, Braithwaite RA, Dawling S. Dosage adjustment from simple nortriptyline spot level predictor tests in depressed patients. *Clin Pharmacokinetics* 1979;4:129–136.
11. Montgomery SA, McAuley R. Rani SJ, Montgomery DB, Braithwaite RA, Dawling S. Amitriptyline plasma concentration and clinical response. *Br Med J* 1979;1:230–231.
12. Giedke H, Gaertner H, Breyer-Pfaff U, Rein W, Axmann D. Amitriptyline and oxaprotiline in the treatment of hospitalised depressive patients. Clinical aspects, psychophysiology and drug

plasma levels. *Eur Arch Psychiatr Neurol Sci* 1986;235:329–338.
13. Breyer-Pfaff U, Gaertner HJ, Kreuter F, Scharek G, Brinkschulte M, Wiatr R. Antidepressive effect and pharmacokinetics of amitriptyline with consideration of unbound drug and 10-hydroxynortriptyline plasma levels. *Psychopharmacology* 1982;76:240–244.
14. Moyes KA, Ray RL, Moyes RB. Plasma levels and clinical improvement—A comparative study of clomipramine and amitriptyline in depression. *Postgrad Med J* 1980;56(Suppl 1):127–129.
15. Vandel S, Vandel B, Sandoz M, Allers G, Bechtel P, Volmat R. Clinical response and plasma concentration of amitriptyline and its metabolite nortriptyline. *Eur J Clin Pharmacol* 1978;14: 185–190.
16. Corona G, Fenoclio L, Pinelli P, Zerbi F. Amitriptyline, nortriptyline plasma levels and therapeutic response in depressed women. *Pharmakopsychiatrie* 1977;10:299–308.
17. Robinson DS, Cooper TB, Ravaris C, et al. Plasma tricyclic drug levels in amitriptyline-treated depressed patients. *Psychopharmacology* 1979;63:223–231.
18. Mahgoub A, Idle JR, Dring LG, Lancaster R, Smith RL. Polymorphic hydroxylation of debrisoquine in man. *Lancet* 1977;2:584–586.
19. Montgomery S, Baldwin D, Fineberg N. The relative toxicity of antidepressants in overdose using reports independent of observer bias. *Neuropsychopharmacology* (in press)
20. Burgess CD. Effects of antidepressants on cardiac function. *Acta Psychiatr Scand* 1981; 63(Suppl 290):370–379.
21. Cassidy S, Henry J. Fatal toxicity of antidepressant drugs in overdose. *Br Med J* 1987;295:1021–1024.
22. Montgomery SA, Pinder RM. Do some antidepressants promote suicide? *Psychopharmacology* 1987;92:265–266.
23. Montgomery SA, McAuley R, Rani SJ, Roy D. Montgomery DB. A double-blind comparison of zimelidine and amitriptyline in endogenous depression. *Acta Psychiatr Scand* 1981;63(Suppl 290);314–327.
24. Walinder J, Carlsson A, Persson R. 5-HT reuptake inhibitors plus tryptophan in endogenous depression. *Acta Psychiatr Scand* 1981;63(Suppl 290):179–190.
25. Wood KM, Swade CC, Coppen AJ. Zimeldine: A pharmacokinetic and pharmacodynamic study in depressive illness. *Br J Clin Pract* 1982#ppl 19:42–47.
26. Wernicke JF, Dunlop SR, Dornseif BE, Zerbe RL. A fixed dose fluoxetine therapy for depression. *Psychopharmacol Bull* 1987;23:164–168.
27. Wernicke JF, Bosomworth JC, Ashbrook E. Fluoxetine at 20 mg per day. I. The recommended and therapeutic dose in the treatment of depression. *Int Clin Psychopharmacol* 1989; 4(Suppl 1):63–68.
28. Montgomery SA, Rani SJ, McAuley R, Roy D. Montgomery DB. The antidepressant efficacy of zimelidine and maprotiline. *Acta Psychiatr Scand* 1981;63(Suppl 290):219–224.
29. Aberg A. Controlled cross-over study of a 5HT uptake inhibiting and an NA uptake inhibiting antidepressant. *Acta Psychiatr Scand* 1981; 63(Suppl 290):244–255.
30. Montgomery SA, James D, Montgomery DB. Pharmacological specificity is not the same as clinical selectivity. In: Dahl SG, Gram LF, Paul SM, Potter WZ, eds. New York: Springer, 1987;179–188.
31. Aberg Widsted A. A double-blind study of zimelidine, a serotonin uptake inhibitor, and desipramine, a noradrenaline uptake inhibitor, in endogenous depression. I. Clinical findings. *Acta Psychiatr Scand* 1982;66:50–65.
32. Barker WA, Scott J, Eccleston D. The Newcastle chronic depression study—Results of a treatment regime. *Int Clin Psychopharmacol* 1987;2: 261–272.
33. Hale AS, Procter AW, Bridges P. Clomipramine, tryptophan and lithium in combination for resistant endogenous depression: Seven case studies. *Br J Psychiatry* 1987;151:213–217.
34. Thomson J, Rankin H, Ashcroft GW, Yates CM, McQueen JK, Cummings SW. The treatment of depression in general practice: A comparison of L-tryptophan, amitriptyline, and a combination of L-tryptophan and amitriptyline with placebo. *Psychol Med* 1982;12:741–752.
35. de Montigny C, Courmoyer G, Morissette R, Langlois R, Caille G. Lithium carbonate addition in tricyclic antidepressant-resistant unipolar depression. *Arch Gen Psychiatry* 1983;40: 1327–1334.
36. Heninger GR, Charney DS, Sternberg DE. Lithium carbonate augmentation of antidepressant treatment. *Arch Gen Psychiatry* 1983;40:1335–1342.
37. Garbutt JC, Mayo JP, Gillette GM, Little KY, Mason GA. Lithium potentiation of tricyclic antidepressant following lack of T_3 potentiation. *J Psychiatry* 1986;143:1038–1039.
38. Grahame Smith DG, Greene AR. The role of brain 5HT in the hyperactivity produced by lithium and MAOI. *Br J Pharmacol* 1976;52:19–26.
39. Committee on Safety of Medicines. Fluvoxamine and fluoxetine—Interaction with monoamine oxidase inhibitors, lithium and tryptophan. *Curr Problems* No 26, 1989.
40. Steiner W, Fontaine R. Toxic reaction following the combined administration of fluoxetine and L-tryptophan: five case reports. *Biol Psychiatry* 1986;21:1067–1071.
41. Kielholtz P, Terzani S, Gastpar M. Treatment for therapy-resistant depressions. *Int Pharmacopsychiatry* 1979;14:94–100.
42. Gagiano GA. The therapeutic efficacy of paroxetine in patients with major depression not responding to antidepressants. *Acta Psychiatr Scand* (in press)
43. Tyrer P, Marsden CA, Casey P, Seivewright N. Clinical efficacy of paroxetine in resistant depression. *J Psychopharmacol* 1987;4:251–257.
44. Glassman AH, Kantor SJ, Shostak M. Depres-

sion, delusions and drug response. *Am J Psychiatry* 1975;132:716–719.
45. Rao VA, Coppen A. Classification of depression and response to amitriptyline therapy. *Psychol Med* 1979;9:321–325.
46. Paykel ES, Price JS, Gillan RU, Palmai G, Chesser ES. A comparative trial of imipramine and chlorpromazine in depressed patients. *Br J Psychiatry* 1968;114:1281–1287.
47. Rickels K, Jenkins BW, Zamostien BZ, Raab E, Kanther M. Pharmacotherapy in neurotic depression. *J Nerv Ment Disord* 1968;145L:475–485.
48. Young JPR, Hughes WC, Lader MH. A controlled comparison of flupenthixol and amitriptyline in depressed outpatients. *Br Med J* 1976;1:1116–1118.
49. Johnson DAW. A double-blind comparison of flupenthixol, nortriptyline, and diazepam in neurotic depressions. *Acta Psychiatr Scand* 1979;59:1–8.
50. Nelson JC, Bowers MB. Delusional unipolar depression: Description and drug treatment. *Arch Gen Psychiatry* 1978;35:1321.
51. Kaskey GB, Nasr S, Meltzer HY. Drug treatment in delusional depression. *Psychiatry Res* 1980;1:267–277.
52. Spiker DG, Weiss JC, Dealy RS, et al. The pharmacological treatment of delusional depression. *Am J Psychiatry* 1985;142:430–436.
53. Hamilton M, White JM. Factors related to the outcome of depression treated with ECT. *J Mental Sci* 1960;106:1031–1041.
54. Carney MWP, Roth M, Garside RF. The diagnosis of depressive syndromes and the prediction of ECT response. *Br J Psychiatry* 1965;111:659–674.
55. Johnstone E, Lawler P, Stevens S, et al. The Northwick Park electroconvulsive therapy trial. *Lancet* 1980;2:1317–1320.
56. Avery D, Lubrano A. Depression treated with imipramine and ECT: The deCarolis study reconsidered. *Am J Psychiatry* 1979;136:559–562.
57. Fink M. ECT: A last resort treatment for resistant depression? In: Zohar J, Belmaker RH, eds. Treating resistant depression. PMA Publishing, 1987.
58. Grahame Smith DG, Greene AR, Costain DW. The mechanism of the antidepressant action of ECT. *Lancet* 1974;1:254.
59. Montgomery SA. Clomipramine in obsessional neurosis: A placebo controlled trial. *Pharmaceut Med* 1980;1:189–192.
60. de Veaugh Geiss J, Landau P, Katz R. Treatment of obsessive compulsive disorder with clomipramine. *Psychiatr Ann* 1989;19:97–101.
61. Montgomery SA, Montgomery DB, Fineberg N. Early response with clomipramine in obsessive compulsive disorder—a placebo controlled study. *Prog Neuro-Psycholpharmacol Biol Psychiatry* 1990;14:719–727.
62. den Boer JA. *Serotonergic mechanisms in anxiety disorders.* den Haag: CIP Gegevens Koninklijke Biblioteek; 1987.
63. Angst J, Dobler-Mikola A. The Zurich Study—A prospective epidemiological study of depressive neurotic and psychosomatic syndromes. *Eur Arch Psychiatry Neurol Sci* 1985;234:408–416.
64. Montgomery SA, Roy D, McAuley R, et al. The prevention of recurrent suicidal acts. *B J Clin Pharmacol* 1983;15:183S–188S.
65. Montgomery SA, Montgomery D, Baldwin D, Green M. Intermittent 3-day depressions and suicidal behavior. *Neuropsychobiology* 1989;22:128–134.
66. Montgomery S. Montgomery D. McAuley R, et al. Maintenance therapy in repeat suicidal behaviour: A placebo controlled trial. *Proceedings 10th International Congress for Suicide Prevention and Crisis Intervention*.1979;227–229.
67. Quitkin FM, Steward JW, McGrath P. et al. Phenelzine versus imipramine in the treatment of probable atypical depression: Defining syndrome boundaries of selective MAOI responders. *Am J Psychiatry* 1988;145:306–311.
68. Keller MB, Shapiro RW. "Double depression": Superimposition of acute depressive episodes in chronic depressive disorders. *Am J Psychiatry* 1982;139:438–442.
69. Keller MB, Lavori PW, Endicott J, Coryell W, Klerman GL. "Double-depression": Two-year follow-up. *Am J Psychiatry* 1983;140:689–694.

11

Fluoxetine Enhancement of Heterocyclic Antidepressants

Jesse S. Rosenthal, Malcolm J. Kaswan, Camille Hemlock, and Arnold Winston

Results obtained with a single agent antidepressant are often less than optimal despite assiduous treatment with close clinical and laboratory monitoring. There appears to be a core of affectively ill patients who are resistant to therapy with a single antidepressant agent, and as many as 21% of patients with major depression treated with conventional antidepressant therapy have failed to respond within 2 years (1). In addition, there is an even larger number of patients who will experience only partial response, with a less than optimal outcome. A variety of clinical approaches to partial responders have evolved, including polypharmacology, electroconvulsive therapy (ECT), and adjunctive antidepressant therapies. Over the years, various agents, such as lithium, thyroid hormones, psychostimulants, amino acid precursors, and anticonvulsants, have been employed as adjuvants to enhance the effect of the primary antidepressant medication (2).

Fluoxetine, a bicyclic third generation antidepressant agent, is reported to be highly specific for serotonergic reuptake blockade. Its effect on dopaminergic and noradrenergic systems is of less clinical significance, and unlike the tricyclic antidepressants (TCAs), it is free of central and peripheral nervous system anticholinergic, antihistaminic, and postsynaptic noradrenergic receptor effects (3). When fluoxetine was given to some patients who experienced only a partial response to an adequate trial of a TCA, a rapid robust clinical response was sometimes observed either within 24 to 72 hours or within a 2 to 3-week period. Similar clinical responses have been reported with lithium augmentation therapy (4,5).

Further documentation of the enhancement effect of fluoxetine on TCAs was reported by Weilburg and Rosenbaum at Harvard Medical School (6). In an open study of 30 depressed patients who experienced minimal response to a variety of heterocyclic antidepressants, the addition of fluoxetine produced a significant improvement in 28 patients (93%). This enhancement effect was observed in patients diagnosed with either major depression, dysthymic disorder, or bipolar type of depression. Moreover, when the heterocyclic compound was discontinued in 12 patients, 8 experienced a clinical relapse that responded when the heterocyclic antidepressant was restarted in conjunction with fluoxetine. We report additional cases of fluoxetine augmentation of TCAs in resistant depressive patients.

Division of Clinical Psychopharmacology, Beth Israel Medical Center, and Mount Sinai School of Medicine, New York, NY 10128.

PATIENT HISTORIES

Patient 1

Mr. S. is a 50-year-old male with a 20-year history of recurrent major depression. Maintenance treatment with lithium, carbamazepine, and various TCAs has failed to prevent recurrence. His acute depressive episodes last approximately 4 to 5 months and follow a predictable time course despite aggressive treatment. During his most recent depression, Mr. S. had been on imipramine 400 mg/day (plasma levels in therapeutic range) for about 2 months, with only partial improvement. Fluoxetine (20 mg/day) was then added to the imipramine. Within 24 hours there was a significant improvement, with distinct symptomatic changes. He reported increased energy, improved sleep, and a large reduction in depressed ruminative thinking. The improvement has been sustained and consistent for 3 months with no indication of relapse. The combination of both drugs was well tolerated, with no adverse effects.

Patient 2

Ms. N. is a 29-year-old female with a 7-year history of chronic major depression with melancholia. Previous treatment attempts with various TCAs of adequate dosage (plasma levels in therapeutic range) had been minimally effective in alleviating symptomatology. Ms. N. had been taking 125 mg/day of desipramine for 3 months when 20 mg per day of fluoxetine was added. Within 48 hours, she reported a notable rise in energy and sense of well-being. This improvement continued over 2 weeks but then spontaneously diminished. An additional 20 mg of fluoxetine was added, with rapid clinical improvement observed over 2 to 3 days. Her improved condition has been sustained over the following 3 months with no alterations of medication. The onset of motor restlessness and hand tremor was observed along with clinical improvement. These side effects responded to low doses of alprazolam (0.5 mg prn) when bothersome.

Patient 3

Mr. Y. is a 58-year-old male with a 4-year history of major depression. Treatment attempts with adequate dosages and trials of various TCAs yielded only moderate results, with no clear-cut remission. He had been on 100 mg per day of nortriptyline (plasma levels in therapeutic range) for 3 months when 20 mg per day of fluoxetine was added. Although there was no immediate change, he reported subtle yet significant reduction of dysphoria, morning anxiety, and sleep disturbance after 2 weeks. This improvement was sustained for several months until we attempted to reduce the nortriptyline by 25 mg. Interestingly, a return of symptomatology was noticed within 72 hours of the nortriptyline reduction and then promptly reversed by reinstatement of the prior combined treatment dosage regimen. The only notable side effect was the onset of moderate daytime sedation, which was eliminated by having the patient take both medications at bedtime.

DISCUSSION

The fact that clinical improvement occurred more rapidly after the addition of fluoxetine than the expected 4- to 6-week response time with fluoxetine alone suggests that some type of pharmacological augmentation is occurring, rather than a simple additive effect of two separate antidepressant agents. This may suggest a mechanism similar to the lithium enhancement of central serotonergic activity when combined with a single antidepressant in some refractory depressives. Furthermore, long-term administration of TCAs is

TABLE 1. *Characteristics of 10 responders to fluoxetine enhancement of heterocyclic antidepressants*

Patient	Sex	Age	Diagnosis	Medication and dosage	Time frame	Interaction side effects
1[a]	M	50	MDD[b]	IMI 400 mg + FLU 20 mg	24 hr	None
2[a]	F	29	MDD	DMI 125 mg + FLU 40 mg	48 hr/2 wk	Restlessness, tremor
3[a]	M	58	MDD	NOR 100 mg + FLU 40 mg	2 wk	Sedation
4	F	38	MDD and OCD	IMI 200 mg + FLU 20 mg	1 wk	Tremor
5	M	35	MDD and chronic pain	DOX 150 mg + FLU 80 mg	48–72 hr	None
6	F	39	MDD	DMI + LITH + FLU 150 mg 600 mg 40 mg	2 wk	None
7	M	42	MDD	DMI 350 mg + FLU 40 mg	72 hr	None
8	F	34	MDD and panic	TRZ 200 mg + FLU 40 mg	72 hr	Sedation
9	F	39	MDD and panic	AMI 75 mg + FLU 20 mg	1 wk	Tremor
10	F	44	MDD	DOX 250 mg + FLU 40 mg	2 wk	None

[a] Patients 1, 2, and 3 are reported in detail in text.
[b] MDD, major depression disorder.

thought to increase sensitivity of postsynaptic 5HT receptors, and we, therefore, speculate that the rapid clinical change seen with fluoxetine augmentation may be secondary to enhancement of already sensitized postsynaptic serotonergic receptors. In this regard, the observation that a response also may occur over a more protracted time period of several weeks is similar to the response described with lithium augmentation therapy (4,5).

Additional evidence supporting a distinct fluoxetine–TCA enhancement effect has been derived from recent animal studies conducted by Baron et al. (7). The simultaneous administration of desipramine and fluoxetine induced a more rapid and increased downregulation of central β-adrenoreceptors than either agent alone in the rat brain. These findings may indicate yet another potential neurochemical mechanism involved with this combination treatment.

Fluoxetine lacks anticholinergic and antihistaminic effects and does not exacerbate preexisting side effects of the TCA with which it is combined. Although it has a low potential for toxicity when combined with TCAs, severe and fatal toxic reactions have been reported when fluoxetine was combined with L-tryptophan (8) and monoamine oxidase inhibitors (9). Additionally, there have been reports suggesting that fluoxetine may delay the hepatic metabolism of other antidepressants, resulting in tricyclic drug accumulation and potential toxicity (10–12). Although we did not observe this pharmacokinetic interaction in our 10 patients (Table 1), we urge caution with this combination and suggest close clinical and TCA blood level monitoring during treatment.

In light of these unique characteristics, the finding that fluoxetine may be a useful adjunct in the treatment of partially responsive depression warrants more systematic investigation.

REFERENCES

1. Keller MB, Klerman GL, Lavori PW, et al. Long-term outcome of episodes of major depression: Clinical and public health significance. *JAMA* 1984;252:758–792.
2. Zucky PM, Biederman J, et al. Adjunct low dose lithium carbonate in treatment-resistant depression: A placebo-controlled study. *J Clin Psychopharm* 1988;8:120–124.
3. Feighner JP. The new generation of antidepressants. *J Clin Psychiatry* 1983;44:49–55.
4. DeMontigny C, Cournoyer G, et al. Lithium carbonate addition to tricyclic antidepressant-resistant unipolar depression. *Arch Gen Psychiatry* 1983;40:1327–1334.
5. Heninger GR, Charney DS, Sternberg DE. Lithium carbonate augmentation of antidepressant treatment. *Arch Gen Psychiatry* 1983;40:1335–1342.
6. Weilburg JB, Rosenbaum JF, et al. Fluoxetine added to non-MAOI antidepressant converts nonresponders to responders: A preliminary report. *J Clin Psychiatry* 1989;50:447–449.
7. Baron BM, Ogden A, Seigel BW, et al. Rapid downregulation of β-adrenoreceptors by coadministration of desipramine and fluoxetine. *Eur J Pharmacol* 1988;154:125–134.
8. Steiner W, Fontaine R. Toxic reaction following the combined administration of fluoxetine and L-tryptophan: five case reports. *Biol Psychiatry* 1986;21:1067–1071.
9. *Physicians desk reference*. Oradell, NJ: Medical Economics, 1988.
10. Bell IR, Cole JO. Fluoxetine induces elevation of desipramine and exacerbation of geriatric non-psychotic depression. *J Clin Psychopharmacol* 1988;8:447–448.
11. Aranow R, et al. Elevated antidepressant plasma levels after addition of fluoxetine. *Am J Psychiatry* 1989;146:911–913.
12. Downs J, et al. Increased plasma tricyclic antidepressant concentrations in two patients currently treated with fluoxetine. *J Clin Psychiatry* 1989;50:226–227.

12

Rapid Downregulation of Cerebral β-Adrenoceptors by Combined Treatment with Imipramine and Mianserin

René Klysner and Arne Geisler

Treatment of rats with polycyclic antidepressants, monoamine oxidase inhibitors (MAOIs), or electroconvulsive therapy (ECT) has repeatedly been shown to reduce cerebral β-adrenoceptor density and β-adrenoceptor-mediated cAMP formation after a period of 1 to several weeks (1,2). The delay in downregulation of cerebral β-adrenoceptors during antidepressant treatment is of the same magnitude as seen in patients before the therapeutic effect occurs and is one of the reasons for the hypothesis that cerebral β-adrenoceptor downregulation may be associated with the antidepressant effect (3).

It has been found that the delay in cerebral β-adrenoceptor downregulation can be reduced if an α_2-adrenoceptor blocking agent is administered concurrently with the antidepressant, and it has, therefore, been suggested that α_2-adrenoceptor antagonists could be valuable adjuncts in antidepressant treatment (4,5).

In the present study, we investigated whether concomitant administration of two antidepressants, one of which is also a potent α_2-adrenoceptor antagonist, could lead to a more rapid downregulation of cerebral β-adrenoceptors than is seen after treatment with either agent alone.

MATERIALS AND METHODS

Male Wistar rats, weighing 180 to 200 g, were treated twice daily with i.p. injections of imipramine hydrochloride (10 mg/kg), mianserin hydrochloride (10 mg/kg), zimelidine hydrochloride (10 mg/kg), yohimbine chloride (2 mg/kg), or a combination of imipramine with either of these drugs. Control animals received a similar volume of saline.

After treatment for 3 or 14 days as indicated, the animals were decapitated in a cold room (4°C) 18 hours after the last injection. Cerebral cortex from the dorsolateral aspects of the brain was immediately frozen and stored at −80°C until receptor determination.

Assessment of ^{3}H-dihydroalprenolol binding to β-adrenoceptors of Scatchard analysis was performed as previously described (6).

^{3}H-Dihydroalprenolol was obtained from New England Nuclear, Dreieich, FRG. Mianserin hydrochloride was donated by Organon A/S, Denmark, zimelidine hydrochloride was a gift from Astra A/S, Denmark, and imipramine hydrochloride was provided by DAK-Laboratories, Denmark. Levo-propranolol was a gift from ICI, UK. All other agents used were of analytical grade.

Statistical analysis was performed by Wilcoxon's test for unpaired differences.

Department of Pharmacology, University of Copenhagen, Copenhagen, Denmark.

TABLE 1. *Effect of treatment with imipramine and mianserin for 3 days on ^{3}H-dihydraoalprenolol binding to β-adrenoceptors in rat cerebral cortex*

Treatment	No. of animals	B_{max} (fmol/mg protein)	K_d (nM)
Control		164 ± 15[a]	0.53 ± 0.06
Imipramine[b]	7	143 ± 11	0.61 ± 0.03
Mianserin	8	158 ± 13	0.50 ± 0.09
Yohimbine	7	158 ± 12	0.50 ± 0.04
Imipramine + Mianserin	6	108 ± 10*	0.46 ± 0.02
Imipramine + Yohimbine	7	115 ± 10*	0.48 ± 0.05

[a]Mean ± SEM.
[b]Yohimbine was given as 2 mg/kg, i.p., twice daily; imipramine and mianserin were given in doses of 10 mg/kg bid.
*$p<0.02$ compared to controls.

RESULTS

Treatment for 3 days with yohimbine or the antidepressants mianserin or imipramine did not have any measurable effect on either β-adrenoceptor density or affinity for ligand in the rat cerebral cortex when the drugs were administered alone (Table 1). In contrast, combined treatment for 3 days with mianserin and imipramine decreased the density of β-adrenoceptors, an effect that was seen also after combined treatment with yohimbine and imipramine (Table 1).

A decrease in β-adrenoceptors in the cerebral cortex was evident after 14 days of treatment with imipramine, either given alone or in combination with mianserin. After 14 days of treatment, mianserin still had no effect on ^{3}H-dihydroalprenolol binding, and the effect of the combined treatment with imipramine and mianserin was not significantly different from that seen after treatment with imipramine alone (Table 2). Zimelidine given either alone or in combination with imipramine for 3 days did not induce changes in the binding of ^{3}H-dihydroalprenolol to cerebral β-adrenoceptors (Table 3).

No alterations in receptor affinity were seen with any of the treatments. In the groups of animals given combined treatment with imipramine and either mianserin or yohimbine, there was a trend toward increased affinity, but it did not in any instance reach statistical significance.

In vitro addition of imipramine, mianserin, or a combination of these (10^{-4} M)

TABLE 2. *Effect of treatment with imipramine and mianserin for 14 days on ^{3}H-dihydroalprenolol binding to β-adrenoceptors in rat cerebral cortex*

Treatment	No. of animals	B_{max} (fmol/mg protein)	K_d (nM)
Control	4[a]	140 ± 15	0.53 ± 0.07
Imipramine[b]	5	102 ± 3*	0.59 ± 0.11
Mianserin	5	137 ± 12	0.53 ± 0.09
Imipramine + mianserin	5	87 ± 6*	0.37 ± 0.06

[a]Means ± SEM.
[b]Drug doses were 10 mg/kg bid given i.p.
*$p<0.05$ compared with controls.

TABLE 3. *Effect of treatment with imipramine and zimelidine for 3 days on ^{3}H-dihydroalprenodol binding to β-adrenoceptors in rat cerebral cortex*

Treatment	No. of animals	B_{max} (fmol/mg protein)	K_d (nM)
Control	6	184 ± 18[a]	0.75 ± 0.23
Zimelidine	5	196 ± 21	0.53 ± 0.10
Imipramine	6	224 ± 17	0.89 ± 0.12
Imipramine + zimelidine	4	200 ± 22	0.74 ± 0.12

[a]Means ± SEM.
[b]Drug doses were 10 mg/kg bid given i.p.

did not change the affinity of the β-adrenoceptors (data not shown).

DISCUSSION

Several studies have demonstrated that chronic treatment with antidepressant drugs leads to decreased density of β-adrenoceptors in the rat brain. The downregulation of β-adrenoceptors is seen after a delay similar to the delay in therapeutic effect seen in humans, and this constitutes one of the bases of the hypothesis that β-adrenoceptors downregulation in the brain may be linked to the alleviation of depression (3).

Much evidence favors the view that the antidepressant-induced downregulation of cerebral β-adrenoceptors is an adaptation to presynaptic actions of the antidepressants, leading to increased synaptic concentrations of NE (2,7,8). The synaptic NE concentration is, among other factors, dependent on α_2-adrenoceptors inhibiting presynaptic NE release (9). Although measurements of α_2-adrenoceptor density after antidepressant treatments have given diverging results (10–12), some antidepressant treatments seem to lead to an apparent α_2-adrenoceptor subsensitivity in the brain (13–15). Such functional subsensitivity may, however, be present in the locus coeruleus rather than on presynaptic terminals in the cerebral cortex (16,17).

It has been speculated that this apparent α_2-adrenoceptor subsensitivity could facilitate β-adrenoceptor downregulation by increasing NE release (5,18). In line with this, it has been found that pharmacological blockade of α_2-adrenoceptors can accelerate the downregulation of β-adrenoceptors during treatment with TCAs or MAOIs (5). This accelerated β-adrenoceptor downregulation has been demonstrated as decreased ligand binding to β-adrenoceptors (4,5,10), decreased cAMP formation (19,20), and decreased β-adrenoceptor-mediated behavioral events. It has been foreseen from these experiments that combination of an antidepressant with an α_2-adrenoceptor antagonist might also accelerate the therapeutic effect of the antidepressant treatments in humans (4,19).

One of the α_2-adrenoceptor blocking agents often used in animal experiments, yohimbine, may, however, not be optimal for use in the treatment of depression, since it has been found to provoke anxiety in humans (21), to induce manic symptoms in depressed patients (22), and to provoke agitation when given in combination with an antidepressant (23). Furthermore, it was found (23,24) that addition of yohimbine to an antidepressant treatment was not advantageous. However, the patients included in these studies seemed nonresponsive to conventional antidepressant medication, impeding the assessment of an earlier response to the antidepressant.

Mianserin, a commonly used antidepressant drug, is a potent α_2-adrenoceptor blocking agent (25) and should, therefore, be expected, like yohimbine, to accelerate the downregulation of cerebral β-adrenoceptors evoked by other antidepressant treatments. The present results demonstrate that combined treatment of rats with mianserin and imipramine causes a reduced density of β-adrenoceptors in the cerebral cortex after only 3 days of treatment, at a time when the effect of imipramine alone was not yet evident. Although a clear tendency to further reduction in β-adrenoceptor density after combined treatment with imipramine and mianserin for 14 days was seen, there was no significant effect on the β-adrenoceptors further than that seen after treatment with imipramine alone.

The rapid downregulation of cerebral β-adrenoceptors after combined treatment with imipramine and mianserin does not seem to be due simply to treatment with two antidepressants, since combined treatment with imipramine and zimelidine did not reduce β-adrenoceptor density in the cerebral cortex after 3 days of treatment. The reason for using zimelidine as a control treatment was that zimelidine has only little affinity for α_2-adrenoceptors in the brain (26), and long-term treatment with either zimelidine or mianserin alone has only minor effects on ^{3}H-dihydroalprenolol binding to β-adrenoceptors (6,27).

CONCLUSION

If downregulation of cerebral β-adrenoceptors is associated with alleviation of depression, as hypothesized, it may thus be advantageous to combine mianserin and imipramine when treating depressed patients, since concomitant treatment of rats with these antidepressants can lead to a much faster downregulation of cerebral β-adrenoceptors than is seen after treatment with imipramine alone. Such a faster onset of action of mianserin in combination with another antidepressant is supported by the observation (28) that during combined treatment with mianserin and isocarboxide, depressive symptoms improved after only 2 to 10 days. At present, a study on the combined effect of mianserin and imipramine in endogenous depression is, thererfore, in progress.

REFERENCES

1. Vetulani J, Stawarz RJ, Dingell JW, Sulser F. A possible common mechanism of action of antidepressant treatments. *Naunyn Schmiedebergs Arch Pharmacol* 1976;293:109–114.
2. Wolfe BB, Harden TK, Sporn JR, Molinoff PB. Presynaptic modulation of β-adrenergic receptors in rat cerebral cortex after treatment with antidepressants. *J Pharmacol Exp Ther* 1978;207:446–457.
3. Sulser F. New cellular mechanisms of antidepressant drugs. In: Fielding S, Effland RC, eds. *New frontiers in psychotropic drug research.* Futura Publishing Company, 1979;29–50.
4. Wiech NL, Ursillo RC. Accleration of desipramine-induced decrease of rat corticocerebral β-adrenergic receptors by yohimbine. *Commun Psychopharmacol* 1980;4:95–100.
5. Scott JA, Crews FT. Rapid decrease in rat brain β-adrenergic receptor binding during combined antidepressant α_2-antagonist treatment. *J Pharmacol Exp Ther* 1983;224.
6. Klysner R, Geisler A, Andersen P. Antidepressants and components of the β-adrenoceptor system: Studies on zimelidine. In: Usdin E, Dahl SG, Gram LF, eds. *Clinical pharmacology in psychiatry* (3rd International Meeting). London: Macmillan Press Ltd, 1983;301–312.
7. Schweitzer JW, Schwartz R, Friedhoff AJ. Intact presynaptic terminals required for β-adrenergic receptor regulation by desipramine. *J Neurochem* 1979;33:3177–3179.
8. Mishra R, Gillespie DD, Lovell RA, Robson RD, Sulser F. Oxaprotiline: Induction of central noradrenergic subsensitivity by its (+)-enantiomer. *Life Sci* 1982;30:XX.
9. Langer SZ. Presynaptic regulation of the release of catecholamines. *Pharmacol Rev* 1981;32:337–362.
10. Johnson RW, Reisine T, Spotnutz S, Wiech N, Ursillo R, Yamamura HI. Effects of desipramine and yohimbine on α_2 and β-adrenoceptor sensitivity. *Eur J Pharmacol* 1980;67:123–127.
11. Smith CB, Garcia-Sevilla JA, Hollingsworth PJ. α_2-Adrenoceptors in rat brain are decreased after long-term tricyclic antidepressant drug treatment. *Brain Res* 1981;210:418–423.
12. Cohen RM, Aulakh CS, Campbell IC, Murphy DL. Functional subsensitivity of α_2-adrenoceptors accompanies reduction in yohimbine binding after clorgyline treatment. *Eur J Pharmacol* 1982;81:145–148.
13. Spyráki C, Fibiger HC. Functional evidence for sub-sensitivity of noradrenergic α_2-receptors after chronic desipramine treatment. *Life Sci* 1980;27:1863–1867.

14. Heal DL, Akagi H, Bowdler JM, Green AR. Repeated electroconvulsive shock attenuates clonidine-induced hypoactivity in rodents. *Eur J Pharmacol* 1981;75:231–237.
15. Sugrue MF. A study of the sensitivity of rat brain α_2-adrenoceptors during chronic antidepressant treatments. *Naunyn Schmiedebergs Arch Pharmacol* 1982;320:XX.
16. Scuvée-Moreau JJ, Svensson TH. Sensitivity in vivo of central α_2 and opiate receptors after chronic treatment with various antidepressants. *J Neural Transm* 1982;54:51–63.
17. Schoffelmeer ANM, Hoorneman EMD, Sminia P, Mulder AH. Presynaptic α_2-and postsynaptic β-adrenoceptor sensitivity in slices of rat neocortex after chronic treatment with various drugs. *Neuropharmacology* 1984;23:115–119.
18. Keith RA, Howe BB, Salama AI. Modulation of peripheral β_1 and α_2-receptor sensitivities by the administration of the tricyclic antidepressant, imipramine, alone and in combination with α_2-antagonists to rats. *J Pharmacol Exp Ther* 1986;236:356–363.
19. Kendall DA, Duman R, Slopis J, Enna SJ. Influence of adrenocorticotropic hormone and yohimbine and antidepressant-induced declines in rat brain neurotransmitter receptor binding and function. *J Pharmacol Exp Ther* 1982;222:566–571.
20. Campbell IC, McKernan RN, Smockcum RWJ, Stephenson JD, Weeramanthri TB. Effect of desipramine, phenoxybenzamine and yohimbine on β-adrenoceptors and cyclic AMP production in the rat brain. *Neuropharmacology* 1984;23:1385–1388.
21. Lader M, Bruce M. States of anxiety and their induction by drugs. *Br J Clin Pharmacol* 1986;22:251–261.
22. Price LH, Charney DS, Heninger GR. Three cases of manic symptoms following yohimbine administration. *Am J Psychiatry* 1984;141:1267–1268.
23. Laakmann G, Dieterle D, Weiss L, Schmauss M. Therapeutic and neuroendocrine studies using yohimbine and antidepressants in depressed patients and healthy subjects. *Adv Biosci* 1982;40:295–301.
24. Charney DS, Price LH, Heninger GR. Desipramine–yohimbine combination treatment of refractory depression. Implications for the β-adrenergic receptor hypothesis of antidepressant action. *Arch Gen Psychiatry* 1986;43:1155–1161.
25. Rose A, McCulloch MW, Sarantos-Laska C, Rand MJ. Effects of mianserin on noradrenergic mechanisms. *J Psychiatr Res* 1984;18:79–88.
26. Hall H, Ögren SO. Effects of antidepressant drugs on different receptors in the brain. *Eur J Pharmacol* 1981;80:393–407.
27. Mishra J, Janowsky A, Sulser F. Action of mianserin and zimelidine on the norepinephrine receptor coupled adenylate cyclase system in brain: Subsensitivity without reduction in β-adrenergic receptor binding. *Neuropharmacology* 1980;19:983–987.
28. Riise IS, Holm P. Concomitant isocarboxazide/mianserin treatment of major depressive disorder. *J Affective Disord* 1984;6:175–179.

13

Combined MAOI-TCA Treatment in Refractory Depression

Atul C. Pande, Margaret M. Calarco, and Leon J. Grunhaus

Although the monoamine oxidase inhibitors (MAOI) were the first antidepressant drugs to be discovered, their popularity has waxed and waned through the years. The efficacy and safety of these drugs have been debated endlessly, and some practitioners appear to disregard them as potentially beneficial agents in the treatment of mood disorders. This belief persists despite evidence of the comparable efficacy of MAOIs and tricyclics (1).

The early literature on MAOIs emphasized the hazards of hypertensive crises, which only later were recognized as being due to the tyramine (cheese) effect. Further hazards were noted with a variety of drug interactions, most notably with other psychotropic drugs, such as the tricyclic antidepressants (TCAs). Hyperpyrexia, hypertensive episodes and delirium were noted, leading to recommendations against the use of TCA-MAOI combinations. Later reports indicated that the order in which the two drugs were introduced was a determinant of whether any serious side effects might develop. In brief, the addition of an MAOI to ongoing TCA treatment seemed to be free of any significant risk as did the simultaneous institution of the two drugs. The gravest risk emerged with the addition of a TCA to ongoing MAOI treatment (2). Once these facts were recognized, more reports began to appear of the successful use of combined treatment in patients previously not responsive to tricyclic therapy.

EFFICACY AND SAFETY OF COMBINED THERAPY

Most of the literature on the use of TCA-MAOI combinations consists of case reports or uncontrolled studies. On this anecdotal basis there seems to be an indication that some patients who have been unresponsive with prior treatment do derive benefit when placed on the combination treatment. However, because in many of these cases the patients did not have a trial of an MAOI alone, it cannot be said with certainty whether they responded to the MAOI-TCA combination or to the MAOI alone after having failed to respond to prior TCA treatment.

Uncontrolled Studies

Several open studies (3–14; M.M. Calarco, L.J Grunhaus, and A.C. Pande, unpublished observations), mostly retrospective, have compared the MAOI-TCA combination against either a single tricyclic, MAOI, or both (Table 1). The almost unanimous conclusion from these studies appears to be that although the combined treatment does not produce an excess of side effects when compared to either drug alone, all treatments are equally effective.

Depression Program, Department of Psychiatry, University of Michigan Medical Center, Ann Arbor, MI 48109-0118.

TABLE 1. Studies of combined MAOI-TCA treatment (excludes single case studies)

Author (ref)	n	Diagnosis	Resistant to TCA	Resistant to MAOI	Resistant to ECT	MAOI/TCA combination	Treatment response	Adverse effects
Uncontrolled studies								
Dally 1965 (3)	8	Depression	+	+	+	AMI[a] 150 mg/day ISO 20–30 mg/day IPR 50–100 mg/day	Good, employable	Weight gain, hypotension, incoordination
Gander 1965 (4)	157	Depression	One or more antidepressants			AMI 150 mg/day PHE 45 mg/day (or others)	62% recovered or improved considerably	Carbohydrate craving in 38%, weight gain
Sargant et al. 1966 (5)	73	Chronic tension states	Many treatments			IPR 75–150 mg/day AMI 75–150 mg/day	86% moderate improvement	Weight gain, hypotension
Kelly et al. 1970 (6)	74	Phobics	???			PHE 30–60 mg/day AMI or TRI	Good	No serious events
Schuckit et al. 1971 (7)	5	Depression	+	+	–	TRA 40 mg/day AMI 100 mg/day	Not reported	No serious events
Winston 1971 (8)	20	Depression	+	+	+	AMI 100 mg/day ISO or TRA	70% had considerable improvement	Weight gain, hypotension
Ray 1973 (9)	84	Depression	—do—			AMI/TRI 25–150 mg TRA or PHE	62% had considerable improvement	Hypotension
Sethna 1974 (10)	10	Atypical depression	+	+	+	PHE 45 mg/day AMI 50–75 mg/day	90% recovery	Fainting, weight gain, ?? mania
Davidson 1974 (11)	14	Depression	Refractory			AMI and TRA	Good	No serious events

Study	N	Diagnosis	Refractory	Regimen	Response	Side effects
Ayd 1975 (12)	55	Depression	Not mentioned	DOX 200 mg/day TRA or PHE	Not reported	Hypotension, constipation
Spiker and Pugh 1976 (13)	201	Depression	???	AMI or IMI TRA, PHE or ISO	Not reported	Hypotension
Schmauss et al. 1988 (14)	94	Depression (ICD-9)	+	TRA 10–30 mg/day AMI 75–250 mg/day (or other cyclics)	68% good or very good response	Less than with single antidepressant drugs
Calarco et al. (unpublished)	10	MDD	Refractory	IMI, NOR, DOX, AMI with PHE	Euthymia in 40%	Not serious
Controlled studies						
Davidson et al. 1978 (15)	19	Depression	+	AMI 100 mg/day plus PHE 45 mg/day vs ECT	ECT superior	Uncomfortable, not serious
Young et al. 1979 (16)	135	Depressed	Not refractory	PHE 45 mg/day or ISO 32 mg/day or TRI 106 mg/day or PHE + TRI ISO + TRI	Trimipramine alone better than other groups	Modest, more insomnia in MAOI or MAOI-TCA groups
White et al. 1980 (17)	30	Depressed	Not refractory	AMI 300 mg/day or TRA 40 mg/day or combination	Single drugs as effective as combination	Equal side effects in all groups
Razani et al. 1983 (18)	60	MDD (DSM-III)	Not refractory	AMI 300 mg/day or TRA 60 mg/day or AMI 150 mg + TRA 30 mg/d	Equal rate of improvement in each group	Similar in all groups
White et al. 1982 (19)	71	MDD (DSM-III)	Not refractory	AMI 300 mg/day or TRA 60 mg/day or AMI 150 mg + TRA 30 mg/day	Equal rate of improvement in each group	Similar in all groups

[a] AMI, amitriptyline; IMI, imipramine; TRI, trimipramine; DOX, doxepin; NOR, nortriptyline; TRA, tranylcypromine; PHE, phenelzine; ISO, isocarboxazid; IPR, iproniazid.

Since the population used for these studies were unselected depressives (both inpatients and outpatients), these data still leave the question of the efficacy of combined therapy in refractory depression unanswered.

Apart from anecdotal reports, a number of uncontrolled series of refractory patients were reported as being treated successfully with combined MAOI-TCA therapy. Dally (3) reported on eight patients treated with amitriptyline combined with iproniazid or isocarboxazid and who had a good response with few serious side effects. Gander (4) reported a series of 157 depressives unresponsive to "one or more" antidepressants of whom 62% responded significantly to combined treatment. Sargant et al. (5) treated 73 patients with "chronic tension states" who were being evaluated for leukotomy. Combined iproniazid and amitriptyline produced at least moderate improvement in 86%, although it should be noted that many patients were receiving concomitant ECT and/or narcosis, thus confounding the attribution of therapeutic benefit to the antidepressant combination alone.

These earlier studies set the stage for many similar reports of combined treatment in various clinical populations of depressives. These studies are summarized in Table 1.

Sethna (10) reported perhaps the first open but prospective study on 10 patients who had either failed to respond or had relapsed soon after treatment with TCAs, MAOIs, and ECT. Two other patients were included who had failed to respond to TCAs or MAOIs but had refused or could not be given ECT. None of the patients were noted to have "endogenous" or "psychotic" features, and all of them had considerable overt anxiety, with many of them fearing being left alone. Furthermore, there was a preponderance of atypical symptoms, such as intact mood reactivity, neurotic features, phobic symptoms, and nonepisodic course of illness. Patients were drug free for 2 weeks and were then treated with a combination of phenelzine 15 mg three times daily and amitriptyline 75 mg at bedtime in 10 patients and 50 mg in 2 patients. Clinical ratings were done on the Hamilton Rating Scale for Depression at baseline and repeated after 3 and 6 weeks of treatment. Significant clinical improvement occurred over the course of treatment, and during a mean follow-up of 16 months, 9 patients continued to be free of depression or anxiety and functioned at work or at home. One patient relapsed after being taken off the combination, and another had fainting attacks that necessitated discontinuation of the drugs. The last subject, who did the least well initially, worsened during follow-up and was hospitalized again.

Among the uncontrolled retrospective studies, Schmauss et al. (14) reported the largest series of therapy-resistant patients, defined as being unresponsive to two single drug trials over 4 weeks each, who were treated with the combination of tranylcypromine with a number of TCAs and tetracyclic agents (amitriptyline, imipramine, dibenzepine, nomifensine, clomipramine, lofepramine, maprotiline). Ninety-four inpatients received the combination treatment, and it is questionable if adequate therapeutic doses of the various agents were employed. Overall, after a mean duration of treatment of 22 days, 31% of patients had a very good therapeutic effect (no depressive symptomatology) and 37% had good effect (little depressive symptomatology). The tranylcypromine-amitriptyline combination was the most effective, with a very good response in 51% and a good response in 27%. Combined therapy produced a nonsignificantly lower frequency of side effects as compared to single drug therapy. However, tranylcypromine combined with nomifensine or clomipramine led to an increase in all side effects. Only 4 patients (4.2%) discontinued the combination due to side effects, such as headaches, weight gain, orthostatic hypotension, and hypertensive crisis.

More recently, we have made similar observations in a small retrospective study as

TABLE 2. *Summary of MAOI-TCA treated patients*

Patient	Age	Sex	Previous episodes	Duration of current episode (weeks)	TCA dose	TCA-MAOI dose	Response
1	44	F	0	468	NOR[a] 125 mg	NOR 125 mg PHE 60 mg	None[b]
2	23	M	0	78	IMI 300 mg	IMI 200 mg PHE 60 mg	None[b]
3	18	F	2	24	NOR 75 mg	NOR 75 mg PHE 45 mg	None[b]
4	59	M	12	40	NOR 175 mg	NOR 125 mg PHE 45 mg	Euthymic[b]
5	37	M	4	47	DOX 275 mg	DOX 200 mg PHE 75 mg	Euthymic
6	46	F	[c]	106	NOR 50 mg	NOR 50 mg PHE 75 mg	Euthymic
7	45	M	2	17	NOR 75 mg	NOR 75 mg PHE 45 mg	None
8	31	F	0	52	AMI 200 mg	AMI 100 mg PHE 45 mg	None
9	24	M	0	150	IMI 600 mg	IMI 600 mg PHE 45 mg	Euthymic
10	41	M	0	52	NOR 125 mg	NOR 125 mg PHE 45 mg	Mild[b]

[a] AMI, amitriptyline; IMI, imipramine; DOX, doxepin; NOR, nortriptyline; PHE, phenelzine.
[b] Refractory to TCA-lithium also.
[c] Number of previous episodes too ill-defined to count.

well (M.M. Calarco, L.J. Grunhaus, and A.C. Pande, unpublished observations). In our sample of 10 patients refractory to previous tricyclic treatment, some noted marked improvement in symptoms while on combined treatment without a concomitant increase in side effects (Table 2). No serious adverse effects were noted (Table 3).

Controlled Studies

Only a few controlled trials of combined treatment in depression have been reported. The first of these by Davidson et al. (15) compared ECT with combined amitriptyline-phenelzine in 19 medication-refractory depressives. ECT was found superior

TABLE 3. *Comparison of adverse effects with TCA alone and MAOI-TCA combinations*

Adverse effects	On TCA alone	On MAOI-TCA
Dizziness	5 (2-R)[a]	3
Insomnia	0	2
Nausea	0	2
Dry mouth	5	4
"Felt drugged"	1	1
Constipation	2	2 (1-R)
Frontal headache	1 (R)	2 (1-R)
Tinnitus	1 (R)	0
Drowsiness	3	3 (1-R)
Increased appetite	1	2
Anorgasmia	0	1
Transient AM confusion	0	2 (1-R)
Hypomania	0	1
Paresthesia	0	1
Blurred vision	1	1
Urinary hesitancy	1	1

[a] R, symptom reported initially, but resolved during treatment.

in efficacy, but no serious adverse effects occurred with the drug regimen. Young et al. (16) compared trimipramine, phenelzine, and isocarboxazid against a combination of trimipramine with an MAOI in 135 outpatients. Although the patients on trimipramine alone did better than the other groups, it is notable that the doses of the MAO inhibitors were relatively low in view of the current dosing practices.

White et al. (17) compared the combination of amitriptyline and tranylcypromine against either drug alone in 30 depressed inpatients who were randomly assigned to open treatment with either of the three drug regimens. Equal therapeutic efficacy and similar frequency of side effects were reported for all three groups. The same investigators (18,19) subsequently confirmed these findings in a double-blind controlled study.

PREDICTORS OF RESPONSE TO COMBINED TREATMENT

The review by White and Simpson (20) examined the predictors of response to combined MAOI-TCA treatment. The bulk of the evidence seemed to suggest that patients with nonendogenous, neurotic, or anxious symptoms along with depression appear to do the best. Interestingly, this profile is similar to the group of MAOI-responsive patients labeled as "atypical" depressives by others (21). Hence, the possibility exists that response to combined MAOI-TCA treatment may be predominantly a response to MAOI.

RECOMMENDATIONS FOR COMBINED TREATMENT

As Cole (22) has appropriately noted in his succinct review of the current situation with antidepressant availability, each new pharmacological approach to the treatment of depressive illness provides a distinct but modest increase in the yield of responsive patients over and above the 70 to 80% who respond to standard tricyclic therapy. It is possible the same truism may hold for the efficacy of combined MAOI-TCA therapy; i.e., some patients not previously responsive to antidepressant drug therapy may respond to this combination. However, the available data suggest that, in direct comparisons, the combination has no superiority over single drug treatment for unselected depressives.

Only a few reports have described the use of combined treatments in patients previously refractory to adequate antidepressant therapy, thus providing insufficient data to clearly establish the efficacy of combined treatment in such patients. Since the possibility must be entertained that refractory patients may respond to the combination, it is reasonable to consider this form of treatment when all other treatments have been found relatively ineffective.

Although the safety of combined treatment is now demonstrated, a systematic protocol is necessary for safe treatment. There are two safe methods for initiating combined drug therapy. The TCA may be started first and raised to a therapeutic level followed by the addition of the MAOI in gradually increasing doses until response occurs or side effects become a limiting factor. Used in this manner, the addition of the MAOI to ongoing but ineffective TCA treatment may be seen as one of the many TCA augmentation strategies (such as the addition of, e.g., lithium or thyroid hormones) often used in refractory depressives. If a clinical response does occur, the possibility needs to be entertained that the response may be to the MAOI alone rather than to the combination. This possibility may be tested by gradually attempting to reduce the dose of the TCA and monitoring potential loss of clinical response. If symptoms begin to reappear, the original effective dose of the TCA should be reinstituted.

A second, probably more popular, method of using combined treatment is to initiate both agents at the same time in gradually increasing doses until either a response occurs or side effects force a ceiling on the dose. In using either of these strategies, it is advisable to avoid certain drug combinations, such as tranylcypromine-chlorimipramine, which are reported to be especially hazardous. Based on pharmacological grounds, Marley and Wozniak (23–26) have suggested that serotonin reuptake inhibitors, such as clomipramine and fluoxetine, should never be combined with an MAOI. This is substantiated by recent reports to the manufacturer (Eli Lilly Laboratories) of severe interactions between MAOIs and fluoxetine. Virtually all other combinations of MAOIs and cyclic antidepressants have been used and found to have no greater adverse effects than single drugs used alone.

REFERENCES

1. Davis JM, Janicak PG, Bruniga K. The efficacy of MAO inhibitors in depression: A meta-analysis. *Psychiatr Ann* 1987;17:825–831.
2. Pare CMB. Combining the antidepressant drugs. *Br Med J* 1965;1:384.
3. Dally PJ. Combining the antidepressant drugs. *Br Med J* 1965;1:384.
4. Gander DR. Combining the antidepressant drugs. *Br Med J* 1965;1:521.
5. Sargant W, Walter CJS, Wright N. New treatment of some chronic tension states. *Br Med J* 1966;1:322–324.
6. Kelly D, Guirguis W, Frommer E, Mitchell-Heggs N, Sargant W. Treatment of phobic states with antidepressants. *Br J Psychiatry* 1970;116:387–398.
7. Schuckit M, Robins E, Feighner J. Tricyclic antidepressants and monoamine oxidase inhibitors. *Arch Gen Psychiatry* 1971;24:509–514.
8. Winston F. Combined antidepressant therapy. *Br J Psychiatry* 1971;118:301–304.
9. Ray I. Combinations of antidepressant drugs in the treatment of depressive illness. *Can Psychiatric Assoc J* 1973;18:399–402.
10. Sethna ER. A study of refractory cases of depressive illness and their response to combined antidepressant treatment. *Br J Psychiatry* 1974;124:265–272.
11. Davidson J. The management of resistant depression. *Br J Psychiatry* 1974;124:219–220.
12. Ayd FJ. Psychotropic drug combinations: Good and bad. In: Greenblatt M, ed. *Drugs in combination with other therapies*. New York: Grune & Stratton, 1975.
13. Spiker DG, Pugh DD. Combining tricyclic and monoamine oxidase inhibitor antidepressants. *Arch Gen Psychiatry* 1976;33:828–830.
14. Schmauss M, Kapfhammer HP, Meyr P, Hoff P. Combined MAO inhibitor and tri (tetra) cyclic antidepressant treatment in therapy-resistant depression. *Prog Neuropsychopharmacol Biol Psychiatry* 1988;12:523–532.
15. Davidson J, McLeod M, Law-Yone B, Linnoila M. A comparison of electroconvulsive therapy and combined phenelzine-amitriptyline in refractory depression. *Arch Gen Psychiatry* 1978;35:639–642.
16. Young JPR, Lader M, Hughes WC. Controlled trial of trimipramine, monoamine oxidase inhibitors, and combined treatment in depressed outpatients. *Br Med J* 1979;4:1315–1317.
17. White K, Pistole T, Boyd JL. Combined monoamine oxidase inhibitor-tricyclic antidepressant treatment: A pilot study. *Am J Psychiatry* 1980;137:1422–1425.
18. Razani J, White KL, White J, et al. The safety and efficacy of combined amitriptyline and tranylcypromine antidepressant treatment. *Arch Gen Psychiatry* 1983;40:657–661.
19. White K, Razani J, Simpson G, et al. Combined MAOI tricyclic antidepressant treatment: A controlled trial. *Psychopharmacol Bull* 1982;18:180–181.
20. White K, Simpson G. Combined MAOI tricyclic antidepressant treatment: A reevaluation. *J Clin Psychopharmacol* 1981;1:264–282 (review).
21. Aarons SF, Frances AJ, Mann JJ. Atypical depression: A review of diagnosis and treatment. *Hosp Comm Psychiatry* 1985;36:275–282.
22. Cole J. Where are those new antidepressants we were promised? *Arch Gen Psychiatry* 1988;45:193–194.
23. Marley E, Wozniak KM. Clinical and experimental aspects of interaction between amine oxidase inhibitors and amine re-uptake inhibition. *Psychol Med* 1983;13:735–749.
24. Marley E, Wozniak KM. Interaction of a nonselective monoamine oxidase inhibitor, phenelzine, with inhibitors of 5-hydroxytryptamine, dopamine or noradrenaline re-uptake. *J Psychiatr Res* 1984;18:173–189.
25. Marley E, Wozniak KM. Interaction of nonselective monoamine oxidase inhibitors, tranylcypromine and nialamide, with inhibitors of 5-hydroxytryptamine, dopamine or noradrenaline re-uptake. *J Psychiatr Res* 1984;18:191–203.
26. Marley E, Wozniak KM. Interactions between relatively selective monoamine oxidase inhibitors and an inhibitor of 5-hydroxytryptamine re-uptake, clomipramine. *J Psychiatr Res* 1984;19:597–608.

14

Use of High Dose Tranylcypromine in Resistant Depression

Jay D. Amsterdam

As many as 30% of depressed patients fail to respond to antidepressant treatment (1,2), and approximately 15% experience a chronic, unremitting, depression (3). The reason for nonresponse to medication often is unclear. However, several factors could account for this situation, including (a) differential effectiveness of specific drugs for treating particular subtypes of depression (e.g., endogenous vs nonendogenous), (b) individual differences in drug metabolism that result in inadequate (or excessive) plasma drug concentrations, (c) insufficient duration of treatment, (d) patient noncompliance, and (e) biochemically distinct subtypes of depression that may respond preferentially to drugs that affect specific neurotransmitter systems (4–8).

However, after controlling for these and other variables (9–11), there remain a substantial number of patients with treatment-resistant depression. Unfortunately, there are no universal treatment algorithms for treating these patients. For example, some authorities suggest using a tricyclic antidepressant (TCA) with a different pharmacological profile for treating patients resistant to an initial TCA (12), whereas others have advocated switching to a monoamine oxidase inhibitor (MAOI) (13). In contrast, several investigators have suggested potentiating an ineffective TCA by adding triiodothyronine (14), lithium carbonate (15), or a MAOI (16,17).

However, aggressive treatment of these patients with drug combinations (18–21), second generation antidepressants (22,23), unconventional antidepressants (21,24,25), or electroconvulsive therapy (ECT) (26) often has met with only partial success. Additionally, there are problems that can arise when treating refractory depressed patients in this fashion. For example, there is an increased potential for drug-drug interactions, as well as an extended time frame required for systematically exploring the variety of treatment options available. The increased morbidity and associated risk of suicide in these patients during long-term antidepressant treatment indicate a pressing need for using first-line antidepressants in a more effective fashion to achieve a safe and rapid therapeutic response.

Because there is evidence that some patients fail to respond to conventional doses of MAOIs as a result of inadequate MAO enzyme inhibition (27), we performed an open-label study with high doses of tranylcypromine sulfate (Parnate), ranging from 90 mg to 180 mg daily, in depressed patients refractory to at least two prior antidepressant treatments.

Depression Research Unit, Department of Psychiatry, Hospital of the University of Pennsylvania, Philadelphia, PA 19104.

TABLE 1. *Descriptive features of patients*

Patient no.	Age (years)	Sex	Diagnosis	HDRS Baseline	HDRS Max dose
1	64	F	Melancholic	37	6
2	27	M	Melancholic	30	30
3	38	M	Nonmelancholic	23	6
4	31	M	Melancholic	21	4
5	33	M	Melancholic	27	16
6	37	M	Melancholic	24	20
7	72	M	Melancholic	21	10
8	31	M	Nonmelancholic	21	10
9	54	F	Nonmelancholic	18	4
10	66	F	Melancholic	23	4
11	50	M	Melancholic	20	11
12	23	F	Melancholic	25	11
13	33	M	Nonmelancholic	23	7
14	41	F	Nonmelancholic	23	10
Mean ± SD	43 ± 16			24 ± 5	10 ± 8

SUBJECTS AND METHODS

Subjects

Fourteen treatment-resistant depressed patients were evaluated. All subjects satisfied DSM-III criteria (28) for major depressive disorder, single or recurrent episode. None of the patients had manic-depressive (bipolar I) illness or delusional depression, and patients with characterological or dysthymic disorder were specifically excluded. Descriptive features of the patients are presented in Table 1. All subjects had a minimum Hamilton Depression Rating Scale (HDRS) (29) score ≥20 on a 21-item scale, and all had a clear history of nonresponse to at least two prior medication treatments during the current episode.

All patients were in good physical health and had no history or evidence of renal, hepatic, endocrinological, cardiovascular, or neurological disease. None of the subjects had any clinically meaningful laboratory or electrocardiographic abnormalities.

Procedure

All subjects discontinued their previous medications for a minimum of 7 days before initiating tranylcypromine treatment, and all were given a strict low tyramine–low dopamine diet before and during therapy. After informed consent was obtained, tranylcypromine was administered in an open-label fashion, with dosing increments dependent on the clinical need and tolerance of the patient. Initial dosing began at 20 mg daily, with 10 mg increments ranging from every third day to weekly intervals. The minimum and maximum tranylcypromine doses were arbitrarily set at 90 mg and 180 mg, respectively, and all patients received doses ≥90 mg for a minimum of 3 weeks, with clinical examinations at regular intervals to record changes in HDRS scores, blood pressure and heart rate, and the presence of adverse events. Side effects were carefully assessed at each interview by the treating physician, and serum hepatic enzyme, renal function tests, and standard electrocardiograms were obtained before treatment and at maximum dosing. With the exception of an occasional sedative for insomnia, no concomitant psychotropic drugs were prescribed.

Statistical Procedures

Complete response to treatment was defined as a ≥50% reduction from baseline HDRS score plus a final HDRS score ≤10.

TABLE 1. Continued

Duration of illness (years)	No. of previous treatments	No. of previous drug combinations	No. of ECT	Max daily dose (mg)
8	14	3	14	120
8	13	5	28	170
8	7	1	12	100
19	3	0	0	130
2.5	7	1	1	120
25	8	1	0	170
9	9	1	0	90
8	6	0	0	120
1.5	7	0	0	120
20	22	5	37	110
1.5	2	0	0	180
14	15	4	0	120
2	5	1	0	120
2	8	0	0	120
9 ± 8	9 ± 5	2 ± 2	7 ± 12	128 ± 27

Partial response was defined as a ≥30% reduction from baseline plus a final HDRS score >10, whereas nonresponders had a reduction <30% from their pretreatment HDRS score (30). Changes in HDRS ratings for the entire group were analyzed by Wilcoxon sign ranks nonparametric test, and changes in physiological measurements were analyzed using a two-tailed paired t-test.

RESULTS

Efficacy

Overall, HDRS scores decreased from 24 ± 5 (range 20–37) to 10 ± 8 (range 4–30) ($z = 3.2, p = 0.001$) at a mean (± SD) daily tranylcypromine dose of 128 ± 27 mg. Seven of 14 subjects (50%) who were previously resistant to an average of nine prior treatments had a complete response, and 3 patients (21%) had a partial response to treatment. Daily tranylcypromine doses for the responders ranged from 90 mg to 130 mg with a mean (±SD) daily dose of 113 ± 14 mg. In contrast, the 4 patients who failed to respond received daily doses ranging from 120 mg to 180 mg (with a mean ±SD of 160 ± 27 mg) for at least 3 weeks. Therapeutic outcome did not appear to be related to the duration of the present episode or to the number of prior treatments.

Adverse Effects

The most frequently reported side effects are shown in Table 2. Four subjects discontinued treatment because of adverse effects. Overall, every patient experienced some mild side effects, and 10 experienced moderate or severe side effects. Although none of the adverse reactions were life threatening and no tyramine reactions were observed, several patients did experience significant events that required discontinuation of treatment. Specifically, patient 1 electively discontinued her dose of 120 mg because of a 28 pound weight gain, patient 2 experienced a single episode of postmicturational syncope at 170 mg, patient 11 experienced an acute confusional state with confabulation and visual hallucinations at 180 mg, and patient 12 had a serotonergic crisis after combining 120 mg of tranylcypromine with 4 g of L-tryptophan (after discontinuing the study protocol for partial response).

The most frequent side effects were sympatholytic (e.g., lightheadedness, impotence, urinary tract symptoms), adrenergic (e.g., sweating, palpitations, insomnia),

TABLE 2. Number of patients reporting side effects to high dose tranylcypromine

Side effect	Mild	Moderate/severe
Sympatholytic		
Lightheadedness/syncope	8	4
Urinary tract	2	1
Impotence	1	2
Flushed/dry mouth	3	—
Blurred vision	2	—
Gastrointestinal		
Weight gain/truncal obesity	2	3
Carbohydrate craving	1	1
Nausea/diarrhea	3	—
Adrenergic		
Sweating/palpitations	6	—
Tremor/ataxia	3	—
Insomnia	7	2
Vivid dreams	—	2
Agitation/headache	4	—
Other		
Tinnitus	2	—
Joint pains	—	1
Sedation	3	1
Slurred speech	1	—
Psychotic reaction	—	1
Hypomania	2	—

and gastrointestinal (e.g., weight gain, carbohydrate craving). The idiosyncratic events (e.g., postmicturational syncope, joint pains, diminished taste perception, confusional state) occurred at higher doses. Interestingly, with the exception of the postmicturational syncope at 170 mg and the confusional state at 180 mg, most autonomic side effects were experienced at low to moderate tranylcypromine doses and diminished or completely disappeared at higher doses. Although the paucity of side effects at high tranylcypromine doses is intriguing, these data must be interpreted with caution because of the limited sample size and open-label nature of the treatment.

Physiological Measures

Maximum doses of tranylcypromine did not appear to produce any significant changes in the mean resting (sitting) or orthostatic (standing) blood pressure and pulse rate measurements when compared to pretreatment values (Table 3).

There was a statistically significant decrease in the mean sitting systolic ($p = 0.002$) and diastolic ($p < 0.001$) blood pressure, as well as in the mean standing systolic ($p < 0.001$) and diastolic ($p = 0.006$) blood pressure at moderate tranylcypromine doses (68 ± 26 mg) when compared to baseline measurements (Table 3). Furthermore, at moderate tranylcypromine doses, the sitting systolic ($p = 0.02$) and diastolic ($p = 0.02$) blood pressure and the standing systolic ($p = 0.009$) and diastolic blood pressure ($p = 0.02$) also were significantly lower compared to measurements at maximum dosing (128 ± 27 mg), suggesting a relative normalization of the drug-induced hypotension at high tranylcypromine doses. There were no differences in the mean pulse rate measurements between the various dose range groups. Finally, maximum doses of tranylcypromine did not appear to alter the pretreatment blood chemistry or electrocardiographic values, even in those patients with severe side effects.

TABLE 3. *Mean ± SD blood pressure and pulse at baseline, moderate, and high dose tranylcypromine*

Blood pressure (BP) and pulse	Pretreatment	Moderate dose (mean 68 ± 26 mg)	Maximum dose (mean 128 ± 27 mg)
Sitting			
Systolic	132 ± 22	109 ± 15[a]	124 ± 16
Diastolic	77 ± 7	67 ± 9[b]	77 ± 11
Pulse	80 ± 12	80 ± 7	83 ± 11
Standing			
Systolic	125 ± 15	99 ± 14[c]	117 ± 17
Diastolic	80 ± 11	70 ± 14[d]	79 ± 11
Pulse	84 ± 12	85 ± 10	88 ± 11

[a]Sitting systolic BP at moderate dose is significantly lower than BP at pretreatment ($t=3.5$, $p=0.002$) and at maximum dose ($t=2.8$, $p=0.02$).
[b]Sitting diastolic BP at moderate dose is significantly lower than BP at pretreatment ($t=4/9$, $p=0.0002$) and at maximum dose ($t=3.0$, $p=0.02$).
[c]Standing systolic BP at moderate dose is significantly lower than BP at pretreatment ($t=6.9$, $p=0.00001$) and at maximum dose ($t=3.0$, $p=0.009$).
[d]Standing diastolic BP at moderate dose is significantly lower than BP at pretreatment ($t=3.3$, $p=0.006$) and at maximum dose ($t=2.7$, $p=0.02$).

DISCUSSION

MAOIs usually have been used for patients who prove to be resistant to TCAs (13,16,17). As a consequence, MAO inhibitors were relegated to secondary treatment status. In addition, early clinical trials often reported MAOIs to be less effective than TCAs (13,27,31), although many of these studies used low doses of the MAOI (27,32). Furthermore, therapeutic profiles for MAOI use have been less clearly defined than for other antidepressant treatments (32). Finally, many clinicians have come to view MAOIs as potentially dangerous drugs that must be used with extreme caution (13).

More recently, however, a meta-analysis of prior placebo-controlled studies found MAOIs to be superior to placebo (32). McGrath et al. (33) reported a superior response to phenelzine versus imipramine in a double-blind, placebo-controlled, crossover design trial in patients resistant to prior TCA treatment. These data suggest that many patients who are TCA nonresponders might be more likely to benefit from a trial of an MAOI compared to retreatment with another TCA. Furthermore, the combination of a TCA and MAOI also has been reported to be more effective than either drug alone (13,16,17) and, with the exception of combining clomipramine and tranylcypromine, may represent a safe alternative in TCA nonresponders (34).

Several recent case reports have suggested that higher than conventional doses of the MAOI tranylcypromine may be a safe and effective treatment for refractory depression (30,35–38). Robinson (30) described a patient with refractory depression who responded at 90 mg of tranylcypromine, whereas Guze et al. (36) and Pearlman (37) described 3 refractory patients who required tranylcypromine doses ranging from 100 mg to 200 mg daily. Interestingly, side effects were uncommon in these patients, and blood pressures remained in the normotensive range.

We previously reported the use of tranylcypromine ranging from 90 mg to 170 mg in seven refractory depressed patients who had failed to respond to at least three prior treatment regiments (Table 1, patients 1–7) (38). Four of seven (57%) had a complete response at a mean daily tranylcypromine dose of 112 ± 16 mg.

In the present study, which extends our

initial sample size, we observed a complete response in 7 of 14 (50%) patients at a mean daily tranylcypromine dose of 113 ± 14 mg (range 90 mg–130 mg). We observed no evidence of hepatotoxicity, although 2 patients did experience an acute confusional episode, and 1 had an episode of postmicturational syncope. For the most part, the patients remained compliant with a fairly restrictive dietary regimen, and as a consequence we observed no tyramine or cheese reactions.

Most adverse effects referrable to functional changes in the autonomic nervous system (e.g., hypotension, impotence, insomnia) were observed at moderate tranylcypromine doses (68 ± 26 mg) and appeared to diminish at maximum (128 ± 27 mg) doses. One possible explanation for this phenomenon could be that at higher plasma concentrations of tranylcypromine, the inherent sympathomimetic (amphetamine-like) activity of the drug overrides the sympatholytic activity of MAO enzyme inhibition. This possibility also may explain, in part, why patients refractory to conventional doses of tranylcypromine respond at higher doses.

In this trial, we specifically chose patients suffering from resistant depression as defined by the most stringent criteria (21). Treatment approaches to patients with this degree of refractory depression have received little systematic attention, in part, because of ethical considerations of treating severely depressed patients in placebo-controlled trials, as well as the difficulty of recruiting large samples sizes of therapy-resistant patients to participate in research studies. As a consequence, rigorously controlled drug studies in refractory depression are uncommon and difficult to perform. Although carefully documented open-label trials can yield important clinical information, caution should be used when applying treatments from uncontrolled studies. In this regard, we examined only a modest sample size, which lacked a parallel placebo group, and this factor places constraints on the conclusions that can be drawn about the specific drug efficacy. Furthermore, we did not measure plasma concentrations of tranylcypromine or percent changes in MAO enzyme inhibition during treatment, and these factors placed limits on our ability to explain the underlying mechanisms of high dose tranylcypromine efficacy in refractory depression.

In conclusion, the substantial response rate to high doses of tranlycypromine in a group of therapy-resistant depressed patients is of obvious clinical importance. In addition, the favorable side effects profile for this treatment approach strengthens its potential usefulness as a promising therapy for resistant depression. We would encourage the performance of larger, placebo-controlled studies in order to assess more fully the potential benefit of high dose tranylcypromine therapy for refractory depression.

ACKNOWLEDGMENTS

This work was supported by funds from the Jack Warsaw Fund for Research in Biological Psychiatry. The author acknowledges the contribution of Neil Berwish, M.D., and Larry Potter, B.A., in the performance of this study, and to Ms. Kathryn Pochi, B.A., for her assistance in the preparation of this manuscript.

REFERENCES

1. Bennett IF. Is there a superior antidepressant? In: Garattini S, Duke MNG, eds. *Antidepressant drugs: Excerpta Medica International Congress Series #122,* Amsterdam: Excerpta Medica, 1967.
2. Thase ME, Kupfer DJ. Characteristics of treatment-resistant depression. In: Zohar J, Belmaker RH, eds. *Treating resistant depression.* New York: PMA Publishing Corp, 1987;23–45.
3. Anath J, Ruskin R. Treatment of intractable depression. *Int Pharmacopsychiatry* 1974;9: 218–229.
4. Asberg M, Cronholm B, Sjoqvist F, Tuck D. Relationship between plasma levels and therapeutic effects of nortriptyline. *Br Med J* 1971;3:331–334.
5. Glassman AH, Perel JM, Shostak M, Kantor S,

Fleiss J. Clinical implications of imipramine plasma levels for depressive illness. *Arch Gen Psychiatry* 1977;34:197–204.
6. Amsterdam JD, Brunswick DJ, Mendels J. The clinical application of tricyclic antidepressant pharmacokinetics and plasma levels. *Am J Psychiatry* 1980;137:653–662.
7. Brunswick DJ, Amsterdam JD, Potter L, Caroff S, Rickels K. Relationship between tricyclic antidepressant plasma levels and clinical response in patients treated with desipramine or doxepine. *Acta Psychiatr Scand* 1983;67:371–377.
8. Aberg-Wistedt A, Jostell KG, Ross SB, Westerlund D. Effects of zimelidine and desipramine on serotonin and noradrenaline uptake mechanisms in relation to plasma concentrations and to therapeutic effects during treatment of depression. *Psychopharmacology* 1981;74:297–304.
9. Alexanderson B, Evans DAP, Sjoqvist F. Steady-state plasma levels of nortriptyline in twins: Influence of genetic factors and drug therapy. *Br Med J* 1969;4:764–768.
10. Asberg M. Treatment of depression with tricyclic drugs—Pharmacokinetic and pharmacodynamic aspects. *Pharmakopsychiatr Neuropsychopharmakol* 1976;9:18–26.
11. Ziegler VE, Biggs JT. Tricyclic plasma levels—Effects of age, race, sex and smoking. *JAMA* 1977;238:2167–2169.
12. Maas JW, Davis J, Hanen I, et al. Pretreatment neurotransmitter metabolites in response to imipramine and amitriptyline treatment. *Psychol Med* 1982;12:37–43.
13. Shawcross C, Tyrer P. The place of monoamine oxidase inhibitors in the treatment of resisting depression. In: Zohar J, Belmaker RH, eds. *Treating resistant depression.* New York: PMA Publishing Corp, 1987;113–129.
14. Goodwin FK, Prange AJ Jr, Post RM, Muscattola C, Lipton MA. L-Triiodothyronine converts tricyclic antidepressant nonresponders to responders. *Am J Psychiatry* 1982;139:334–338.
15. Joyce PR, Hewland HR, Jones AV. Rapid response to lithium in treatment-resistant depression. *Br J Psychiatry* 1983;142:204–205.
16. Sethna ER. A study of refractory cases of depressive illness and their response to combined antidepressant treatment. *Br J Psychiatry* 1974;124:265–271.
17. Davidson J, McLeod M, Law-Yone B, Linnoila M. A comparison of electroconvulsive therapy and combined phenelzine-amitriptyline in refractory depression. *Arch Gen Psychiatry* 1978;35:639–642.
18. Stern SL, Mendels J. Drug combinations in the treatment of refractory depression: A review. *J Clin Psychiatry* 1981;42:368–373.
19. Feighner JP, Herbstein J, Damlouji N. Combination MAOI, TCA, and direct stimulant therapy of treatment-resistant depression. *J Clin Psychiatry* 1985;46:206–209.
20. de Montigny C, Corunoyer G, Morissette R, Langlois R, Caille R. Lithium carbonate addition in tricyclic antidepressant-resistant unipolar depression. *Arch Gen Psychiatry* 1983;40:1337–1344.
21. Amsterdam JD, Berwish N. Treatment of refractory depression with combination reserpine and tricyclic antidepressant therapy. *J Clin Psychopharmacol* 1987;7:238–242.
22. Berwish NJ, Amsterdam JD. An overview of investigational antidepressants. *Psychosomatics* 1989;30:1–18.
23. Zis AP, Goodwin FK. Novel antidepressants and the biogenic amine hypothesis of depression. The case of iprindol and mianserin. *Arch Gen Psychiatry* 1979;36:1097–1107.
24. Lecrubier Y, Puech AJ, Jouvent R, Simon P, Widlocher D. A β-adrenergic stimulant salbutamol vs chlorimipramine in depression. A controlled study. *Br J Psychiatry* 1980;136:354–358.
25. Amsterdam JD, Kaplan M, Potter L, Bloom L, Rickels K. Adinazolam, a new triazolobenzodiazepine, and imipramine in the treatment of major depressive disorder. *Psychopharmacology* 1986;88:484–488.
26. Fink M. ECT: A last resort treatment for resistant depression? In: Zohar J, Belmaker RH, eds. *Treating resistant depression.* New York: PMA Publishing Corp, 1987;163–173.
27. Tyrer P. Towards rational treatment with monoamine oxidase inhibitors. *Br J Psychiatry* 1976;128:354–360.
28. American Psychiatric Association Committee on Nomenclature and Statistics. *Diagnostic and statistical manual on mental disorders,* 3rd ed. Washington DC: American Psychiatric Association, 1980.
29. Hamilton M. A rating scale for depression. *J Neurol Neurosurg Psychiatry* 1960;23:56–62.
30. Robinson DS. High dose monoamine inhibitor therapy. *JAMA* 1983;250:2212.
31. Quitkin F, Rifkin A, Klein DF. Monoamine oxidase inhibitors. A review of antidepressant effectiveness. *Arch Gen Psychiatry* 1979;35:749–760.
32. Davis JM, Janicak PG, Bruninga K. The efficacy of MAO inhibitors in depression: A meta-analysis. *Psychiatr Ann* 1987;17:825–831.
33. McGrath PJ, Stewart JW, Harrison W, Quitkin FM. Treatment of tricyclic refractory depression with a monoamine oxidase inhibitor antidepressant. *Psychopharmacol Bull* 1987;23:169–172.
34. Oefele KV, Grohmann R, Ruther E. Adverse drug reactions in combined tricyclic and MAOI therapy. *Pharmacopsychiatry* 1986;19:243–244.
35. Shopsin B, Kline NS. Monoamine oxidase inhibitors: Potential for drug abuse. *Biol Psychiatry* 1976;11:451–456.
36. Guze BH, Baxter LR Jr. Refractory depression treated with high doses of a monoamine oxidase inhibitor. *J Clin Psychiatry* 1987;48:31–32.
37. Pearlman C. High dose tranylcypromine in refractory depression. *J Clin Psychiatry* 1987;48:424–433.
38. Amsterdam JD, Berwish NJ. High dose tranylcypromine therapy in refractory depression. *Pharmacopsychiatry* 1989;22:21–25.

15

Treatment-Resistant Bipolar Affective Disorder: Phenomenological Characteristics, Pathophysiological Mechanisms, and Novel Therapies

Richard L. Hauger, Michael R. Irwin, Renee M. Dupont, and Demitri F. Papolos

The division of pathological affective states into the opposite polarities of mania and melancholia and the reciprocal relationship between these phases of bipolar disorder have been recognized since antiquity. In the nineteenth century, French psychiatrists first defined a distinct cyclical affective disorder alternating between pathological mood states of opposite polarity. However, many years passed before the concept of circular or cyclic folly was expanded into the affective syndrome of manic-depressive insanity by the German psychiatrist Emil Kraepelin in his 1921 landmark study (1). Kraepelin's broad concept of bipolar affective disorder as an endogenous, recurrent mood and rate disorder consisting of manic "excitability" and depressive "inhibition" phases encompassed many forms of major affective illness, including all clinical manias, most depressive states, periodic and circular psychoses, character psychopathology if a significant mood disturbance was present, and affective delirious states (amentia).

In 1957, Karl Leonhard narrowed the boundaries of manic-depressive illness by defining depressive disorders as "bipolar" if a manic episode had been experienced at some point and "unipolar" in the absence of mania (2). This nosological separation of depressive illness into bipolar and unipolar segregates established mania as the central phenomenological discriminator in affective disorders. However, recent studies have emphasized that the recurrent nature of major affective disorders (especially the recurrent form of unipolar depression, which is distinct from nonrecurrent depressive illnesses) had not been fully recognized in the United States (3–5). This situation was the result of a too rigid application of Leonhard's definition of nonbipolar depression as any mood disorder that could not be formally defined as the full syndrome of classic manic-depressive illness.

Over the past 15 years, the limits of manic-depressive illness have gradually reverted to Kraepelin's original concept. For example, depression is now defined as bipolar on the basis of the intensity and duration of past manic episodes (3–7). In this nomenclature, bipolar I disorder is present if at least one overt mania has been expressed. If the expression of manic symptoms has been less intense and for brief periods, the manic-depressive syndrome is defined as bipolar II. Although this latter

---

Department of Psychiatry, University of California San Diego, La Jolla, CA 92161.
The work described herein was done as part of our employment with the federal government and is therefore in the public domain.

distinction has been controversial, recent studies have supported the hypothesis that certain forms of bipolar II syndrome are separate from bipolar I on the basis of a distinct relapse pattern. For example, only 4% of bipolar II patients experience a frank manic episode over 2 years, whereas 43% of bipolar I patients become manic during the same period (8,9). Bipolar II disorder, however, does not differ from bipolar I with respect to the number of depressive recurrences based on evidence that both syndromes have a similar propensity for multiple episodes of major depression (8,9).

The return to the Kraepelinian view has led also to the inclusion of mild cases of affective dysregulation, disorders of temperament, and recurrent depression in the bipolar spectrum (10–12). These soft bipolar illnesses include not only recurrent major depression with a family history of classic bipolar disorder (bipolar III) but also the interconnected syndromes of subaffective dysthymia (chronic dysthymia, hypersomnia, and Schneiderian depressive character traits), irritability temperament (mixed states of subsyndromic depression and hypomania), cyclothymic temperament (recurrent, brief cycles of hypomania and subsyndromic depression), and hyperthymia (frequent episodes of subsyndromic hypomania, chronically decreased need for sleep, and Schneiderian hypomanic character traits). Hypomania in soft bipolar illnesses usually is induced by tricyclic antidepressants (TCAs), whereas the depressive phase has a seasonal pattern of relapse with a lesser magnitude and duration (10–12). It has also been suggested that the newly identified syndrome of "seasonal affective disorder" may be another subclinical variant of bipolar illness (13). However, recent work has indicated that the majority of patients with winter depressions do not experience hypomania or mania or have a family history of bipolar illness (14,15).

The cited studies emphasize that the presence of a bipolar diathesis is a crucial determinant of the course of affective illness and the responses to antidepressant and antimanic therapies, even when this vulnerability is only expressed as manic symptomatology of the smallest intensity and duration or as a family history of bipolarity. Although lithium therapy is highly efficacious in classic bipolar I disorder, 20 to 30% of bipolar patients with good compliance do not respond to lithium prophylaxis against affective relapse (7,16–20). Manic-depressive illness also is associated with a high risk for suicide, which becomes greater in the setting of refractory bipolar depression. Therefore, it is imperative that current therapeutic approaches be improved significantly. The revised typology for manic-depressive illness is leading to a more accurate phenomenology of treatment-resistant bipolar affective disorders and the development of more specific pharmacotherapies. This chapter focuses on recent research into pathophysiological mechanisms and new therapies for treatment-resistant bipolar disorder.

PHENOMENOLOGY OF LITHIUM PROPHYLAXIS AND LITHIUM-RESISTANT BIPOLAR DEPRESSION

Antidepressant and Prophylactic Effects of Lithium

Lithium therapy has been firmly established as an effective antidepressant treatment for bipolar depression because of its ability to reduce the incidence of an affective relapse (17,19–22). Earlier studies recommended lithium prophylaxis if bipolar patients had experienced two or more episodes within the past 2 years. However, this criterion excluded too many bipolars who benefit from lithium maintenance therapy. In 1981, Angst proposed that the risk of two affective relapses over the next 5 years in an actively ill bipolar patient was sufficient criterion for initiating lithium prophylaxis (23). The 1985 NIMH Consensus Conference has now recommended even more frequent use of lithium prophylaxis in bipolar illness (21).

Important determinants of lithium responsivity are a past history of a therapeutic effect of lithium and a positive family history for bipolar illness (18,24–26). A role for familial and genetic factors in therapeutic responses to lithium is supported by a high concordance rate for lithium responsivity in bipolar monozygote and dizygotic twins (27,28). A family history of psychotic depression (possibly due to the genetic link between bipolar disorder and certain forms of psychotic and delusional depression) and suicide in a first degree relative may also predict positive prophylactic responses on lithium (24,29). Akiskal has emphasized that an early age of onset, a sudden emergence of affective symptoms in a bipolar episode, a family history of bipolar illness, and psychotic features in a patient's first depressive episode prognosticate positive lithium responses (10–12).

Lithium Response in Bipolar Subtypes

Kukopulos et al. have classified the course of the bipolar disorder as follows: (a) mania-depression-free interval (MDI) course (mania, often severe, begins the bipolar cycle followed by usually a moderate depression and then a euthymic period), (b) depression-mania-free interval (DMI) (initial depressive phase, which can be severe, followed by switch into mania or hypomania, often very rapid, and then a free interval), (c) irregular (IRR) (no regular affective sequence in the cycle), and (d) continuous circular (CC) (episodes of depression and mania or hypomania alternate without any free intervals) (30–32). The best suppression of affective episodes by lithium was observed in the MDI course. Four additional studies have confirmed these findings of a high response rate (approximately 90%) to lithium in the MDI form of bipolar I and II disorder (18,24,33–35).

The poorest response to lithium prophylaxis was in the CC bipolar patients, many of whom were rapid cyclers (30–32). Only 33% of the DMI bipolars (the majority being bipolar II) had a good response to lithium prophylaxis (30–32). Lithium resistance probably resulted from the induction of a postdepressive hypomania by antidepressant treatment during the depressive phase. Therefore, excellent acute antimanic responses and affective prophylaxis to lithium occur in bipolars with the following cycle sequence: mania, depressive phase, and then a euthymic interval. The opposite cycling pattern of depression followed by a switch into mania can be found in lithium nonresponders.

Antidepressant therapy in DMI bipolars promotes treatment-resistant cycling (30–32,36). However, antidepressants may be beneficial in the postmanic depression of MDI bipolars. The rates of mania are not increased by imipramine treatment of depression-prone bipolar I patients on lithium maintenance (37,38). In contrast, remitted bipolar I patients with mania-proneness exhibit more frequent manic relapses on imipramine. Therefore, one should refrain from the use of antidepressants in the premanic depression of DMI bipolars. Lithium nonresponders in the DMI subtype may be converted to lithium responders following withdrawal from antidepressant medication (36,39,40).

Lithium Therapy and Treatment-Resistant Rapid Cycling

Rapid cycling bipolars exhibit the highest incidence of lithium nonresponsiveness (7,30–32,36,39,41). The continuous circular course of bipolar illness can be divided as follows: (a) bipolars with a high frequency of affective relapses (≥ two depressive or hypomanic recurrences per year) and (b) bipolars who have continuous but long affective states (e.g., one prolonged cycle of depression and hypomania over 1 year without any intervening period of euthymia) (30–32). In general, a good lithium response occurs when manias last longer than 3 months, followed by a brief depression. Bipolars with more rapid cycling into and out of hypomania/mania (e.g., manic episodes less than 3 months) have poor responses to lithium, regardless of the length of the depressive episodes. These findings indicate that brief manic intervals, but not short depressions, predict lithium-resistant bipolar illness.

A crucial mechanism generating rapid cycling may be the switch into a postdepressive hypomania caused by TCA therapy followed by tricyclic-induced acceleration of cycling (30–32,36,40). The increased cycling would then decrease the length of manic phases to less than 3 months, a situation noted previously to be treatment-resistant. Therefore, tricyclics should not be used to treat depression in bipolars at risk for rapid cycling. If the pre-rapid cycling course was characterized by mania preceding (but not following) depression, antidepressants should be discontinued and a full trial of lithium instituted. It should be remembered that Schou first demonstrated the antidepressant action of lithium in a bipolar patient experiencing more than 10 affective episodes per year (20,42). The importance of a therapeutic lithium trial in rapid cyclers off antidepressants is further emphasized by reports that lithium can be therapeutic in patients with a 48-hour periodic psychosis (20,43,44).

Lithium can cause subclinical or clinical hypothyroidism. This antithyroid effect of lithium can lead to the development of treatment-resistant depression or to overt rapid cycling (45,46). Since treatment with lithium and thyroxine, especially in the setting of thyroid hypofunction, can be beneficial in rapid cyclers, thyroid hormone supplementation may convert lithium-insensitive rapid cyclers to lithium responders (45,46). Small increases in basal TSH secretion or increased TSH responses to TRH can be used as indices for thyroid therapy in bipolar disorder. However, thyroid supplementation must be used cautiously, since thyroid hormones can induce mania and have adverse cardiovascular effects.

A paradoxical increase in the frequency of affective episodes can occur infrequently in bipolars receiving lithium. Lithium resistance also can result from the rare situation of lithium-induced rapid cycling (46,47). Another cause of the induction of mania is the addition of lithium to potentiate TCA trial (48). This situation provides another example how tricyclic therapy can nullify the therapeutic effect of lithium in bipolars. However, lithium added to an antipsychotic–antidepressant regimen has been reported to augment antidepressant action in bipolars with a refractory psychotic depression (49). The combined use of lithium, neuroleptic, and antidepressant has little therapeutic effect in unipolar psychotic depressives (49).

PHENOMENOLOGY AND TREATMENT OF LITHIUM-RESISTANT MANIA

Antimanic Effects of Lithium

A series of open lithium trials and four placebo-controlled, double-blind studies have conclusively established the following: (a) lithium possesses a specific antimanic action in bipolar patients, (b) the general response rate to lithium in bipolars is 70 to 80%, (c) the antimanic effect of lithium is delayed, usually requiring 6 to 10 days of lithium therapy during acute mania, and (d) lithium exhibits a high degree of antimanic prophylaxis when administered continuously to bipolars (4,19,20,50–53). However, the 20 to 30% of acutely manic patients who fail to respond to lithium and bipolar patients who are insensitive to lithium prophylaxis constitute a significant population of treatment-resistant bipolar illness.

Phenomenological Predictors of Lithium-Resistant Manic States

Early studies on lithium efficacy have indicated that a positive antimanic response to lithium is associated with classic mood-congruent manic symptoms, including euphoric and elated mood, flight of ideas, pressure of speech, accelerated psychomotor rate, and grandiose ideation even when delusional (4,54). A poor response to lithium has been observed in bipolars with a predominant mood of dysphoria rather than euphoria, incomplete auditory hallucinations, some degree of formal thought disorder, high scores on rating scales for "destructiveness" and paranoia, and a premorbid constitution of depressive withdrawal (4,54).

The Role of Cyclothymia in Treatment-Resistant Bipolar Disorder

Although the premorbid character of certain lithium responders can be cyclothymic, Kraepelin had earlier noted a poor course of illness in manic-depressives with an intrinsic cyclothymic temperament (1). A recent study has shown that the presence of cyclothymic swings in bipolar illness, schizophrenia, and nonaffective/nonpsychotic psychiatric disorders is associated with a poor response to treatment (55). This finding suggests that subaffective cyclothymic mood swings may reflect excessive CNS responsiveness to stressful stimuli.

Treatment Outcome in Mania with Psychotic Features

In a landmark review, Pope and Lipinski reexamined lithium responsivity in bipolars with schizophrenic-like psychotic symptoms (e.g., schizoaffectives) versus classic bipolar manics (56). They found no difference in the lithium responses of good-prognosis schizoaffective patients compared to classic bipolars. In fact, they discovered that first rank symptoms were present in 20 to 40% of acute manic episodes. Other studies have observed that mood-incongruent psychotic symptoms (e.g., grandiose, paranoid, and/or bizarre delusions, auditory or visual hallucinations) present in young bipolar I patients during the course of their illness were associated with longer remissions on lithium maintenance therapy (57). Therefore, bipolars who develop psychotic manias may be more lithium-sensitive than the 30% of bipolar I patients who never experience psychotic symptoms (57,58).

The prevalence of narrowly defined formal thought disorder in mania has been investigated recently. In general, flight of ideas is the most common manic ideation, and formal thought disorder is rare. The infrequent manic patients exhibiting formal thought disorder have an earlier age of bipolar onset, mood lability, denudative behaviors, catatonic symptoms, and higher schizophrenia scores (e.g., delusions of persecution, auditory hallucinations and first rank symptoms) (59). These findings suggest that mania with formal thought disorder is a more severe form of bipolar disorder. Nevertheless, the treatment response for mania with formal thought disorder is similar to mania without thought disorder, and the treatment outcome for both forms of mania is significantly better than a schizophrenia episode during an index admission (59).

Frank psychotic symptoms, such as auditory hallucinations, formal thought disorder, Schneiderian first rank symptoms, and catatonic features (i.e., posturing and negativism), can occur in manic episodes that are lithium-responsive (4,6,12). However, poverty of speech content and vagueness in a patient's ideation do appear to discriminate acute schizophrenia episodes from mania. Conversely, patients who exhibit emotional blunting in the context of a full manic syndrome follow a course of illness resembling schizophrenia (60). Mania with emotional blunting has a poor response to lithium and requires the addition of a neuroleptic at high doses for a therapeutic effect.

The Adjunctive Use of Neuroleptics with Lithium in Treatment-Resistant Mania

A dopaminergic mechanism for mania has been proposed previously (61). Dopamine-active psychostimulants, such as amphetamine, and the dopamine agonist bromocriptine can precipitate mania in bipolars (61–64). Conversely, the inhibition of the dopamine-synthesizing enzyme tyrosine hydroxylase with α-methyl-p-tyrosine reduces mania (65). The reduction of neuronal norepinephrine stores by dopamine β-hydroxylase inhibition has no antimanic effect (66). In contrast, the depletion of dopamine by reserpine can produce behavioral sedation and depression (4,64,67).

In a comprehensive review of neuroleptic therapy in bipolar disorder, the phenothiazine chlorpromazine was found to decrease psychomotor hyperactivity more rapidly than lithium, consistent with dopamine's important regulatory effect on psychomotor behavior (68). Lithium, however, was specific for normalizing manic ideation and stabilizing mood (68). The butyrophenone haloperidol has a more accelerated effect on manic psychosis and agitation, consistent with haloperidol's higher affinity for brain dopaminergic D_2 receptors. A substantial reduction in acute manic symptoms was produced by the specific dopamine receptor antagonist pimozide in bipolar I patients with high CSF HVA levels (69). This antimanic response, which occurred within 2 to 5 days, was more rapid than pimozide's antipsychotic effects. Conversely, the augmentation of dopaminergic neurotransmission by amphetamine or the dopamine receptor agonist piribedil can induce mania that rapidly responds to pimozide (62,69). It is interesting to note that poor antidepressant responses to piribedil occur in patients with high basal levels of CSF HVA (62,70).

Therefore, rapid control of extreme psychomotor hyperactivity or nonaffective delusions in mania can be accomplished by the addition of neuroleptics to lithium therapy until the antimanic effect of lithium emerges. However, the chronic administration of neuroleptics in bipolars should be avoided, since patients with affective disorders are at the highest risk for the development of tardive dyskinesia (71). Often, neuroleptic doses are increased in treatment-resistant bipolar disorder in the hopes of producing an antimanic response in a refractory manic psychosis. The risk of neuroleptic malignant syndrome is high in these situations where antipsychotics are added to a regimen of multiple psychotropic medications in treatment-resistant bipolars.

Neuroleptic therapy has been associated with depressive episodes refractory to lithium (31,32). It has been proposed that rapid cyclers may improve on a regimen of lithium and neuroleptics following antidepressant discontinuation. Other studies have observed more severe and prolonged depressions following antipsychotic administration to manic bipolars (31). The combination of lithium with carbamazepine or lithium with valproic acid has already been successful in rapid cyclers (39). The addition of the anticonvulsants carbamazepine or valproic acid to lithium would be preferable to a lithium–neuroleptic regimen for acute antimanic and maintenance therapy of manic psychosis and treatment-resistant bipolar illness.

Novel Therapies for Mania and Bipolar Prophylaxis

Antimanic Effects of Clonazepam

The addition of clonazepam to a lithium regimen is beneficial when increased sedation and sleep are required during the slow onset of lithium's acute antimanic action (39,72). Clonazepam alone can also reduce manic symptoms in nonpsychotic bipolars who cannot tolerate lithium or who are lithium nonresponders (39,72–75). However, clonazepam does not appear to be an effective treatment for recurrent psychotic mania, bipolars with delusional depression, psychotic mixed mania, or rapid cycling (39,75). The efficacy of clonazepam in lithium-resistant, nonpsychotic mania may be related to its very high affinity for central benzodiazepine receptors (76). Clonazepam may also stabilize mood by enhancing lithium's facilitation of serotonergic neurotransmission, an effect that does not involve inhibition of presynaptic serotonin reuptake or any interaction at postsynaptic 5HT receptors (75). Clonazepam's antimanic action could also be mediated by its anticonvulsant and antikindling effects. Clonazepam's hypnotic properties would abolish the progressive sleep deprivation during the evolution of a manic episode. Sleep loss may be an important generator of mania (77). In contrast to clonazepam's action at the central GABA–benzodiazepine–chloride ionophore complex, carbamazepine preferentially interacts at "peripheral-type" benzodiazepine receptors (76).

The Use of Spironolactone for Antimanic Maintenance Therapy

Spironolactone is a competitive antagonist of the biological response to mineralocorticoids via its binding to aldosterone receptor sites to form an inactive receptor complex that cannot attach to nuclear acceptor sites. The presence of ^{3}H-spironolactone uptake in the hypothalamus suggests that this drug acts at mineralocorticoid sites in the CNS (78). Over 10 years ago, an open study demonstrated that spironolactone was an effective maintenance therapy in six lithium-responsive bipolar patients who were changed to 100 mg/day of spironolactone because of lithium-induced side effects (78). Over the next 1 ½ years, these bipolar patients did not experience any manic recurrences during spironolactone therapy. Spironolactone also may prove to be beneficial in treatment-resistant bipolar illness.

STRUCTURAL BRAIN ABNORMALITIES AND TREATMENT-RESISTANT BIPOLAR AFFECTIVE DISORDER

Cerebral Ventricular Size

Ventricular enlargement and abnormal attenuation values in subcortical regions have been measured in bipolar patients using pneumoencephalography and computed tomography (CT) (79–81). Pathologically enlarged cerebral ventricles in bipolar disorder have been associated with an older age at the onset of affective illness, the presence of delusions, and other "positive" psychotic symptoms during the depressive state, increased frequency of affective relapses requiring hospitalization, and psychosocial deterioration. Other studies have not observed a correlation between high VBR values and these treatment-resistant parameters (82).

Cerebral atrophy and ventricular dilation can also occur during Cushing's syndrome and corticosteroid therapy (83). Prolonged exposure of the CNS to high levels of glucocorticoids has been associated with the loss of neurons in the hippocampus (84). Since abnormally high levels of urinary free cortisol over a 24-hour period and nonsuppression of cortisol secretion after 1 mg of dexamethasone have been demonstrated in bipolars with increased ventricular size, neurotoxicity from cortisol hypersecretion may contribute to the development of treatment-resistant affective states (85,86).

Brain Changes Measured by Magnetic Resonance Imaging

The inconsistent CT findings in affective disorders may have resulted from methodological problems. Recent work has examined structural brain changes in bipolar disorder with magnetic resonance imaging (MRI), a method superior to CT because of its increased contrast resolution and ability to detect small structural abnormalities. We

TABLE 1. Description of clinical variables in bipolar and normal subjects[a]

	Bipolars with normal MRI	Bipolars with abnormal MRI	Controls
Age (years)	37 ± 10[b]	36 ± 10	41 ± 10
Age of onset (years)	25 ± 7.5	26 ± 6.9	—
Number of hospitalizations	2.0 ± 2.0	3.7 ± 1.2*	—
Hospitalization with history of psychosis	70 ± 48%	78 ± 44%	—
Neuroleptic use[c]	0.8 ± 0.8	1.2 ± 0.97	—
Hamilton Rating Scale for Depression	8.3 ± 7.2	13.8 ± 6.9**	0.7 ± 0.7**

[a]From refs. 87, 88.
[b]Mean ± SD.
[c]0, no use; 1, 6 months or less; 2, more than 6 months; 3, long-term use.
*$p<0.05$ vs bipolar patients with normal MRI scan.
**$p<0.10$ vs bipolar patients with normal MRI scan.

have demonstrated the presence of small subcortical signal hyperintensities on MRI in 9 of 20 bipolars with no past history of significant medical illnesses, substance abuse, or head injury (Table 1) (87,88). One bipolar, a 26-year-old graduate student, had an arachnoid cyst displacing the left temporal lobe. Clinically, such hyperintensities are seen in a number of pathological states, such as cerebral ischemia, multiple sclerosis, and inflammatory disease. However, the MRI abnormalities in the bipolars were not correlated with age and did not appear to be caused by known arteriosclerotic vessel disease (87,88). In fact, some of the bipolar patients with subcortical signal hyperintensities on MRI were the youngest in age.

Although the cause is not clear, it is evident that these abnormalities were correlated in post hoc analyses with increased numbers of hospitalizations, increased depression rating scales, and a trend toward impairment on tests of recall memory (Table 1) (87,88). A significant correlation between high VBR measures and subcortical leukoencephalopathy recently has been established. The persistent increases in depressive symptoms suggest that bipolars with MRI abnormalities will have a higher incidence of dysphoric mood and mixed affective psychopathology.

These structural abnormalities may represent the end of a continuum of a process affecting all bipolar patients or may delineate a subgroup of treatment-resistant bipolar patients. Since structural abnormalities also can be detected in chronic schizophrenics who are refractory to neuroleptics, these changes may be a general predictor of treatment resistance and mental deterioration in psychiatric illness. Ventricular enlargement in chronic schizophrenics has been associated with "negative symptoms," whereas "positive" (i.e., psychotic) symptoms can occur in patients with affective disorders and increased VBR (86). Therefore, brain changes in subcortical and ventricular structures may have a different influence on the course of bipolar illness compared to schizophrenia.

TREATMENT-RESISTANT ASPECTS OF MIXED AFFECTIVE STATES AND DYSPHORIC MANIA

Phenomenological Characteristics

Transitional Affective Symptoms in Classic Bipolar States

Kraepelin first described the presence of mixed states in bipolar episodes, which he regarded as having a relatively poor prognosis. He noted that anxiety, typical symptoms of depression, such as "ideas of sin and persecution," and "hypochondriacal delusions," could be present in "depressive mania," and bipolar depressives could manifest flight of ideas (1). Later studies recorded transient periods of tearfulness, depression, and suicidal ideation at the peak of mania (12,58,89). Affective lability and racing thoughts can occur also during the switch from mania to a typical bipolar depressive state of hypersomnia and psychomotor retardation (12,89,90). With regard to the presence of racing thoughts, the classic manic symptom of increased rate of thinking often can occur in depression but is found rarely in schizophrenic patients (90). Although more than 60% of bipolar patients can experience such transitional affective states, true mixed affective states, dysphoric mania, and extreme rapid cycling are rare.

Mixed Affective States

The coalescence in mixed affective states of opposing pathological mood polarities has been reported to be present in approximately 30% of bipolars in a typical mood disorders clinic. Mixed states generally have a poor treatment outcome because of the high incidence of lithium nonresponsiveness (91–93). Since female manic patients have a higher frequency of depressive symptoms, women who are lithium nonresponders should be examined for the presence of mixed mania. Mixed mania also can be associated with a high incidence of alcohol and sedative abuse, the presence of a superimposed neuropsychiatric illness (e.g., closed head injury, a major neurological disease, perinatal brain injury), and adolescent bipolar illness (between the ages of 12 and 19) (93).

Himmelhoch has divided mixed manic states into Kraepelinian mixed mania and true bipolar illness complicated with comorbidity (91,93). Since the Kraepelinian course for mixed mania involves the merger of anhedonic depression with severe manic states, the bipolar cycle in these patients may be arrested at the switch point from depression to mania. The hypothesis is consistent with the continuum theory that a "depressive core" is at the center of a manic state (94). The Kraepelinian mixed states have a better treatment response than mixed mania, where neuropsychiatric comorbidity has impaired CNS adaptational responses.

Dysphoric Mania

Dysphoric mania (e.g., the presence of high ratings of irritable not euphoric mood, anger, and anxiety during a manic episode) has an incidence of 46% among treatment-refractory bipolars and is associated with poor response to lithium (95). Dysphoric mania can be found frequently in female bipolar patients. However, unlike the typical course of bipolar disorder in women, patients with dysphoric mania have more persistent manic episodes, infrequent affective relapses, and long periods of cycling between mania and depression due to reduced mood switching (95). In dysphoric mania, the depression/mania ratio (e.g., the Bunney-Hamburg scales for global depression rating divided by the mania rating at peak severity) significantly correlates with the depression severity during the manic episode but not with manic severity or the presence of psychosis, anger, or anxiety (95).

Extreme Forms of Rapid Cycling Bipolar Disorder

In the early 1900s, the first reports of extreme rapid cycling appeared, including Bleuler's account of a manic-depressive patient with a 50-hour mood cycle (96). Although this form of rapid cycling is rare, there have been approximately 20 case reports in the world literature describing bipolar disorder characterized by 48-hour cycles of mania and depression and a high incidence of treatment resistance (4,44,96,97). Urinary excretion of 17-hydrocorticosteroids in a female bipolar patient with a 48-hour cycle was lowest over the manic interval and at high levels during depression (44).

Pharmacotherapy for Dysphoric Mania and Mixed Affective States

Carbamazepine

Bipolar patients with dysphoric and anxious manic episodes generally are lithium nonresponders. A positive therapeutic effect of carbamazepine in acute mania has been correlated significantly with very high global ratings of mania, dysphoria, and anxiety, an increased incidence of rapid cycling ($\geq$ 4 episodes/year) in the previous year before admission, and the presence of psychosis (95). Lithium resistance have been demonstrated in patients with dysphoric bipolar syndromes characterized by paroxysmal EEG abnormalities and substance abuse, who later exhibited antimanic responses to carbamazepine (93).

The efficacy of carbamazepine in dysphoric mania may be related to its ability to decrease high levels of CSF NE in acutely manic patients (39,95). In this regard, very high levels of CSF NE have been measured during dysphoric mania (95,98). Antimanic responses to carbamazepine correlate with a large reduction in CSF NE levels. Carbamazepine, which has some degree of antidepressant action, does not alter the lower levels of CSF NE and MHPG in bipolar depression. Therefore, the antidysphoric action of carbamazepine may be mediated by its attenuation of central noradrenergic hyperactivity. Carbamazepine also may augment brain serotonergic neurotransmission and diminish dopaminergic function in the CNS. These pharmacological effects may contribute to carbamazepine's efficacy in certain forms of bipolar disorder (99).

A carbamazepine trial is indicated in bipolar patients with mania proneness or dysphoric mania who are lithium nonresponsive. If lithium nonresponders become well with the addition of carbamazepine, lithium can be withdrawn to evaluate whether a specific carbamazepine response or lithium–carbamazepine synergism has occurred. Although both rapid cyclers and dysphoric manics are lithium-nonresponsive, rapid cycling bipolars experience less manic dysphoria, psychosis, and anxiety (39,95). Rapid cyclers also have more frequent affective episodes than do dysphoric bipolars. These phenomenological differences suggest that lithium-resistant syndromes that are responsive to carbamazepine have different pathophysiology.

Clonidine

Mixed mania is associated also with hyperactivity of central noradrenergic neurons (88,98). The α_2-receptor agonist clonidine can inhibit NE release by acting at presynaptic autoreceptors. Studies have demonstrated antimanic responses to clonidine in lithium-resistant mixed bipolar states (100). Clonidine alone or in combination with lithium or neuroleptics also can be an effective antimanic therapy in other bipolars with acute mania who failed to respond to adequate trials of lithium or antipsychotics (100,101). However, a comparison of clonidine to lithium indicates that lithium possesses more antimanic activity than clonidine in lithium-sensitive bipolar I patients (101).

Neuroendocrine Pathophysiology in Mixed Bipolar Illness and Dysphoric Mania

Hypercortisolism is a frequent neuroendocrine manifestation of endogenous depression (84,102–108). Furthermore, dexamethasone often does not suppress cortisol secretion in depressed patients because of the overactivity of the hypothalamic-pituitary-adrenal (HPA) axis (102,103,108–111). The dexamethasone suppression test (DST) does not possess a high sensitivity or specificity for discriminating major depression from other psychiatric disorders (109). Therefore, cortisol nonsuppression may reflect a general stress pathophysiology shared by many neuropsychiatric illnesses. However, very high rates of DST nonsuppression (69–100%) have been observed in psychotic affective states, mixed bipolar disorder, and dysphoric mania (109,110, 112,113). In contrast, DST nonsuppression is rare in classic euphoric mania (109). Therefore, secretory overactivity of the HPA axis may be a stress-sensitive state marker for mixed affective syndrome and dysphoric, but not euphoric, mania.

ROLE OF HPA AXIS PATHOPHYSIOLOGY IN TREATMENT-RESISTANT BIPOLAR DISORDER

Affective Responses to Stress

Bipolar Depression

A great deal of research has attempted to elucidate the pathophysiological relationship between affective disorders and stress. The hypothesis has been that depression results from defective or exhausted adaptational responses to stress necessary for the maintenance of affective homeostasis. Several retrospective studies have demonstrated that major depression frequently is preceded by stressful life events, supporting the hypothesis that exposure to significant stressors 1 to 6 months previously increases the incidence of a depressive episode by fivefold to sixfold (64,114–116). There is no evidence that chronic stress has primary depressogenic effects (115). Therefore, stress can repetitively precipitate depressive episodes in depression-prone individuals predisposed to affective dysregulation, but stress does not appear to have a direct etiological role.

The homeostatic termination of HPA axis activation is a normal process of adaptation to chronic stress (117–120). A corollary hypothesis for the role of stress in depression pathophysiology is that the failure of adaptational responses to stress occurs in patients who later develop an affective relapse. This maladaptation results in an excessive activation of psychoneuroendocrine and affective behavioral centers in the CNS. It has been proposed that this pathological hyperactivity of the stress response results from the loss of "counterregulatory restraint" (102).

Mania

Less research has been conducted on the role of stress in the development of hypomania and mania. Psychoanalytical concepts of mania proposed that mania was a defense whereby loss was denied (64). Mania occurring in widows experiencing acute bereavement has been viewed as support for this hypothesis. A controlled study has demonstrated that stressors involving loss or threat can precipitate mania (121). In addition to the pathological role of psychosocial stress, psychotropic factors, such as antidepressant administration, abrupt antidepressant withdrawal, endocrine perturbations (e.g., hyperthyroidism, high dose corticosteroid therapy, postpartum cessation of female sex steroid hypersecretion), and disruption of circadian rhythms, also may act like stressors and induce hypomania/mania (15,40,77,122). The driving force for manic switches in these conditions may be a sleep deprivation mechanism (77). If stress induction of mood cycling is the basis for the first several bipolar episodes, sensitization can occur that leads to increased vulnerability to subthreshold stimuli (117,123–125).

HPA Axis Dysregulation in Bipolar Disorder

Basal Adrenocortical Secretion

Cortisol hypersecretion and cortisol nonsuppression both occur in bipolar depression (44,104,105,109,110). The magnitude of HPA axis hyperactivity in bipolar patients does not appear to be significantly different from the degree of DST nonsuppression and the diurnal patterns of high adrenocortical secretion measured in unipolar depression (104,109,110). Increased corticotropin-releasing factor (CRF) levels have been measured in the lumbar CSF of depressed patients compared to normal controls and nonaffective psychiatric patients (102,106,108). The highest CSF concentrations of CRF have been measured in DST nonsuppressors (106). A reduction in the CRF receptor concentration also has been measured in the cerebral cortex of suicide victims, many of whom were depressed (108). These findings suggest that increased CRF drive at or above the level of the hypothalamus may occur during depression. Recently, corticosteroid receptor downregulation in the hippocampus in the context of CRF hypersecretion has been proposed as a model for hypercortisolism in depression (84).

Cortisol hypersecretion has been reported to be absent during mania despite high urinary corticosteroid levels and hypercortisolemia being measured in the same bipolar patients during the depressive phase of the cycle (44,104,126). Mean urinary free cortisol also is significantly lower in mania compared to adrenal secretory activity in normal controls and euthymic bipolars (104). Although these data suggest a differential regulation of the HPA axis in mania versus bipolar depression, the classic studies of Edward Sachar demonstrated pathologically high plasma cortisol levels over a 24-hour secretory period in severe mania (105). Since cortisol hypersecretion was not observed in hypomania, the intensity of the manic episode may be an important influence on the HPA axis.

Pituitary-Adrenal Responses to Corticotropin-Releasing Factor

Several studies have demonstrated that depressed patients exhibit a blunted or diminished ACTH secretory response to an i.v. injection of CRF (102,103,106,107,127). This pituitary hyporesponsivity to CRF in depression could result from increased negative feedback due to cortisol hypersecretion or desensitization of the pituitary corticotroph. Adrenocortical responses to CRF are normal or proportionally higher than CRF-stimulated cortisol release in control subjects (102,106,107). This effect may result from adrenal hypertrophy and increased sensitivity of the adrenal cortex to CRF.

Pituitary-adrenal responses to CRF in mania also have been investigated. Consistent with the normal secretory activity or hypoactivity of the adrenal cortex during the manic phase of the bipolar cycle, the magnitude of ACTH and cortisol responses to CRF in mania is similar to responses in control subjects (106). A study of serial pituitary-adrenal responses to CRF after dexamethasone has revealed that CRF-stimulated ACTH and cortisol release are significantly reduced following a tricyclic-induced switch into mania or during clinical remission (103). Since dexamethasone could not suppress pituitary-adrenal responses to CRF during depression, CRF overdrive was not dampened by exposure to negative glucocorticoid feedback. This situation may result from brain-pituitary feedback receptors in depressed patients being subsensitive to the inhibitory effects of corticosteroids. Normalization of the negative feedback system appears to occur in euthymia or mania (103). In this regard, it is interesting to note that the antimanic carbamazepine has been reported to increase ACTH responses to CRF in bipolars (103).

The Role of Sensitization Mechanisms in Treatment-Resistant Bipolar Disorder

Chronic exposure to a psychotropic stimulus, which activates or arouses the CNS, can produce a hypersensitivity of cerebral responses to novel stimuli (117,123–125). For example, chronic restraint stress in lab-

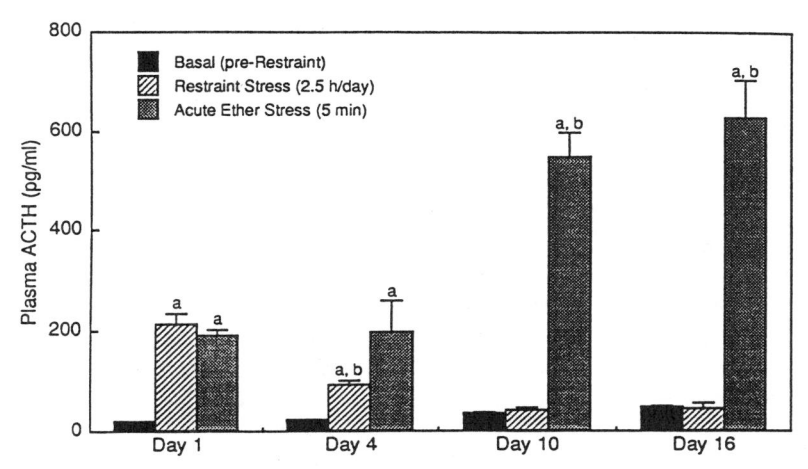

FIG. 1. Sensitization of plasma ACTH responses to acute ether stress (5 min) following chronic intermittent immobilization stress (2.5 hour restraint/day). ACTH values across the treatment groups were significantly different ($F=80.1$, df 11,221, $p<0.001$ by one-way ANOVA). By one-way ANOVA or unpaired Student's t-test, statistically significant differences are as follows: [a]$p<0.001$ vs nonstressed control; [b]$p<0.001$, vs day 1 restraint; [c]$p<0.05$ vs nonstressed control. Since chronic stress downregulates CRF receptors in the anterior pituitary, the increased pituitary corticotroph response to novel stressful stimuli involves the facilitation of stimulatory inputs to CRF-releasing neurons in the hypothalamus and the integrative actions of CRF and other ACTH regulators at the post-CRF receptor level. (From ref. 118.)

oratory animals can greatly enhance the ACTH response to acute ether stress (Fig. 1) (118–120). Likewise, chronic psychostimulant administration in laboratory animals can produce behavioral sensitization—a state characterized by greatly enhanced motoric responses to the same dose of psychostimulant that, when given earlier as the first injection, produced a much smaller increase in locomotion and stereotypy (117,123–125,128). The development of behavioral sensitization is most likely mediated by chronic stimulant-induced changes in mesolimbic and mesocortical dopaminergic neurotransmission and leads to a cross-sensitization to stress (128).

Post and Weiss have proposed an important model of treatment-resistant bipolar illness based on kindling and sensitization mechanisms for the augmentation of affective recurrences (123–125,129). Similar to stress sensitization, sensitization of vulnerable bipolar patients to external stressors and endogenous stimuli would precipitate full affective episodes, when previously these stimuli had been subthreshold. A sensitization pattern to psychosocial stresses has been observed in bipolar patients (121). Post and Weiss also make the interesting proposal that early in the course of bipolar illness, affective relapse would be more effectively prevented by lithium therapy (123–125,129). Lithium-resistant phases of bipolar illness emerge later, manifested as frequent affective relapses or rapid cycling. These lithium-resistant phases are hypothesized to result from sensitization responses to repetitive stressors or pharmacological switching stimuli. After sensitization, bipolars would be responsive to anticonvulsants, such as carbamazepine (123–125,161).

Recent work has demonstrated that the CRF-pituitary-adrenal axis can modulate behavioral sensitization to amphetamine. Adrenalectomy blocks behavioral sensitization to amphetamine (130). Therefore, corticosteroid receptor activation is required for amphetamine sensitization of brain dopaminergic systems. It is conceivable that corticosteroid hypersecretion in bipolar depression could contribute to treatment-resistant processes by augmenting CNS sensitization to stress and stimulants.

The intracerebroventricular administration of the CRF receptor antagonist significantly attenuates chronic amphetamine-induced sensitization of both locomotor activity and stereotypy (131). Behavioral sensitization to amphetamine is greatly diminished by the peripheral administration of a CRF antiserum (131). CRF immunoneutralization abolishes HPA axis responses to the i.v. injection of amphetamine (Fig. 2) and to stress (132). Consequently, affective kindling may be an important mechanism for CNS sensitization in treatment-resistant bipolar disorder. The prophylactic treatment of bipolar patients with long-acting CRF antagonists may prevent this progression.

NOVEL ANTIDEPRESSANT THERAPIES FOR BIPOLAR DISORDER

MAO Type A-Selective Monoamine Oxidase Inhibitors in Treatment-Resistant Bipolar Depression and Rapid Cycling

Clorgyline

Clorgyline exerts a selective, irreversible inhibition of the MAO-A enzyme that preferentially deaminates NE and 5HT in the CNS (133). Chronic administration of clorgyline downregulates $5HT_1$ serotonergic receptors and delays the phase-position for the circadian rhythm of α- and β-adrenergic, opiate, and benzodiazepine receptors in rat brain (133–136). When clorgyline was administered to rapid cycling bipolars at low doses (2.5 to 10 mg/day), alone or in combination with lithium carbonate, the frequency and severity of the mood cycles

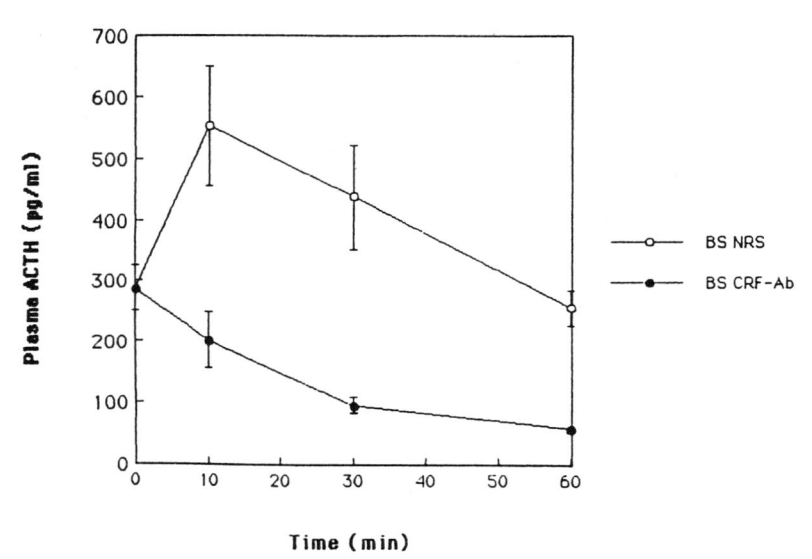

FIG. 2. Effect of CRF immunoneutralization on the stimulation of ACTH secretion by the intravenous injection of amphetamine. Baseline i.v. blood samples were obtained via an indwelling jugular cannula at the 0 time point in adult male Sprague-Dawley rats (7 rats/group). Immediately afterward, either normal rat serum (NRS) plus 5 mg/kg amphetamine (○———○) or rat CRF antiserum (CRF-ab) plus 5 mg/kg amphetamine (●———●) was coinjected i.v. CRF immunoneutralization abolished i.v. amphetamine-induced ACTH release without altering locomotor or stereotypy responses. In contrast, amphetamine stimulated large increases in plasma ACTH levels in rats pretreated with NRS. (From Hauger et al., submitted for publication).

were dramatically reduced resulting in prolonged periods of remission (137,138).

Low-dose clorgyline treatment in bipolar depression and in rapid cycling bipolar illness results in a substantial reduction in the whole body turnover of NE (Fig. 3), presumably resulting from increased autoreceptor inhibition and resultant decreases in noradrenergic activity (137–139). The administration of low doses of clorgyline has little effect on the neuronal metabolism of 5HT but significantly reduces urinary HVA levels. High doses (30 μg/day) of clorgyline can decrease CSF HVA (133). Norepinephrine and cardiovascular responses to clonidine were not blunted during low-dose clorgyline therapy, suggesting that the regulation of presynaptic α_2-receptor density or sensitivity in treatment-refractory bipolar depression is neither necessary nor sufficient for antidepressant effect (137,140). Low-dose clorgyline, many antidepressants, lithium, and ECT all have in common the ability to reduce NE turnover (137–141).

Noradrenergic centers function in the CNS as "modulator of incoming signals" (139,141). Recently, Potter proposed that the dysregulation of the brain NE system in depression diminishes the ability of NE to suppress "spontaneous, noisy, nonfunctional" neuronal firing in other neurotransmitter systems (5,139,141). This situation would impair the "focusing" and "targeting" of neurotransmission in the brain. Without noradrenergic enhancement of neuronal transmitting efficiency by increasing the "gain" of neurotransmission in brain afferent and efferent pathways (i.e., increasing the signal/noise ratio), affective homeostasis can not be maintained and pathological mood responses are precipitated by endogenous or environment stressors. Depression or more rapid cycling could result from pathological hyperresponsiveness of brain noradrenergic systems to stress due to a more rigid processing of noise as signal (139,141). Effective therapies for bipolar disorder would increase the flexibility of the brain noradrenergic system. This therapeutic effect may be reflected by the reduction of total NE output to clorgyline and other antidepressants. Therefore, the antidepressant-induced restoration of "noradrenergic synaptic efficiency" increases the signal/noise ratio of relevant neuronal inputs "restabilizing" central neurotransmission, which regulates mood via noradrenergic "focusing" mechanisms (5,139,141).

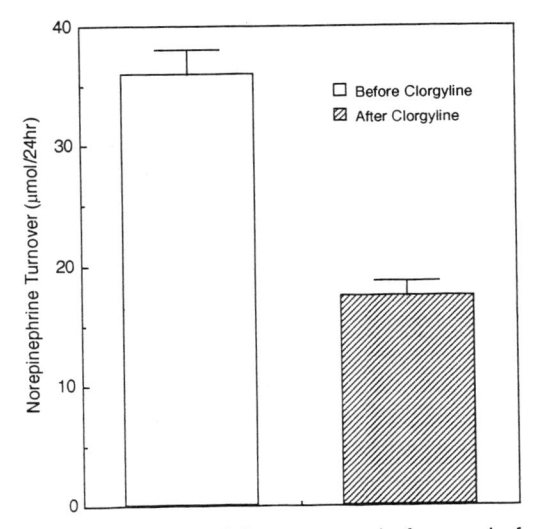

FIG. 3. Norepinephrine turnover before and after low-dose clorgyline treatment (2.5–10 mg/day) in bipolar patients. Whole body turnover of norepinephrine (NE) was calculated as the sum (μmol/24 hour) of the urinary levels of NE, normetanephrine, vanillylmandelic acid, and MHPG measured by GC/MS assay. These data are a subset of NE turnover values from a published study of NE output and α_2 adrenergic responses to clonidine in unipolar and bipolar patients receiving low-dose clorgyline treatment. (From ref. 137.)

There is a lower incidence of manic switches at the 5 to 10 mg clorgyline dose range even in the absence of lithium (137,138). This finding and the cessation of rapid cycling on clorgyline suggest that clorgyline facilitation of noradrenergic synaptic efficiency is not associated with cycle acceleration. Zimelidine and lithium decrease total NE turnover and output without inducing mania or rapid cycling (141, 142). In contrast, TCAs, such as desmethylimipramine, which also reduce NE turnover, precipitate manic switches and rapid cycling in bipolar depressives (36,40, 122). Therefore, the facilitation of noradrenergic synaptic efficiency by antidepressants may be a therapeutic mechanism in bipolar depression that is not associated with the induction of mania or rapid cycling. A reduction in dopamine turnover also may be important for the antidepressant action of clorgyline and tranylcypromine in treatment-resistant bipolars (138).

Moclobemide

Recent studies have demonstrated that moclobemide, a benzamide derivative that produces a rapidly reversible inhibition of the MAO-A enzyme, also is an effective antidepressant in bipolar depression (143, 144).

New Generation Antidepressants in the Treatment of Bipolar Depression

Fluoxetine and Clomipramine

Fluoxetine is a selective inhibitor of presynaptic 5HT reuptake without any appreciable affinity for binding to muscarinic cholinergic, α-adrenergic, and histaminergic receptors in the brain (134,136,140). The initial receptor studies indicated that fluoxetine did not downregulate postsynaptic β-noradrenergic receptors with chronic administration using homogenate binding assays (134,140). However, a recent autoradiographic study has observed a significant downregulation of β-adrenergic receptors in layer IV of the frontoparietal cortex (145). The augmentation of serotonergic neurotransmission is an important mechanism mediating fluoxetine's therapeutic effects in depression and obsessive-compulsive disorder (136,140). The combination of fluoxetine with TCAs also can accelerate the downregulation of postsynaptic β-adrenergic receptors and desensitization of cAMP responses to isoproterenol in the cerebral cortex. Although this regimen may cause a more rapid antidepressant response or convert antidepressant nonresponders to responders, fluoxetine interferes with the oxidative metabolism of antidepressants, resulting in marked increases in the circulating levels of nortriptyline and desipramine (140). Fluoxetine also may impair the demethylation of antidepressants, such as imipramine, amitriptyline, and doxepin, resulting in toxic accumulation of these medications.

The combination of clomipramine, L-tryptophan, and lithium has produced antidepressant responses in treatment-resistant bipolar depression (146). Fluoxetine has been administered with L-tryptophan in bipolar depressives, but a serotonergic syndrome has occurred with this regimen (147). In addition, the combined use of fluoxetine and lithium can cause neurotoxicity (148). L-Tryptophan potentiation of antidepressants has been associated with serious hematological disorders, and the combination of L-tryptophan with trazadone can precipitate hypomania (140,149,150). Consequently, these regimens should not be used in the treatment of refractory bipolar disorders.

However, the combination of the 5HT-active antidepressants fluoxetine and trazadone may be an effective therapy for treatment-resistant depression. Serotonergic neurotransmission does not appear to be an important mediator for the switch process in bipolar depressives (64). For example, measures of central serotonergic function are low in both phases of the bipolar cycle. In addition, in the same bipolar patients, zimelidine does not induce mania and rapid cycling, whereas desipramine, which selectively acts on the NE transporter, produces manic switches and cycle acceleration (142). Several months of clomipramine administration only produces a very slow switching of mood in some bipolar patients, which most likely results from increasing levels of noradrenergic-active metabolites (140).

A significant antidepressant response has been observed in a bipolar I patient who had a history of dysphoric mania and prolonged periods of a treatment-resistant depression (R. L. Hauger et al., unpublished observations). The use of carbamazepine may have prevented the induction of mania by trazadone and fluoxetine. Since carbamazepine may augment brain serotonergic neurotransmission and possibly diminish dopaminergic function, carbamazepine may increase the antidepressant activity of fluoxetine by potentiating 5HT neuronal activity (99). Manic switches may be inhibited by carbamazepine's toning down of dopaminergic neurotransmission. However, the combined regimen of fluoxetine, trazadone, and carbamazepine should be used cautiously in treatment-resistant bipolar depressives until future controlled studies determine its efficacy and safety in treatment-resistant bipolar depression.

Bupropion

The unicyclic aminoketone bupropion preferentially inhibits the presynaptic reuptake of dopamine (136,140,151). Bupropion possesses only weak affinities for the noradrenergic and serotonergic transporters. Unlike most antidepressant therapies, bupropion does not desensitize NE-sensitive adenylate cyclase or produce β-adrenergic receptor and serotonergic $5HT_2$ receptor downregulation (134,136,152).

In 1983, three bipolar I depressives maintained on bupropion for 1 year, in the absence of lithium therapy, had no manic or depressive recurrences (153). However, a subsequent study observed the induction of mania by bupropion when two bipolar I patients also were taking pseudoephedrine and a nonprescription cold medication (154).

Recent studies have examined the antidepressant effects of bupropion in bipolar versus unipolar depression. Excellent antidepressant responses were observed in a small group of bipolar and unipolar depressives in the absence of lithium carbonate, although the antidepressant response rate was higher in unipolars (75%) than in bipolars (43%) (140,151,154). In depressed patients who did not respond to bupropion, the circulating concentrations of plasma HVA were increased from 52.1 ± 5.7 to 70.9 ± 5.6 pmol/ml. These posttreatment levels are in the range of plasma HVA values measured in unmedicated schizophrenic patients with active psychotic symptoms (151). Although it is not certain whether increased plasma HVA reflects changes in brain dopaminergic neurotransmission, certain bipolar depressives may be bupropion nonresponders due to the psychotomimetic effects of bupropion-induced overactivity of central dopaminergic neurons.

Bupropion can cause a psychosis in bipolar depressives with high plasma HVA (151,155). This property is consistent with the previous observation that a poor response to the experimental antidepressant piribedil, a dopamine receptor agonist, occurred in depressed patients with high basal levels of CSF HVA (70). Furthermore, psychotic states with paranoid delusions, visual and auditory hallucinations, and thought disorder have been precipitated in bipolar I and II depressives receiving bupropion, whereas psychosis emerged in a rapid cycler treated with bupropion, lithium maintenance, and L-thyroxine (140,151, 155). Bupropion treatment has resulted also in psychotic relapses in schizoaffective patients (156). Consequently, bupropion should not be used in bipolar patients who have experienced a previous episode of psychotic depression or mania.

Idazoxan

An interesting case study recently described a significant antidepressant response to the selective α_2-receptor antagonist idazoxan in treatment-resistant bipolar depressives (157). The occupancy of presynaptic α_2-receptor sites by an α_2-antagonist would block the negative feedback of NE release by synaptic NE and result in increased terminal NE release. A twofold increase in circulating basal levels of plasma NE (0.53 ± 0.11 to 1.2 ± 03 nmol/L) occurred over the first 3 to 5 days of idazoxan administration (60 mg/day) and persisted for at least 4 to 6 weeks of idazoxan administration (120 mg/day) (157). Parallel increases in NE levels were observed in the cerebrospinal fluid and urine during the sustained antidepressant response to idazoxan.

Low levels of supine plasma and CSF NE have been measured in bipolar depression (139,141). Consequently, antidepressant responses in bipolar depressives may result from medications, such as idazoxan, that increase the firing rate of presynaptic NE neurons and the synaptic accumulation of NE. Although idazoxan did not induce mania or rapid cycling in the study, noradrenergic neurotransmission is believed to increase at the onset of mania, and the idazoxan-induced NE release could precipitate manic switches. Since such an antidepressant response continued after the addition of lithium to idazoxan, the combination of lithium maintenance therapy with idazoxan may ensure a prolonged period of remission in bipolar illness without manic switches. In addition to selective α_2-receptor antagonists, α_1-receptor agonists and selective inhibitors of presynaptic NE reuptake may prove to be therapeutic antidepressants in treatment-resistant bipolar depression.

S-Adenosyl-Methionine

S-Adenosyl-methionine (SAM), a sulfonium compound that serves as a methyl donor for many methyl transfer reactions in cells, enhances neurotransmitter synthesis, particularly the formation of serotonin (140). In open trials and controlled studies, i.v. SAM has produced rapid antidepressant responses with psychomotor activation (i.e., motor hyperactivity and insomnia induction) in depressed patients (140,158–161). When the effects of i.v. SAM were compared to oral or i.v. imipramine treatment in tricyclic-sensitive depressives, an antidepressant response to SAM occurred within 4 to 7 days. In contrast, the earliest antidepressant responses to i.v. imipramine occur at 2 weeks. Three cases of treatment-resistant chronic depression, however, have not responded to i.v. SAM (140).

Fourteen days of i.v. SAM administration in depressed patients increases CSF levels of 5HIAA, HVA, and SAM while decreasing serum prolactin levels. In healthy volunteers, 1 week of i.v. SAM reduces heart rate and plasma NE responses to standing without any changes in circulating levels of plasma MHPG (140,141). Consequently, the antidepressant action of SAM may involve the activation of central dopaminergic and serotonergic neurotransmission and the attenuation of peripheral noradrenergic responsivity.

In bipolar depressives, i.v. SAM treatment can rapidly cause hypomanic and manic switches. The incidence of hypomania/mania induction during i.v. SAM treatment of bipolar depression has been reported to be approximately 80%. In a recent study in depressed patients, oral SAM induced a manic episode in a patient who had no previous history of mania (158–160). Therefore, SAM may be contraindicated as an antidepressant therapy in mania-prone bipolars due to its propensity for precipitating switches and its potential for inducing rapid cycling.

SUMMARY

The monovalent action of most antidepressants represents a therapeutic crux in the treatment of bipolar disorder. Most antidepressants, particularly the tricyclics, produce the unidirectional response of changing a depression to the basal euthymic mood state. Although this psychotropic valency of action is ideal for pure unipolar depression, monovalent antidepressants result in counterdepressive overshoots to hypomania or mania in bipolar depressives and certain recurrent unipolars. Such a psychopharmacological effect is not acutely therapeutic and may induce long-term pathological forms of cycling in bipolar illness.

There are exceptions to this generalization about antidepressant action. ECT possesses a bivalent action on bipolar illness. ECT is both antidepressant and antimanic, although it can cause transitory hypomanic switches. New hope for the development of nonswitching antidepressants for bipolar depression has been increased by the unique antidepressants, idazoxan, a selective α_2-antagonist, and the dopamine reuptake blocker bupropion, both of which have not as yet induced mania in bipolars.

However, lithium still remains the most effective medication for bipolar disorder because of its acute antimanic and antidepressant and chronic anticycling actions. Consequently, lithium is a true euthymoregulator, which acts as a mood stabilizer rather than a monovalent antidepressant. This unique action of lithium may be derived from its action on the mediation of neurotransmitter action via G-protein transduction and phosphatidylinositol second messenger systems in the CNS. Future research should be directed at the development of agents that selectively act on components of these cellular transduction systems. The possible development of such medications raises great expectations for the effective treatment of the many patients who suffer from treatment-resistant and intractable forms of bipolar illness.

Finally, bipolar depression and mixed bipolar states can be associated with cortisol hypersecretion and defects in the negative feedback system for glucocorticoids in the CNS. There is evidence for increased brain CRF drive in the depressive phase of bipolar affective disorder. Therefore, the CRF-pituitary-adrenocortical axis may have an important pathophysiological role in the sensitization of bipolar illness and in the etiology of other treatment-resistant mechanisms. The development of high affinity and long-acting CRF receptor antagonists and antiglucocorticoid agents may provide new therapies that will prevent the development of refractory bipolar disorders.

REFERENCES

1. Kraepelin E. *Manic depressive insanity and paranoia,* translated by RM Barclay. Edinburgh: E & S Livingstone, 1921.
2. Leonhard K. Aufeiling der Endogenen Psychosen, 2nd ed. Berlin: Akademik Verlag, 1959.
3. Goodwin FK, Jamison KR. The natural course of manic-depressive illness. In: Post RM, Ballenger, eds. *Neurobiology of mood disorders.* Baltimore: Williams & Wilkins, 1984;20–38.
4. Goodwin FK, Jamison KR. Pathophysiology: Critical evaluation, integration, and future directions. In: Goodwin FK, Jamison KR, eds. *Manic-depressive illness.* New York: Oxford University Press, 1990.
5. Goodwin FK. The biology of recurrence: New directions for the pharmacologic bridge. *J Clin Psychiatry* 1989;44:253–255.
6. Dunner DL, Clayton PJ. Drug treatment of bipolar disorder. In: Meltzer HY, ed. *Psychopharmacology: The third generation of progress.* New York: Raven Press, 1987;1077–1083.
7. Dunner DL, Fleiss JL, Fieve RR. Lithium carbonate prophylaxis failure. *Br J Psychiatry* 1976;129:40–44.
8. Coryell W, Andreasen N, Endicott J, Keller M. The significance of past mania and hypomania in the course and outcome of major depression. *Am J Psychiatry* 1987;144:309–315.
9. Coryell W, Keller M, Endicott J, Andreasen N, Clayton P, Hirschfeld RM. Bipolar II illness: Course and outcome over a five year period. *Psychol Med* 1989;19:129–141.
10. Akiskal HS. The clinical significance of the "soft" bipolar spectrum. *Psychiatr Ann* 1986; 16:667–671.
11. Akiskal HS. New insights into the nature and heterogeneity of mood disorders. *J Clin Psychiatry* 1989;50:6–10.
12. Akiskal HS. Diagnostic considerations in the treatment of mood disorders. In: *Treatments of psychiatric disorders: A task force report of the American Psychiatric Association, vol 3.* Washington, DC: American Psychiatric Association, 1989.
13. Rosenthal NE. Seasonal affective disorder: A description of the syndrome and preliminary findings with light therapy. *Arch Gen Psychiatry* 1984;41:72–80.
14. Lewy AJ, Sack RL, Singer CM, White DM, Hoban TM. Winter depression and the phase-shift hypothesis for bright light's therapeutic

effects. History, theory, and experimental evidence. In: Rosenthal NE, Blehar MC, eds. *Seasonal affective disorders and phototherapy.* New York: Guilford Press, 1989;295–310.
15. White DM, Lewy AJ, Sack RL, Blood ML, Wesche DL. Is winter depression a bipolar disorder? *Comp Psychiatry* 1990;31:196–204.
16. Abou-Saleh MT, Coppen A. Who responds to prophylactic lithium? *J Affective Disord* 1986; 10:115–125.
17. Baastrup PC, Paulsen JC, Schon M. Prophylactic lithium: Double-blind discontinuation in manic-depressive disorders. *Lancet* 1970;2: 326–330.
18. Maj M, Pirozzi R, Starace F. Previous pattern of course of the illness as a predictor of response to lithium prophylaxis in bipolar patients. *J Affective Disord* 1989;17:237–241.
19. Schou M. Lithium treatment: A refresher course. *Br J Psychiatry* 1986;149:541–547.
20. Schou M. Lithium prophylaxis: Myths and realities. *Am J Psychiatry* 1989;146:573–576.
21. NIMH/NIH Consensus Conference Statement. Mood disorders: Pharmacological prevention of recurrences. *Am J Psychiatry* 1985;1142: 469–476.
22. Prien RF, Kupfer DJ, Mansky PA, et al. Drug therapy in the prevention of recurrences in unipolar and bipolar affective disorder. *Arch Gen Psychiatry* 1984;41:1096–1104.
23. Angst J. Clinical indications for a prophylactic treatment of depression. *Adv Biol Psychiatry* 1981;7:218–229.
24. Maj M, Del Vecchio M, Starace F, Pirozzi R, Kemali D. Prediction of affective psychoses response to lithium prophylaxis. *Acta Psychiatr Scand* 1984;69:37–44.
25. Mendlewicz J, Fieve RR, Stallone F. Relationship between effectiveness of lithium therapy and family history. *Am J Psychiatry* 1973;130: 1011–1013.
26. Prien RF, Caffey EM, Klett CJ. Factors associated with treatment success in lithium carbonate prophylaxis. *Arch Gen Psychiatry* 1974; 31:189–192.
27. Mendlewicz J. Prediction of treatment outcome: Family and twin studies in lithium prophylaxis and the question of lithium red blood cell/plasma ratio. In: Cooper TB, Gershon S, Kline NS, Schon M, eds. *Lithium controversies and unresolved issues.* Amsterdam: Excerpta Medica, 1979.
28. Mendlewicz J, Verbanck S, Linkowski P. Lithium accumulation in erythrocytes of manic-depressive patients: An in vivo twin study. *Br J Psychiatry* 1978;133:436–444.
29. Weissman MM, Prusott BA, Merikangas KR. Is delusional depression related to bipolar disorder? *Am J Psychiatry* 1984;141:892–893.
30. Kukopulos A, Caliari B, Tondo A, et al. Rapid cyclers, temperament, and antidepressants. *Comp Psychiatry* 1983;24:249–258.
31. Kukopulos A, Reginaldi D, Laddomada P, Floris G, Serra G, Tondo L. Course of manic-depressive cycle and changes caused by treatments. *Pharmacopsychiatry* (1980);13:156–157.
32. Kukopulos A, Reginaldi D, Laddomada P, Floris G, Serra G, Tondo L. Course of the manic-depressive cycle and changes caused by treatments. *Pharmacopsychiatry* 1980;13:157–167.
33. Grof E, Haag M, Grof P, Haag H. Lithium response and the sequence of episode polarities: Preliminary report on a Hamilton sample. *Prog Neuropsychopharmacol Biol Psychiatry* 1987; 11:199–203.
34. Haag M, Heidorn A, Haag H, Greil W. Response to stabilizing lithium therapy and sequence of affective polarity. *Pharmacopsychiatry* 1986;19:278–279.
35. Haag H, Heidorn A, Haag M, Greil W. Sequence of affective polarity and lithium response: Preliminary report on Munich sample. *Prog Neuropsychopharmacol Biol Psychiatry* 1987;11:205–208.
36. Wehr TA, Goodwin FK. Can antidepressants cause mania and worsen the course of affective illness? *Am J Psychiatry* 1987;144:1403–1411.
37. Quitkin FM, Kane J, Rifkin A, Ramos-Lorenzi J, Nayak DV. Prophylactic lithium carbonate with and without imipramine for bipolar I patients. *Arch Gen Psychiatry* 1981;38:902–907.
38. Quitkin FM, Rabkin JG, Prien RF. Bipolar disorder: Are there manic-prone and depression-prone focus? *J Clin Psychopharmacol* 1986;6: 167–172.
39. Post RM. Approaches to treatment-resistant bipolar affectively ill patients. *Clin Neuropharmacol* 1988;11:93–104.
40. Wehr TA, Goodwin FK. Rapid cycling in manic-depressives induced by tricyclic antidepressants. *Arch Gen Psychiatry* 1979;36:555–559.
41. Dunner DL, Patrick V, Fieve RR. Rapid cycling manic-depressive patients. *Compr Psychiatry* 1977;18:561–566.
42. Schou M. Lithiumterapi ved mani: Praktiske retningslmeir. *Nord Med* 1956;55:790–794.
43. Baastrup PC, Schou M. Lithium as a prophylactic agent: Its effect against recurrent depressions and manic-depressive psychosis. *Arch Gen Psychiatry* 1967;16:162–173.
44. Bunney WE Jr, Hartmann EL. Study of a patient with 48-hour manic-depressive cycles. Part II. Strong positive correlation between endocrine factors and manic defense patterns. *Arch Gen Psychiatry* 1965;12:619–625.
45. Bauer MS, Whybrow PC. The effect of changing thyroid function on cyclic affective illness in a human subject. *Am J Psychiatry* 1986;143: 633–636.
46. Cowdry RW, Wehr TA, Zis AP, Goodwin FK. Thyroid abnormalities associated with rapid cycling bipolar illness. *Arch Gen Psychiatry* 1983;40:414–420.
47. Squillace K, Post RM, Savard R, Ervin M. Life charting of the longitudinal course of recurrent affective illness. In: Post RM, Ballenger JL, eds. *Neurobiology of mood disorders.* Baltimore: Williams & Wilkins, 1984.
48. Price LH, Charney DS, Heninger GR. Manic symptoms following addition of lithium to an-

tidepressant treatment. *J Clin Psychopharmacol* 1984;4:361–362.
49. Nelson JC, Mazure CM. Lithium augmentation in psychotic depression refractory to combined drug treatment. *Am J Psychiatry* 1986;143:363–366.
50. Maggs R. Treatment of manic illness with lithium carbonate. *Br J Psychiatry* 1963;109:56–65.
51. Schou M, Juel-Nielsen, Stromgren E, Voldby H. The treatment of manic psychoses by the administration of lithium salts. *J Neurol Neurosurg Psychiatry* 1954;17:250–260.
52. Stokes PE, Shamoian CA, Stoll PM, Patton MJ. Efficacy of lithium as acute treatment of manic-depressive illness. *Lancet* 1971;1:1319–1325.
53. Tyrer SP. Lithium in the treatment of mania. *J Affective Disord* 1985;8:251–257.
54. Taylor MA, Abrams R. Acute mania. *Arch Gen Psychiatry* 1975;32:863–871.
55. Fichter CG, Grossman LS, Harrow M, Goldberg JF, Klein DN. Cyclothymic mood swings in the course of affective disorders and schizophrenia. *Am J Psychiatry* 1989;146:1149–1154.
56. Pope HG, Lipinski JF. Diagnosis in schizophrenia and manic-depressive illness: A reassessment of the specificity of "schizophrenic" symptoms in the light of current research. *Arch Gen Psychiatry* 1978;35:811–828.
57. Rosenthal NE, Rosenthal LN, Stallone F, Fleiss J, Dunner DL, Fieve RR. Psychosis as a predictor of response to lithium maintenance treatment in bipolar affective disorder. *J Affective Disord* 1979;1:237–248.
58. Carlson GA, Goodwin FK. The stages of mania—A longitudinal analysis of the manic episode. *Arch Gen Psychiatry* 1973;28:221–228.
59. Jampala VC, Taylor MA, Abrams R. The diagnostic implications of formal thought disorder in mania and schizophrenia: A reassessment. *Am J Psychiatry* 1989;146:459–463.
60. Jampala VC, Abrams R, Taylor MA. Mania with emotional blunting: Affective disorder or schizophrenia? *Am J Psychiatry* 1985;142:608–612.
61. Gerner RH, Post RM, Bunney WE Jr. A dopaminergic mechanism in mania. *Am J Psychiatry* 1976;133:1177–1180.
62. Post RM, Jimerson DC, Silberman EK. Amphetamine and piribedil in affective illness. *Psychopharmacol Bull* 1980;16:57–59.
63. Johnson JM. Treated mania exacerbated by bromocriptine. *Am J Psychiatry* 1981;138:980–982.
64. Whybrow PC, Akiskal HS, McKinney WT Jr. *Mood disorders: Toward a new psychobiology.* New York: Plenum Press, 1984;119–150.
65. Brodie HKH, Murphy DL, Goodwin FK, Bunney WE Jr. Catecholamines and mania: The effect of α-methyl-paratyrosine on manic behavior and catecholamine metabolism. *Clin Pharmacol Ther* 1971;12:218–224.
66. Sack RL, Goodwin FK. Inhibition of dopamine β-hydroxylase in manic patients. *Arch Gen Psychiatry* 1974;31:649–654.
67. Willner P. Dopamine and depression. *Brain Res Rev* 1983;6:211–224.
68. Goodwin FK, Zis AP. Lithium in the treatment of mania. *Arch Gen Psychiatry* 1979;36:840–844.
69. Post RM, Jimerson DC, Bunney WE Jr, Goodwin FK. Dopmaine and mania: Behavioral and biochemical effects of the dopamine receptor blocker pimozide. *Psychopharmacology* 1980;67:297–305.
70. Post RM, Gerner RH, Carman JS, et al. Effects of a dopamine agonist piribedil in depressed patients: Relationship of pretreatment homovanillic acid to antidepressant response. *Arch Gen Psychiatry* 1978;35:609–615.
71. Casey DE. Tardive dyskinesia and affective disorders. In: Gardos G, Casey DE, eds. *Tardive dyskinesia and affective disorders.* Washington, DC: American Psychiatric Press, Inc., 1984.
72. Freinhar JP, Alvarez WH. Use of clonazepam in two cases of acute mania. *J Clin Psychiatry* 1985;46:29–30.
73. Aronson TA. Clonazepam treatment of five lithium-refractory patients with bipolar disorder. *Am J Psychiatry* 1989;146:77–80.
74. Chouinard G. Clonazepam in acute and maintenance treatment of bipolar affective disorder. *J Clin Psychiatry* 1987;48 (Suppl):29–37.
75. Sachs GS, Rosenbaum JF, Jones L. Adjunctive clonazepam for maintenance treatment of bipolar affective disorder. *J Clin Psychopharmacol* 1990;10:42–47.
76. Weiss SRB, Post RM, Patel J, Marangos PJ. Differential mediation of the anticonvulsant effects of carbamazepine and diazepam. *Life Sci* 1985;36:2413–2419.
77. Wehr TA. Sleep loss: A preventable cause of mania and other excited states. *J Clin Psychiatry* 1989;50 (suppl 12):8–16.
78. Hendler NH. Spironolactone prophylaxis in manic-depressive disease. *J Nerv Ment Dis* 1978;166:517–520.
79. Pearlson GS, Garbacz DJ, Tompkins RT, et al. Clinical correlates of lateral ventricular enlargement in bipolar affective disorder. *Am J Psychiatry* 1984;141:253–256.
80. Roy-Byrne PP, Post RM, Kellner CH, Joffe RT, Uhde TW. Ventricular-brain ratio and life course of illness in patients with affective disorder. *Psychiatr Res* 1988;23:277–284.
81. Standish-Barry HMAS, Bouras N, Bridges PK, Bartlett JR. Pneumoencephalographic and computerized axial tomography scan changes in affective disorder. *Br J Psychiatry* 1982;141:614–617.
82. Nasrallah HA, McCalley-Whitters M, Pfohl B. Clinical significance of large cerebral ventricles in manic males. *Psychiatry Res* 1984;13:151–156.
83. Bentson JR, Reta M, Winter J, Wilson G. Steroids and apparent cerebral atrophy on computer tomography scan. *J Comput Assist Tomogr* 1978;2:16–23.
84. Sapolsky RM, Plotsky PM. Hypercortisolism and its possible neural bases. *Biol Psychiatry* 1990;27:937–952.

85. Kellner CH, Rubinow DR, Gold PW, Post RM. Relationship of cortisol hypersecretion to brain CT scan alterations in depressed patients. *Psychiatr Res* 1983;8:191–197.
86. Lukins DJ, Lewine RRJ, Meltzer HY. Lateral ventricular size, psychopathology, and medication response in the psychoses. *Biol Psychiatry* 1984;19:29–44.
87. Dupont RM, Jernigan TL, Butters N, et al. Subcortical abnormalities detected in bipolar affective disorder using magnetic resonance imaging: Clinical and neuropsychological significance. *Arch Gen Psychiatry* 1990;47:55–59.
88. Dupont RM, Jernigan TL, Gillin JC, Butters N, Delis DC, Hesselink JR. Presence of subcortical signal hyperintensities in bipolar patients detected by MRI. *Psychiatry Res* 1987;21:357–358.
89. Kotin J, Goodwin FK. Depression during mania: Clinical observations and theoretical implications. *Am J Psychiatry* 1972;129:679–686.
90. Braden W, HO CK. Racing thoughts in psychiatric inpatients. *Arch Gen Psychiatry* 1981;38:71–75.
91. Himmelhoch JM. Mania: The dual nature of elation. In: Giannini AJ, ed. *The biological foundation of clinical psychiatry.* New York: Medical Examination Publishing Company, 1986;116–130.
92. Secunda SK, Swann A, Katz MM, Koslow SH, Croughan J, Chang S. Diagnosis and treatment of mixed mania. *Am J Psychiatry* 1987;144:96–98.
93. Himmelhoch JM, Garfinkel ME. Sources of lithium resistance in mixed mania. *Psychopharmacology Bull* 1986;22:613–620.
94. Court J. Manic-depressive psychosis: An alternative conceptual model. *Br J Psychiatry* 1968;114:1523–1530.
95. Post RM, Rubinow DR, Uhde TW, et al. Dysphoric mania. *Arch Gen Psychiatry* 1980;46:353–358.
96. Paschalis C, Pavlou A, Papadimitriou GN. A stepped forty-eight hour manic-depressive cycle. *Br J Psychiatry* 1980;137:332–336.
97. Hanna SM, Jenner FA, Pearson IB. The therapeutic effect of lithium carbonate on a patient with a forty-eight hour periodic psychosis. *Br J Psychiatry* 1972;121:271–280.
98. Swann AC, Secunda SK, Katz MM, Koslow SH. Mania: Amines, symptoms, and response to lithium. In: Swann AC, ed. *Mania: New research and treatment.* Washington, DC: American Psychiatric Association Press, 1986;177–200.
99. Elphick M, Yang J-D, Cowen PJ. Effects of carbamazepine on dopamine- and serotonin-mediated neuroendocrine responses. *Arch Gen Psychiatry* 1990;47:135–140.
100. Zubenko GS, Cohen BM, Lipinski JF Jr, Jonas JM. Clonidine in the treatment of mania and mixed bipolar disorder. *Am J Psychiatry* 1984;141:1617–1618.
101. Giannini AJ, Pascarzi GA, Loiselle RH, Price WA, Giannini MC. Comparison of clonidine and lithium in the treatment of mania. *Am J Psychiatry* 1986;143:1608–1609.
102. Gold PW, Goodwin FK, Chrousos G. Clinical and biochemical manifestations of depression: Relation to the neurobiology of stress. *N Engl J Med* 1988;319:413–420.
103. Holsboer F, von Bardeleben U, Heuser I, Steiger A. Human corticotropin-releasing hormone challenge tests in depression. In: Schatzberg AF, Nemeroff CB, eds. *The hypothalamic-pituitary-adrenal axis: Physiology, pathophysiology, and psychiatric implications.* New York: Raven Press, 1988;79–100.
104. Rubinow DR, Post RM, Gold PW, Ballenger JC, Wolff EA. The relationship between cortisol and clinical phenomenology of affective illness. In: Post RM, Ballenger JC, eds. *Neurobiology of mood disorders.* Baltimore: Williams & Wilkins, 1980;271.
105. Sachar EJ. Twenty-four-hour cortisol secretory patterns in depressed and manic patients. *Brain Res* 1970;42:81–91.
106. Gold PW, Kling MA, Demitrack MA, et al. Clinical studies with corticotropin releasing hormone: Implications for hypothalamic-pituitary-adrenal dysfunction in depression and related disorders. *Curr Topics Neuroendocrinol* 1988;8:55–77.
107. Amsterdam JD, Maislin G, Gold P, Winokur A. The assessment of abnormalities in hormonal responsiveness at multiple levels of the hypothalamic-pituitary-adrenocortical axis in depressive illness. *Psychoneuroendocrinology* 1989;14:43–62.
108. Owens MJ, Nemeroff CB. The neurobiology of corticotropin-releasing factor: Implications for affective disorders. In: Schatzberg AF, Nemeroff CB, eds. *The hypothalamic-pituitary-adrenal axis: Physiology, pathophysiology, and psychiatric implications.* New York: Raven Press, 1988;1–35.
109. Arana GW, Baldessarini RJ, Ornsteen M. The dexamethasone suppression test for diagnosis and prognosis in psychiatry. *Arch Gen Psychiatry* 1985;42:1193–1204.
110. Evans DL, Nemeroff CB. The clinical use of the dexamethasone suppression test in DSM-III affective disorders: Correlation with the severe depressive subtypes of melancholia and psychosis. *J Psychiatr Res* 1987;21:185–194.
111. Carroll BJ. The dexamethasone suppression test for melancholia. *Br J Psychiatry* 1982;140:292–304.
112. Evans DL, Nemeroff CB. The dexamethasone suppression test in mixed bipolar disorder. *Am J Psychiatry* (1983);140:615–617.
113. Krishnan RR, Maltbie AA, Davidson JRT. Abnormal cortisol suppression in bipolar patients with simultaneous manic and depressive symptoms. *Am J Psychiatry* 1983;140:203–205.
114. Anisman H. Vulnerability to depression: Contribution of stress. In: Post RM, Ballenger JC, eds. *Neurobiology of mood disorders.* Baltimore: Williams & Wilkins, 1984;407–427.

115. Breslau N, Davis GC. Chronic stress and major depression. *Arch Gen Psychiatry* 1986;43:309–314.
116. Willner P. Animal models of depression: An overview. *Pharmacol Ther* 1989;45:425–455.
117. Antelman SM. Stressor-induced sensitization to subsequent stress: Implications for the development and treatment of clinical disorders. In: Kalivas PW, Barnes CD, eds. *Sensitization in the nervous system*. NJ: Telford Press, 1988;227–254.
118. Hauger RL, Lorang M, Irwin M, Aguilera G. CRF receptor regulation and sensitization of ACTH responses to acute ether stress during chronic intermittent immobilization stress. *Brain Res* 1990 532:34–40.
119. Hauger RL, Millan MA, Lorang M, Harwood JP, Aguilera A. Corticotropin releasing factor receptors and pituitary-adrenal responses during immobilization stress. *Endocrinology* 1988;123:396–405.
120. Keller-Wood ME, Dallman MF. Corticosteroid inhibition of ACTH secretion. *Endocrine Rev* 1984;5:1–24.
121. Ambelas A. Psychologically stressful events in the precipitation of manic episodes. *Br J Psychiatry* 1979;135:15–21.
122. Wehr TA, Sack DA, Rosenthal NE, Cowdry RW. Rapid cycling affective disorder: Contributing factors and treatment responses in 51 patients. *Am J Psychiatry* 1988;145:179–184.
123. Post RM, Weiss SRB. Sensitization, kindling, and anticonvulsants in mania. *J Clin Psychiatry* 1989;50 (Suppl 12):23–30.
124. Post RM, Weiss SRB. Kindling and manic-depressive illness. In: Bolwig TG, Trimble MR, eds. *The clinical relevance of kindling*. Chichester: John Wiley & Sons Ltd., 1989;209–230.
125. Post RM, Weiss SRB, Pert A. Animal models of mania. In: Willner P, Scheel-Kruger J, eds. *The mesolimbic dopamine system: From motivation to action*. Chichester: John Wiley & Sons Ltd., 1990.
126. Rizzo N, Fox HM, Laidlaw JC, Thorn GW. Concurrent observations of behavior changes and of adrenocortical variations in a cyclothymic patient during a period of 12 months. *Ann Intern Med* 1954;41:798–815.
127. Risch SC, Golshan S, Rapaport MH, et al. Neuroendocrine effects of intravenous ovine corticotropin-releasing factor in affective disorder patients and normal controls. *Biol Psychiatry* 1988;23:755–758.
128. Koob GF, Bloom FE. Cellular and molecular mechanisms of drug dependence. *Science* 1988;242:715–723.
129. Post RM. Sensitization and kindling perspectives for the course of affective illness: Toward a new treatment with the anticonvulsant carbamazepine. *Pharmacopsychiatry* 1990;23:3–17.
130. Rivet J-M, Stinus L, LeMoal M, Mormede P. Behavioral sensitization to amphetamine is dependent on corticosteroid receptor activation. *Brain Res* 1989;498:149–153.
131. Cole BJ, Cador M, Stinus L, Koob GF, LeMoal M. Endogenous CRF: Role in stress- and amphetamine-induced sensitization of forebrain dopamine systems. *Soc Neurosci Abstr* 1989;14:252.
132. Rivier CL, Plotsky PM. Mediation by corticotropin releasing factor (CRF) of adenohypophysial hormone secretion. *Annu Rev Physiol* 1986;48:475–494.
133. Murphy DL, Aulakh CS, Garrick NA, Sunderland T. Monoamine oxidase inhibitors as antidepressants: Implications for the mechanism of action of antidepressants and the psychobiology of the affective disorders and some related disorders. In: Meltzer HY, ed. *Psychopharmacology: The third generation of progress*. New York: Raven Press, 1987;545–552.
134. Hauger RL, Paul SM. Neurotransmitter receptor plasticity: Alterations by antidepressants and antipsychotics may explain their clinical effects. *Psychiatric Ann* 1983;13:399–407.
135. Wirz-Justice A, Kafka MS, Naber D, et al. Clorgyline delays the phase-position of circadian neurotransmitter receptor rhythms. *Brain Res* 1982;241:115–122.
136. Goodman WK, Charney DS. Therapeutic applications and mechanisms of action of monoamine oxidase inhibitor and heterocyclic antidepressant drugs. *J Clin Psychiatry* 1985;46:6–22.
137. Hauger RL, Scheinin M, Siever LJ, Linnoila M, Potter WZ. Dissociation of norepinephrine turnover from α_2 responses after clorgyline. *Clin Pharmacol Ther* 1988;43:32–38.
138. Potter WZ, Murphy DL, Wehr TA, Linnoila M, Goodwin FK. Clorgyline. *Arch Gen Psychiatry* 1982;39:505–510.
139. Potter WZ. Norepinephrine as an "umbrella" neuromodulator. *Psychosomatics* 1986;27(Suppl 11):5–9.
140. Rudorfer MV, Potter WZ. Antidepressants: A comparative review of the clinical pharmacology and therapeutic use of the "newer" versus the "older" drugs. *Drugs* 1989;37:713–718.
141. Potter WZ, Rudorfer MV, Linnoila M. New clinical studies support a role of norepinephrine antidepressant action. In: *Perspectives in psychopharmacology*. New York: Alan R. Liss Inc., 1988;495–513.
142. Extein IL, Potter WZ, Wehr TA, Goodwin FK. Rapid mood cycles after a noradrenergic but not a serotonergic antidepressant. *Am J Psychiatry* 1979;136:1602–1603.
143. Baumhackl U, Biziere K, Fischbach R, et al. Efficacy and tolerability of moclobemide compared with imipramine in depressive disorder (DSM-III): An austrian double-blind multicentre study. *Br J Psychiatry* 1989;155(suppl 6):78–83.
144. Versiani M, Oggero U, Alterwain P, et al. A double-blind comparative trial of moclobemide v. imipramine and placebo in major depressive episodes. *Br J Psychiatry* 1989;155(suppl 6):72–77.
145. Byerley WF, McConnell EJ, McCabe RT, Daw-

sen TM, Grosser BI. Decreased β-adrenergic receptors in rat brain after chronic administration of the selective serotonin uptake inhibitor fluoxetine. *Psychopharmacology* 1988;94:141–143.
146. Hale AS, Procter AW, Bridges PK. Clomipramine, tryptophan and lithium in combination for resistant endogenous depression: Seven case studies. *Br J Psychiatry* 1987;151:213–217.
147. Steiner W, Fontaine R. Toxic reaction following the combined administration of fluoxetine and L-tryptophan: Five case reports. *Biol Psychiatry* 1986;21:1067–1071.
148. Thienhaus OJ. A case of severe lithium toxicity induced by combined fluoxetine and lithium carbonate. *Am J Psychiatry* 1989;146:278.
149. Hertzman PA, Blevins WL, Mayer J, Greenfield B, Ting M, Gleich GJ. Association of the eosinophilia-myalgia syndrome with the ingestion of tryptophan. *New Engl J Med* 1990;322:869–873.
150. Patterson BD, Srisopark MM. Severe anorexia and possible psychosis or hypomania after trazodone-tryptophan treatment of aggression. *Lancet* 1989;1:1017.
151. Golden RN, Rudorfer MV, Sherer MA, Linnoila M, Potter WZ. Buproprion in depression. *Arch Gen Psychiatry* 1988;45:139–149.
152. Ferris RM, Beaman OJ. Bupropion: A new antidepressant, the mechanism of action of which is not associated with downregulation of postsynaptic β-adrenergic, serotonergic (5HT$_2$), α$_2$-adrenergic, imipramine, and dopaminergic receptors. *Neuropharmacology* 1983;22:1257–1267.
153. Shopsin B. Bupropion's prophylactic efficacy in bipolar affective illness. *J Clin Psychiatry* 1983;44 (Sec 2):163–169.
154. Wright G, Galloway L, Kim J, Dalton M, Miller L, Stern W. Bupropion in the long-term treatment of cyclic mood disorders: Mood stabilizing effects. *J Clin Psychiatry* 1985;46:22–25.
155. Golden RN, James SP, Sherer MA, Rudorfer MV, Sack DA, Potter WZ. Psychoses associated with bupropion treatment. *Am J Psychiatry* 1985;142:1459–1462.
156. Goode DJ, Manning AA. Comparison of bupropion alone and with haloperidol in schizoaffective disorder, depressed type. *J Clin Psychiatry* 1983;44:253–255.
157. Osman OT, Rudorfer MV, Potter WZ. Idazoxan: A selective α$_2$-antagonist and effective sustained antidepressant in two bipolar depressed patients. *Arch Gen Psychiatry* 1989;46:958–959.
158. Bell KM, Plon L, Bunney WE Jr, Potkin SG. S-Adenosylmethionine treatment of depression: A controlled clinical trial. *Am J Psychiatry* 1988;145:1110–1114.
159. Kagan BL, Sultzer DL, Rosenlicht N, Gerner RH. Oral S-adenosylmethionine in depression: A randomized, double-blind, placebo-controlled trial. *Am J Psychiatry* 1990;147:591–595.
160. Lipinski JF, Cohen BM, Frankenburg F, et al. Open trial of S-adenosylmethionine for treatment of depression. *Am J Psychiatry* 1984;141:448–450.
161. Bottiglieri T, Laundy M, Martin R, et al. S-Adenosylmethionine influences monoamine metabolism. *Lancet* 1984;2:224.

16

Anticonvulsants as Adjuncts or Alternatives to Lithium in Refractory Bipolar Illness

Robert M. Post

Treatment of the bipolar depressed patient raises unique problems in comparison with the unipolar depressed patient because of concern that traditional antidepressants may induce a manic episode or rapid or continuous cycling. Substantial clinical experience and a considerable literature (1–4) indicate that some bipolar patients are indeed susceptible to the induction of mood swings by certain antidepressants. For example, in our refractory bipolar patient population, 35% showed definite or likely induction of mania, 34% demonstrated cycle shortening, and 17% showed induction of continuous cycling on tricyclic (TCA) or heterocyclic antidepressants. Those who showed likely manic induction (compared with those who did not, or where mania was unlikely attributable to the TCA) were more likely to have experienced rapid mood cycling in the year before NIMH admission and stayed longer in the hospital, suggesting a more severe course of illness.

As is implied in the foregoing discussion, treatment of the depressive episode in a bipolar patient should deal with two temporal perspectives: (a) early relief of symptoms associated with the acute episode, and (b) attention to the longitudinal course of the illness with regard to the potential for recurrent mood swings and the need for prophylaxis. Therefore, treatments associated with the potential for long-term prophylaxis of both manic and depressive episodes might be expected to have a higher priority in the treatment of bipolar depressed patients than heretofore considered. In this regard, considerable evidence suggests an acute and prophylactic efficacy for carbamazepine in the treatment of manic episodes and for preventing recurrent depressive episodes. Given this emerging spectrum of clinical efficacy, carbamazepine deserves special attention in the treatment of the depressed bipolar patient. Other anticonvulsants also are mentioned briefly, but little data exist regarding their acute and long-term efficacy in the treatment of bipolar disorder.

CARBAMAZEPINE IN THE TREATMENT OF ACUTE DEPRESSION

To date, we have evaluated 54 patients in a double-blind clinical trial of carbamazepine in depression, and 17 showed at least a moderate degree of response (5). Although this rate of response would not be considered robust in unselected populations, it is higher than that observed following placebo in our group of treatment-refractory patients. Several other points are noteworthy and are illustrated in Fig. 1. For example, in the treatment-responsive group, there was little evidence of clinical improvement in the first week of treatment, but gradual improvement did occur thereafter, with maximum improvement demon-

---

Biological Psychiatry Branch, National Institute of Mental Health, Bethesda, MD 20892.

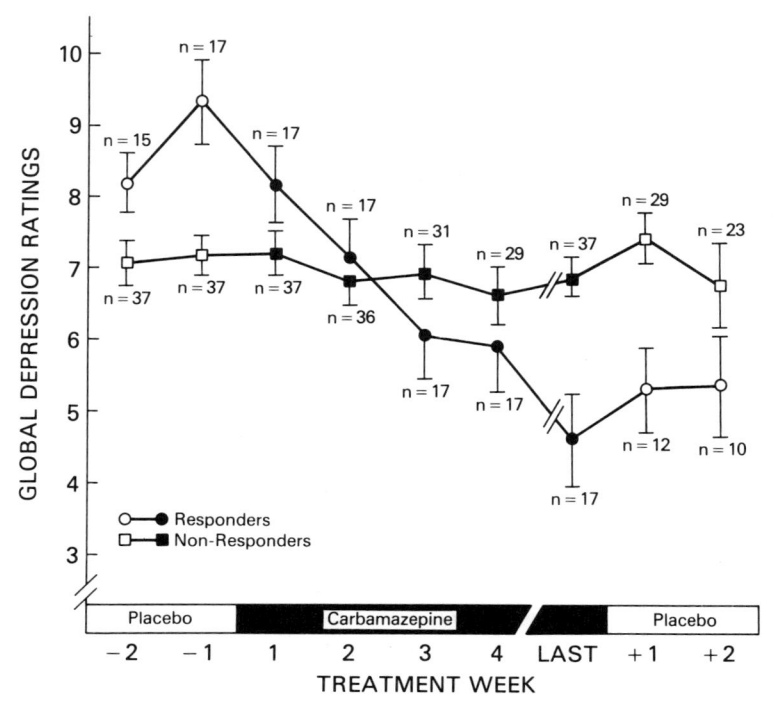

FIG. 1. Antidepressant course in marked response to carbamazepine.

strated by the fourth, fifth, or sixth week of treatment. This time lag in onset of antidepressant efficacy with carbamazepine in the responder group parallels that observed with traditional TCAs and monoamine oxidase inhibitor (MAOI) drugs. It is also noteworthy that the patients with more severe depression in the initial baseline placebo week before active treatment with carbamazepine were among those who showed the more substantial antidepressant response. In the patients who failed to respond to carbamazepine, there was little evidence of a withdrawal syndrome following carbamazepine discontinuation. Moreover, in contrast to many patients who did respond to carbamazepine for acute treatment of mania and showed rapid relapse following drug discontinuation (6), the antidepressant responders to carbamazepine often showed little evidence of deterioration on drug withdrawal.

In addition to severity of depression, other potential predictors of acute antidepressant response to carbamazepine include a history of discrete affective episodes rather than chronic depression (5). In addition, several factors not associated with acute antidepressant response to carbamazepine are particularly noteworthy. Neither minor EEG abnormalities nor a history of prominent paraepileptic or psychosensory symptoms usually associated with psychomotor seizures was predictive of acute antidepressant response. In contrast to antimanic responders (6), a negative family history of affective illness was not a predictor of antidepressant response. Although an association with acute antidepressant response to sleep deprivation and later antidepressant response to carbamazepine was originally noted, this relationship has not continued to be demonstrated in the larger series of patients and deserves further clinical investigation.

The antidepressant efficacy of carbamazepine compared with standard treatment modalities deserves further study using randomized assessment of patients. Most of the patients who responded to carbamazepine in our series previously had been refractory to other antidepressant agents, including lithium and more traditional TCAs and MAOIs. Thus, studies using crossover designs would be helpful not only in delineating the relative efficacy of carbamazepine against other agents but also in assessing whether there are different clinically responsive subgroups of patients who respond selectively to some agents and not others. Our initial data are not inconsistent with the observations of Neumann et al. (7) and of Prasad (8) but do not specifically address the question of antidepressant efficacy relative to other antidepressant agents. Similarly, despite substantial clinical research on the acute antidepressant effects of lithium carbonate, this treatment approach continues to remain a subject of some controversy. Thus, at present, the initial clinical profile of both lithium and carbamazepine indicates well-documented acute antimanic properties but less robust acute antidepressant effects.

Carbamazepine Dose, Blood Levels, and Side Effects

Conventional doses of carbamazepine in the treatment of epilepsy and trigeminal neuralgia range from 400 mg/day to 1600 mg/day. The dose and blood level range for the treatment of depression appear to be within a similar range. However, treatment of individual patients should be directed at attaining optimal dose and blood level in the absence of clinical side effects. Since there is an extremely wide range of carbamazepine doses and blood levels at which side effects are observed across different patients, this individualized dose titration approach appears critical for optimum management of carbamazepine. We suggest very slow increases in doses starting at 100 or 200 mg/day at night and holding or reducing doses should side effects emerge. These typically may be sedation, dizziness, ataxia, or diplopia several hours after an initial dose when peak blood levels are obtained. Should these side effects occur, maintenance of the same dose of transient dose reduction may be sufficient to obviate these difficulties. After 2 to 3 weeks of treatment, carbamazepine induces hepatic microsomal enzymes that increase the metabolism of the drug, and a dose that was initially poorly tolerated during the first several weeks of treatment ultimately may be tolerated easily after more chronic administration.

Within the dose range employed, we failed to observe a consistent relationship between carbamazepine blood levels and degree of clinical response (9). This lack of relationship supports the appropriateness of dose titration rather than the use of standardized approaches to bring all patients within a small range, particularly in the absence of a well-delineated therapeutic window.

A variety of commonly used drugs may increase carbamazepine blood levels substantially. These include erythromycin and its antibiotic congeners; the calcium channel blockers, verapamil and diltiazem (but not apparently nifedipine); the MAOI antituberculosis drug, isoniazid (but not other MAOIs, such as tranylcypromine); and several other agents, including propoxyphene. Thus, patients should be warned about the use of these agents in combination, since they may cause substantial increases in carbamazepine blood levels. Cimetidine may transiently cause mild increases, which are usually of little clinical concern. Valproate may increase the amount of carbamazepine epoxide in blood, but usually this is without clinical consequence.

LITHIUM AND CARBAMAZEPINE COMBINATION TREATMENT: EFFICACY AND SIDE EFFECTS

More than 50% of our patients who were inadequate responders to the antidepressant effects of carbamazepine showed a substantial clinical improvement when lithium carbonate was added on a blinded basis (10). The rapid onset of antidepressant response to lithium potentiation appeared to represent a true potentiation, since the response occurred faster than in other patients who show antidepressant responses to lithium alone and was faster in onset than that observed in successful potentiation of the antimanic effects of carbamazepine (10). The lithium doses used in this study were 300 to 1500 mg/day, with mean ($\pm$ SEM) blood levels of 0.7 ± 0.03 mEq/L and ranging between 0.2 and 1.0 mEq/L. Thus, these data are consistent with a large literature regarding lithium potentiation of other antidepressant medications (10).

Rapid onset of effect was reported by de Montigny et al. (11,12), although slower onset has been observed by Price et al. (13).

What remains to be seen is whether patients on lithium will also demonstrate a potentiation effect when carbamazepine is added to the treatment regimen. Potentiating the combination of lithium and carbamazepine with TCAs and MAOIs, although commonly attempted, also remains to be systematically examined.

Many side effects of lithium are not of particular concern in relation to carbamazepine. Carbamazepine possesses its own profile of side effects, including pruritic rash in 10 to 15% of psychiatric patients, dizziness, ataxia, sedation, or diplopia (which are dose-related and easily avoidable with slow increases in dose or dose reduction), mild white count suppression, and the ability to induce hyponatremia, hypocalcemia, and, more rarely, atrioventricular (AV) block. Very rare side effects of serious medical concern include idiosyncratic development of agranulocytosis, aplastic anemia, various types of hepatitis, water intoxication, and a rare allergic syndrome associated with lymphadenopathy.

The effect of lithium plus carbamazepine on the white count is of particular interest. The mild to moderate benign suppression of total white count that occurs with carbamazepine is completely reversed when lithium carbonate is introduced. Values not only return to baseline but also exceed the initial medication-free values (unpublished observations). These data are consistent with the original report of Brewerton et al. (14) and the study of Joffe et al. (15).

Whether lithium would have salutary effects against more rare idiosyncratic hematological reactions remains to be determined but is doubtful. These serious hematological effects, in contrast to the consistent small degrees of white count suppression, are extraordinarily rare. Pisciotta (16,17) estimated these to occur at a rate of 1 in 10,000 to 40,000 patients. More recent estimates of Pellock et al. (18) suggest that the incidence may be of the order of 8 patients in 1 million or 1 in 125,000 for either agranulocytosis or aplastic anemia.

The FDA-approved guidelines in the product package insert recently have been changed from a recommendation of monitoring on a frequent basis to a more flexible schedule. It would appear prudent to obtain baseline complete blood counts and follow these until becoming convinced that only benign white count suppression was occurring and the other hematological indices remained within normal limits. The patient should be instructed to call the physician should potential physical signs of severe hematological suppression develop, such as fever, rash, sore throat, petechiae, or bleeding.

The effect of lithium-carbamazepine in combination on thyroid hormones is particularly instructive. In this case, two potentially antithyroidal agents have an additive effect in reducing circulating levels of T_4, free T_4, and T_3 (10). However, in spite of this increased suppression of circulating thyroid hormones, the degree of TSH increase observed with the combination is similar if not less than that observed on lithium alone. This suggests that the antithyroid effects of carbamazepine, which are not usually associated with clinical hypothyroidism, occur by a different mechanism than those of lithium and that when the combination is used, it is the lithium-induced increases in TSH that are being observed.

It is of considerable theoretical interest that patients who show the most robust clinical antidepressant response to carbamazepine also show the greatest decrements in circulating levels of T_4 and free T_4 ($r = -0.56$, $n = 36$, $p = 0.0004$). These data are similar to observations by Baumgartner et al. (19), who reported that decrements in thyroid indices were related to clinical response to clomipramine and maprotiline. These data are not placed easily in the context of the general view that hypothyroidism may be associated with rapid cycling (20,21). The degree to which prior or concurrent lithium treatment accounted for this association in the study of Cowdry et al. (20) is uncertain. In contrast to those findings, Joffe et al. (22) and our group found no relationship of initial medication-free thyroid indices and degree of rapid cycling (23). In fact, when we examined the last medication-free thyroid indices before beginning pharmacotherapy, we observed a weak but statistically significant relationship between higher levels of free T_4 and T_4 and degree of rapid cycling ($r = 0.22$, $n = 103$, $p < 0.05$). If one split the groups on the basis of rapid cycling (four or more episodes/year) and nonrapid cycling (less than four episodes/year), the rapid cyclers showed significantly higher levels of both T_4 and free T_4. Viewed from this perspective, it is possible that the relative antithyroidal effects of lithium and carbamazepine could be related to or be a marker of their clinical effectiveness (24).

In a similar fashion, Joffe et al. (24) postulated that the acute effects of T_3 potentiation in the treatment of depression could be conceptualized as providing a relatively antithyroidal effect. When T_3 is given, levels of circulating T_4 are suppressed by a feedback mechanism. Since circulating levels of T_4 appear to be the main mechanism of providing thyroid hormone to the brain by active uptake of circulating T_4 and intracellular conversion to T_3, it is possible that T_3 potentiation (via its suppressive effect on T_4) also could be acting as a relative thyroid-suppressing mechanism, at least for cerebral thyroid metabolism. This interesting proposition remains to be tested directly in animals, given the complex regulatory mechanisms to maintain thyroid homeostasis. The integrated effect of giving T_3 on circulating T_4 levels and cerebral metabolism certainly deserves further careful clinical and basic investigation.

Initial clinical data, however, suggest the possible use of T_3 potentiation of ongoing antidepressant responses to a variety of treatment modalities (see ref. 25 for review). One would suggest the use of T_3 instead of T_4 for this acute antidepressant potentiation for several reasons. Most of the clinical trials have used T_3, and data of Joffe et al. (26) suggest that T_3 potentiation is more effective than T_4 potentiation when the two drugs were given on a randomized basis in treatment-refractory depressed patients.

Although we have not observed a similar antidepressant response with T_3 potentiation of carbamazepine in nonresponders compared to that of lithium potentiation, we have seen some apparent responders to thyroid potentiation. Thus, it may be practical to attempt thyroid potentiation with triiodothyronine 25 or 50 µg in the A.M. before considering switching antidepressant modalities or potentiation by lithium carbonate.

The effects of lithium and carbamazepine on fluid and electrolyte function are worthy of comment. Whereas lithium produces diabetes insipidus, carbamazepine has been used to treat this syndrome. However, carbamazepine will not reverse lithium-induced diabetes insipidus. Its effect appears to be exerted at or near the vasopressin receptor, whereas the antivasopressin effects of lithium appear beyond the receptor by interfering with adenylate cyclase function. It remains to be directly demonstrated whether carbamazepine has a different set of effects on tests of learning, memory, and cognition in comparison with lithium (27).

CARBAMAZEPINE PROPHYLAXIS FOR RECURRENT BIPOLAR DEPRESSION

Decreased frequency and duration of recurrent depressive as well as manic episodes have been observed in a series of our bipolar patients treated with carbamazepine alone or in combination with previously ineffective drugs and followed in a naturalistic study. In preliminary analysis of a group of 22 patients followed for an average of more than 4 years on carbamazepine, we observed that half the patients showed a pattern of stable prophylaxis, whereas half began to demonstrate a pattern of escape from adequate carbamazepine prophylaxis during the second, third, or fourth year of the study.

In preclinical models, we have elucidated a syndrome of conditioned tolerance to the anticonvulsant effects of carbamazepine on amygdala-kindled seizures (28). This tolerance can be reversed by a period of seizures with no treatment or by administering carbamazepine after rather than before kindled seizures occur. We currently are exploring the possibility that conditioned tolerance could develop also in nonseizure syndromes, such as trigeminal neuralgia or affective illness, and account for some instances of progressive loss of efficacy. Should the preclinical findings on contingent tolerance be relevant, they might suggest that temporary discontinuation of a drug that has lost efficacy could be associated with renewed responsiveness when the drug is restarted.

Our data on long-term prophylaxis in a subgroup of patients are consistent with the earlier work of Okuma et al. (29), indicating that a subgroup of patients will show a moderate to excellent response when carbamazepine is used either alone or, usually, in combination with previously ineffective treatment modalities (in most instances, lithium carbonate). The double-blind study of Okuma et al. (30) showed a trend toward increased efficacy of carbamazepine in the prevention of depressive episodes compared with placebo. These data are consistent with the controlled data of Watkins et al. (31) and an open study of Kishimoto and Okuma (32), who found that lithium nonsignificantly decreased the number of depressions per year from 1.8 ± 1.5 to 1.4 ± 1.5, and carbamazepine decreased them to 0.9 ± 1.5 ($p<0.025$ paired t-test carbamazepine vs control). However, further double-blind controlled clinical trials of the relative efficacy of carbamazepine, lithium, and the combination, as well as study of possible clinical predictors of response, appear indicated. Preliminary data of Joffe (unpublished observations) from an open study suggest that more rapid cycling patients may respond better to carbamazepine compared with lithium and that patients who show a pattern of continuous cycling may be among those who require the combination.

The role of adjunctive agents, including thyroid potentiation, for the long-term management of patients with recurrent depression, also deserves further study. Following the observations of Gjessing (33) and Stancer and Persad (34), hypermetabolic doses of thyroid might prevent recurrent episodes of periodic catatonia and affective swings. Systematic trials by Wehr et al. (35) and Bauer and Whybrow (36) suggested a possible use of thyroid augmentation in some rapid cycling, treatment-refractory bipolar patients.

OTHER ANTICONVULSANTS FOR TREATMENT-REFRACTORY BIPOLAR PATIENTS

Although valproic acid (37) and clonazepam (38) exert antimanic efficacy, their clinical use in the depressed phase of bipolar illness remains to be further delineated in systematic controlled studies. Preliminary evidence suggests that some rapid cycling patients who do not respond adequately to carbamazepine may respond to valproic acid (37,39,40). However, in the study of Puzynski and Klosiewicz (41), depressed phases of the illness did not respond as adequately as manic phases, and some patients experienced an increased frequency of recurrent depressive episodes. The number of manic episodes decreased 57.1% on valproate, but depressive episodes showed only a 19.1% reduction. The use of clonazepam in prophylaxis of bipolar patients also awaits further clinical documentation, particularly in light of reports that some benzodiazepines may precipitate depression in patients with panic attacks (42,43).

Although claims for the antidepressant efficacy of phenytoin have been widely touted (44), systematic studies of this anticonvulsant in patients with major affective disorders have not been performed.

Both the acute and long-term efficacy of GABA-active agents, such as progabide and its congeners, remains to be systematically explored (45,46). Our preliminary evidence suggests that the $GABA_B$ agonist L-baclofen is ineffective in the treatment of depression, although it is effective in the treatment of trigeminal neuralgia.

Calcium channel blockers, with the exception of nimodipine and flunarazine, are not widely recognized for their anticonvulsant efficacy. Nonetheless, they remain of considerable interest as potential treatment options for the refractory bipolar depressed patient in light of recent reports of their acute antimanic effectiveness.

Hoschl and Kozeny (47) reported that verapamil was as effective as haloperidol alone or in combination with lithium in the treatment of acute mania but that it was ineffective in depression, where it was equal to placebo and inferior to amitriptyline or other standard antidepressant treatments.

The anticonvulsant treatment with the clearest profile of clinical efficacy in refractory depression remains electroconvulsive therapy (ECT) (48). It has been amply demonstrated that electroconvulsive seizures (ECS) in both patients and laboratory animals exert potent anticonvulsant effects. In patients, there is often an increase in the threshold for seizures with repetition of ECS, with some patients becoming refractory even at maximal settings (49–52). We have found that ECS in the rat potently will inhibit the development of amygdala-kindled seizures as well as inhibit these seizures once they are fully developed (53). Others have demonstrated that an anticonvulsant principle is released into CSF of animals experiencing major seizures, and when CSF is transferred from these animals, it exerts an anticonvulsant effect in the recipient animal that is naloxone reversible, suggesting the possibility that this principle is an endogenous opiate (54). Regardless of the mechanism of the anticonvulsant effects of ECS, which have been postulated to involve a variety of neurotransmitter and neuropeptide systems, it is evident that this modality is among the most potent in treating patients with refractory depression. Clearly, it remains a treatment for further clinical and theoretical investigation in the refractory bipolar patient.

LIFE CHARTING LONGITUDINAL COURSE OF MANIC-DEPRESSIVE ILLNESS: A POSSIBLE DIFFERENTIAL PHARMACOTHERAPY AS A FUNCTION OF STAGE OF EVOLUTION OF ILLNESS

Elsewhere we have discussed the importance of considering the longitudinal course of the illness in the overall assessment and treatment of the bipolar patient with recurrent or refractory illness (55,56). We believe that this life charting technique (57–59) has many derived practical clinical benefits as well as leading one to consider that pharmacotherapy may differ in various stages of bipolar illness. For example, there is considerable evidence that lithium is less effective in rapidly cycling bipolar patients compared to patients with slower cycle frequencies (60–62). Conversely, preliminary data from several laboratories suggest that carbamazepine may be more effective in patients with rapid cycling (6,32 R.T. Joffe, unpublished observations). The relative clinical efficacy of carbamazepine in patients earlier in the course of illness and in those who are not lithium refractory requires further clinical study.

The possibility exists that different agents might be more effective in different stages of manic-depressive illness, in a fashion similar to preclinical animal models, such as electrophysiological kindling (56). In these animal models for the progressive evolution of affective syndromes (63), there is clear-cut evidence that the time frame of pharmacological intervention may be associated with the efficacy of a given agent. For example, in cocaine-induced behavioral sensitization, neuroleptics given on day 1 before a high dose of cocaine (40 mg/kg) block the development of cocaine-induced behavioral sensitization, whereas when given on day 2 before a low challenge dose of cocaine, they are insufficient to block the expression of cocaine-induced behavioral sensitization (64). Other pharmacological agents do not show this dissociation. For example, the benzodiazepine diazepam and the α_2-noradrenergic agonist clonidine appear effective in both the development and the expression of cocaine-induced behavioral sensitization, and carbamazepine is ineffective in this animal model in both early (development) and late (expression) phases of sensitization (55).

In contrast, carbamazepine is effective in some stages of kindling but not others, and this varies according to the type of kindling (56). It blocks the development of cocaine- and lidocaine-induced kindled seizures but is ineffective at blocking these seizures once they are in the completed phase or following acute high doses. Pinel (65) has demonstrated that in the late, spontaneous phases of electrical kindling, there is differential responsivity to pharmacological agents, with animals responding to phenytoin but not diazepam, whereas earlier in the development of the kindling, the response profile was the opposite. Similar principles may obtain in the differential treatment of early, mid, and late (rapid cycling) phases of manic-depressive illness (56).

CONCLUSIONS

A variety of treatment modalities are now available for the lithium-resistant bipolar depressed patient. Systematization of the database and identification of possible clinical and biological markers of which patient may respond to which treatment most optimally remains an issue of high clinical and theoretical priority. Evaluation of the course of illness and the temporal relationship between symptom development and pharmacological intervention may be relevant for appropriate clinical assessment. New treatment modalities obviously are needed for the small but substantial percentage of patients with refractory illness.

It is hoped that through a combination of recent neuroscience advances, serendipity, and systematic preclinical investigation and clinical studies, a new range of treatment options will emerge for this group of patients. In a short span of several decades, we have progressed from an era where no effective treatment modality existed for the bipolar patient to lithium as the only treatment to the present, where a host of pharmacological interventions is available. We look forward to the development of new and more specific treatment alternatives for affectively ill patients so that the potentially devastating consequences of illness can be ameliorated.

REFERENCES

1. Wehr TA, Goodwin FK. Can antidepressants cause mania and worsen the course of affective illness? *Am J Psychiatry* 1987;144:1403–1411.

2. Wehr TA, Goodwin FK. Do antidepressants cause mania? *Psychopharmacol Bull* 1987;23:61–65.
3. Bunney WE Jr, Wehr TR, Gillin JC, et al. The switch process in manic-depressive psychosis. *Ann Intern Med* 1977;87:319–335.
4. Kukopulos A, Reginaldi D, Laddomada P, et al. Course of the manic-depressive cycle and changes caused by treatments. *Pharmakopsychiatria* 1980;13:156–167.
5. Post RM, Uhde TW, Roy-Byrne PP, et al. Antidepressant effects of carbamazepine. *Am J Psychiatry* 1986;143:29–34.
6. Post RM, Uhde TW, Roy-Byrne PP, et al. Correlates of antimanic responses to carbamazepine. *Psychiatry Res* 1987;21:71–83.
7. Neumann J, Seidel K, Wunderlich H-P. Comparative studies of the effect of carbamazepine and trimipramine in depression. In: Emrich HM, Okuma T, Muller AA, eds. *Anticonvulsants in affective disorders*. Amsterdam: Excerpta Medica, 1984;160–166.
8. Prasad AJ. Efficacy of carbamazepine as an antidepressant in chronic resistant depressives. *J Indian Med Assoc* 1985;183:235–237.
9. Post RM, Uhde TW, Ballenger JC, et al. CSF carbamazepine and its -10,11-epoxide metabolite in manic-depressive patients: Relationship to clinical response. *Arch Gen Psychiatry* 1983;40:673–676.
10. Kramlinger KG, Post RM. The addition of lithium carbonate to carbamazepine: Antidepressant efficacy in treatment-resistant depression. *Arch Gen Psychiatry* 1989;46:794–800.
11. de Montigny C, Elie R, Caille G. Rapid response to the addition of lithium in iprindole-resistant unipolar depression: A pilot study. *Am J Psychiatry* 1985;142:220–223.
12. de Montigny C, Grunberg F, Mayer A, et al. Lithium induces rapid relief of depression in tricyclic antidepressant drug non-responders. *Br J Psychiatry* 1981;138:252–256.
13. Price LH, Charney DS, Heninger GR. Variability of response to lithium augmentation in refractory depression. *Am J Psychiatry* 1986;143:1387–1392.
14. Brewerton TD. Lithium counteracts carbamazepine-induced leukopenia while increasing its therapeutic effect: A case report. *Biol Psychiatry* 1986;21:677–685.
15. Joffe RT. Hematological effects of lithium potentiation of carbamazepine in patients with affective illness. *Int Clin Psychopharmacol* 1988;3:53–57.
16. Pisciotta AV. Carbamazepine: Hematologic toxicity. In: Woodbury DM, Penry JK, Pippenger C, eds. *Antiepileptic drugs*. New York: Raven Press, 1982;533–541.
17. Pisciotta AV. Hematologic toxicity of carbamazepine. In: Penry JK, Daly DD, eds. *Complex partial seizures and their treatment: Advances in neurology, vol 11*. New York: Raven Press, 1975;355–368.
18. Pellock JM. Carbamazepine side effects in children and adults. *Epilepsia* 1987;28:64S–70S.
19. Baumgartner A, Graf K-J, Kurten I, et al. The hypothalamic-pituitary-thyroid axis in psychiatric patients and healthy subjects: Part 3: The TRH test and thyroid hormone determinations as predictors of therapeutic response and long-term outcome in major depression and schizophrenia. *Psychiatr Res* 1988;24:306–315, 324–332.
20. Cowdry RW, Wehr TA, Zis AP, et al. Thyroid abnormalities associated with rapid-cycling bipolar illness. *Arch Gen Psychiatry* 1983;40:414–420.
21. Bauer MS, Whybrow PC. Thyroid hormones and the central nervous system in affective illness: Interactions which may have clinical significance. *Integrative Psychiatry* 1988;6:75–85.
22. Joffe RT, Kutcher SP, MacDonald C. Thyroid function and lithium treatment in bipolar affective disorder. In: *Proceedings of the 2nd British lithium Congress*. [Sept 6–9, 1987, Wolverhampton, England]. Oxford: IRL Press, 1988.
23. Post RM, Kramlinger KG, Joffe RT, et al. Effects of carbamazepine on thyroid function. Abstracts, American Psychiatric Assoc, 140th Annual Meeting, Chicago, May 9–14, 1987, Symposium 104-D, 1987;142.
24. Joffe RT, Roy-Byrne PP, Uhde TW, et al. Thyroid function and affective illness: A reappraisal. *Biol Psychiatry* 1984;19:1685–1691.
25. Joffe RT, Post RM. Experimental treatment for affective disorder. In: Berger PA, Brodie KH, eds. *American handbook of psychiatry, vol. 8*. New York: Basic Books, 1986;386–407.
26. Joffe RT, Singer W. A comparison of triiodothyronine and thyroxine in the potentiation of tricyclic antidepressants. *Psychiatry Research* 1990;32:241–251.
27. Joffe RT, MacDonald C, Kutcher SP. Lack of differential cognitive effects of lithium and carbamazepine in bipolar affective disorder. *J Clin Psychopharmacol* 1988;8:425–428.
28. Weiss SRB, Post RM. Development and reversal of conditioned inefficacy and tolerance to the anticonvulsant effects of carbamazepine. *Epilepsia* in press.
29. Okuma T, Kishimoto A, Inoue K, et al. Antimanic prophylactic effects of carbamazepine on manic-depressive psychosis. *Folia Psychiatr Neurol Jpn* 1973;27:283–297.
30. Okuma T, Inanaga K, Otsuki, S. A preliminary double-blind study of the efficacy of carbamazepine in prophylaxis of manic-depressive illness. *Psychopharmacology* 1981;73:95–96.
31. Watkins SE, Callender K, Thomas DR, et al. The effect of carbamazepine and lithium on remission from affective illness. *Br J Psychiatry* 1987;150:180–182.
32. Kishimoto A, Okuma T. Antimanic and prophylactic effects of carbamazepine in affective disorders. Abstracts of the 4th World Congress of Biological Psychiatry, Sept 8–13, 1985, Philadelphia, 1985;363, Abstract 506.4.
33. Gjessing LR. Academic address: A review of periodic catatonia. *Biol Psychiatry* 1975;8:23–45.
34. Stancer HC, Persad E. Treatment of intractable

rapid-cycling manic-depressive disorder with levothyroxine. *Arch Gen Psychiatry* 1982;39: 311-312.
35. Wehr TA, Sack DA, Cowdry RW. Thyroid-axis abnormalities in bipolar depression. Abstracts, IVth World Congress of Biological Psychiatry, Sept 8-13, 1985, Philadelphia, 1985;326, Abstract 414.6.
36. Bauer MS, Whybrow PC. Rapid cycling bipolar affective disorder. II. Treatment of refractory rapid cycling with high-dose levothyroxine: A preliminary study. *Archives of General Psychiatry* 1990;47:435-440.
37. Emrich HM, Dose M, von Zerssen D. Action of sodium-valproate and of oxcarbazepine in patients with affective disorders. In: Emrich HM, Okuma T, Muller AA, eds. *Anticonvulsants in affective disorders.* Amsterdam: Excerpta Medica, 1984;45-55.
38. Chouinard G, Young SN, Annable L. Antimanic effect of clonazepam. *Biol Psychiatry* 1983;18: 451-466.
39. Post RM, Uhde TW. Anticonvulsants in non-epileptic psychosis. In: Trimble MR, Bolwig TG, eds. *Aspects of epilepsy and psychiatry.* Chichester, England: John Wiley & Sons Ltd, 1986; 177-212.
40. McElroy SL, Keck PE Jr, Pope HG Jr. Sodium valproate: Its use in primary psychiatric disorders. *J Clin Psychopharmacol* 1987;7:16-24.
41. Puzynski S, Klosiewicz L. Valproic acid amide as a prophylactic agent in affective and schizoaffective disorders. In: Emrich HM, Okuma T, Muller AA, eds. *Anticonvulsants in affective disorders.* Amsterdam: Excerpta Medica, 1984; 68-75.
42. Pollack MH, Tesar GR, Rosenbaum JF, et al. Clonazepam in the treatment of panic disorder and agoraphobia: A one-year follow-up. *J Clin Psychopharmacol* 1986;6:302-304.
43. Lydiard RB, Laraia MT, Ballenger JC, et al. Emergence of depressive symptoms in patients receiving alprazolam for panic disorder. *Am J Psychiatry* 1987;144:664-665.
44. Dreyfus J. *A remarkable medicine has been overlooked.* New York: Simon & Schuster, 1981.
45. Morselli PL, Fournier V, Macher JP, et al. Therapeutic action of progabide in depressive illness: A controlled clinical trial. In: Bartholini G, Lloyd KG, Morselli PL, eds. *GABA and mood disorders.* [Laboratoires d'Etudes et de Recherches Synthelabo (L.E.R.S.) Monograph Series, vol. 4.] New York: Raven Press, 1986;119-126.
46. De Maio D. Progabide in mania: Preliminary observations. Proceedings of the IXth International Union of Pharmacology (IUPHAR) Congress, Paris, Aug 6-7, 1984.
47. Hoschl C, Kozeny J. Verapamil in affective disorders: A controlled, double-blind study. *Biol Psychiatry* 1989;25:128-140.
48. Fink M. Theories of the antidepressant efficacy of convulsive therapy (ECT). In: Post RM, Ballenger JC, eds. *Neurobiology of mood disorders.* Baltimore: Williams & Wilkins, 1984;721-730.

49. Hinkle PE, Coffey CW, Weiner RD, et al. Use of caffeine to lengthen seizures in ECT. *Am J Psychiatry* 1987;144:1143-1148.
50. Coffey CE, Weiner RD, Hinkle PE, et al. Augmentation of ECT seizures with caffeine. *Biol Psychiatry* 1987;22:637-649 (published erratum appears in *Biol Psychiatry* 1987;22:1299).
51. Shapira B, Lerer B, Gilboa D, Drexler H, Kugelmass S, Calev A. Facilitation of ECT by caffeine pretreatment. *Am J Psychiatry* 1987; 144:1199-1202.
52. Sackeim HA, Decina P, Portnoy S, Neeley P, Malitz S. Studies of dosage, seizure threshold, and seizure duration in ECT. *Biol Psychiatry* 1987;22:249-268.
53. Post RM, Putnam F, Uhde TW, Weiss SRB. ECT as an anticonvulsant: Implications for its mechanism of action in affective illness. In: Malitz S, Sackeim HA, eds. *Electroconvulsive therapy: Clinical and basic research issues.* Annals of the New York Academy of Sciences, vol. 462. New York: NY Academy of Sciences, 1986;376-388.
54. Holaday JW, Tortella FC, Long JB, Belenky GL, Hitzeman RJ. Endogenous opioids and their receptors: Evidence for involvement in the postictal effects of electroconvulsive shock. *Ann NY Acad Sci* 1986;462:124-139.
55. Post RM, Rubinow DR, Ballenger JC. Conditioning, sensitization, and kindling: Implications for the course of affective illness. In: Post RM, Ballenger JC, eds. *Neurobiology of mood disorders.* Baltimore: Williams & Wilkins, 1984; 432-466.
56. Post RM, Rubinow DR, Ballenger JC. Conditioning and sensitization in the longitudinal course of affective illness. *Br J Psychiatry* 1986;149:191-201.
57. Squillace KM, Post RM, Savard R, Erwin M. Life charting of the longitudinal course of affective illness. In: Post RM, Ballenger JC, eds. *Neurobiology of mood disorders.* Baltimore: Williams & Wilkins, 1984;38-59.
58. Roy-Byrne PP, Post RM, Uhde TW, Porcu T, Davis D. The longitudinal course of recurrent affective illness: Life chart data from research patients at the NIMH. *Acta Psychiatr Scand* 1985;71(Suppl 317):3-34.
59. Post RM, Roy-Byrne PP, Uhde TW. Graphic representation of the life course of illness in patients with affective disorder. *Am J Psychiatry* 1988;145:844-848.
60. Goodnick PJ, Fieve RR, Schlegel A, Baxter N. Predictors of interepisode symptoms and relapse in affective disorder patients treated with lithium carbonate. *Am J Psychiatry* 1987;144:367-369.
61. Bouman TK, Niemantsverdriet-van Kampen JG, Ormel J, Slooff CJ. The effectiveness of lithium prophylaxis in bipolar and unipolar depressions and schizo-affective disorders. *J Affective Disord* 1986;11:275-280.
62. Hanus H, Zapletalek M. The prophylactic lithium treatment in affective disorders and the possibilities of the outcome prediction. *Sb Ved Pr Lek Fak Univ Karlovy* 1984;27:5-75.

63. Post RM. Non-homologous animal models of affective illness: Clinical relevance of sensitization and kindling. In: Koob GF, Ehlers CL, Kupfer D, eds. *Animal models of depression.* Boston: Birkhauser Inc., 1989;30–54.
64. Weiss SRB, Post RM, Pert A, Woodward R, Murman D. Context-dependent cocaine sensitization: Differential effect of haloperidol on development versus expression. *Pharmacol Biochem Behav* 1989;34:655–661.
65. Pinel JP. Effects of diazepam and diphenylhydantoin on elicited and spontaneous seizures in kindled rats: A double dissociation. *Pharmacol Biochem Behav* 1983;18:61–63.

17

A Review of Psychostimulants in Elderly Patients with Refractory Depression

David Gurevitch,[1] Curtis A. Bagne,[1] Eliezer Perl,[2] and Manuel S. Dumlao[1]

Psychostimulants were an important pharmacological treatment for depression starting in the mid 1930s and later were used as active control agents to evaluate antidepressants that have become standard therapies (1,2). More recently, stimulants fell into disrepute primarily because of concern about dependency and potential for abuse (3,4). Current resurgent interest in the antidepressant effects of stimulants is represented by recent reviews (5–8) and clinical research reports. These agents are of interest because of their therapeutic profile, the remaining need for antidepressant therapies, as probes for elucidating nervous system function and psychopathology (9,10), and as test agents to predict antidepressant response (11,12).

This chapter reviews some aspects of psychostimulant therapy that are relevant for treatment of depressed or apathetic elderly patients. Many of the studies described patients who were "chronic," "intractable," "refractory," or "treatment-resistant" without using any standard working definition. However, we agree with the comment by Chiarello and Cole about psychostimulant therapy for depressed patients that the "findings are tantalizing but decidedly inconclusive" (6, p. 288).

The second part of this chapter presents results from a pilot study of the antidepressant effects of pemoline in an elderly population. The pilot study demonstrates a measure of benefit or harm that would allow us to conduct more definitive evaluations of drugs used to manage chronic disorders that impair function.

REVIEW

Early Studies

Several studies were conducted in the 1930s before the introduction of modern antidepressants and recent definitions of depression.

Myerson reported seven patients representing a larger series in whom twice daily doses of 10 to 20 mg amphetamine sulfate generally ameliorated depressive states (13). Response was rapid but short-lived. Myerson also reported two patients in whom the effect was judged to be adverse and commented that drug effects tended to be variable and difficult to anticipate (13). Davidoff and Reifenstein reported improvement in 30% of manic-depressive patients in depressed phase with 10 to 30 mg amphetamine sulfate per day (14). Anderson studied the responses of 27 hospitalized depressed patients on 5 to 45 mg daily doses of amphetamine sulfate (15). As other investigators before and after, he noted great variability of response but stated that a

---

[1]Lafayette Clinic, Detroit, MI 48207.
[2]The Talbieh Hospital, Jerusalem 91100, Israel.

"small minority of cases seem to benefit definitely" (15, p. 64).

Dub and Lurie used a longitudinal double-blind design with repeated drug challenges and large samples of repeated assessments to evaluate 5 to 10 mg daily doses of amphetamine in 48 depressed females, ages 18 to 75, who had been institutionalized from 10 months to 26 years (16). Treatment appeared to be quite remarkably and consistently effective.

Methylphenidate (Ritalin), which was introduced in the 1950s, provided an alternative to the amphetamines. Reports on the use of methylphenidate in doses up to 60 mg/day suggested that the drug was effective in a majority of cases over a broad age range (17–20). These studies, on a total of 318 patients, reported improvement in 60 to 70% of the subjects. It should be noted that the patient group was heterogeneous, and only one of these studies was placebo controlled.

Controlled Studies for Depressed Patients

Satel and Nelson provided a comprehensive review of studies reported since 1956 on the effects of stimulants on depression (8). There were no controlled studies on the effect of stimulants for geriatric patients with primary depression. Two lines of evidence come closest to addressing the problem of treatment-resistant depression in the elderly. This section reviews controlled evaluations of stimulants in depressed patients who were not generally elderly. The following section reviews controlled studies in which stimulants were evaluated for geriatric patients.

Doust et al. reported a placebo-controlled, double-blind study of the antidepressant effects of imipramine, iproniazid, and amphetamine in 24 refractory patients (21). Amphetamine was not found to be significantly effective, and the individual reactions to drugs were variable. A placebo-controlled crossover study of amphetamine in 40 chronically depressed patients was reported by the General Practice Research Group (22). The majority of patients were diagnosed as endogenously depressed, with symptom durations of 1 to 2 years. Amphetamines were found to have slight effect in the chronically depressed. Hare et al. treated 43 patients in a crossover design comparing amphetamine, 10 mg/day, phenelzine 60 mg/day, and placebo (23). Each drug was given for a period of 2 weeks. Neither active drug was more effective than placebo on a 5-point nonstandardized clinical scale.

Overall et al. compared the efficacy of dextroamphetamine to tranylcypromine in 51 men using a randomized parallel group design (2). These study patients had a variety of depressive disorders, and the age range was 29 to 70. Tranylcypromine was found to be somewhat more effective as judged by subjective patients ratings, but both drugs were found to be equally beneficial by professional raters.

Controlled Studies in Elderly Depressed Patients

The studies reviewed in this section addressed relatively homogeneous geriatric patient populations (Table 1). Landman et al. reported on the efficacy and safety of methylphenidate, 30 mg/day, for 61 chronically depressed subjects (24). Many of these patients were suffering from a variety of physical disorders. Patients on methylphenidate were found to be significantly improved, with few side effects. Insomnia, restlessness, and slight tremor were seen in 7% of the patients. Kaplitz studied the efficacy of methylphenidate in 44 "withdrawn, apathetic geriatric patients" in a double-blind, randomized design (25, p. 271). Following a 2-week pretreatment period, subjects who received methylphenidate 20 mg/day over 6 weeks demonstrated significant improvement as measured on the Mental Status Check List (MSCL),

TABLE 1. Controlled studies of stimulants in geriatric patients

Study	Design	Subjects	Age (average)	Type of assessment	Improved (%)
Landman et al. 1958 (24)	Double-blind, crossover, methylphenidate/placebo	61	70	Clinical impression	61%
Kaplitz 1975 (25)	Double-blind, parallel group, methylphenidate/placebo	44	77	Global evaluation, MSCL, NOSIE	76%

Nurses' Observation Scale for Inpatient Evaluation (NOSIE), and clinical evaluation. Clear-cut response to the stimulant was in the absence of side effects, suggesting the possibility of increasing the dose "when a greater response is desired" (25, p. 276).

Combination Therapies

Table 2 summarizes five studies in which psychostimulants were evaluated in combination with other drugs for the treatment of refractory depression (26–30). Wharton et al. used a longitudinal design and reported on "patients with recurrent refractory psychotic depressive illness" (26, p. 1619). Methylphenidate appeared to increase blood levels of tricyclic antidepressants (TCA). It was reported that "five of the seven patients treated with the combination therapy had prompt, striking, complete clinical remissions" (26, p. 1621). A case report by Cooper and Simpson replicated these results (27). A case report by Drimmer et al. found clinical improvement without a change in serum desipramine level (28). Feighner et al. reported that combinations of drugs involving stimulants, monoamine oxidase inhibitors (MAOIs), and TCAs were generally safe and effective for patients with "intractable" depression (29). Depressive symptomatology appears to have improved in about 25 of the 34 patients summarized in Table 2 who received treatment combinations including stimulants.

Depressed, Medically Ill Patients

Treatment of medically ill patients is complicated by the fact that conventional antidepressants may be contraindicated or ineffective. Eight reports about the use of stimulants are summarized in Table 3 (31–38). These studies were primarily case reports and chart reviews. A total of 139 patients was reported. A majority of these patients were elderly. Antidepressants, in

TABLE 2. Psychostimulants in combination with other drugs for treatment of depression

Study	Subjects	Age[a]	Drug combination	Outcome
Wharton et al. 1971 (26)	7	$\bar{x} = 55$ 43–69	Imipramine or nortriptyline/methylphenidate	5/7 improved
Cooper and Simpson 1973 (27)	1	61	Imipramine/methylphenidate	Improved
Drimmer et al. 1983 (28)	1	39	Desipramine/methylphenidate	Improved
Lehmann et al. 1971 (30)	12	$\bar{x} = 72$ 61–82	Meperidine/dextroamphetamine	8/12 improved
Feighner et al. 1985 (29)	13	$\bar{x} = 51$ 33–77	MAOI/stimulant with or without TCA	10/13 improved

[a]$\bar{x}$ = mean.

TABLE 3. *Psychostimulants in treatment of depressed medically ill patients*

Study	Subjects	Age[a]	Medical diagnosis	Outcome
Katon and Raskind 1980 (34)	3	$\bar{x} = 79$ 73–85	Various illnesses	Good response
Kaufman and Murray 1982 (35)	3		Various illnesses	Good response
Kaufman et al. 1984 (36)	5	$\bar{x} = 65$ 57–73	Various diagnoses	Good response
Kaufman et al. 1984 (37)	4	$\bar{x} = 62$ 52–71	Cardiac conduction defect (CHF)	Good response
Fisch 1985 (38)	3	$\bar{x} = 75$ 70–79	Various diagnoses	Good response
Woods et al. 1986 (31)	66	$\bar{x} = 72$ 37–87	Various illnesses	73% some improvement 48% marked/moderate improvement
Fernandez et al. 1987 (32)	30	$\bar{x} = 57$ 30–99	Cancer	76% marked/moderate improvement
Lingam et al. 1988 (33)	25	$\bar{x} = 78$	Stroke	52% improvement

[a] $\bar{x}$ = mean.

most cases TCAs, were attempted but failed to improve the patient's affective status or could not be used because of complicating medical problems. Three of the studies, including 121 patients, reported an improvement in depressive symptoms in 52 to 76% of the subjects, with rapid response, generally within 48 hours, and few side effects (31–33).

Overview

Two authors have offered treatment guidelines for depressed medically ill and depressed elderly patients (39,40). Stimulants should be considered after standard therapies have been exhausted. Psychostimulants may produce rapid antidepressant effect with few untoward effects.

Literature that deals specifically with therapeutic strategies for treatment-resistant depression is scant. Only recently have some authors dealt with this subgroup of depressed patients. Ayd and Zohar listed three groups of patients who may benefit from the use of psychostimulants—chronic dysphorics, chronic unipolar depressives, and medically ill depressed geriatric patients (7). The authors concluded that amphetamines and methylphenidate may be safe and effective in such patients. Kennedy and Joffe suggested that psychostimulants should be limited to terminally ill patients, although they may be used as a single therapy in treatment-resistant patients (41). Satel and Nelson concluded that controlled studies of stimulants in the treatment of primary depression did not demonstrate the efficacy of these drugs (8). However, these drugs may be efficacious for depressed patients who are treatment resistant, medically ill, or geriatric. Stimulants were found to be as safe as TCAs. Subgroup hypotheses, derived from clinical experience and post hoc analyses, need to be substantiated by randomized prospective studies.

PEMOLINE PILOT STUDY

Pemoline, a mild central stimulant with little abuse potential, has been used infrequently as an antidepressant. It was, however, reported to be helpful in moderately depressed adults (42–44).

Six nonbipolar depressed (DSM-III-R) patients without psychotic features, aged 65 to 85, participated in this open-label study. On admission, all patients had Hamilton Depression Rating Scale scores of 16 or above. Tricyclics were either contraindicated, not tolerated, or not effective. All subjects were inpatients of the Geriatric Service at Lafayette Clinic and, on admission, had evaluations, including history, complete physical and neurological examinations, laboratory tests (SMA, CBC, thyroid function tests and urinalysis), and ECG.

Psychotropic medications were washed out for 1 to 2 weeks before administration of pemoline. During the study, only chloral hydrate was permitted for insomnia. Pemoline was given in doses of 17.5 mg twice daily for 1 to 2 weeks before the dose was increased to 37.5 mg twice daily for an additional 2 or 3 weeks.

Weekly ratings were performed before and during therapy, using the Inventory of Psychic and Somatic Complaints in the Elderly (IPSC-E) (45). Repeated measures of dose levels and response variable levels were used to compute values of a measure of the apparent benefit or harm of therapy. Values of this measure were computed for each of the 15 response variables derived from the IPSC-E and for each patient. Benefit and harm scores essentially measure longitudinal associations between variables. These scores have the following characteristics: (a) scores of zero indicate no evidence for treatment effect, (b) positive scores provide evidence for benefit, and negative scores provide evidence for harm, (c) each score is from a distribution of potential scores with a mean of 0 and a standard deviation of 1, and (d) score magnitudes can increase without limit as the number of repeated assessments increases. A measure of overall benefit for each patient was computed by averaging the standardized symptom-specific benefit scores.

Table 4 shows the raw dose and response data, with the corresponding benefit score for each response variable. Notice how the magnitudes and signs of the scores quantify evidence for benefit and harm. The proce-

TABLE 4. *Pemoline dose and levels of 10 response variables for one patient: the benefit/harm score is shown for each response variable*

Week	Pemoline dose	Sleep	Paranoid ideation	Energy loss	Depression	Memory
1	0	7	3	18	15	20
2	37.5	9	3	18	16	15
3	37.5	7	3	14	15	13
4	75.0	5	5	10	9	12
5	75.0	6	6	12	17	13
6	75.0	4	9	18	17	13
Benefit scores		3.00	−3.00	1.58	−1.58	2.24

Week	Pemoline dose	Agitation	Attention	Confusion	Anxiety	Disorientation
1	0	7	5	4	21	4
2	37.5	5	8	4	16	4
3	37.5	6	4	4	19	4
4	75.0	6	4	4	21	4
5	75.0	10	6	5	24	4
6	75.0	6	5	3	19	4
Benefit scores		1.41	1.00	0	0	0

dure for computing benefit scores has been submitted for the Proceedings of the Fourth International Conference on Pharmacoepidemiology (46).

Results

The overall benefit score for each patient was positive, indicating some evidence for benefit from pemoline therapy. Mean overall benefit (0.627) was significantly different from 0 ($t = 5.3$, $df = 5$, $p < 0.01$).

Figure 1, a benefit/harm profile, shows the average (plus or minus 1 SD) benefit score across six patients for each of the 15 response variables. When benefit was tested for individual response variables, statistically significant beneficial effects were identified for energy loss ($t = 9.12$, $p < 0.01$), memory ($t = 8.30$, $p < 0.01$), and sleep ($t = 2.69$, $p < 0.05$). The apparent adverse effect of pemoline on paranoid ideation was not statistically significant.

DISCUSSION

Many antidepressants are contraindicated, not effective, or not tolerated for many patients with manifestations of depression, especially elderly and medically ill patients. This has led clinicians and researchers to reconsider psychostimulants as antidepressants.

The literature reviewed cites instances of apparently rapid and dramatic improvement in response to stimulant therapy. However, the group averages of clinical trials seldom reveal statistically significant beneficial effects. The problem, often discussed in the stimulant literature, appears to be heterogeneity of patient response (47). Heterogeneity of response diminishes statistical power and makes it difficult to identify treatment effects. We need to implement new procedures that are available for revealing criteria that can be used to identify patients who respond consistently and preferentially to specific therapies.

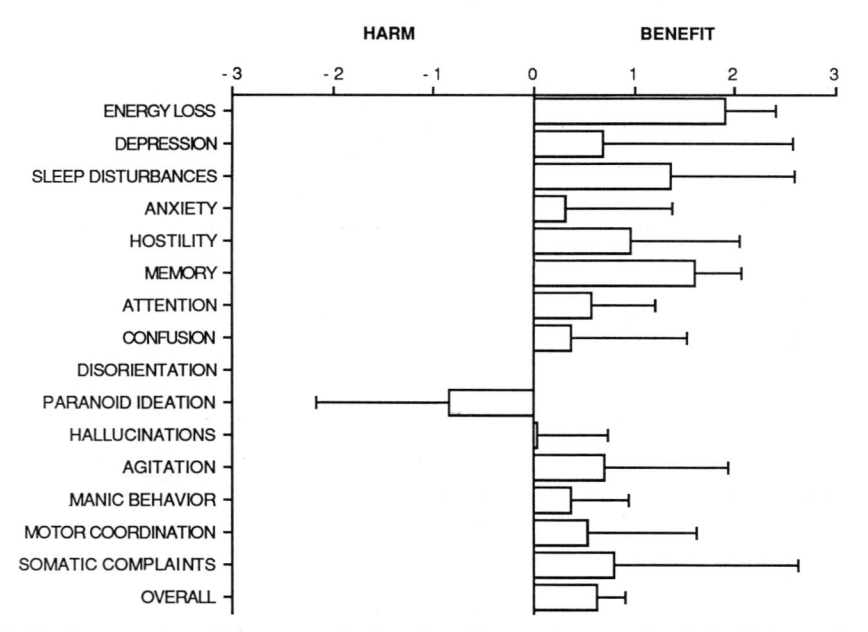

FIG. 1. Average benefit/harm profile for six patients who were treated with pemoline.

The pilot study we presented indicated that pemoline, and possibly other stimulants, may be promising treatments for some depressed patients. In addition, the procedure for measuring the apparent benefit or harm of therapy can be an important part of the solution to the problem of evaluating pharmacotherapy when there is heterogeneity of response.

Identifying Subgroups of Responders

One key to identifying homogeneous subgroups of responders is to obtain a more valid, reliable, and precise measure of each patient's response. The first part of this task is to collect data for individual patients using a N of 1 clinical trial (48) or other intensive design (49). Data from these trials could be evaluated with the benefit scoring procedure demonstrated in the pilot study. Randomized, double-blind N of 1 designs would help ensure that values of the measure of apparent response are valid indicators of actual response. In addition, this approach, unlike most clinical trials, would help separate drug responders from placebo responders.

There are two major ways in which benefit scoring increases the reliability of measuring each patient's response. First, unlike subjective global judgments, benefit scoring is reproducible and operationally defined. Second, benefit scoring can be applied to samples of repeated assessments that are large enough to provide a reliable indicator of each patient's response. The Dub and Lurie study (16) is an example of a longitudinal design with multiple drug challenges, performed under double-blind conditions, that yielded large samples of repeated assessments. Such designs exploit the same principle by which response to drug withdrawal and rechallenge is used to evaluate adverse drug reactions (50). The pilot study demonstrated how benefit scores from repeated measures studies can be analyzed with simple statistical procedures. The authors are not aware of other published clinical trials that have used measures of benefit and harm, computed from both dose and response variable data, as outcome variables.

A second key to identifying more homogeneous groups of drug responders is to profile benefit and harm across more representative samples of response variables that are affected by therapy. Response profiles deal with the independence of effect on different response dimensions that was observed by Silberman et al. in their report on heterogeneity of amphetamine response in depressed patients (47). Clusters of similar patient-specific response profiles would be used to help identify diagnostic criteria for more homogeneous groups of responders.

The proposed strategy for identifying subgroups of responders addresses a fundamental weakness in the stimulant literature. It provides a means whereby a series of studies could lead to the progressive identification of more homogeneous diagnostic groups. The same strategy could be applied to other drugs used to manage chronic disorders that impair function and are prevalent among the elderly.

CONCLUSION

The literature on the antidepressant effects of psychostimulants is top heavy with review and commentary. Nevertheless, a consensus seems to be emerging that stimulants may be safe and effective for some depressed patients who are elderly, treatment resistant, or medically ill. When used judiciously, stimulants appear to be safe when administered either alone or in combination with other antidepressants. In addition, study of responses to these agents can contribute to a working knowledge of nervous system function. However, research on the role of stimulants in therapy does not seem to have become progressively more productive. As Mattes concluded after a recent double-blind trial of methylphenidate in mildly depressed patients, "the paradigm which can consistently demonstrate a stimulant effect continues to elude us" (51, p. 527).

Progress in this area and specific recommendations for therapy depend on new research strategies. More specifically, progress is likely to flow from a new measure of the apparent benefit or harm of therapy that was demonstrated in this chapter, in combination with longitudinal, multiple N of 1 clinical trial designs.

ACKNOWLEDGMENT

The authors would like to thank Ms. Alice Yancey for manuscript preparation.

REFERENCES

1. Overall JE, Hollister LE, Pokorny AD, Casey JF, Katz G. Drug therapy in depressions: Controlled evaluation of imipramine, isocarboxazide, dextroamphetamine-amobarbital, and placebo. *Clin Pharmacol Ther* 1962;3:16–22.
2. Overall JE, Hollister LE, Shelton J, Johnson M, Kimbell I. Tranylcypromine compared with dextroamphetamine in hospitalized depressed patients. *Dis Nerv Syst* 1966;27:653–659.
3. Edison GR. Amphetamines: A dangerous illusion. *Ann Intern Med* 1971;74:605–610.
4. Tinklenberg JR. A clinical view of the amphetamines. *Am Fam Physician* 1971;4:82–86.
5. Wittenborn JR. Antidepressant use of amphetamines and other psychostimulants. *Mod Probl Pharmacopsychiatry* 1982;18:178–195.
6. Chiarello RJ, Cole JO. The use of psychostimulants in general psychiatry. *Arch Gen Psychiatry* 1987;44:286–295.
7. Ayd FJ, Zohar J. Psychostimulant (amphetamine or methylphenidate) therapy for chronic and treatment-resistant depression. In: Zohar J, Belmaker RH, eds. *Treating resistant depression*, New York: PMA Publishing, 1987;343–355.
8. Satel SL, Nelson JC. Stimulants in the treatment of depression: A critical overview. *J Clin Psychiatry* 1989;50:241–249.
9. vanPraag HM, Kits TP, Schut T, Dijkstra P. An attempt at indirect evaluation of the noradrenaline hypothesis. *Behav Neuropsychiatry* 1969;1:17–24.
10. Joyce PR, Donald RA, Nicholls G, Livesey JH, Abbott RM. Endocrine and behavioural responses to methylphenidate in depression. *Psychol Med* 1986;16:531–540.
11. Goff DC. The stimulant challenge test in depression. *J Clin Psychiatry* 1986;47:538–543.
12. Joyce PR. Mood response to methylphenidate and the dexamethasone suppression test as predictors of treatment response to zimelidine and lithium in major depression. *Biol Psychiatry* 1985;20:598–604.
13. Myerson A. Effect of benzedrine sulfate on mood and fatigue in normal and in neurotic persons. *Arch Neurol Psychiatry* 1936;36:816–822.
14. Davidoff E, Reifenstein EC. The results of eighteen months of benzedrine sulfate therapy in psychiatry. *Am J Psychiatry* 1939;95:945–969.
15. Anderson EW. Further observations on benzedrine. *Br Med J* 1938;2:60–64.
16. Dub LA, Lurie LA. Use of benzedrine in the depressed phase of the psychotic state. *Ohio State Med J* 1939;35:39–45.
17. Natenshon AL. Clinical evaluation of Ritalin. *Dis Nerv Syst* 1956;17:392–396.
18. Jacobson A. The use of Ritalin in psychotherapy of depressions of the aged. *Psychiatr Q* 1958;32:474–483.
19. Kerenyi AB, Koranyi EK, Sarwer-Foner GJ. Depressive states and drugs-III. Use of methylphenidate (Ritalin) in open psychiatric settings and in office practice. *Can Med Assoc J* 1960;83:1249–1254.
20. Jaffe GV. Depression in general practice. *Practitioner* 1961;186:492–495.
21. Doust JWL, Lewis DJ, Miller A, Sprott D, Wright RLD. Controlled assessment of antidepressant drugs, including Tofranil. *Can Psychiatr Assoc J* 1959;4:S190–S194.
22. General Practice Research Group. Dexamphetamine compared with an inactive placebo in depression. *Practitioner* 1964;192:151–154.
23. Hare EH, Dominian J, Sharpe L. Phenelzine and dexamphetamine in depressive illness. *Br Med J* 1962;1:9–12.
24. Landman ME, Preisig R, Perlman M. A practical mood stimulant. *J Med Soc NJ* 1958;55:55–58.
25. Kaplitz SE. Withdrawn, apathetic geriatric patients responsive to methylphenidate. *J Am Geriatr Soc* 1975;23:271–276.
26. Wharton RN, Perel JM, Dayton PG, Malitz S. A potential clinical use for methylphenidate with tricyclic antidepressants. *Am J Psychiatry* 1971;127:1619–1625.
27. Cooper TB, Simpson GM. Concomitant imipramine and methylphenidate administration: A case report. *Am J Psychiatry* 1973;130:721.
28. Drimmer EJ, Gitlin MJ, Gwirtsman HE. Desipramine and methylphenidate combination treatment for depression: Case report. *Am J Psychiatry* 1983;140:241–242.
29. Feighner JP, Herbstein J, Damlouji N. Combined MAOI, TCA, and direct stimulant therapy of treatment-resistant depression. *J Clin Psychiatry* 1985;46:206–209.
30. Lehmann HE, Ananth JV, Geagea KC, Ban TA. Treatment of depression with Dexedrine and Demerol. *Curr Ther Res* 1971;13:42–49.

31. Woods SW, Tesar GE, Murray GB, Cassem NH. Psychostimulant treatment of depressive disorders secondary to medical illness. *J Clin Psychiatry* 1986;47:12–15.
32. Fernandez F, Adams F, Holmes VF, Levy JK, Neidhart M. Methylphenidate for depressive disorders in cancer patients. *Psychosomatics* 1987;28:455–461.
33. Lingam VR, Lazarus LW, Groves L, Oh SH. Methylphenidate in treating poststroke depression. *J Clin Psychiatry* 1988;49:151–153.
34. Katon W, Raskind M. Treatment of depression in the medically ill elderly with methylphenidate. *Am J Psychiatry* 1980;137:963–965.
35. Kaufmann MW, Murray GB. The use of d-amphetamine in medically ill depressed patients. *J Clin Psychiatry* 1982;43:463–464.
36. Kaufmann MW, Cassem NH, Murray GB, Jenike M. Use of psychostimulants in medically ill patients with neurological disease and major depression. *Can J Psychiatry* 1984;29:46–49.
37. Kaufmann MW, Cassem N, Murray G, MacDonald D. The use of methylphenidate in depressed patients after cardiac surgery. *J Clin Psychiatry* 1984;45:82–84.
38. Fisch RZ. Methylphenidate for medical in-patients. *Int J Psychiatry Med* 1985;15:75–79.
39. Veith RC. Depression in the elderly: Pharmacologic considerations in treatment. *J Am Geriatr Soc* 1982;30:581–586.
40. Gerner RH. Present status of drug therapy of depression in late life. *J Affective Disord* 1985;1:S23–S31.
41. Kennedy SH, Joffe RT. Pharmacological management of refractory depression. *Can J Psychiatry* 1989;34:451–456.
42. Rickels K, Gordon PE, Gansman DH, Weise CC, Pereira-Ogan JA, Hesbacher PT. Pemoline and methylphenidate in mildly depressed outpatients. *Clin Pharmacol Ther* 1970;11:698–710.
43. Elizur A, Wintner I, Davidson S. The clinical and psychological effects of pemoline in depressed patients—A controlled study. *Int Pharmacopsychiatry* 1979;14:127–134.
44. Kagan G. Clinical trial of pemoline in general practice. *Br J Clin Pract* 1974;28:375–378.
45. Raskin A, Gershon S, Crook TH, Sathananthan G, Ferris S. The effects of hyperbaric and normobaric oxygen in cognitive impairment in the elderly. *Arch Gen Psychiatry* 1978;35:50–56.
46. Bagne CA. Assessing the effects of prolonged and variable drug exposures on human functioning. In: Edlavitch S, ed. *Proceedings of the Fourth International Conference on Pharmacoepidemiology.* (in press).
47. Silberman EK, Reus VI, Jimerson DC, Lynott AM, Post RM. Heterogeneity of amphetamine response in depressed patients. *Am J Psychiatry* 1981;138:1302–1307.
48. Guyatt G, Sackett D, Taylor W, Chong J, Roberts R, Pugsley S. Determining optional therapy—Randomized trials in individual patients. *N Engl J Med* 1986;314:889–892.
49. Chassan JB. *Research design in clinical psychology and psychiatry,* 2nd ed. New York: Irvington, 1979.
50. Kramer MS, Leventhal JM, Hutchinson TA, Feinstein AR. An algorithm for the operational assessment of adverse drug reactions: I. Background, description, and instructions for use. *JAMA* 1979;242:623–633.
51. Mattes JA. Methylphenidate in mild depression: A double-blind controlled trial. *J Clin Psychiatry* 1985;46:525–527.

ns*18*

Lithium Augmentation for Refractory Depression in Old Age

C.L.E. Katona and E.J.L. Finch

Depression is common in the elderly and can present considerable problems in diagnosis and management. Outcome often is relatively poor, with high rates of chronicity and suicide and an excess mortality from other causes. It is likely to be underdiagnosed and undertreated in this patient population. However, an energetic approach to diagnosis and management of depression in the elderly may improve this poor prognosis.

Elderly patients who fail to recover despite adequate antidepressant treatment are a particular problem in view of the relatively high risk of adverse effects from drug combinations.

PREVALENCE OF DEPRESSION IN OLD AGE

Over 25 years ago, Kay et al. (1) studied a sample of community and institutionalized elderly subjects in the UK and found a prevalence of mild "affective disorders and neurosis" of 6.2% and of severe mood disorders of 10%. Endogenous affective disorder was estimated to occur in between 1.3% and 3% of subjects. Subsequent epidemiological studies have reported prevalence rates ranging from as high as 34.5% (2) to as low as 1% (3). This variability has depended on the criteria for caseness and the methodology used for sample selection and the eliciting of diagnostic symptoms. Self-completed rating scales, particularly those with high scores for somatic symptoms, tended to generate high prevalence rates, whereas standard diagnostic criteria, such as DSM-III (4), tended to underdiagnose depression in elderly subjects. These individuals were less likely to complain of depressed mood and change in appetite or interests but more likely to somatize their feelings. The use of semi-structured interviews and diagnostic algorithms designed specifically for the elderly, such as the GMS-AGECAT package (5), has considerably improved the validity of recent epidemiological studies and resulted in more consistent findings. Studies in Australia (6), the US (7), and the UK (7,8) all have yielded similar prevalence rates for depressive caseness, as well as suggesting that DSM-III criteria are relatively insensitive to depression in the elderly. Katona and Bell, in a recent review (9), determined an overall prevalence of about 3% for DSM-III major depressive disorder and 10 to 20% for mild, but still disabling, depressive symptomatology.

PROGNOSIS

There is now substantial evidence that the outcome of depressive illness in old age is relatively poor. Two-year follow-up stud-

University College and Middlesex School of Medicine and Whittington Hospital, London, UK.

ies of hospitalized patients (10,11) suggest that chronic morbidity and mortality rates have changed little since a similar study by Roth (12) published in 1955.

Using more detailed measures of outcome, Murphy (13) studied 124 depressed elderly patients. At 1-year follow-up, only 33% were well, whereas over 50% had persistent symptoms or at least one relapse, and 14% were dead. Poor outcome was found to be associated with severity and duration of the initial illness, the presence of delusions, poor physical health, and adverse life events. In a similar but retrospective study, Baldwin and Jolley (14) followed up 100 elderly patients over 1 year and found that more than half were well and only 8% were dead. They suggested that the difference between their findings and those of Murphy (13) might be explained by the use of ECT in 48% of their subjects and only 15% of Murphy's. This is supported by the finding that elderly patients receiving ECT have a high rate of lasting recovery (15).

Murphy et al. (16), in a longer follow-up of her original sample compared with age-matched controls, found that the depressed group had a higher 4-year mortality, even after controlling for the effect of concurrent physical illness. In this sample, excess mortality was by natural causes, although the risk of suicide in elderly depressed patients is increased.

In the UK, 30% of suicides occur in persons over 65 years of age, who represent only 15% of the population. Barraclough (17), in a detailed retrospective analysis of elderly suicides, found that depression almost invariably could be diagnosed. The subjects tended to have depressive illnesses of only mild to moderate severity but almost always consulted their general practitioners in the weeks preceding death.

MANAGEMENT

Baldwin (18) had emphasized the importance of active treatment (drugs, ECT, and social intervention) in influencing the prognosis of depression in the elderly. Any such intervention must be preceded by a thorough clinical and social assessment, preferably in the patient's home.

Core clinical features of depression in the elderly usually are similar to those seen in younger patients. Elderly patients may have sleep and appetite disturbance, diurnal variation of mood, social withdrawal, and psychomotor retardation, as well as delusions of poverty or loss. Extreme agitation and depressive stupor also are relatively common in the elderly. Patients often are unable to express their depressive preoccupations in words, tending instead to somatize them in the form of pain and other hypochondriacal features, frequently complaining of loss of memory and poor concentration. On objective assessment, cognitive function usually is much less impaired than patients' complaints would suggest. A minority of patients do have profound memory impairment and loss of self-care skills. Such depressive pseudodementia can give rise to real difficulty in differential diagnosis. Short duration, preserved insight, the absence of dysphasia, and a lack of excuses for poor performance are pointers toward a primary diagnosis of depression.

Acute management of depression in the elderly patient should involve both physical and psychosocial treatment approaches. Antidepressant drugs and psychotherapy both have been found effective (19).

In general, antidepressants should be initiated at low doses and the dosage increased slowly. Not uncommonly, the maximum tolerated dose may be lower than that in younger patients, but second and third generation antidepressants with fewer anticholinergic side effects may reduce the incidence of confusional states and urinary retention. Postural hypotension resulting from adrenergic blockade also may limit antidepressant dosing. Furthermore, compliance may be poor in these patients, and this factor can be mitigated by switching to a single daily dose regimen with close supervision. Major tranquilizers may be a useful adjunct to antidepressants in delusional depression, where the combination may be comparable in efficacy to ECT (20) and in modifying severe agitation. Major tranquilizers should, however, be given for as short a time as possible to minimize the risk of tardive dyskinesia, which is particularly high in the elderly.

ECT may be very effective in elderly patients, particularly those with depressive delusions or marked retardation. Memory disturbance following ECT is more likely in the elderly, though this may be minimized by unilateral nondominant electrode placement (21). The anesthetic risk is also greater in elderly patients, but this has to be balanced against the risks of TCAs and especially those of untreated depression.

There is a clear link between social isolation and depression in the elderly (22). This can contribute to the persistence of depressive symptoms and, in turn, be alleviated by encouraging home visits and visits from good neighbors as well as day center attendance. Bereavement counseling may be useful, as can cognitive and brief, focused psychotherapy. In elderly patients who are recovering from acute episodes of depression, risk of relapse may be reduced by continued antidepressant treatment or by attendance at psychotherapeutic support groups (23).

REFRACTORY DEPRESSION

As many as two thirds of elderly patients will have some response to initial antidepressant treatment. In those who fail to respond, the treatment plan must be reviewed with particular reference to the appropriateness of prior treatment, management strategies, the adequacy and duration of prior antidepressant dosage (at least 6 weeks at maximum tolerated dose), and compliance with the prescribed treatment regimen. In addition, the identification of factors that might cause or contribute to depression is vital. Several pharmacological strategies for resistant depression can be considered in refractory cases (24), although the risk of side effects is considerably greater in the elderly.

LITHIUM AUGMENTATION

Lithium, which appears effective in the prophylaxis of depression in elderly patients with unipolar illness as well as reducing the relapse rate of bipolar depression (25), also has been used in the treatment of refractory depression to augment partial or absent response to prior antidepressants. To date, most studies have evaluated its use in general adult populations but have not specifically examined its efficacy in the elderly. Katona (26) reviewed case reports, open studies, and placebo-controlled trials of lithium augmentation and found that a response rate of about 60% could be expected when lithium was added to TCAs, monoamine oxidase inhibitors (MAOIs), or second generation antidepressants. The mechanism for augmentation is unclear, but lithium may enhance serotonergic neurotransmission in neurons previously sensitized by antidepressant drug treatment.

Lithium augmentation has received relatively little formal evaluation in elderly depressed patients. We have reviewed the case reports of lithium augmentation cited by Katona (26) to identify elderly subjects (Table 1). Of the 36 cases reported, 14 were over 60 years of age. Only one article (27) specifically evaluated elderly patients. All the elderly cases reported had unipolar depressive illnesses, and from the reports, it was possible to ascertain that 1 of the 14 had only a partial response and the rest a complete response to lithium augmentation.

The conclusions that can be drawn from these studies are clearly limited. Only clinical criteria for identifying cases were used in all studies except one (28), which used the RDC (29). Initial antidepressant treatment often was not given for an adequate length of time for failure of response to be

TABLE 1. Case reports of lithium augmentation in the elderly[a]

Reference	Age of subject (years)	Antidepressant	Response	Comments
Madakasira (32)	71	Phenelzine	Complete	300 mg lithium used
Kushnir (27)	83	Maprotiline	Complete	300 mg lithium used
	65	Desipramine	Complete	300 mg lithium used
	93	Desipramine	Complete	300 mg lithium used
	78	Desipramine	Complete	300 mg lithium used
	87	Trazadone	Complete	150 mg lithium used
Pande and Max (44)	82	Imipramine	Complete	Hypotension
Schrader and Levien (31)	73	Clomipramine	Complete	Deluded; no response to ECT or neuroleptics
Nelson and Byck (28)	75	Phenelzine	Partial	Used RDC (29) criteria
Weaver (45)	73	Maprotiline + T_3	Complete	Developed muscle weakness and tremor
Pai et al. (30)	72	Amitriptyline	Complete	Effective in delusional depression
	64	Dothiepin	Complete	
	69	Mianserin	Complete	
Hale et al. (46)	60	Clomipramine	Complete	

[a] From ref. 26.

unequivocal. Pai et al. (30) included 3 subjects over 60 years old and emphasized that lithium was effective in patients with delusional depression. Schrader and Levien (31) confirmed this, showing that lithium could be effective in delusional depression despite the failure of both ECT and combinations of TCAs and major tranquilizers. Both Kushnir (27) and Madakasira (32) used relatively low serum lithium levels (less than 0.4 mmol/L). This may be particularly important in the elderly, in whom toxic effects of lithium are both more likely and more disabling. Kushnir (27) emphasized that lithium augmentation was possible even in the physically ill elderly, describing a lasting remission in a 93-year-old man with atrial fibrillation and carcinoma of the colon and prostate.

In general, these case reports suggest that the addition of lithium augmentation at low doses and low serum levels in elderly patients with refractory depression may be both feasible and effective.

Most of the open studies of lithium augmentation reviewed by Katona (26) give only mean ages of subjects, although it may be inferred that some of the subjects were elderly. Nelson and Mazure (33) gave the mean ages of their subjects as 55.3 ± 13.9 for unipolar patients and 51.1 ± 10.6 for bipolars. Price et al. (34) included two elderly patients and suggested that even where lithium augmentation failed, the subsequent addition of tranylcypromine sometimes produced a favorable clinical response. In a small study by de Montigny et al. (35), two elderly patients responded to lithium augmentation of iprindole.

Three placebo-controlled studies are discussed by Katona (26). Only one of these (36) specifically included elderly patients; there were 4 of a total of 15. All subjects showed statistically significant improvement following lithium augmentation that was better than placebo, although the magnitude of change was small. The specific response rate in the elderly patients was not reported.

TOXICITY AND ADVERSE EFFECTS OF LITHIUM IN THE ELDERLY

Although the question of toxicity risk is of particular importance in evaluating the feasibility of lithium augmentation in the elderly, there has been no study looking specifically at such adverse effects. Work has been done on the effects of lithium in the prophylaxis of bipolar illness in elderly patients. Smith and Helms (37) looked at the adverse effects of lithium therapy in patients aged 65 and over and compared them with those under 65. A retrospective chart review was done on 15 elderly patients with a mean age of 70 years. No difference was found in the total number of side effects, but there was a significantly greater incidence of more serious side effects, mainly neurotoxicity, which resulted in confusion and disorientation in 43% of the sample. However, the serum lithium levels were relatively high, ranging from 0.86 to 1.26 mEq/L.

Roose et al. (38) reviewed data from 31 patients over 60 years old and compared them with a younger group also on lithium prophylaxis. They found a significantly higher incidence of toxicity in the elderly group and commented that this occurred more rapidly and at lower serum lithium levels. They recommended using serum levels of 0.6 to 0.7 mEq/L and did not find clinical effectiveness to be lower. Jefferson (39) commented that as well as monitoring blood levels, careful clinical observation was necessary, since episodes of toxicity could occur in the elderly at blood levels conventionally regarded as therapeutic. Himmelhoch et al. (40) noted that in patients with neurological problems, such as parkinsonism, neurotoxicity could occur at low serum levels.

These studies have a general relevance to the use of lithium in combination with antidepressants in refractory depression but are of limited relevance to the specific question of lithium augmentation, since they do not address possible toxicity associated with lithium-antidepressant combinations.

PATIENTS AND METHODS

We performed a retrospective evaluation of treatment and outcome in consecutive referrals to a catchment psychogeriatric service during the period April 1986 to November 1987 (41). The patients all lived in a defined catchment area in Islington, North London. They were included if on case note review they fulfilled ICD-9 (42) criteria for manic depressive psychosis (296) or depressive neurosis (300.4) and if they scored 10 or more on the Information/Orientation scale of the Clifton Assessment Procedures for the Elderly (43). Subjects were excluded if they had received specific specialist psychiatric treatment for the index episode before referral. Demographic variables, treatment episodes with TCAs, MAOIs, and lithium, and overall outcome (good, intermediate, or poor) were recorded.

Fifty-nine patients (10 men, 49 women, age range 65–93, mean age 76.7) were included in the evaluation. In 9 patients, lithium augmentation was attempted. All of these subjects had failed to respond to an adequate trial of a TCA, and 4 also had failed to respond to ECT. Table 2 shows the demographic and illness characteristics of those who improved with TCAs, those who were given TCAs but failed to respond, and those who were given lithium following TCA failure. There were no significant differences in demographic characteristics among the groups. Lithium augmentation was successful initially in 6 of 9 subjects. We noted episodes of toxicity associated with the combination of lithium and antidepressants in 4 subjects, and lithium had to be discontinued in 2 of them. One 78-year-old woman had an episode of postural hypotension and tremor that responded to a decrease in dose to 200 mg daily (resulting in a blood level of 0.68 mEq/L), and another 83-year-old woman who was partially blind had an episode of toxicity characterized by dizziness and associated with a blood level of 1.13 mmol/L. This was thought to be the result of an accidental overdose. One of our subjects had to be taken off lithium, since her renal function and congestive cardiac failure were deteriorating. Another 65-year-old woman experienced substantial weight gain on lithium, but she could tolerate this.

TABLE 2. Retrospective study of lithium augmentation in the elderly[a]

	Lithium-treated group	TCA responders	TCA failures
Number	9	18	9
Age Mean (range)	76 (65–83)	76 (65–91)	79 (65–85)
Sex (M/F)	2/7	2/16	2/7
Length of episode (weeks: median, range)	80 (5–260)	138 (3–>999)	203 (4–>999)
Diagnosis (296/300.4)	7/2	11/7	9/0
Outcome (good/ intermediate, or poor)[b]	7/2	14/4	0/9

[a] From ref. 41.
[b] overall χ^2 test: $\chi^2 = 16.8$; $df = 2$; $p<0.001$; A vs C, B vs C: $p<0.01$ (Fisher's exact test).

One subject failed to respond despite an adequate trial of lithium augmentation.

At initial follow-up after a period of 3 to 20 months (median 6 months), 7 of 9 subjects in the lithium group were well, 1 had a partial response, and 1 was still depressed. The lithium group fared as well as the TCA responders at follow-up and did significantly better ($p < 0.01$) than the TCA failures. We have now followed up the lithium-treated group for an additional 18 months. One patient has died (from carcinoma of the lung), and of the remaining 8, 5 are well, 2 have had a modest response, and 1 is still depressed. Of the 5 with a good outcome, 3 are still on lithium. This is in keeping with the recent report (47) of long-term outcome of lithium augmentation in younger subjects.

Generally, we have found that the use of regular blood level monitoring aimed at keeping serum lithium levels within the range 0.4 to 0.8 mEq/L, associated with regular clinical examination and liaison as necessary with geriatric physicians, enabled most patients to remain safely on their drug. Lithium therapy is, however, a relatively regimented treatment strategy involving outpatient attendance, blood and side effect monitoring, and pretreatment screening. In our study, we were unable to control for social interventions, including occupational therapy, nursing and psychology input, and domiciliary follow-up. It is possible that we selected for lithium augmentation those antidepressant nonresponders with a relatively good underlying prognosis. This is, however, unlikely, since the lithium-treated group in our study had a relatively high prevalence of delusions (5/9), which have been shown to be a predictor of poor outcome (13).

CONCLUSIONS

Lithium augmentation is a potentially hazardous treatment in elderly subjects in view of its low therapeutic ratio. In common with other studies, we found that a number of our patients were unable to tolerate lithium. We have, however, found that lithium augmentation appears to be as likely to produce a clinical response in elderly as in younger subjects with refractory depression and to be associated with a relatively good prognosis. This may contribute to improving the relatively poor outlook of elderly patients with refractory depression and thus clearly merits further prospective evaluation.

REFERENCES

1. Kay DWK, Beamish P, Roth M. Old age mental disorders in Newcastle upon Tyne. Part I: A study of prevalence. *Br J Psychiatry* 1964;110: 146–158.
2. Raymond EF, Michals TJ, Steer RA. Prevalence and correlates of depression in elderly persons. *Psychol Rep* 1980;47:1055–1061.

3. Myers JK, Weissman MM, Tischler GL, et al. Six month prevalence of psychiatric disorders in three communities. *Arch Gen Psychiatry* 1984; 41:959–967.
4. American Psychiatric Association. *Diagnostic and statistical manual of mental disorders,* 3rd ed. Washington, DC: American Psychiatric Association, 1980.
5. Copeland JMR, Dewey ME, Griffiths-Jones HM. Computerized psychiatric diagnostic systems and case nomenclature for elderly subjects. *Psychol Med* 1986;16:89–99.
6. Kay DWK, Henderson AS, Scott R, Wilson J, Richwood D, Grayson DA. Dementia and depression among the elderly living in the Hobart community: The effect of diagnostic criteria on the prevalence rates. *Psychol Med* 1985;15:771–778.
7. Copeland JMR, Gurland BJ, Dewey ME, Kelleher MJ, Smith AMR, Davidson IA. Is there more dementia depression and neurosis in New York? *Br J Psychiatry* 1987;151:466–474.
8. Copeland JMR, Dewey ME, Wood N, Searle R, Davidson IA, McWilliam C. Range of mental illness among the elderly in the community: Prevalence in Liverpool using the GMS-AGECAT package. *Br J Psychiatry* 1987;150:815–823.
9. Katona CLE, Bell GT. Depression and dysphoria in old age. In: Akiskal HS, Burton SW, eds. *Dysthymia: A new concept in chronic mild depression.* London: Gaskell, 1990;49–68.
10. Christie AB. Changing patterns in mental illness in the elderly. *Br J Psychiatry* 1982;140:154–159.
11. Blessed G, Wilson ID. The contemporary natural history of depression in old age. *Br J Psychiatry* 1982;141:59–67.
12. Roth M. The natural history of mental disorders in old age. *J Ment Sci* 1951;101:281–301.
13. Murphy E. The prognosis of depression in old age. *Br J Psychiatry* 1983;142:111–119.
14. Baldwin RC, Jolley DJ. The prognosis of depression in old age. *Br J Psychiatry* 1986;149:574–583.
15. Godber C, Rosenvinge H, Wilkinson D, Smithies J. Depression in old age: Prognosis after ECT. *Int J Geriatr Psychiatry* 1987;2:19–24.
16. Murphy E, Smith R, Lindesay J, Slattery J. Increased mortality rate in late life depression. *Br J Psychiatry* 1988;152:347–353.
17. Barraclough BM. Suicide in the elderly. In: Kay DWK, Walk A, eds. *Recent developments in psychogeriatrics.* Ashford: Headley Brothers, 1971;87–97.
18. Baldwin B. Late life depression: Undertreated? *Br Med J* 1988;296:519.
19. Jarvik LF, Mintz J, Steuer J, Gerner R. Treating geriatric depression: A 26-week interim analysis. *J Am Geriatr Soc* 1982;30:713–717.
20. Spiker DG, Perel JM, Hanin I, et al. The pharmacological treatment of delusional depression. *J Clin Psychopharmacol* 1986;6:339–342.
21. Fraser RM, Glass IB. Unilateral and bilateral ECT in elderly patients. *Acta Psychiatr Scand* 1980;62:13–31.
22. Murphy E. Social origins of depression in old age. *Br J Psychiatry* 1982;141:135–142.
23. Ong YK, Martineau F, Lloyd C, Robbins I. A support group for the depressed elderly. *Int J Geriatr Psychiatry* 1987;2:119–123.
24. Katona CLE, Barnes TRE. Pharmacological strategies in depression. *Br J Hosp Med* 1985; 38:168–171.
25. Abou-Saleh M, Coppen A. The prognosis of depression in old age: The case for lithium therapy. *Br J Psychiatry* 1983;143:527–528.
26. Katona CLE. Lithium augmentation in refractory depression. *Psychiatr Dev* 1988;2:153–171.
27. Kushnir SL. Lithium—Antidepressant combinations in the treatment of depressed, physically ill geriatric patients. *Am J Psychiatry* 1986;143: 378–379.
28. Nelson JC, Byck R. Rapid response to lithium in phenelzine non-responders. *Br J Psychiatry* 1982;111:85–86.
29. Spitzer RL, Endicott J, Robins E. Research Diagnostic Criteria: Rationale and reliability. *Arch Gen Psychiatry* 1979;36:17–24.
30. Pai M, White AC, Deane AG. Lithium augmentation in the treatment of delusional depression. *Br J Psychiatry* 1986;148:736–738.
31. Schrader GD, Levien HM. Response to sequential administration of clomipramine and lithium carbonate in treatment-resistant depression. *Br J Psychiatry* 1985;147:573–575.
32. Madakasira S. Low dose potency of lithium in antidepressant augmentation. *Psych J Univ Ottowa* 1986;11:107–109.
33. Nelson CJ, Mazure CM. Lithium augmentation in psychotic depression refractory to combined drug treatment. *Am J Psychiatry* 1986;143:363–366.
34. Price LH, Charney DS, Heninger GR. Variability of response to lithium augmentation in refractory depression. *Am J Psychiatry* 1986;143: 1387–1392.
35. de Montigny C, Gruneberg F, Mayer A, Deschenes JP. Lithium induces rapid relief of depression in tricyclic antidepressant drug non-responders. *Br J Psychiatry* 1981;138:252–256.
36. Heninger GR, Charney DS, Sternberg DE. Lithium carbonate augmentation of antidepressant treatment. *Arch Gen Psychiatry* 1983;40:1335–1342.
37. Smith RE, Helms PM. Adverse effects of lithium therapy in the acutely ill elderly patient. *J Clin Psychiatry* 1982;43:94–99.
38. Roose SP, Bone S, Haidorher C, Dunner D, Fieve PR. Lithium treatment in older patients. *Am J Psychiatry* 1979;136:843–844.
39. Jefferson JW. Lithium and affective disorder in the elderly. *Comp Psychiatry* 1983;24:166–178.
40. Himmelhoch JM, Neil JF, May SJ, Fuchs CZ, Licata SM. Age, dementia, dyskinesias and lithium response. *Am J Psychiatry* 1980;137:941–945.
41. Finch EJL, Katona CLE. Lithium augmentation in the treatment of refractory depression in old age. *Int J Geriatr Psychiatry* 1989;4:41–46.
42. World Health Organization. *International Classification of Diseases (1975 revision).* Geneva: World Health Organization, 1977.
43. Pattie AH, Gilleard CJ. *The Clifton Assessment*

Procedures for the Elderly. Beckenham: Hodder and Stoughton, 1979.
44. Pande AD, Max P. A lithium-tricyclic combination for treatment of depression. *Am J Psychiatry* 1985;142:1228–1229.
45. Weaver KEC. Lithium for delusional depression. *Am J Psychiatry* 1983;140:962–963.
46. Hale AS, Procter AW, Bridges PK. Clomipramine, tryptophan and lithium in combination for resistant endogenous depression: Seven case studies. *Br J Psychiatry* 1987;151:213–217.
47. Nierenberg AA, Price LH, Charney DS, Heninger GR. After lithium augmentation: A retrospective follow-up of patients with antidepressant-refractory depression. *J Affective Disord* 1990;18:167–175.

19

Thyroid Hormone Potentiation of Antidepressants

Russell T. Joffe[1] and William Singer[2]

Approximately one third of patients with major depression do not improve satisfactorily while receiving an initial trial of a tricyclic antidepressant (TCA) (1). Several other treatment options are available for these nonresponders, including an alternative TCA, a monoamine oxidase inhibitor (MAOI), or electroconvulsive therapy (ECT) (1). However, these alternatives often have limitations that militate against their clinical application, and all involve a considerable delay in the onset of therapeutic action (1).

Over the last 20 years, several synergistic treatments have been described that may provide a more rapid antidepressant response when added to the TCA in nonresponding patients. Among these strategies, the addition of the thyroid hormone, triiodothyronine (T_3), has been suggested to provide a fast, safe, and easy method of treating refractory depression. In this chapter, we provide a critical review of the current literature examining thyroid hormone potentiation of antidepressants, and we evaluate the possible mechanism of action of thyroid hormone in augmenting antidepressant treatment in light of recent data on the use of thyroid hormone by the brain. Finally, we present a summary of recent data from our laboratory that shows differential effects of T_3 and thyroxine (T_4) in augmenting the response to TCAs.

TRIIODOTHYRONINE POTENTIATION OF TRICYCLIC ANTIDEPRESSANTS

Prange et al. were the first to study the use of T_3 in the treatment of depressed patients (2). They initially described the use of small amounts of T_3 to accelerate the response to TCA in depressed women (2). However, in a subsequent study, they showed that the addition of small amounts of T_3 could convert TCA nonresponders to responders within a short period of time (2). Since these initial studies, others have confirmed the observation that small amounts of T_3 could convert TCA nonresponders to responders in a substantial proportion of patients. These studies are summarized in Table 1. They demonstrate that between 5 and 50 µg of T_3 can produce a rapid antidepressant response when added to a TCA in some treatment nonresponders.

The open studies (3–7) strongly support the efficacy of T_3 in converting TCA nonresponders to responders, whereas the data from the controlled studies (8,11) are less conclusive. Although Goodwin et al. (8) reported that two thirds of their patients had a rapid antidepressant response when T_3 was added to one of several TCAs, both Thase et al. (10) and Gitlin et al. (11) could not confirm an antidepressant response with T_3 potentiation. In this regard, Thase

---

[1]Department of Psychiatry, Clarke Institute of Psychiatry, and the University of Toronto, Ontario, Canada.
[2]Department of Endocrinology, St. Michael's Hospital, and the University of Toronto, Ontario, Canada.

TABLE 1. Studies of T_3 potentiation of tricyclic antidepressants

Study	n	Tricyclic	T_3 dose	Design	Result
Earle 1970 (3)	25	Imipramine or amitriptyline	25 μg	Open	14/25 improved
Banki 1975 (4)	52	Several	20–40 μg	Open	39/52 improved
Banki 1977 (5)	33	Amitriptyline	20 μg	Partially controlled	23/33 improved
Ogura et al. 1974 (6)	44	Several	20–30 μg	Open	29/44 improved
Tsutsui et al. 1979 (7)	11	Several	5–25 μg	Open	10/11 improved
Goodwin et al. 1982 (8)	12	Several	25–50 μg	Double-blind	8/12 improved
Schwarcz et al. 1984 (9)	8	Desipramine	25–50 μg	Open	4/8 improved
Thase et al. 1985 (10)	20	Imipramine	25 μg	Partially controlled	5/20 improved
Gitlin et al. 1986 (11)	16	Imipramine	25 μg	Double-blind placebo-controlled	T_3 no different from placebo

et al. (10) found that only 25% (5 of 20) of patients with major depression who failed a trial of imipramine converted to responders when 25 μg of T_3 was added. Similarly, Gitlin et al. (11) were unable to demonstrate an overall difference between T_3 and placebo when these were added to a TCA in 16 treatment-resistant patients. However, the latter study used a crossover design in which T_3 and placebo were administered for only 2 weeks. This design may have limited the ability to demonstrate differences between drug and placebo, and the 2-week duration may have been too short a time frame to assess thyroid hormone potentiation. Although the controlled studies are less convincing, they are only three and involve small patient samples. On the other hand, a substantial clinical experience combined with the open-label studies strongly supports the observation that small doses of T_3 can rapidly convert some TCA nonresponders to responders (Table 1).

The mechanism of action of T_3 in potentiating the response to TCAs remains largely unknown. The small doses of T_3 used have been shown not to alter the pharmacokinetics of the TCAs (12). The effect of thyroid hormones on catecholamine systems in brain (13) also have been proposed as their mechanism of antidepressant action. Alternatively, it is possible that alterations in cerebral thyroid hormone levels may lead to alterations in mood.

T_4 is the main circulating thyroid hormone (14). T_4 is converted to T_3 in order to mediate its psychological effects (14). Because T_4 may be regarded as a precursor of T_3, it has been assumed that T_4 would have similar effects to T_3 in the potentiation of TCAs. Although Targum et al. (15) found that T_3 and T_4 both were effective in potentiating TCAs in selected patients with evidence of subclinical hypothyroidism, there have been no systematic studies directly comparing the antidepressant-potentiating effect of T_3 and T_4 in euthyroid depressed patients. Therefore, the comparable efficacy of these two thyroid hormones remains largely conjectural. Recent data on the regulation of thyroid hormone levels in the central nervous system and on the differential use of various thyroid hormones by brain have led to our reevaluation of whether T_3 and T_4 may have comparable efficacy in the augmentation of TCAs.

THE BRAIN AND THYROID HORMONE

Recent data suggest that thyroid hormones have a direct and important effect on mature brain function (16,17). First, the nuclear T_3 receptor, the site of initiation of thyroid hormone action, is widely distributed in adult brain (18). Second, thyroid hormone is actively taken up and concentrated by synaptosomes in discrete brain areas (19). Last, rigid homeostatic mechanisms maintain cerebral thyroid hormone levels within narrow limits, even in the presence of extreme alterations in peripheral thyroid function (20).

Animal studies suggest that T_3 and T_4 may have differential effects on cerebral thyroid hormone levels (14). In peripheral organs, the T_3 available for receptor binding is derived directly from plasma T_3 (20). In brain, however, 80% of T_3 available for receptor binding is derived from the intracerebral conversion of T_4 to T_3 (20). Therefore, under physiological conditions, the brain does not directly use T_3 (21). In other words, plasma T_3 is the main determinant of T_3 content of peripheral organs, whereas plasma T_4 is the main determinant of cerebral T_3 content (22). Therefore, the administration of small doses of T_3 would raise plasma T_3 levels but, by negative feedback on the hypothalamic-pituitary-thyroid axis, would suppress plasma T_4 and possibly result in a relative cerebral thyroid hypofunction (23). On the other hand, administration of T_4 would lead to increases in plasma T_4 and increased cerebral thyroid hormone levels. We have, therefore, hypothesized (23) that T_3 and T_4 would have opposite effects on cerebral thyroid hormone levels and, consequently, on brain functions that might affect mood. The effects of T_3 administration would be hypothesized to be similar to the effects of other antidepressant treatments, i.e., lowering of cerebral thyroid hormone levels (23). In order to support this hypothesis (23), we carried out a randomized double-blind study of T_3 versus T_4 augmentation of TCAs.

SUBJECTS AND METHODS

Subjects comprised consecutive outpatients attending the Mood Disorders Clinic at St. Michael's Hospital in Toronto. All subjects fulfilled RDC (24) for primary nonpsychotic unipolar major depressive disorder on a structured interview using the Schedule for Affective Disorders and Schizophrenia-Lifetime Version (SADS-L) (25). All patients had failed an initial trial of imipramine or desipramine during the current episode and had a score of 16 or more on the 17-item Hamilton Rating Scale for Depression (HDRS). All patients were evaluated by a physical examination and routine biochemical screening for the absence of any medical disorder, particularly thyroid disease, which would exclude them from study.

Patients were assigned randomly to receive either 37.5 µg of T_3 or 150 µg of T_4 in a single unmarked capsule administered once a day. The dose of T_4 used takes into account the relative potency of T_3 as compared to T_4 (21). During the 3-week duration of the thyroid hormone potentiation trial, no change was made in the dose of desipramine or imipramine.

At baseline, before randomization, and at weekly intervals, the subjects were evaluated by a trained rater on the HDRS as well as the Beck Depression Inventory (BDI). At the time of each evaluation, blood samples were obtained for measurement, by standard radioimmunoassay, of T_4, free T_3, T_3, T_3 resin uptake (T_3RU) and thyrotropin (TSH). The coefficients of variation for these assays are, respectively, 4.6%, 6.5%, 5%, and 3%. The Free Thyroxine Index (FTI) was calculated as the product of the T_4 and the T_3RU.

Response to thyroid hormone was defined as a 50% or more reduction in HDRS scores between baseline and the end of the 3-week trial. The difference in overall response rate to the two thyroid hormones was determined by Fisher Exact Test. A series of two-way analyses of variance (AN-

OVA) with repeated measures was used to assess possible differences in effect of these two thyroid hormones on mood scores as well as on thyroid function tests. For the HDRS and BDI scores, percentage change between baseline and each week was used in order to avoid the confounding effect of baseline depression scores on the change in mood ratings across the 3 weeks of the study.

RESULTS

Thirty-eight subjects, 14 males and 24 females, completed the study. Seventeen subjects (M:F 8:9) received T_3, and 21 subjects (M:F 6:15) received T_4. Four of 21 subjects responded to T_4, whereas 9 of 17 subjects responded to T_3 ($p = 0.026$, Fisher Exact Test).

By ANOVA, there was a small but statistically significant main effect of thyroid hormone type ($F = 4.18$, $p < 0.05$) and an effect of time ($F = 6.28$, $p < 0.001$) on the HDRS percent change scores. Furthermore, a statistically significant difference in mean percent change scores on the HDRS with T_3 as compared with T_4 was evident at week 3 ($-40.1 \pm 24.6\%$ vs $-22.1 \pm 26.8\%$, $t = 2.03$, $df = 36$, $p < 0.05$). No significant difference was noted in the effect of T_3 and T_4 on the BDI.

As expected, the two thyroid hormones had significantly different effects on thyroid function tests. Evaluation of thyroid function tests during the trial showed that the administration of T_4 as compared with T_3 was associated with significantly greater increases in plasma T_4 and FTI levels, whereas there were no significant differences in either TSH or T_3RU levels between the two thyroid hormones. With T_3 treatment, free T_3 levels were significantly higher in the T_3- as compared with the T_4-treated patients.

Responders could not be distinguished from nonresponders to thyroid hormone potentiation by mean pretreatment depression ratings, any measurements of thyroid function at baseline, or mean change in any thyroid function tests between baseline and the end of the trial.

DISCUSSION

Our study suggests that T_4 and T_3 may have differential effects in the augmentation of response to TCAs. In a 3-week trial, we observed that T_3 was significantly more effective than T_4 in converting TCA nonresponders to responders.

There are several possible explanations for our findings. First, it is possible that the antidepressant response noted with thyroid hormone may have been due to the delayed effect of the antidepressants rather than to the specific augmenting effect of the thyroid hormones. However, this would fail to explain the differential response to T_3 and T_4. Second, it is possible that thyroid hormones were effective because of the presence of varying degrees of subclinical hypothyroidism in the depressed patients. However, only a very small percentage of depressed patients have subclinical hypothyroidism (26), and there is no convincing evidence to suggest that thyroid replacement therapy is effective in patients with subclinical hypothyroidism (27).

T_3 and T_4 have considerable differences in half-life. The half-life of T_3 is approximately 12 hours, whereas that of T_4 is approximately 1 week (21). However, a differential effect between these two hormones was evident only at the third week of treatment, so that the differences in hormone half-life are unlikely to account for their differential effect during a 3-week trial. It is possible that our data indicate a true differential effect with T_3, as compared with T_4, in the conversion of TCA nonresponders to responders. Further data are required to confirm these preliminary observations and to investigate the mechanisms whereby T_3 and T_4 exert their differential effects on mood and brain neurotransmission.

REFERENCES

1. Klein DE, Gittelman R, Quitkin F, eds. *Diagnosis and drug treatment of psychiatric disorders*, 2nd ed. Baltimore: Williams & Wilkins, 1980.
2. Prange AJ Jr, Loosen PT. Thyroid hormone and antidepressants. In: Costae, Racheni G, eds. *Typical and atypical antidepressants: Clinical practice*. New York: Raven Press, 1982;289–296.
3. Earle BV. Thyroid hormone and tricyclic antidepressants in resistant depression. *Am J Psychiatry* 1970;126:1667–1669.
4. Banki CM. Triiodothyronine in the treatment of depression. *Orv Hetil* 1975;116:2543–2547.
5. Banki CM. Cerebral spinal fluid amine metabolites after combined amitriptyline-triiodothyronine treatment of depressed women. *Eur J Clin Pharmacol* 1977;11:311–315.
6. Ogura C, Okuma T, Uchida Y. Combined thyroid (triiodothyronine)-tricyclic antidepressant treatment in depressive states. *Fol Psychiat Neurol Jpn* 1974;28:179–186.
7. Tsutsui S, Yamazaki Y, Namba T. Combined therapy of T_3 and antidepressants in depression. *J Int Med Res* 1979;7:138–146.
8. Goodwin FK, Prange AJ Jr, Post RM. Potentiation of antidepressant effects by L-triiodothyronine in tricyclic nonresponders. *Am J Psychiatry* 1982;139:34–38.
9. Schwarcz G, Halaris A, Baxter L. Normal thyroid function in desipramine nonresponders compared to responders by the addition of L-triiodothyronine. *Am J Psychiatry* 1984;141:1614–1616.
10. Thase ME, Kupfer DJ, Jarrett DB. Response to T_3 and imipramine resistant depression. *Proc Am Psychiatry Assoc* 1985;Abstract NR120.
11. Gitlin MJ, Weiner H, Fairbanks L. Failure of T_3 to potentiate tricyclic antidepressant response. *J Affective Disord* 1987;13:267–272.
12. Garbutt JC, Malekpour B, Brunswick D. Effects of triiodothyronine on drug levels and cardiac function in depressed patients treated with imipramine. *Am J Psychiatry* 1979;136:980–982.
13. Whybrow PC, Prange AJJ. A hypothesis of thyroid-catecholamine-receptor interaction. *Arch Gen Psychiatry* 1981;38:106–113.
14. Larsen PR. Thyroid-pituitary interaction. *N Engl J Med* 1982;306:23–32.
15. Targum SD, Greenberg RD, Harmon RL. Thyroid hormone and TRH tests in refractory depression. *J Clin Psychiatry* 1984;45:345–346.
16. Dratman MB, Crutchfield FL. Synaptosomal ^{125}I-triiodothyronine after intravenous ^{125}I-thyroxine. *Am J Physiol* 1978;235:E638–E647.
17. Dratman MB, Crutchfield FL. Normally high levels of T_3 generated from T_4 in brain markedly increased by hypothyroidism: Contrasting the minimum responses in other tissues. *Endocrinology* 1980;106 (Suppl):223.
18. Oppenheimer JH. Thyroid hormone action at the cellular level. *Science* 1979;203:971–979.
19. Dratman MB, Futesku Y, Crutchfield FL. Iodine-125-labeled triiodothyronine in rat brain: Evidence for localization in discreet neural systems. *Science* 1982;215:309–312.
20. Dratman MB, Crutchfield FL. Contrasting effects of hyperthyroidism on formation of labeled 3,3,5-triiodothyronine (T_3) in brain and liver after i.v. 125-I-thyroxine (T_4). Program of the Annual American Thyroid Association 56, San Diego, California.
21. Larsen PR, Silva JE, Kaplan MM. Relationship between circulating and intracellular thyroid hormones: Physiological and clinical implications. *Endocrine Rev* 1981;2:87–102.
22. Crantz FR, Silva JE, Larsen PR. An analysis of the sources and quantity of 3,5,3-triiodothyronine specifically bound to nuclear receptors in rats cerebral cortex and cerebellum. *Endocrinology* 1982;110:367–375.
23. Joffe RT, Roy-Byrne PP, Post RM. Thyroid function and affective illness: A reappraisal. *Biol Psychiatry* 1984;19:1685–1691.
24. Spitzer RL, Endicott J, Robins E. Research Diagnostic Criteria: Rationale and reliability. *Arch Gen Psychiatry* 1978;35:773–782.
25. Spitzer RL, Endicott J. *Schedule for Affective Disorders in Schizophrenia-Lifetime Version (SADS-L)*, 3rd ed. New York: New York State Psychiatric Institute, 1978.
26. Gold NS, Pottash ALC, Extein I. Hypothyroidism and depression. Evidence from complete thyroid function evaluation. *JAMA* 1981;245:1919–1922.
27. Bell GM, Todd WTA, Forfar JC. End-organ responses to thyroxine therapy in subclinical hypothyroidism. *Clin Endocrinol* 1985;22:83–89.

20

Rapid Cycling Bipolar Disorder: Clinical Features, Treatment, and Etiology

Mark S. Bauer and Peter C. Whybrow

In 1974, Dunner and Fieve provided the first definition of rapid cycling in a study of treatment outcome in bipolar illness (1). They found that bipolar patients with four or more affective episodes per year failed lithium treatment at a much higher rate than did those with fewer episodes. They coined the term "rapid cycling" to identify such bipolar patients, emphasizing the poor response of this group to lithium carbonate.

This definition became widely accepted in clinical and research usage and served to focus attention on a subset of bipolar patients with a particularly poor prognosis. However, little is known about these patients as a group. Several studies have investigated individual aspects of rapid cycling (e.g., relationship to antidepressant use or endocrine status). Yet except for one recent report (2), there has been little progress since the description of the original sample (3,4) in producing a coherent clinical picture of rapid cycling. Nevertheless, psychopharmacological research must focus substantial attention on such refractory groups in the coming decades (5).

Affective Disorders Program, Department of Psychiatry, University of Pennsylvania, Philadelphia, PA 19104.

CLINICAL CHARACTERISTICS OF RAPID CYCLING

Phenomenology of Rapid Cycling

Rapid cycling, defined as four or more affective episodes in 12 months, may be specific to the bipolar forms of affective illness. Dunner et al. (3) reported that 40 of 390 patients with bipolar disorder exhibited a rapid cycling course, compared to none of 84 unipolar depressives. Similarly, Prien et al. (6) found a rapid cycling course in bipolar but not unipolar subjects. Our own data (7) indicate that although some patients with rapid cycling may exhibit only depressive episodes during a period of observation, they meet criteria for bipolar disorder by virtue of past manic or hypomanic episodes. These findings are consistent with the formulation by Coryell et al. (8) proposing that although unipolar depression tends toward chronicity, the natural history of bipolar illness is characterized by recovery and relapse.

Patient Characteristics

Rapid cycling occurs with equal frequency in bipolar type I and type II patients (4). Clinical characteristics do not distinguish rapid cycling from nonrapid cycling bipolar patients during depressive (3) or manic or hypomanic episodes (9), although rapid cycling patients may exhibit a dysphoric manic profile less frequently than other bipolar patients (10).

Rapid cycling occurs predominantly in women, with 80 to 95% of rapid cycling patients being female in most (1,2,7,11) but not all (12) studies. No other patient characteristics distinguish rapid cycling from nonrapid cycling bipolar patients (13), including age, age of onset of affective symptoms, or duration of affective symptoms.

Prevalence of Rapid Cycling in Bipolar Illness

Dunner's original study reported a prevalence of 13% (1), although estimates have ranged from 4.2% (6) to 27% (11) depending on the criteria used. Although prevalence estimates derived from such studies depend on referral patterns to those study centers, it is clear that rapid cycling is not a rare phenomenon in secondary or tertiary care centers.

Rapid cycling may be underrecognized in general psychiatric practice as well. Its complex clinical picture often can masquerade as a nonaffective disorder. For example, many rapid cycling patients eventually referred to our program at some time carried the diagnosis of borderline personality disorder, usually on the basis of their frequent changes in mood and the concurrent changes in interpersonal relationships.

Risk Factors for Rapid Cycling

Rapid cycling has been associated with a variety of neuropsychiatric disturbances, such as multiple sclerosis (14) and subnormal intelligence (15). However, it is not likely that such features account for a large proportion of rapid cycling, nor do these lead specifically to a rapid cycling outcome. There is evidence from several studies that three factors may be associated with a rapid cycling course: gender, antidepressant use, and hypothyroidism.

Women comprise 80 to 95% of rapid cycling patients in most (1,2,7,11) though not all (12) studies. This is in contrast to the even sex distribution in bipolar illness in general (16). Although menstrually related mood changes have been described in some rapid cycling patients (7,17), most affective episodes occur without temporal relationship to the menstrual cycle (7). Further, rapid cycling occurs in both premenopausal and postmenopausal women and can continue through menopause (2). Thus, although the association between gender and rapid cycling is strong, there does not appear to be a strong link with fluctuations of gonadal axis function.

Antidepressants have been well documented to induce or exacerbate rapid cycling (2,11,18–20) and may contribute to frequency of episodes in 33 to 51% of rapid cycling patients (2). Data from our series (7) indicate that patients with antidepressant-induced rapid cycling are not distinguishable from spontaneously rapid cycling patients on clinical characteristics, thyroid status, or outcome, suggesting that patients with spontaneous and antidepressant-induced rapid cycling do not represent distinct clinical groups. Rather, these patients may represent a continuum of severity of risk, as may be the case for bipolar patients with antidepressant-induced versus spontaneous manic or hypomanic episodes.

The most common thyroid axis abnormality in unselected bipolar patients is a blunted TSH response to TRH infusion (21). In contrast, the most common finding in rapid cycling bipolars is hypothyroidism or related evidence of thyroid hypofunction. Rapid cycling patients have been shown to have an increased incidence of hypothyroidism during treatment with lithium carbonate (22), a higher prevalence of hypothyroidism from various causes (7,23), and a greater increase in TSH in response to treatment with lithium carbonate (23) than nonrapid cycling bipolars. Wehr et al.

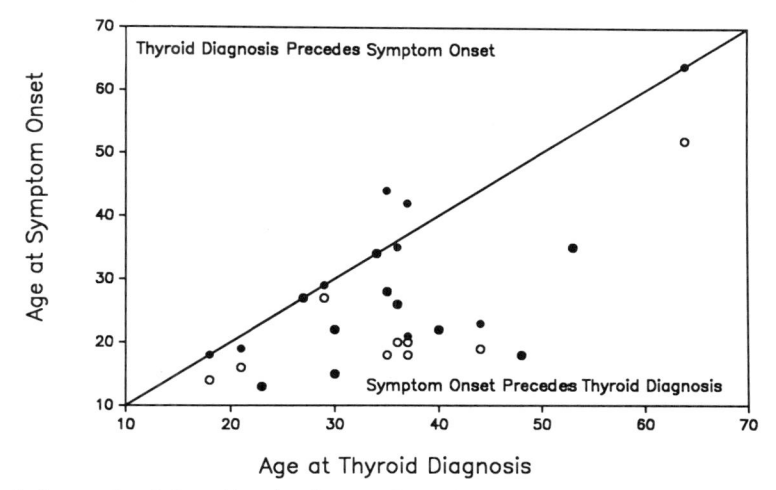

FIG. 1. Age of diagnosis of thyroid axis abnormalities (horizontal axis) is graphed against age of onset of either rapid cycling (●) or nonrapid cycling (○) affective symptoms. Each of 19 patients with thyroid abnormalities is, therefore, represented by two symbols, one representing the temporal relationship of thyroid diagnosis to onset of rapid cycling and one representing the temporal relationship of thyroid diagnosis to the onset of affective illness. The solid diagonal line represents concurrent onset of both thyroid and affective symptoms, such that points above the line represent patients in whom the diagnosis of thyroid abnormality preceded onset of mood symptoms and points below the line represent patients whose thyroid abnormalities followed the onset of affective symptoms. In no patients did thyroid abnormalities predate the onset of noncyclic affective illness. Yet in 8 of these 19, thyroid abnormalities predated or occurred within a year of rapid cycling, suggesting that thyroid alterations may be involved in the pathogenesis of rapid cycling but not in affective illness in general in this sample.

(2) also found very high rates of hypothyroidism in rapid cycling bipolars, but this was not different from a comparison group of refractory nonrapid cycling bipolar patients.

Results of our investigations (7) substantiate the association of hypothyroidism with rapid cycling. Specifically, we have found that grade I, usually clinically evident, hypothyroidism occurs disproportionately in rapid cycling compared to nonrapid cycling bipolar illness. Importantly, this association is independent of potential confounding factors, such as lithium use and gender.

The time course of development of thyroid abnormalities during bipolar illness relative to onset of rapid cycling further supports a pathogenic role for lowered thyroid function in rapid cycling. As summarized in Fig. 1, the onset of affective symptoms in patients who will eventually develop rapid cycling preceded the diagnosis of thyroid abnormalities in all 19 patients studied. However, thyroid abnormalities antedated or appeared concurrently with the onset of the rapid cycling pattern in 8 of the 19 (42%). This temporal association of thyroid abnormalities with rapid cycling, but not with affective symptoms in general, is consistent with thyroid hypofunction as a risk factor for rapid cycling (7).

Natural History and Treatment Response in Rapid Cycling

Rapid cycling patients experience many more episodes over the course of their illness than do nonrapid cycling bipolar patients. The magnitude of the difference is striking: rapid cycling patients at the NIMH had experienced 56.7 episodes since the onset of their illness compared to 8.2 for non-rapid cycling bipolar patients (24).

Poor prognosis has been a hallmark of rapid cycling. It is clear that the majority of rapid cycling patients do not respond to treatment with lithium carbonate. Dunner and Fieve's initial study of rapid cycling (1) found that 59% of nonrapid cycling bipolars responded to lithium treatment, whereas only 18% of rapid cycling patients did so. This increased failure rate among rapid cycling patients has been demonstrated in several more recent studies (2,6,25). Interestingly, two early studies indicate that bipolar patients with a cyclic course whose episode frequently is less than four per 12 months also respond poorly to lithium (1,26), raising the question of whether lack of response to lithium is simply a function of episode frequency or whether nonresponsiveness to lithium in some way relates to the temporal pattern of affective episodes.

Antidepressants (2,18–20) and perhaps other agents that affect monoaminergic neurotransmitter systems (13) can increase episode frequency in rapid cycling. However, Wehr et al. (2) found that only 14% of rapid cycling patients entered remission when their antidepressants were discontinued, despite continued lithium therapy. Thus, since spontaneous remissions are rare and state-of-the-art pharmacotherapy induces remission in less than a third of rapid cycling patients (2), the natural history of rapid cycling appears to be that of chronic affective illness whose course may be modulated by antidepressants and other pharmacological agents.

Alternative treatment strategies have been suggested in numerous case reports (reviewed in 13,27). Most of the agents mentioned also show up in the more extensive series of Wehr et al. (2), usually with dismal results. However, promising results have been described with two agents, carbamazepine and high dose thyroid hormone.

As summarized in detail in Chapter 16, a number of studies have supported a role for the anticonvulsants, particularly carbamazepine, in the treatment of various aspects of bipolar illness (28–31). Open and double-blind studies indicate that carbamazepine has acute antimanic effects (32–34) and may be preferable to lithium in the treatment of mania with a dysphoric component (10). There is additional, though not unequivocal, evidence that carbamazepine has acute antidepressant effects as well (35), effects that are not dependent on the presence of electroencephalographic abnormalities (30). In addition, carbamazepine is not effective in treating panic disorder (36), suggesting some degree of specificity for affective illness.

Prien and Gelenberg (5) recently reviewed the studies of carbamazepine as a prophylactic agent in bipolar disorder. They point out that there have been few prospective double-blind trials and only one comparing carbamazepine to placebo. However, the weight of the evidence from the double-blind trials and from studies with other design paradigms studying several hundred patients indicates that carbamazepine does have some efficacy in prophylaxis of bipolar illness.

Because most of those studies investigated bipolar patients refractory to lithium carbonate, it may be assumed that the samples contained a high proportion of rapid cycling patients. However, there are few data addressing the issue of efficacy of anticonvulsants specifically in rapid cycling. Of interest in this regard is the study of Kishimoto et al. (29) indicating that patients with a rapid cycling course may respond better to carbamazepine than patients with a nonrapid cycling course and the recent open label trial of sodium valproate by Calabrese et al. (31).

Genetic Factors in Rapid Cycling

Several studies indicate that families of rapid cycling probands differ from those of other affectively ill patients. Dunner et al.

(3) found higher rates of affective illness in first degree relatives of rapid cycling than in nonrapid cycling bipolar II patients, although there was no difference among bipolar I groups. Nurnberger et al. (37) reported no difference in rates of rapid cycling or affective illness in relatives of rapid cycling versus nonrapid cycling affective (predominantly schizoaffective) patients but did not differentiate between bipolar I and II and schizoaffective probands.

Wehr et al. (2) found that first degree relatives of rapid cycling patients had somewhat higher rates of unipolar illness (40% vs 26%) and somewhat lower rates of bipolar illness (26% vs 37%) than did those of nonrapid cycling bipolar patients. However, rapid cycling occurred only in families of rapid cycling probands (13% vs 0%). Interestingly, rapid cycling families had nearly double the rate of alcoholism found in nonrapid cycling families (30% vs 16%).

In an initial family history study of 83 first degree relatives of 19 bipolar I and II rapid cycling probands (38), we found affective illness in 41% of first degree relatives, similar to the rates Dunner et al. described for bipolar II patients. Unlike Dunner's findings, bipolar I families were more heavily loaded for affective illness than were bipolar II families (52% vs 36%). Similar to Wehr's data, we found alcoholism in approximately 30% of relatives.

In summary, most studies of families of rapid cycling patients find rates of affective illness in excess of the 25% usually found in bipolar illness in general (39). Further, the rates noted are probably underestimates, in view of the low sensitivity of the family history method (39). These studies suggest that rapid cycling bipolars comprise a high risk, as well as high morbidity, clinical group.

TEMPORAL MORPHOLOGY OF RAPID CYCLING

We have been interested in the pattern of clinical symptoms over time in rapid cycling patients for several reasons. First, careful description of the occurrence, course, and resolution of episodes may lead to greater insight into the pathogenesis of the syndrome. Second, better delineation of the temporal morphology of rapid cycling may aid in the identification of subgroup patients with distinct etiologies or patterns of treatment response. Third, the design of treatment protocols for this complex group may be optimized by taking into account the temporal pattern of affective symptoms at baseline and during treatment. Thus far, researchers have been limited to relatively crude indices of baseline pathology and treatment response (40).

Rapid cycling often has been considered explicitly or implicitly to be a cyclic illness (4,13,18–20,41). However, evidence for the periodic nature of the illness is scant beyond the descriptions of the patients with classic 48-hour cycling, who are quite rare (42). Most empiric evidence suggests a more complex pattern. Dunner et al. (3) noted that affective episodes tended to come in doublets or triplets, whereas Kukopulis et al. (25) reported prognostic differences depending on the sequence of mood states.

Data from our group indicate that rapid cycling, defined by the Dunner-Fieve criterion, encompasses a diverse group, including those who experience a repetitive sequence of affective episodes as well as those who have four discrete episodes scattered over 12 months (7). Further, some patients, though bipolar, may exhibit only depressive episodes for certain periods of rapid cycling. Thus, the hallmark of rapid cycling does not appear to be a truly periodic course but a course characterized by frequent episodes. This actually was recognized initially by Kraeplin (43), who made his observations before the introduction of modern pharmacotherapy that could further complicate analysis of the course of rapid cycling:

> The different varieties of course taken by manic-depressive insanity ... have been analyzed into a series of clinical sub-vari-

eties, specially by Falret and Baillarger, who first made us more intimately acquainted with this disease; these sub-varieties are intermittent mania and melancholia, regular and irregular type, folie alterne, folie a double forme, folie circulaire continue. *I think that I am convinced that that kind of effort at classification must of necessity wreck on the irregularity of the disease. The kind and duration of the attacks and the intervals by no means remain the same in the individual case but may frequently change, so that the case must be reckoned always to new forms* (p. 139). [italics added]

About this question it must first be remarked that no border line at all can be drawn between the strictly periodic forms and those which run an irregular course. Of special significance for this question is the fact, that a periodicity, in some degree satisfying, exists in numerous cases only for a certain part of the course, that it develops first in the course of the malady or even again disappears (p. 188).

Observation of rapid cycling patients for extended periods of time bears out Kraeplin's early impressions. For example, a 4-month outpatient record of daily mood ratings for a typical rapid cycling woman on constant medication regimen is illustrated in Fig. 2. At times during this 120-day period, the patient exhibited a fairly periodic course, whereas at other times, the pattern appears much more disorganized. This variability is reflected in the power spectrum generated from the raw mood data (Fig. 3), in which several peaks appear. There is no single dominant peak, and the power is distributed over a broad range of frequencies. More specifically, the power spectrum exhibits the property of increasing cumulative power with decreasing frequency, known as 1/f behavior, that is characteristic of chaotic systems (44). Chaotic behavior, which has been described in numerous normal and pathological biological systems (45,46), is characterized by a complex but nonrandom pattern that is driven by deterministic and, theoretically, fully describable systems (47).

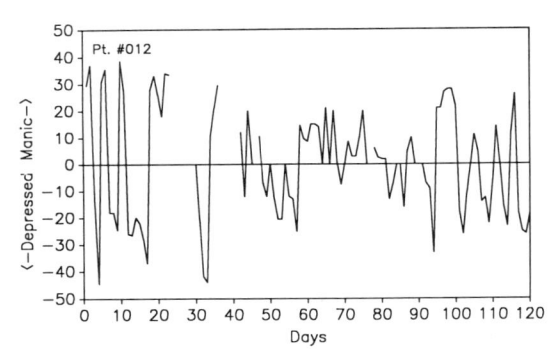

FIG. 2. Patient No. 012 was followed using a daily analog mood rating scale. She was asked to rate her mood daily on a 100 mm line from −50 (worst ever felt) to +50 (best ever felt) with 0 being euthymia. Points below the line, reflecting severity of depressive symptoms, correlated 0.68 with clinician-administered Hamilton Depression Rating Scale, and points above the line, reflecting manic symptoms, correlated 0.59 with Young Mania Rating Scale. During this time, psychotropic medications included lithium, carbamazepine, and replacement dose thyroxine.

Importantly, we have found evidence for a low dimensional chaotic attractor in the mood records of five of six rapid cycling patients studied thus far and in none of normal controls (48). The major implication of find-

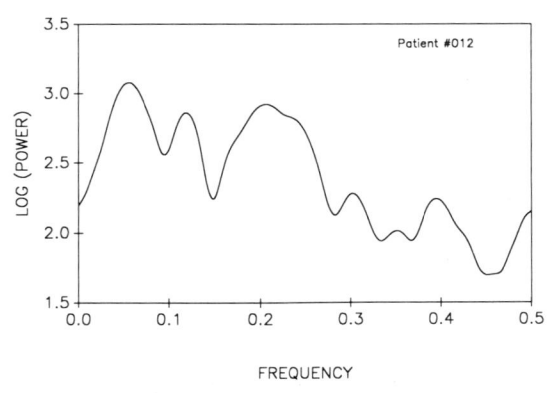

FIG. 3. Power spectrum was generated using statistical package BMDP-PC program 1T, Time Series Analysis, using bandwidth = 0.0583 with linear interpolation for missing data.

ing such chaotic processes in rapid cycling is that seemingly disorganized behavior, such as that illustrated in Fig. 1, actually is produced by a coherent underlying system.

RAPID CYCLING AS A DISTINCT CLINICAL SYNDROME

Kendell (49) has pointed out that the delineation of homogeneous patient groups on phenomenological grounds is an essential step in investigating the pathophysiology of a psychiatric disorder and in targeting specific groups for specific treatment modalities. Based on the original Dunner-Fieve criterion of four or more affective episodes per year (1), the diagnosis of rapid cycling can be made reliably using descriptive, atheoretical criteria. The recent development of instruments for retrospective (24) and prospective (9) tracking of affective episodes should further improve our ability to describe this syndrome.

The clinical pattern of symptoms in rapid cycling, poor outcome, and heavy family loading for affective illness and perhaps alcoholism all support the existence of rapid cycling as a distinct clinical syndrome within bipolar disorder, according to the criteria of Robins and Guze (50). Support is provided also by the association of rapid cycling with the specific risk factors enumerated previously. A further piece of evidence comes from viewing clinical characteristics associated with rapid cycling according to the schema of Kendell (49). He proposed that psychiatric syndromes with similar symptom profiles could be distinguished if there exist "points of rarity" in the frequency distribution of some laboratory or clinical characteristic that appears in the two syndromes in varying degree or if a "nonlinear relationship" (Kendell's term) (Fig. 4) holds between that characteristic and some feature that could separate the two syndromes (e.g., nonsuppression of cortisol after dexamethasone, outcome). Interestingly, the relationship between gen-

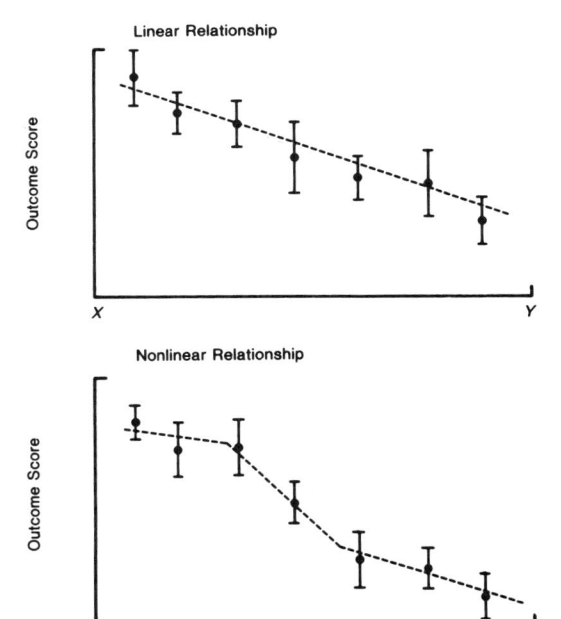

FIG. 4. Suppose that two affective syndromes share a spectrum of some characteristic (e.g., percentage dexamethasone nonsuppression or, as illustrated here, outcome), with one syndrome high on that characteristic and the other low. Further, suppose that the two syndromes represent a spectrum of some set of symptoms (e.g., severity of some single symptom, relative prominence of some symptom compared to another). Kendell proposed that if there was a continuous, linear relationship between the outcome characteristic and the symptom spectrum (**top**), no support was provided for separating patients into two separate syndromes. Rather, they appear to represent two ends of the same continuum. If, however, there is a discontinuity or nonlinearity in the relationship between the variables (**bottom**), then the two ends of the spectrum may represent fundamentally distinct disorders. (Reprinted with permission from ref. 49.)

der and episode frequency in bipolar illness appears to provide an example of such a nonlinearity. Most studies of unselected bipolar patients indicate that approximately 50% are women (16). As illustrated in Fig. 5, a similar proportion of rapid cycling patients with 4 to 11 episodes per year are women. However, the proportion of

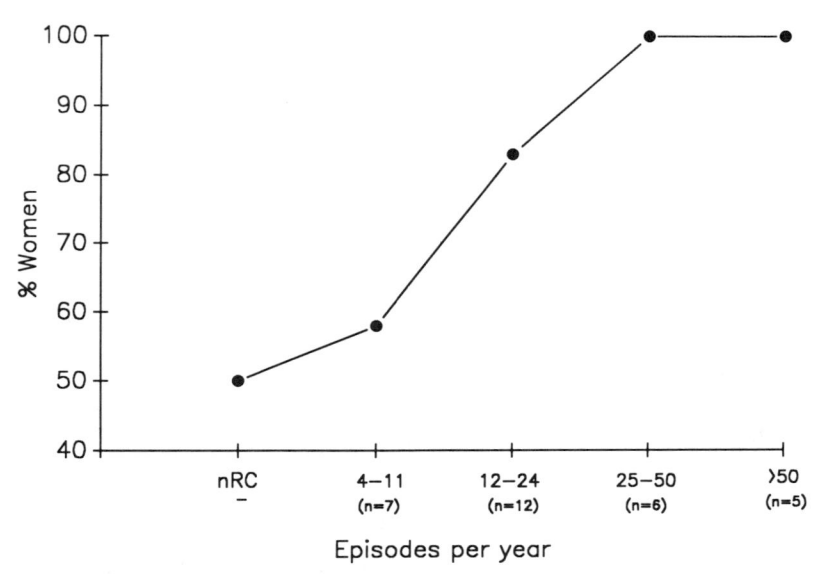

FIG. 5. Data from our initial sample have been reanalyzed to illustrate the relationship between gender and episode frequency. Most studies of unselected bipolar populations indicate that approximately 50% of bipolar patients are women. This is similar to the 58% proportion in rapid cycling patients with 4 to 11 episodes per year. However, the proportion of women increases markedly at ⩾ 12 episodes per year. This may reflect a nonlinearity (49) in the relationship between gender and episode frequency in bipolar illness, providing further support for the delineation of rapid cycling as a distinct form of bipolar illness.

women increases dramatically as episode frequency increases beyond 11 episodes per year, demonstrating a nonlinearity in the relationship between episode frequency and percentage of women. Whether the optimal cutoff for episode frequency in rapid cycling is closer to 12 than 4 episodes per year remains to be determined by subsequent studies using multiple research strategies. Nonetheless, the existence of this break in linearity supports the separation of rapid cycling as a distinct clinical entity.

TREATMENT OF REFRACTORY RAPID CYCLING WITH HIGH DOSE THYROXINE

Stancer and Persad (51) treated 10 rapid cycling patients in an open trial with high doses of thyroxine or triiodothyronine in conjunction with as-needed neuroleptics. Complete remission was reported in 5 women, with an additional woman experiencing a decrease in frequency and severity of affective episodes. There was no change in affective symptoms in 1 man and a 3-month remission in another. All were clinically euthyroid with normal serum thyroxine and triiodothyronine levels at the outset. Hatotani et al. (52) described several cases in which triiodothyronine in combination with other medications induced remission in otherwise refractory rapid cycling.

Our own experience in open and placebo-controlled trials of high dose thyroxine in the treatment of refractory rapid cycling also has yielded promising results (40). We treated 11 patients with refractory rapid cycling in a structured treatment protocol involving the use of high dose thyroxine in addition to existing pharmacotherapy. Patients entered the trial taking lithium ($n=6$), lithium plus carbamazepine ($n=2$), antidepressants ($n=2$), or a benzodiazepine

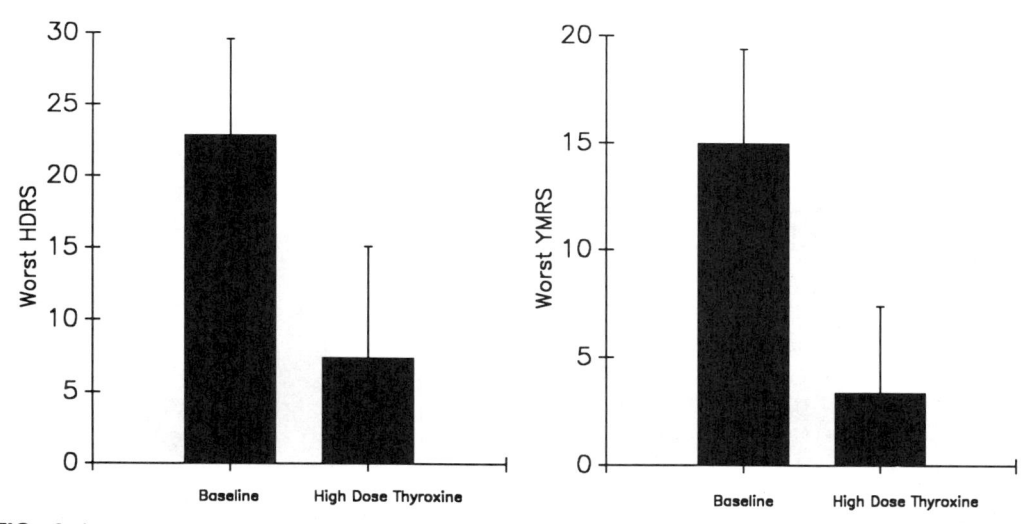

FIG. 6. Improvement during treatment with high dose thyroxine is reflected in decreases of the worst scores during baseline compared to worst scores during treatment for both depression and mania ($p<0.001$ for each, by paired t-test). HDRS, Hamilton Depression Rating Scale; YMRS, Young Mania Rating Scale.

($n=1$). These medications, on which they were documented prospectively to continue a rapid cycling course, were held constant. Thyroxine was added in an open fashion in increasing doses until clinical response or until side effects precluded further increase. Ten of 11 patients responded, defined by reduction in Hamilton depression rating and Young mania rating scores to ≤ 50% of baseline. Group scores on both worst (Fig. 6) and mean (Fig. 7) depression and mania scales declined significantly. Response occurred without regard to presence of baseline thyroid abnormalities.

It is of interest that thyroid function evaluation at the time of clinical response revealed serum total and free thyroxine levels above the normal range in 9 of 10 responders, although triiodothyronine levels were within the normal range and serum TSH levels were not suppressed in all cases (Fig. 8). Thus, behavioral response occurred before complete suppression of TSH production and appeared to be a function of increased thyroxine and not triiodothyronine levels. This effect occurred at a wide range of thyroxine doses (0.15–0.35 mg/day) that were somewhat lower than those used by Stancer and Persad (51). The treatment was well tolerated, with minimal side effects and no evidence of the hypermetabolism originally documented in Gjessing's use of high doses of desiccated thyroid gland or thyroxine in the treatment of periodic catatonia (53).

Subsequent to clinical response, four patients agreed to double-blind or single-blind placebo crossover to determine the role of thyroxine in their clinical response. Three of the four relapsed within 3 weeks of withdrawal of high dose thyroxine (40).

This treatment approach differs from that of Stancer and Persad, who reported using thyroid hormones alone, in that we have used high dose thyroxine as an adjuvant treatment, usually in addition to lithium or lithium plus carbamazepine. This may explain the difference between our positive results and the failure of Wehr et al. (2) to find efficacy of high dose thyroxine treatment, since that group used high dose thyroxine alone (S. James, personal communication, 1988).

To summarize treatment strategies for

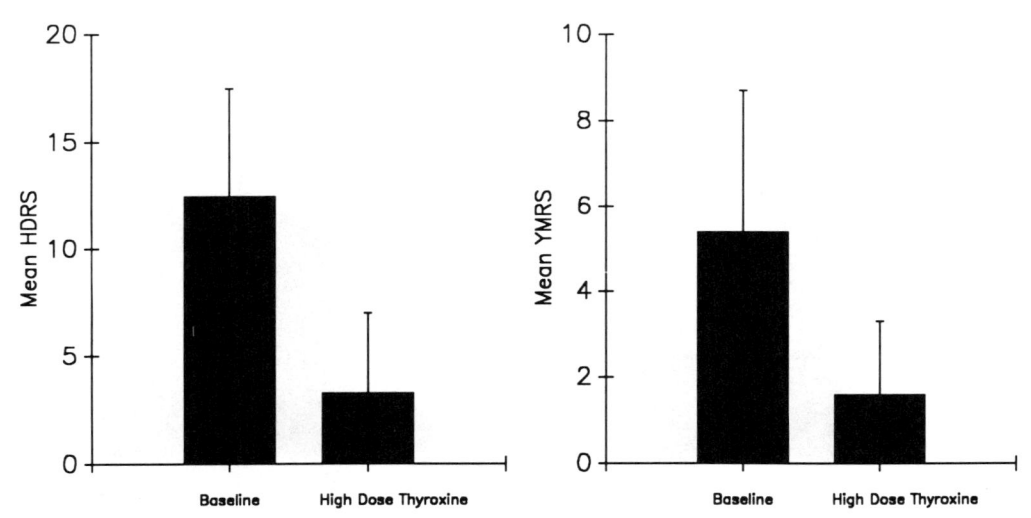

FIG. 7. Improvement during treatment with high dose thyroxine is reflected also in decreases in mean scores on rating scales for depression ($p<0.004$) and mania ($p<0.04$). Mean ratings for each of the measures are the average scores for all ratings performed during the periods of observation, whether or not the patient was in an affective episode. HDRS, Hamilton Depression Rating Scale; YMRS, Young Mania Rating Scale.

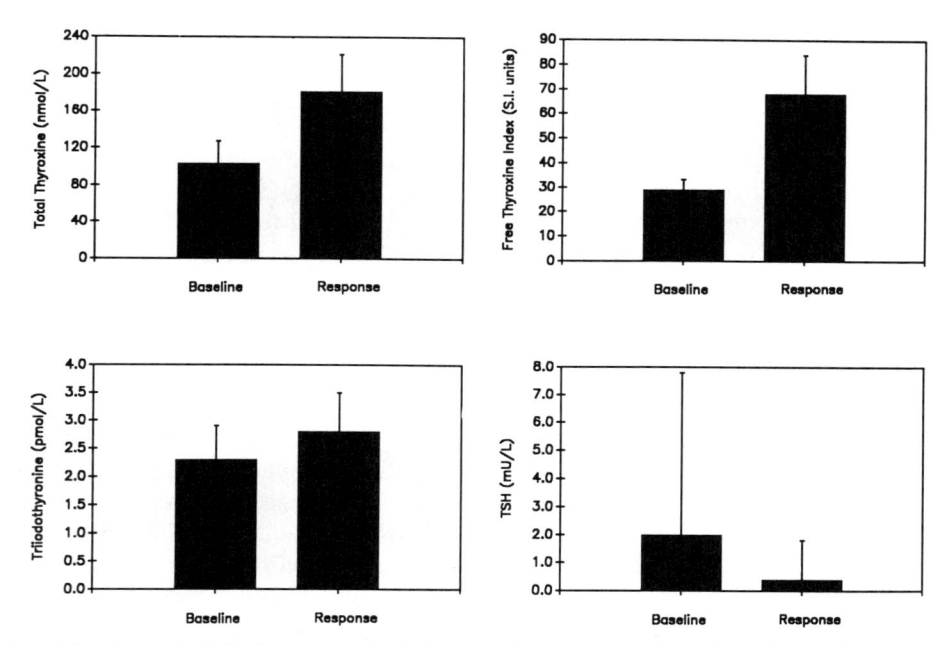

FIG. 8. At the time of clinical response, total serum thyroxine and free thyroxine index were significantly increased ($p<0.001$ for each, paired t-test), as expected, with high dose thyroxine treatment. However, triiodothyronine levels were not significantly changed ($p=0.10$). Although serum TSH was decreased ($p<0.003$, Wilcoxon signed rank test), not all patients had completely suppressed TSH levels (range <0.2–1.8 mIU/L). Thus, clinical response is more closely related to changes in serum thyroxine parameters than to triiodothyronine, whereas changes in TSH are not related to, or lag behind, behavioral response.

rapid cycling, the hallmark of rapid cycling remains nonresponsiveness to lithium. Cautious optimism is warranted regarding initial results with anticonvulsants, such as carbamazepine and valproic acid, and with high dose thyroxine. However, general acceptance of these therapeutic alternatives must await confirmation in prospective double-blind trials.

THEORIES OF RAPID CYCLING

Three theories, not necessarily mutually exclusive, have been presented to explain the occurrence of rapid cycling in bipolar illness. These theories focus on circadian rhythm abnormalities (13,41,42), kindling and behavioral sensitization (54,55), and thyroid axis abnormalities (7,40).

Circadian Rhythms and Rapid Cycling

The theory that rapid cycling results from abnormalities of the circadian timekeeping system derives primarily from two sorts of data: (a) that rapid cycling is a cyclic affective illness, and (b) that rapid cycling patients have abnormalities in the generation or entrainment of circadian rhythms.

The most striking examples of rapid cycling are indeed those in which a periodic pattern is found. Such patients can exhibit a mood cycle with a single periodicity, such as the patients with a 48-hour cycle described by Bunney and Hartmann (56) and Jenner et al. (57). Alternatively, several discrete periodicities can be seen in mood records of some patients (42). However, most patients studied with mood symptom logs for extended periods of time do not show single periodicities in their affective symptoms (48). Further, rapid cycling patients, though bipolar, can exhibit months of only depressive cycling (7) as well as various other patterns (3,25). Thus, as Kraeplin (43) concluded about bipolar illness in general, temporal patterns of rapid cycling are protean and as a rule do not manifest a truly periodic course.

What is the evidence that circadian rhythms are abnormal in rapid cycling? Initial theories (13,41) were built on the evidence that 48-hour periods of activity accompany the switch from depression into mania in rapid cycling (20,41). This was considered to be a manifestation of a 48-hour sleep–wake cycle driven by an endogenous circadian pacemaker. This sleep–wake pacemaker in rapid cycling patients was thought to have an abnormally long period that caused it to uncouple from the temperature pacemaker and the entraining light–dark cycle. This slippage then resulted in extended wakefulness and a switch from depression into mania.

Although the data are strong supporting extended wakefulness during the switch from depression to mania in some rapid cycling patients (20,41), inspection of the activity data presented does not reveal true 48-hour sleep–wake cycles. Similarly, we are not aware of data supporting dissociation of sleep and temperature rhythms in rapid cycling nor data supporting a change in phase-angle of any circadian rhythms to the entraining light–dark cycle in rapid cycling that is not due to masking effects. Thus, despite the intriguing and clinically important changes in the sleep–wake cycle during the switch process in rapid cycling, the link of these findings specifically to the circadian system remains to be established.

A more recent theory is that rapid cycling may result from dissociation of circannual rhythms from photic or temperature-related seasonal cues (42). Although there is some commonality between rapid cycling and seasonal affective disorder in that the latter is also a form of quasi-cyclic affective illness that is probably bipolar (see discussion in 58), the theory of rapid cycling as a disorder or circannual timekeeping rests more on analogies with hibernating rodents (42) than on data from the clinical group in question.

Nonetheless, involvement of the circadian timekeeping system appears likely, since such factors have been demonstrated in other forms of bipolar illness. For instance, light sensitivity may be altered in bipolar patients (59,60) and their relatives (61). In addition, there is evidence for the involvement of light in the pathogenesis of (62) and recovery from (63) seasonal affective disorder. Thus, while strict circadian and circannual theories of rapid cycling appear at this time to be a procrustean bed in which to lay that disorder, the circadian timekeeping system remains a promising area for future research.

Kindling/Sensitization and Rapid Cycling

Post et al. (54,55) have proposed that an autonomous pattern of frequent affective episodes, as occurs in rapid cycling, may develop from increasing sensitization of an individual to actual, anticipated, or imagined environmental stressors. This process was proposed to be similar to (a) kindling, wherein subthreshold convulsant stimuli can decrease the threshold for seizures and eventually lead to spontaneous convulsions, and (b) behavioral sensitization, wherein repeated exposure to pharmacological stimuli can decrease the threshold for specific behavioral responses.

There are several attractive aspects to the kindling/sensitization hypothesis of rapid cycling. The model is supported by the increased frequency of episodes with each episode in bipolar illness in general (64,65) and the possible association of affective episodes in bipolar illness with environmental stressors early, but not later, in its course (55). Further support for this hypothesis is provided by the response of rapid cycling and other bipolar patients to carbamazepine, which has antikindling properties in animals (55).

However, there are several problems with the kindling/sensitization hypothesis as it applies to rapid cycling. As with the circadian rhythms hypothesis, there are as yet few data from the clinical group in question to support the existence of kindling/sensitization phenomena in rapid cycling patients. The decrease in interepisode interval with successive episodes in bipolar illness and the possible association of environmental stressors with episodes early in the course of illness may admit of many explanations and do not specifically support a kindling/sensitization model. Other specific clinical aspects, such as the view of hypomania as a "conditioned compensatory response" to depression (55), although well grounded in psychoanalytical theory, currently have little empiric support.

Kindling itself appears to be a complex process. For example, carbamazepine blocks kindling effects only for certain stimuli at certain stages of development of kindling (55). It is difficult to interpret behavioral sensitization processes in animals in a way that could explain important clinical aspects of rapid cycling. For instance, lithium, but not carbamazepine, blocks cocaine-induced behavioral responses (55), suggesting that behavioral sensitization-related processes actually may be less applicable to rapid cycling patients, who are lithium-resistant, than to other bipolar patients.

Nevertheless, the kindling/sensitization hypothesis provides a powerful intellectual framework for understanding recurrent affective episodes in the context of neurochemical, environmental, and psychodynamic factors. In addition, the theory supplies an interpretation of the very important finding of clinical efficacy of anticonvulsants in affective illness.

Thyroid Function and Rapid Cycling

We have proposed that relative deficiency of thyroid hormone effect in the brain leads to a rapid cycling in bipolar illness (7,40). By this hypothesis, the brain becomes thyroprivic due either to decreased thyroid hormone delivery to the brain, as in hypothyroidism, or to decreased uptake or altered metabolism of thyroid hormone in the brain, with normal serum levels of thyroid hormone.

This hypothesis is based on the higher incidence of hypothyroidism during lithium treatment (22), the higher prevalence of hypothyroidism due to various causes (7,23), and the disproportionate increase in TSH levels (23) in rapid cycling compared to nonrapid cycling bipolar patients. We have suggested further that the association with hypothyroidism actually may explain the high proportion of rapid cycling patients who are female, since women are severalfold more likely than men to develop hypothyroidism (66) and, on this basis, may develop rapid cycling. Additional support for this hypothesis comes from treatment studies indicating that high doses of thyroxine (40,51) and perhaps triiodothyronine (51,52) ameliorate rapid cycling.

There are several problems with the thyroid hypothesis of rapid cycling. First, Wehr et al. (2) found high rates of hypothyroidism in both rapid cycling and refractory nonrapid cycling bipolar patients. Thus, hypothyroidism may lead to a refractory course in other forms of refractory bipolar illness as well. Rather than compromise the thyroid hypothesis, this finding suggests that more research is needed in understanding the role of the thyroid axis in other types of refractory affective illness.

Second, the majority of rapid cycling patients do not have clinically evident hypothyroidism, suggesting that gross compromise in thyroid hormone delivery to the brain cannot explain rapid cycling in most cases. However, there are several steps in thyroid hormone processing within the brain that can be disrupted by drugs used to treat bipolar illness. For example, lithium inhibits the conversion of thyroxine to triiodothyronine in neural and pituitary tissue (67), indicating that lithium has central antithyroid effects distinct from its peripheral goiterogenic effects. Interestingly, tricyclic antidepressants, which can induce or exacerbate rapid cycling (2,18–20), disrupt the uptake of thyroxine into the brain and its conversion to triiodothyronine (68). Thus, disruption of central thyroid effects may underline the association of rapid cycling with antidepressant use as well as with gender.

One major advantage of the thyroid hypothesis is the amount of supporting evidence from the clinical population of interest. However, unlike the other theories, specific mechanisms by which thyroid alterations lead to rapid cycling have not been proposed. Although extensive theorizing would quickly outstrip currently available empirical data, several areas for further investigation can clearly be targeted. One area of important research is thyroid interactions with the neurotransmitter systems (69). A second approach is the development of imaging techniques to measure directly iodothyronine levels in brain. Third, the role of thyroid hormones in the control of circadian rhythm and kindling/sensitization processes may provide better explanations for rapid cycling than any single avenue of research alone.

RAPID CYCLING AND CHAOS THEORY

The presence of chaotic attractors in mood patterns of rapid cycling patients (48) suggests a powerful heuristic model for understanding rapid cycling and perhaps other forms of recurrent affective illness as well. Physiological systems studied over time may manifest steady state, oscillatory, or chaotic behavior depending on the nature of the system. This is in distinction to the random noise present in all biological systems and similar to many physical and chemical processes (46). Under the appropriate conditions, oscillatory systems can come to rest in a steady state, although not all systems in steady state are capable of oscillation. Similarly, systems that are capable of chaotic behavior can oscillate or reach steady state, although only not all physiological systems can become chaotic.

Although complex to define mathematically, there are several properties by which chaotic systems can be identified. One such property is the existence of attractors, as found in the mood records of rapid cycling patients. Three additional properties that may have important clinical relevance are predicted in a system capable of displaying chaotic behavior: (a) the type of behavior displayed by the system, however complex, is driven by an underlying system that can be mathematically described in terms of its parameters and initial conditions, (b) small changes in these parameters can lead to vastly different patterns of behavior, and (c) discrete perturbations of such systems at one point in time can cause long-lasting, complex changes in the behavior of the system.

Parameters in Chaotic Systems

Figure 9 illustrates one of the most studied and fundamental examples of a simple chaotic system (47). This equation has had wide applicability in biology, from describing changes in brain enzyme activity to describing population fluctuations in predator–prey relationships (45,70,71). It can be seen that the output of the system is described by a simple equation. It is characteristic of such systems that small changes in the constant, r, lead to very different types of behavior of the system, including steady state, periodic fluctuations, and apparently disorganized behavior.

Viewing rapid cycling in terms of this model suggests that certain clinical aspects of rapid cycling may be understood in terms of three properties outlined previously. At the most fundamental level, the complex episode pattern of rapid cycling is neither random nor stimulus-driven but can be explained by simple underlying systems.

Further, behavior can be changed dramatically by small changes in the underlying system, as changes in the constant, r, demonstrate. The system can move from steady state to periodic to chaotic behavior, yet each pattern is driven by the same underlying process. A chaotic model could, therefore, explain both classic periodic cycling (56,57) and the variable mood patterns of the majority of rapid cycling patients (7,48).

The effects of therapeutic agents in rapid cycling may be understood in terms of changes in system parameters. Both the detrimental effects of antidepressants and the beneficial effects of thyroxine and carbamazepine in rapid cycling may be described in terms of changes in such parameters. This raises the interesting possibility that all bipolar illness, and perhaps normal behavior as well, can be described by chaotic principles. Rapid cycling bipolars, non-rapid cycling bipolars, and normals may differ only in terms of the constants of the systems driving their moods, and therapeutic manipulations in the clinical populations may be understood in terms of altering such constants to produce long-term changes in behavior.

Discrete Perturbations in Chaotic Systems

The third property of chaotic systems, not illustrated in Fig. 9, is that discrete perturbations of such systems can induce long-term changes in their behavior. Those stimuli, although not modifying the underlying parameters of the system, may drive the system into steady state, periodic fluctuations, or chaotic behavior (44).

Three clinical implications result from this property. First, discrete stressors may produce long-lasting perturbations of the system. This may underlie the hypothesized role of environmental stressors initially in the course of bipolar illness (55,72). However, the chaos model need not invoke increasing sensitivity of the system to stressors as proposed by the kindling/sensitization hypothesis. Rather, such long-lasting effects set into motion by discrete stimuli (i.e., stressors) are expected in systems displaying chaotic dynamics, as has

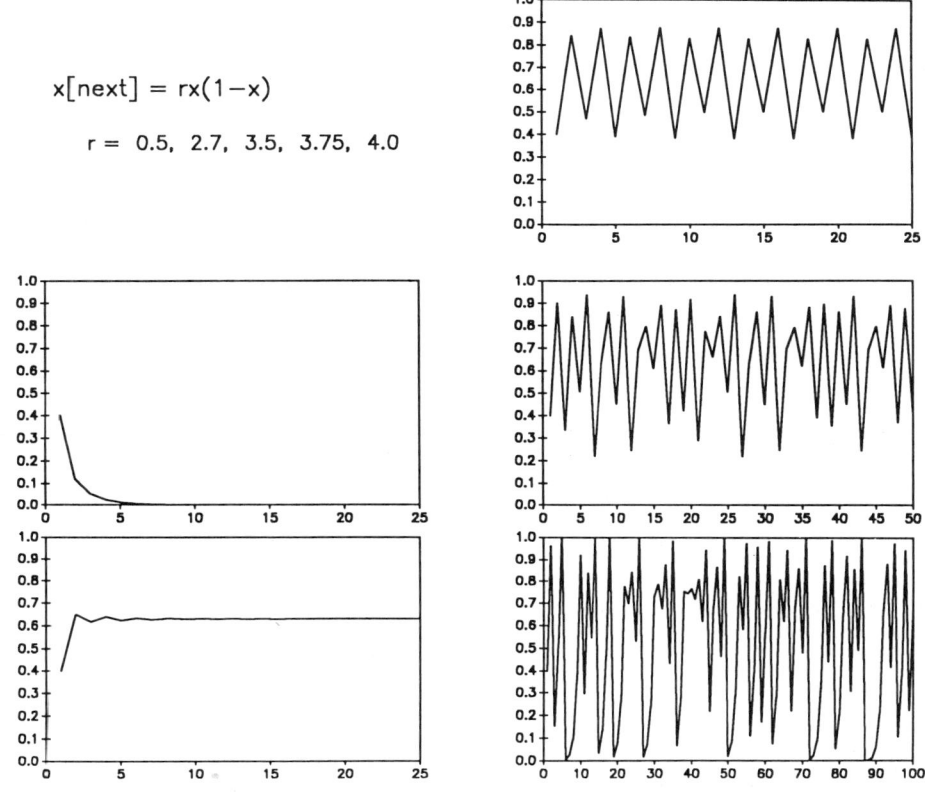

FIG. 9. Complex behavior can be produced by simple changes in simple systems, in this case depending on small changes in the value of the force constant, r. With $r = 0.5$, x[next] goes to zero quickly, whereas with $r = 2.7$, steady state is achieved. With further increases in r, the system exhibits periodic behavior ($r = 3.5$) and subsequently becomes more and more unpredictable ($r = 3.75$ and $r = 4.0$).

been shown for numerous other physiological systems (45). Additionally, chronic exposure to stressors might induce chronic alterations in the physiology of susceptible persons, thereby changing system parameters as outlined previously.

Second, a very effective way to induce chaotic behavior in such systems is to drive a periodic system with an oscillating stimulus of somewhat different period (45). If abnormalities of the circadian timekeeping system do exist in rapid cycling, such abnormalities could predispose susceptible patients to develop a chaotic episode pattern when exposed to appropriate periodic environmental stimuli, such as changes in the light–dark cycle. Thus, rhythmic environmental, or perhaps internal, factors may lead to complex patterns of behavior, despite the fact that those behavior patterns themselves are not rhythmic.

Third, the timing of pharmacological or other interventions may be crucial in determining whether the system is driven to steady state or fluctuates even more widely. In the coming decades, we may find ourselves developing shorter-acting drugs that can be pulsed at particular phases of the illness to complement those longer-acting treatments that alter system parameters.

ACKNOWLEDGMENTS

Preparation of this chapter was supported by Physician Scientist Award MH00720 and a Young Investigator Award from the National Alliance for Research in Schizophrenia and Depression (NARSAD) to MSB, and a NARSAD Established Investigator Award to PCW.

REFERENCES

1. Dunner D, Fieve R. Clinical factors in lithium carbonate prophylaxis failure. *Arch Gen Psychiatry* 1974;30:229–233.
2. Wehr T, Sack D, Rosenthal N, Cowdry R. Rapid cycling affective disorder: Contributing factors and treatment responses in 51 patients. *Am J Psychiatry* 1988;145:179–184.
3. Dunner D, Patrick V, Fieve R. Rapid cycling manic depressive patients. *Compr Psychiatry* 1977;18:561–565.
4. Dunner D. Rapid cycling bipolar manic depressive illness. *Psychiatr Clin North Am* 1979;2:461–467.
5. Prien R, Gelenberg A. Alternative to lithium for preventive treatment of bipolar disorder. *Am J Psychiatry* 1989;146:840–848.
6. Prien R, Kupfer D, Mansky P, et al. Drug therapy in the prevention of recurrences in unipolar and bipolar affective disorders: Report of the NIMH Collaborative Study Group comparing lithium carbonate, imipramine, and a lithium carbonate-imipramine combination. *Arch Gen Psychiatry* 1984;41:1096–1104.
7. Bauer M, Whybrow P, Winokur A. Rapid cycling bipolar affective disorder, I: Association with grade I hypothyroidism. *Arch Gen Psychiatry* 1990;47:427–432.
8. Coryell W, Keller M, Endicott J, Andreasen N, Clayton P, Hirschfeld R. Bipolar II illness: Course and outcome over a five year period. *Psychol Med* 1989;19:129–141.
9. Bauer M, Crits-Christoph P, Ball W, et al. A self-rating instrument for tracking both poles of affective illness. *Biol Psychiatry Suppl* 1990;27:139.
10. Post R, Rubinow D, Uhde T, et al. Dysphoric mania. Clinical and biological correlates. *Arch Gen Psychiatry* 1989;46:353–358.
11. Tondo L, Laddomada P, Serra G, Minnai G, Kukopulos A. Rapid cyclers and antidepressants. *Int Pharmacopsychiatry* 1981;16:119–123.
12. Joffe R, Kutcher S, MacDonald C. Thyroid function and bipolar affective disorder. *Psychiatry Res* 1987;25:117–121.
13. Roy-Byrne P, Joffe R, Uhde T, Post R. Approaches to the evaluation and treatment of rapid-cycling affective illness. *Br J Psychiatry* 1984;145:543–550.
14. Kellner C, Davenport Y, Post R, Ross R. Rapidly cycling bipolar disorder and multiple sclerosis. *Am J Psychiatry* 1984;141:112–113.
15. Jones P, Berney T. Early onset rapid cycling bipolar affective disorder. *J Child Psychiatry* 1987;28:731–738.
16. Weissman M, Boyd J. The epidemiology of affective disorders. In: Post R, Ballenger J, eds. *Neurobiology of mood disorders*. Baltimore: Williams & Wilkins, 1985;60–75.
17. Price W, DiMarzio L. Premenstrual tension syndrome in rapid-cycling bipolar affective disorder. *J Clin Psychiatry* 1986;47:415–417.
18. Wehr T, Goodwin F. Rapid cycling between mania and depression caused by maintenance tricyclics. *Psychopharmacol Bull* 1979;15:17–19.
19. Wehr T, Goodwin F. Tricyclics modulate frequency of mood cycles. *Chronobiologia* 1979;6:377–385.
20. Wehr T, Goodwin F. Rapid cycling in manic-depressives induced by tricyclic antidepressants. *Arch Gen Psychiatry* 1979;36:555–559.
21. Amsterdam J, Winokur A, Lucki I, et al. A neuroendocrine test battery in bipolar patients and healthy subjects. *Arch Gen Psychiatry* 1983;40:515–521.
22. Cho J, Bone S, Dunner D, Colt E, Fieve R. The effect of lithium treatment on thyroid function in patients with primary affective disorder. *Am J Psychiatry* 1979;136:115–116.
23. Cowdry R, Wehr T, Zis A, Goodwin F. Thyroid abnormalities associated with rapid cycling bipolar illness. *Arch Gen Psychiatry* 1983;40:414–420.
24. Roy-Byrne P, Post R, Uhde T, Porcu T, Davis D. The longitudinal course of recurrent affective illness: Life chart data from research patients at the NIMH. *Acta Psychiatrica Scand* 1985;71 (Suppl 317):3–34.
25. Kukopulos A, Reginaldi D, Laddomada P, Floris G, Serra G, Tondo L. Course of the manic-depressive cycle and changes caused by treatments. *Pharmakopsychiatry* 1980;13:156–167.
26. Stancer H, Furlong W, Godse D. A longitudinal investigation of lithium as a prophylactic agent for recurrent depressions. *Can Psychiatr Assoc J* 1970;15:29–40.
27. Alarcon R. Rapid cycling affective disorders: A clinical review. *Compr Psychiatry* 1985;26:522–540.
28. Okuma T, Inanaga K, Otsuki S, et al. A preliminary double-blind study of the efficacy of carbamazepine in prophylaxis of manic-depressive illness. *Psychopharmacology* 1981;73:95–96.
29. Kishimoto A, Ogura C, Hazama H, Inoue K. Long-term prophylactic effects of carbamazepine in affective disorders. *Br J Psychiatry* 1983;43:327–332.
30. Post R. Approaches to treatment-resistant bipolar affectively ill patients. *Clin Neuropharmacol* 1988;11:93–104.

31. Calabrese J, Delucchi G. Spectrum of efficacy of valproate in 55 patients with rapid-cycling bipolar disorder. *Am J Psychiatry* 1990;147:431–434.
32. Emrich H, Dose M, von Zerssen D. The use of sodium valproate, carbamazepine, and oxcarbazepine in patients with affective disorders. *J Affective Disord* 1985;8:243–250.
33. Lerer B, Moore N, Meyendorff E, Cho S, Gershon S. Carbamazepine versus lithium in mania: A double-blind study. *J Clin Psychiatry* 1987;48:89–93.
34. Post R, Uhde T, Roy-Byrne P, Joffe R. Correlates of antimanic response to carbamazepine. *Psychiatry Res* 1987;21:71–83.
35. Post R, Uhde T, Roy-Byrne P, et al. Antidepressant effects of carbamazepine. *Am J Psychiatry* 1986;143:29–34.
36. Uhde T. Stein M, Post R. Lack of efficacy of carbamazepine in the treatment of panic disorder. *Am J Psychiatry* 1988;145:1104–1109.
37. Nurnberger J, Guroff J, Hamovit J, Berrettini W, Gershon E. A family study of rapid-cycling bipolar illness. *J Affective Disord* 1988;15:87–91.
38. Price R, Whybrow P, Bauer M. Unpublished observations.
39. Weissman M, Kidd K, Prusoff B. Variability in rates of affective disorders in relatives of depressed and normal probands. *Arch Gen Psychiatry* 1984;41:1136–1143.
40. Bauer M, Whybrow P. Rapid cycling bipolar affective disorder, II: Treatment of refractory rapid cycling with high dose thyroxine, a preliminary study. *Arch Gen Psychiatry* 1990;47:435–440.
41. Wehr T, Goodwin F, Wirz-Justice A, Breitmaier J, Craig C. 48-hour sleep–wake cycles in manic-depressive illness: Naturalistic observations and sleep deprivation experiments. *Arch Gen Psychiatry* 1982;39:559–565.
42. Wehr T. Causes and treatments of rapid cycling affective disorder. In: Amsterdam J, ed. *Antidepressant therapies: Applications for the outpatient practitioner.* New York: Marcel Dekker, 1989.
43. Kraeplin E. *Manic-depressive insanity and paranoia,* 1921 ed., trans: Barclay R. Birmingham, AL: Classics of Psychiatry and Behavioral Science, 1989.
44. Ruelle D. Strange attractors. *Math Intelligencer* 1980;2:126–137.
45. Mackey M, Glass L. Oscillation and chaos in physiological control systems. *Science* 1977;287–289.
46. Glass L, Mackey M. *From clocks to chaos: The rhythms of life.* Princeton, NJ: Princeton University Press, 1988.
47. Feigenbaum M. Universal behavior in nonlinear systems. *Los Alamos Sci* 1980;1:4–27.
48. Gottschalk A, Bauer M, Whybrow P. Evidence for a chaotic attractor in bipolar affective disorders. *Biol Psychiatry Suppl* 1990;27:99A.
49. Kendell R. The choice of diagnostic criteria for biological research. *Arch Gen Psychiatry* 1982;39:1334–1339.
50. Robins E, Guze S. Establishment of diagnostic validity in psychiatric illness: Its application to schizophrenia. *Am J Psychiatry* 1970;126:107–111.
51. Stancer H, Persad E. Treatment of intractable rapid-cycling manic-depressive disorder with levothyroxine: Clinical observations. *Arch Gen Psychiatry* 1982;39:311–312.
52. Hatotani N, Kitayama I, Inoue K, Nomura J. Psychoendocrine studies of recurrent psychoses. In: Hataotani N, Nomura J, eds. *Neurobiology of periodic psychoses.* Tokyo: Igaku-Shoin, 1984;77–92.
53. Gjessing R. Rhythm and periodicity. In: Gjessing L, Jenner A, eds. *Contribution to the somatology of periodic catatonia.* Oxford: Pergamon Press, 1976;209–215.
54. Post R, Rubinow D, Ballenger J. Conditioning, sensitization, and kindling: Implications for the course of affective illness. In: Post R, Ballenger J, eds. *Neurobiology of mood disorders.* Baltimore: Williams & Wilkins, 1985;432–466.
55. Post R, Rubinow D, Ballenger J. Conditioning, sensitization, and the longitudinal course of affective illness. *Br J Psychiatry* 1986;149:191–201.
56. Bunney W, Hartmann E. Study of a patient with 48-hour manic-depressive cycles: I. An analysis of behavioral factors. *Arch Gen Psychiatry* 1965;12:611–625.
57. Jenner F, Gjessing L, Cox J, Davies-Jones A, Hullin R, Hanna S. A manic depressive psychotic with a persistent forty-eight hour cycle. *Br J Psychiatry* 1967;113:895–910.
58. Blehar M, Rosenthal N. Seasonal affective disorders and phototherapy. Report of a National Institute of Mental Health-sponsored workshop. *Arch Gen Psychiatry* 1989;46:469–474.
59. Lewy A, Wehr T, Goodwin F, Newsome D, Rosenthal N. Light suppresses melatonin secretion in humans. *Science* 1980;210:1267–1269.
60. Lewy A, Nurnberger J, Wehr T, et al. Supersensitivity to light: Possible trait marker for manic-depressive illness. *Am J Psychiatry* 1985;142:725–727.
61. Nurnberger J, Berrettini W, Tamarkin L, et al. Supersensitivity to melatonin suppression by light in young people at high risk for affective disorder. A preliminary report. *Neuropsychopharmacology* 1989;1:217–223.
62. Lewy A, Sack R, Miller L, Hoban T. Antidepressant and phase-shifting effect of light. *Science* 1987;235:352–354.
63. Terman M, Terman J, Quitkin F, McGrath P, Stewart J, Rafferty B. Light therapy for seasonal affective disorder. A review of efficacy. *Neuropsychopharmacology* 1989;2:1–22.
64. Angst J. Course of affective disorders. In: van Praag, ed. *Handbook of biological psychiatry.* New York: Marcel Dekker, 1981;225–242.
65. Goodwin F and Jamison K. The natural course

of manic depressive illness. In: Post R, Ballenger J, eds. *Neurobiology of mood disorders*. Baltimore: Williams & Wilkins, 1985.
66. Tunbridge W, Evered D, Hall R, et al. The spectrum of thyroid disease in a community: The Whickham Survey. *Clin Endocrinol* 1977;7:481–493.
67. St. Germain D. Regulatory effect of lithium on thyroxine metabolism in murine neural and anterior pituitary tissue. *Endocrinology* 1987;120:1430–1438.
68. Dratman M, Crutchfield F. Effect of desipramine on the conversion of thyroxine to triiodothyronine in rat brain. In: Usdin E, Kopin I, eds. *Catecholamines basic and clinical*. New York: Pergamon Press, 1978.
69. Whybrow P, Prange A. A hypothesis of thyroid-catecholamine-receptor interaction: Its relevance to affective illness. *Arch Gen Psychiatry* 1981;38:106–113.
70. Mandell A, Knapp S, Ehlers C, Russo P. The stability of constrained randomness: Lithium prophylaxis at several neurobiologic levels. In: Post R, Ballenger J, eds. *Neurobiology of mood disorders*. Baltimore: Williams & Wilkins, 1985;744–776.
71. Gleick J. *Chaos: Making a new science*. New York: Penguin Press, 1987.
72. Paykel E. Life events and early environment. In: Paykel E, ed. *Handbook of affective disorders*. New York: Guilford Press, 1982;146–161.

21

Estrogen and Refractory Depression

Barbara B. Sherwin

Epidemiological studies have consistently documented a 2:1 female/male ratio in the prevalence of affective illness (1). This sex difference is not due to genetic transmission of the disorder (2), to sex differences in help-seeking behavior (3), to experience and reaction to stressful life events (4), or to differential exposure to the factors related to depression (5). Nor is the sex difference in the prevalence of depressive illness attributable to the tendency for physicians to detect more psychiatric illness in women than in men (6).

It is clear that some women are at greater risk for the development of a depressive episode subsequent to a change in their circulating levels of the sex steroids during various reproductive events. For example, at the time that estradiol and progesterone levels reach a nadir premenstrually, 35% of women report moderate affective and physical symptoms and 3% experience severe, incapacitating symptoms (7). Second, subsequent to the 100-fold decrease in circulating levels of estradiol and progesterone following childbirth, 50 to 70% of women experience a mild, transient mood disturbance between the third and tenth postpartum day, 10 to 21% develop a major depressive episode within the first 3 months, and 0.1 to 0.2% develop postpartum psychosis (8). Finally, during the perimenopausal years when estradiol levels are declining drastically, 79% of women who seek medical care have physical symptoms and 65% have varying degrees of depression (9).

Over half a century ago, several investigators reported that exogenous estrogen alleviated depression in postmenopausal women (10–12). Neurobiological effects of estrogen that have been elucidated during the past decade provide a scientific basis for possible biological mechanisms of action of this sex steroid on affective states and are reviewed here. In addition, clinical studies of estrogenic effects on mood in nonclinical and in clinical populations, although relatively few in number, also are discussed with regard to the therapeutic use of estrogen in refractory depression.

NEUROBIOLOGICAL EFFECTS OF ESTROGEN

Estrogen has both inductive and direct effects on neurons. This hormone induces ribonucleic acid (RNA) and protein synthesis via genomic mechanisms, which, in turn, cause changes in levels of specific gene products, such as neurotransmitter synthesizing enzymes (13). Other prolonged neuronal regulatory effects include the expression of gonadal hormone receptors in specific brain areas. On the other hand, direct effects of estrogen on the brain appear to take place more rapidly. For example, estrogens can alter the electrical activity of neurons in the hypothalamus (14).

Autoradiographic studies have demonstrated that neurons that contain specific

---

Departments of Psychology and Obstetrics and Gynecology, McGill University, Montreal, Quebec H3A 1B1, Canada.

cytosolic receptors for estrogen are found in specific areas of the brain, predominantly in the pituitary, hypothalamus, limbic forebrain (including the amygdala and lateral septum), and the cerebral cortex (15). Moreover, a number of neurotransmitter systems, including serotonergic, cholinergic, dopaminergic, GABAergic, adrenergic, and opioid systems, have been suggested to be responsive to estrogen, although not all of these effects have been demonstrated in vivo or at physiological conditions (16).

There is increasing evidence of abnormal indoleamine metabolism in depressed patients, manifested by a reduced level of 5-hydroxytryptamine (5HT) and 5-hydroxyindole-acetic acid (5HIAA) in the brain and decreased levels of 5HIAA in the cerebrospinal fluid (17,18). In accordance with Schildkraut's biogenic amine hypothesis of depression (19), a decrease in 5HT levels centrally may precipitate depression. There are at least two ways in which estrogen may influence neurotransmitter amine levels. First, it has been demonstrated in the rat that exogenous estrogen decreases monoamine oxidase (MAO) activity in the amygdala and hypothalamus (13). Since MAO is the enzyme that catabolizes 5HT, the net effect of estrogen administration would be to maintain higher brain 5HT levels. Indeed, there is clinical evidence to support this theory. In normal premenopausal women, mean levels of plasma MAO activity before the thermal nadir (when estradiol levels are high) were lower than levels measured after the thermal nadir (postovulation), when estradiol levels had decreased (20). In healthy untreated postmenopausal women, plasma MAO activity was greater and estradiol levels lower compared to enzyme and hormone values observed during the luteal phase of the cycle in regularly menstruating women. Moreover, premenopausal depressed women with regular menstrual cycles had higher levels of plasma MAO activity compared to nondepressed women (21). Briggs and Briggs (22) likewise reported that, in healthy women with regular menstrual cycles, plasma MAO activity was negatively correlated with estradiol concentrations. To the extent that similar events occur centrally, brain 5HT levels would increase as a function of higher estradiol levels.

There is also some evidence that in depressed, regularly cycling women, exogenous estrogen has a beneficial impact on both plasma MAO levels and mood. Klaiber et al. (21) administered 5 mg of conjugated equine estrogen (Premarin) from days 1 to 25 and 10 mg medroxyprogesterone acetate (Provera) from days 21 to 25 to 14 depressed women whose mean age was 28.7 years. During the portion of the cycle when only estrogen was being taken, plasma MAO activity was significantly lower by the third and fourth treatment cycles compared to pretreatment levels. Although changes in affect were not quantified in this uncontrolled study, patients spontaneously reported improvement in mood after estrogen treatment. Taken together, these studies provide evidence that the estrogenic influence on MAO levels documented in rat brain (13) also occur in the plasma of human females.

A second mechanism that may explain the effect of estrogen on mood is that tryptophan, the precursor of 5HT, is displaced from its binding sites to plasma albumin by estrogens in vitro and in vivo (23), thereby increasing free tryptophan in the brain. In 1976, Aylward (24) found a significant negative correlation between depression scores and free plasma tryptophan levels in bilaterally oophorectomized women and an amelioration in their depression scores subsequent to estrogen administration. In a double-blind study, nine women taking lithium were given either conjugated equine estrogen 1.25 mg or placebo daily for 3 months, following which they were crossed-over to the other treatment for an additional 3 months (25). There was a significant increase in the level of free plasma tryptophan when the patients were receiving estrogen compared to placebo. However, the mild affective morbidity of these patients was unaffected by either treatment.

Recently, perimenopausal women with mild depressive symptoms were compared to a similar group whose depression scores were within the normal range (26). Platelet 5HT content was significantly lower in the depressed group and in the subgroup of women who had experienced previous depressive episodes compared to the controls. However, plasma free tryptophan levels did not differ between groups, and a positive correlation between estradiol and platelet 5HT levels was evident only in the euthymic control group. In four women with depressive symptoms, platelet and blood 5HT levels increased moderately after 3 months of estrogen and progestin therapy (doses not reported) coincident with a decrease in their depression scores. The fact that the concentration of plasma free tryptophan did not account for the low platelet 5HT values in the depressed group before treatment suggests that reduced 5HT levels in depression may be partially attributable to reduced platelet 5HT uptake. It should be noted that the failure to standardize the hormone replacement regimen in this study complicates the interpretation of its findings.

EFFECTS ON NEUROTRANSMITTER RECEPTORS

Estrogen enhances central NE availability (27) and sensitizes dopamine receptors (28). Chronic estrogen treatment reduces β-adrenergic receptors in rat cortex (29), an effect similar to that observed with chronic antidepressant treatment. Moreover, 72 hours after estrogen was administered to ovariectomized rats, there was an increase in muscarinic acetylcholine receptors in ventromedial and anterior hypothalamic nuclei (30).

The demonstration that long-term antidepressant treatment induces consistent changes in adrenergic and serotonergic receptor sensitivities suggests that modulation of receptor sensitivity may be a mechanism of action common to tricyclic antidepressants, MAO inhibitors, and electroconvulsive therapy (31). To the extent that estrogen has antidepressant effects, its involvement in the regulation of 5HT receptors would help to explain the phenomenon. When ovariectomized rats received estradiol, followed 48 hours later by progesterone, increased 5HT uptake and content were observed in brain raphe nuclei (32). Another study found biphasic effects on the density of 5HT receptors throughout the brain of ovariectomized female rats who were given estrogen (33). One to two hours after estradiol injection, an acute reduction in 5HT receptor density was evident throughout the brain. However, by 72 hours postinjection, there was a selective increase in 5HT receptor density in brain regions known to contain estrogen receptors, namely, the hypothalamus, preoptic area, and amygdala.

Kendall et al. (34) reported an estrogen-dependent decrease in $5HT_2$ receptor binding in rat frontal cortex during long-term imipramine administration. Castration abolished this decline, which was reversed by estrogen or testosterone but not by the nonaromatizable androgen, dihydrotestosterone. This suggests that the receptor responses to some antidepressant drugs are dependent, at least in part, on the hormonal state of the animal. Thus, estrogen may have a facilitatory role in drug-resistant depressive patients similar to that proposed for lithium carbonate (35).

Advances in neuroscience during the past decade have suggested yet another mechanism whereby estrogen may influence mood. The presence of tritiated imipramine binding sites in rat and human brain and platelets has been well established (36). These binding sites are thought to modulate the presynaptic uptake of 5HT in both tissues (37). Many investigators have found a decrease in the density (B_{max}) but no change in the affinity (K_d) of these binding sites in brain and platelets of depressed patients (38,39), and the density of platelet tritiated imipramine binding sites is now widely regarded as a biological correlate of depression. It has been reported that tritiated imipramine binding and tritiated 5HT uptake increased by 20 to 30% in the frontal cortex and hypothalamus of ovariectomized rats following 12 days of treatment with estradiol (40).

Recent evidence suggests that the estrogenic enhancement of the B_{max} of tritiated imipramine binding sites may be dose-dependent. Whereas changes in binding site density did not occur in association with fluctuating estradiol levels during normal menstrual cycles (41) or following treatment of postmenopausal women with physiological doses of estradiol (42), a significant increase in the density of tritiated imipramine binding sites on platelets was apparent in oophorectomized women given pharmacological doses of estradiol (43).

Consideration of the psychotropic and neurobiological properties of progesterone also is important in the study of estrogenic influences on mood. Progesterone levels fluctuate during the menstrual cycle. This steroid is an important component of oral contraceptive preparations and also is administered frequently to postmenopausal women in association with estrogen in order to prevent endometrial hyperplasia. Whereas estrogen increases the electrical excitability of the brain, progesterone decreases it, acting as an anticonvulsant (44). Progesterone also has sedative and hypnotic effects (45) and, at high doses, induces deep sleep (46). Furthermore, whereas estradiol reduces plasma MAO activity, progestins increase it (47).

CLINICAL STUDIES IN NONPSYCHIATRIC POPULATIONS

Several studies of nonpsychiatric populations of postmenopausal women have reported on changes in affect as a function of circulating estradiol levels. In a prospective investigation, premenopausal women received either an estrogen-androgen combined drug (E-A), estrogen-alone (E), androgen-alone (A), or placebo (PL) for 3 months following bilateral oophorectomy and were randomly crossed over to another treatment for an additional 3 months after a 1-month intervening placebo phase (48). Women who underwent hysterectomy but whose ovaries were retained served as an additional control group (CON). In both treatment phases, women who received PL had higher depression scores on the Multiple Affect Adjective Checklist compared to those of the hormone-treated groups, to the CON group, and to their own preoperative scores in association with their lower plasma levels of estradiol and testosterone (Fig. 1).

A second study investigated otherwise healthy surgically menopausal women who had undergone hysterectomy and bilateral oophorectomy for benign disease approximately 4 years before their recruitment (49). Those who had been receiving either an E-A or an E preparation long-term (one injection per month for the previous 2 years) had more positive moods and higher levels of plasma estradiol than an untreated oophorectomized control group. Women who were given estradiol plus testosterone felt more composed, elated, and energetic than those who were given E alone (Fig. 2). These findings confirmed that mood covaries with circulating estradiol and testosterone levels in healthy, nondepressed women.

Thus, both of these studies (48,49) suggest a positive relationship between mood and estradiol levels in nonpsychiatric populations treated with physiological doses of the hormone. The discrepancy between these results and those of other studies may be due to their failure to control for endocrine status (50), psychiatric illness and the use of psychotropic drugs (51), and malignant disease (52). Interestingly, 9 of 10 postmenopausal women whose pretreatment

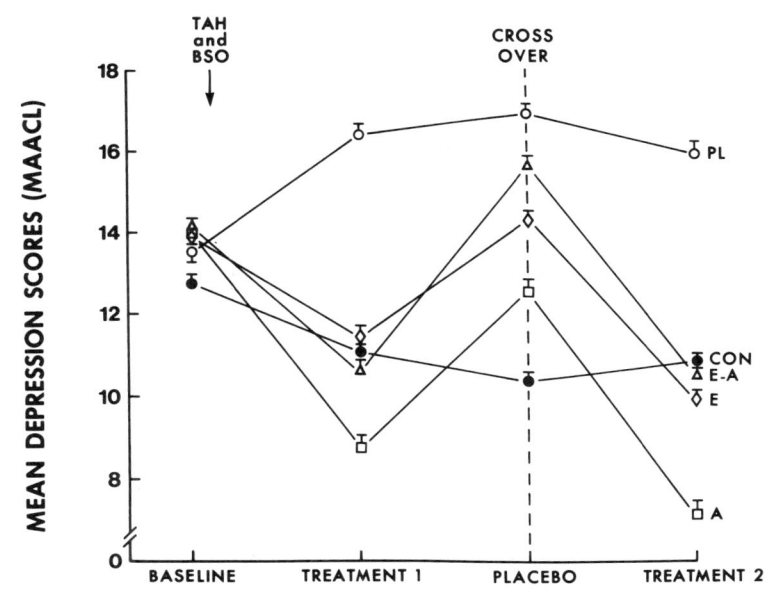

FIG. 1. Mean depression scores (± SEM) on the Multiple Affect Adjective Checklist (MAACL). The treatment groups are estrogen-androgen (E-A, △), estrogen (E, ◇), androgen (A, □), placebo (PL, ○), and hysterectomy control (CON, ●). (From ref. 48.)

scores were less than 18 on the Beck Depression Inventory improved with conjugated equine estrogen 1.25 mg daily, whereas 6 of the 10 women who had pretreatment scores above 20 at baseline actually became more depressed with the same treatment (53). Taken together, these findings suggest that the administration of estrogen in doses conventionally used to treat menopausal symptoms enhances mood in nondepressed women but is therapeutically ineffective with respect to mood disturbances of a clinical magnitude when it is given alone.

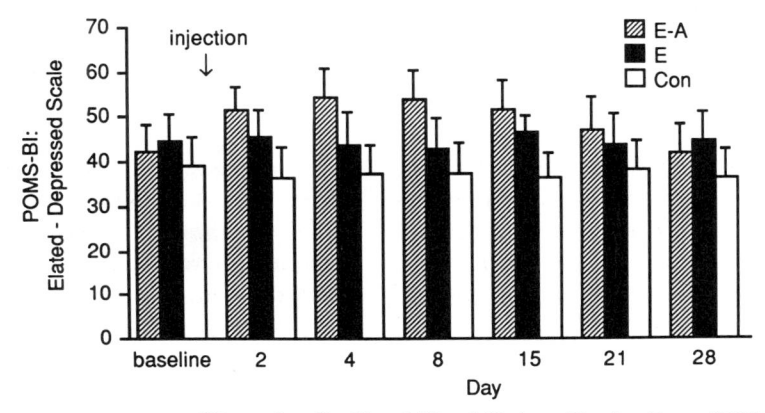

FIG. 2. Mean group scores ± SD on the Profile of Mood States: Bipolar Form (POMS:BI) Elated-Depressed Scale. (From ref. 49.)

ESTROGEN AND REFRACTORY DEPRESSION

Although there have been surprisingly few systematic investigations of the use of estrogen in refractory depression, several controlled studies and case reports serve to provide some (albeit inconsistent) evidence of its effects. The reports in the literature pertain (a) to the administration of estrogen alone to women with refractory depression, (b) to the use of estrogen as an adjunct to antidepressant treatment, and (c) to the use of both estrogen and progestin as adjuncts to a variety of psychotropic drugs.

Only one study in which depressed patients were given sex steroids but no other medication could be located (54). The women who participated were inpatients diagnosed as having recurrent unipolar major depressive disorders that had been resistant (for at least the 2 preceding years) to conventional treatments, such as antidepressant drugs, electroshock therapy, and psychotherapy. Over 60% had a history of suicidal attempts, and all expressed suicidal thoughts at the time of their recruitment. Fifteen of the 23 women randomly assigned to the estrogen group were premenopausal, as were 12 of the 17 women in the placebo group. The other subjects were postmenopausal. Of the 23 women who received estrogen, 5 were given (after daily increases) a maximum dose of 15 mg conjugated equine estrogen (Premarin) per day, 6 received a maximum daily dose of 20 mg, and 12 were given a maximum daily dose of 25 mg Premarin. In addition, premenopausal patients had 2.5 mg medroxyprogesterone acetate (Provera) added to the Premarin from days 21 to 25 of each treatment month to induce menses. Hamilton Depression Rating Scale scores decreased significantly by the third month in the estrogen group, whereas depression scores maintained stability across time in the placebo-treated group. Although the improvement in mood scores was statistically significant, posttreatment scores still indicated moderate depression. Plasma MAO activity also decreased with estrogen but not with placebo treatment. The considerable variability in response to estrogen administration in these women with refractory depression was apparently not related to the fact that some also received a progestin, since neither menopausal status nor age were significantly related to amount of improvement.

Considering that the results of this study constitute an impressive demonstration of the antidepressant effect of estrogen, it should be acknowledged that they were achieved with large pharmacological doses of the hormone. We have reported recently that although 0.625 mg Premarin induced physiological levels of estradiol and estrone, circulating hormone levels following ingestion of 1.25 mg Premarin were supraphysiological (55). It will be recalled that in the Klaiber et al. (54) study, daily doses of Premarin ranged from 15 to 25 mg per day, which is 12 to 20 times the recommended dose for postmenopausal hormone replacement therapy.

In 1976, Prange et al. (56) investigated whether estrogen might enhance the antidepressant effect of imipramine. Thirty women with unipolar depression randomly received either placebo ($n=10$), 150 mg imipramine and placebo ($n=10$), 150 mg imipramine and 50 µg ethinyl estradiol ($n=5$), or 150 mg imipramine and 25 µg ethinyl estradiol ($n=5$). After 1 week of treatment, women who received 50 µg ethinyl estradiol and imipramine were substantially improved, but by day 14, they showed signs of toxicity similar to those reported with imipramine overdosage (e.g., hypotension, drowsiness, coarse tremor, dry mouth). On the other hand, patients who received 25 µg ethinyl estradiol and imipramine improved slightly (although nonsignificantly) faster than patients who received only imipramine while showing no enhanced toxicity.

A second study investigated the interaction between imipramine and conjugated equine estrogen in 11 women between the ages of 26 and 74 years whose depression had been refractory to treatment with antidepressant drugs (57). After 2 weeks on 200 mg imipramine/day, half were given Premarin and half were given placebo for one treatment cycle and were then crossed over to the other treatment for another month. Premarin was given in incremental doses of 1.25 mg/day for 2 days, 2.5 mg/day on days 3 and 4, and 3.75 mg/day on days 5 to 21. The dose was then decreased in similar fashion during the next 5 days. On day 26, norethistrone acetate 10 mg/day was given to the 3 premenopausal women for 5 days to induce menses. Overall, no improvement in depression (as measured by the Hamilton Depression Rating Scale) occurred with either estrogen or placebo. However, one patient improved strikingly after 1 week on estrogen, and her depression remitted completely after 2 weeks. Another women with bipolar disease developed a manic episode 9 days after the addition of estrogen. Possible order effects of treatments were not controlled for by the statistical analyses. Interestingly, no toxic effects of the supraphysiological doses of conjugated equine estrogens added to imipramine were seen in these patients.

Several case reports suggest the possibility of beneficial effects of adding oral contraceptives (containing both estrogen and progestin) to antidepressants for the treatment of refractory depression. A 35-year-old women with bipolar illness who had experienced two manic and four depressive episodes in the previous year while being treated with 200 mg imipramine/day experienced a considerable improvement in depressive symptoms when Ortho-Novum 1/50 (1 mg norethindrone and 0.5 mg mestranol) was added to the antidepressant (58). She remained euthymic on this regimen by the ninth month of follow-up. In another report, the addition of Ovral (0.5 mg norgestrel and 50 µg ethinyl estradiol) to lithium, L-tryptophan, and Premarin 1.25 mg, resulted in the abatement of a refractory depressive episode in a 56-year-old woman (59). A new depressive episode that began when the oral contraceptive was changed to a lower dose combination (0.15 mg norgestrel and 30 µg ethinyl estradiol) was only slightly improved with the reinstitution of Ovral but remitted completely with the addition of medroxyprogesterone acetate 5 mg/day. Similarly, a 49-year-old woman with bipolar illness whose depressive episode was resistant to lithium and L-tryptophan became euthymic after Ovral and haloperidol were added (59). The discontinuation of haloperidol and the replacement of Ovral by Premarin 1.25 mg precipitated a manic episode. Her mood was subsequently stabilized by treatment with clonazepam, lithium, tryptophan, Ovral, and medroxyprogesterone acetate 5 mg/day.

SUMMARY

This review suggests that estrogen may facilitate antidepressant response as well as possess antidepressant properties. There is also evidence that under some circumstances, estrogen has a useful adjunctive role in the treatment of women with refractory depression. The mood-enhancing effect of this steroid may reside in its ability to increase the concentration of neurotransmitters or to increase their bioavailability at the neuronal synapse. Which neurotransmitter(s) and which neuronal mechanisms predominantly account for the hormonal effect on mood remain to be elucidated.

Two issues in the extant literature on the use of estrogen in refractory depression merit attention. Prange et al. (56) observed toxic side effects when 50 µg ethinyl estradiol but not when 25 µg ethinyl estradiol was added to 150 mg imipramine. Although the mechanism of the ethinyl estradiol/imipramine interaction has not been fully delineated, long-term use of oral contraceptives in humans has resulted in inhibition of hepatic microsomal enzymes (60). Studies with norethindrone in mice demonstrate added accumulation of imipramine in the brain and other tissues because of impaired metabolism (61). It has been suggested that the interaction may be dose-related, since contraceptive products containing 30 μg ethinyl estradiol may not inhibit microsomal enzymes to the same degree as those that contain 50 μg ethinyl estradiol (62). Indeed, in the Prange et al. study (56), women who received 25 μg ethinyl estradiol plus imipramine did not display toxicity. There is also reason to believe the ethinyl estradiol/imipramine interaction may be specific to this synthetic estrogen. When large doses of natural conjugated equine estrogens (57) or oral contraceptives containing other synthetic estrogens (58) were added to antidepressant drugs, no toxic effects of their interaction were observed. These findings suggest that natural estrogens or synthetic estrogens other than ethinyl estradiol may be the preparations of choice for use as adjunctive treatment for depression.

Second, there are several reports of precipitation of manic episodes in women with bipolar illness when estrogen was added to their antidepressant regimens for the treatment of a refractory depressive episode (57,59). Rapid cycling also occurred in a 72-year-old woman with refractory depression but no history of bipolar illness 5 days after 4.375 mg Premarin was added to an antidepressant drug (dibenzepin, 480 mg/day) (63). On the other hand, in two women with bipolar illness, cycling was abolished and a stable euthymic state was induced when an oral contraceptive was administered or when medroxyprogesterone acetate was given in addition to estrogen and antidepressant drugs (59). These reports suggest that progestins may obviate mood cycling in women with bipolar illness being treated with estrogen for a depressive episode. Why the administration of progestins in association with estrogens seems to induce this stabilizing effect on mood in patients with bipolar disease is not clear. It is tempting to speculate that the opposite effects of estrogen and progestin on brain electrical excitability (44) and on MAO levels (47) may provide one possible explanation.

In view of the prevalence of refractory depression and of its associated debilitation and mortality and considering also the encouraging findings from the few controlled studies and case reports in the literature, the adjunctive use of estrogen in this disorder merits further investigation. Future studies employing rigorous methodologies to investigate the relative efficacy of specific doses of the sex steroids and their mechanisms of action in both unipolar and bipolar depressive illness are urgently needed to provide clinical guidelines for treatment.

ACKNOWLEDGMENTS

The preparation of this chapter was supported by Grant MA-8707 from the Medical Research Council of Canada.

REFERENCES

1. Weissman MM, Klerman GL. Sex differences and the epidemiology of depression. *Arch Gen Psychiatry* 1977;34:98–111.
2. Merikangas KR, Weissman MM, Pauls DL. Genetic factors in the sex ratio of major depression. *Psychol Med* 1985;15:63–69.
3. Dohrenwend BP, Dohrenwend BS. Reply to Grove and Tudor's comment on sex differences in psychiatric disorders. *Am J Sociol* 1977;82:1136–1145.
4. Kessler RC, Reuter JA, Greenley JR. Sex differences in the use of psychiatric outpatient facilities. *Social Forces* 1979;58:557–571.
5. Radloff LS, Rai DS. Susceptibility and precipitating factors in depression: Sex differences and similarities. *J Abnorm Psychol* 1979;88:174–181.
6. MacIntyre S, Oldman D. Coping with migraine. In: Davis A, Horobin G, eds. *Medical encounters*. London: Croom Helm, 1977;61–72.
7. Andersch B, Wendestam C, Hahn L, Ohman R. Premenstrual complaints. I. prevalence of premenstrual symptoms in a Swedish urban population. *J Psychosom Obstet Gynaecol* 1986;5:39–49.
8. Kendell RE, Wainwright S, Hailey A, Shannon B. The influence of childbirth on psychiatric morbidity. *Psychol Med* 1976;6:297–302.
9. Anderson E, Hamburger S, Liu JH, Rebar RW. Characteristics of menopausal women seeking assistance. *Am J Obstet Gynecol* 1987;156:428–433.
10. Frank RT, Goldberger MA, Solomon UJ. The menopause: Symptoms, hormonal status, and treatment. *NY J Med* 1936;36:1363–1375.

11. Hawkinson LF. The menopausal syndrome: A thousand consecutive patients treated with estrogen. *JAMA* 1938;111:390–393.
12. Weisbader H, Kurzrok R. The menopause: A consideration of the symptoms, etiology, and treatment by means of estrogen. *Endocrinology* 1983;23:32–38.
13. Luine VN, Khylchevskaya RI, McEwen B. Effect of gonadal steroids on activities of monoamine oxidase and choline acetylase in rat brain. *Brain Res* 1975;86:293–306.
14. Kelly MJ, Moss RL, Dudley CA, Fawcett CP. The specificity of the response of preoptic-septal area neurons to estrogen: 17-β-estradiol vs. 17-α-estradiol and the response of extrahypothalamic neurons. *Exp Brain Res* 1977;30:43–52.
15. McEwen BS. The brain as a target organ of endocrine hormones. In: Kreiger DT, Hughes JC, eds. *Neuroendocrinology*. Sunderland, MA: Sinauer Assoc, 1980;33–42.
16. McEwen BS, Biegon A, Fischette CT, Luine VN, Parsons B, Rainbow TC. Towards a neurochemical basis of steroid hormone action. In: Martini L, Ganong W, eds. *Frontiers in neuroendocrinology*. New York: Raven Press, 1984; 1153–1176.
17. Murphy DL, Campbell I, Costa JL. Current status of the indoleamine hypothesis of affective disorders. In: Lipton MA, DiMascio A, Killam KF. eds. *Psychopharmacology: A generation of progress*. New York: Raven Press, 1978;1235–1247.
18. Coopen A, Wood K. 5-Hydroxytryptamine in the pathogenesis of affective disorders. In: Ho BT, Schoolar JC, Usdin E, eds. *Serotonin in biological psychiatry*. New York: Raven Press, 1982;249–259.
19. Schildkraut JJ. The catecholamine hypothesis of affective disorders: A review of supporting evidence. *Am J Psychiatry* 1965;122:509–522.
20. Klaiber EL, Kobayashi Y, Broverman DM, Hall F. Plasma monoamine oxidase activity in regularly menstruating women and in amenorrheic women receiving cyclic treatment with estrogens and a progestin. *J Clin Endocrinol Metab* 1971;33:630–638.
21. Klaiber EL, Broverman DM, Vogal W, Kobayashi Y, Moriarty D. Effects of estrogen therapy on plasma MAO activity and EEG driving responses of depressed women. *Am J Psychiatry* 1972;128:1492–1498.
22. Briggs M, Briggs M. Relationship between monoamine oxidase activity and sex hormone concentration in human blood plasma. *J Reprod Fertil* 1972;29:447–450.
23. Aylward M. Plasma tryptophan levels and mental depression in postmenopausal subjects: Effects of oral piperazine-oestrone sulfate. *IRCS Med Sci* 1973;1:30–34.
24. Aylward M. Estrogens, plasma tryptophan levels in perimenopausal patients. In: Campbell S, ed. *The management of the menopause and postmenopausal years*. Baltimore: University Park Press, 1976;135–147.
25. Coppen A, Wood K. Tryptophan and depressive illness. *Psychol Med* 1978;8:49–57.
26. Guicheney P, Léger D, Barrat J, et al. Platelet serotonin content and plasma tryptophan in peri- and postmenopausal women: Variations with plasma oestrogen levels and depressive symptoms. *Eur J Clin Invest* 1988;18:297–304.
27. Paul SM, Axelrod J, Saaveda JM, Skolnick P. Estrogen-induced afflux of endogenous catecholamines from the hypothalamus in vitro. *Brain Res* 1979;178:479–505.
28. Chiodo LA, Caggiula AR. Substantia nigra dopamine neurons: Alterations in basal discharge rates and autoreceptor sensitivity induced by estrogen. *Neuropharmacology* 1983;22:593–599.
29. Wagner HR, Crutcher KA, Davis JN. Chronic estrogen treatment decreases β-adrenergic responses in rat cerebral cortex. *Brain Res* 1979;71:147–151.
30. Rainbow TC, DeGroff G, Luine VN, McEwen BS. Estradiol-17 β increases the number of muscarinic receptors in hypothalamic nuclei. *Brain Res* 1980;198:239–243.
31. Charney DS, Menkes DB, Heninger GR. Receptor sensitivity and the mechanism of action of antidepressant treatment. *Arch Gen Psychiatry* 1981;38:1160–1180.
32. Cone RI, Davis GA, Coy RW. Effects of ovarian steroids on serotonin metabolism within grossly dissected and microdissected brain regions of the ovariectomized rat. *Brain Res Bull* 1981;7: 639–644.
33. Biegon A, McEwen BS. Modulation by estradiol of serotonin receptors in brain. *J Neurosci* 1982;2:199–205.
34. Kendall DA, Stancel GM, Enna SJ. The influence of sex hormones on antidepressant-induced alterations in neurotransmitter receptor binding. *J Neurosci* 1982;2:354–350.
35. de Montigny C, Grunberg F, Mayer A, Deschenes JP. Lithium induces rapid relief of depression in tricyclic antidepressant drug non-responders. *Br J Psychiatry* 1981;138:252–256.
36. Raisman R, Briley M, Langer SZ. Specific tricyclic antidepressant binding sites in rat brain. *Nature* 1979;281:148–150.
37. Paul SM, Rehavi M, Skolnick P, Goodwin FK. High affinity binding of antidepressants to biogenic amine transport sites in human brain and platelet: Studies in depression. In: Post RM, Ballenger JC, eds. *Neurobiology of mood disorders*. Baltimore: Williams & Wilkins, 1984; 846–853.
38. Raisman R, Briley MS, Bouchami F, Sechter D, Zarifian E, Langer SZ. ³H-Imipramine binding and serotonin uptake in platelets from untreated depressed patients and control volunteers. *Psychopharmacology* 1982;77:332–335.
39. Suranyi-Cadotte BE, Wood PL, Schwartz G, Nair PVN. Altered platelet ³H-imipramine binding in schizoaffective and depressive disorders. *Biol Psychiatry* 1983;18:923–927.
40. Rehavi M, Sepcuti H, Weizman A. Upregulation of imipramine binding and serotonin uptake by estradiol in female rat brain. *Brain Res* 1987; 410:135–139.
41. Poirier MF, Benkelfat C, Galzin AM, Langer SZ. Platelet ³H-imipramine binding and steroid

hormone concentrations during the menstrual cycle. *Psychopharmacology* 1986;88:86–89.
42. Best NR, Barlow DH, Rees MP, Cowan PJ. Lack of effect of estradiol implant on platelet imipramine and 5-HT$_2$ receptor binding in menopausal subjects. *Psychopharmacology* 1989;98:561.
43. Sherwin BB, Suranyi-Cadotte BE. Up-regulatory effect of estrogen on platelet ^{3}H-imipramine binding sites in surgically menopausal women. *Biol Psychiatry* 1990;28:339–348.
44. Bäckström T. Estrogen and progesterone in relation to different activities in the central nervous system. *Acta Obstet Gynaecol Scand* 1977;66:1–17.
45. Arafat ES, Hargrove JT, Maxson WS, Desiderio DM, Wentz AC, Anderson RN. Sedative and hypnotic effects of oral administration of micronized progesterone may be mediated through its metabolites. *Am J Obstet Gynecol* 1988;159:1203–1209.
46. Merryman W, Boiman R, Barnes L, Rothchild I. Progesterone "anesthesia" in human subjects. *J Clin Endocrinol Metab* 1954;14:1567–1569.
47. Klaiber EL, Kobayashi Y, Broverman DM, Hall F. Plasma monoamine oxidase activity in regularly menstruating women and in amenorrheic women receiving cyclic treatment with estrogens and a progestin. *J Clin Endocrinol* 1971;33:630–638.
48. Sherwin BB, Gelfand MM. Sex steroids and affect in the surgical menopause: A double-blind, crossover study. *Psychoneuroendocrinology* 1985;10:325–335.
49. Sherwin BB. Affective changes with estrogen and androgen replacement therapy in surgically menopausal women. *J Affective Disord* 1988;14:177–187.
50. Strickler RC, Borth R, Cecutti A, et al. The role of oestrogen replacement in the climacteric syndrome. *Psychol Med* 1977;7:631–639.
51. Dennerstein L, Burrows GD, Hyman GJ. Hormone therapy and affect. *Maturitas* 1979;1:247–259.
52. Chakravarti S, Collins WP, Newton JR. Endocrine changes and symptomatology after oophorectomy in premenopausal women. *Br J Obstet Gynaecol* 1977;84:769–775.
53. Schneider MA, Brotherton PL, Hailes J. The effect of exogenous oestrogens on depression in menopausal women. *Med J Aust* 1977;2:162–163.
54. Klaiber EL, Broverman DM, Vogel W, Koboyashi Y. Estrogen therapy for severe persistent depression in women. *Arch Gen Psychiatry* 1979;36:550–554.
55. Sherwin BB, Gelfand MM. A prospective one-year study of estrogen and progestin in postmenopausal women: Effects on clinical symptoms and lipoprotein lipids. *Obstet Gynecol* 1989;73:759–766.
56. Prange AJ Jr, Wilson IC, Breese GR, Lipton MA. Hormonal alteration of imipramine response: A review. In: Sachar EJ, ed. *Hormones, behavior and psychopathology*. New York: Raven Press, 1976;41–67.
57. Shapira B, Oppenheim G, Zohar J, Segal M, Malach D, Belmaker RH. Lack of efficacy of estrogen supplementation to imipramine in resistant female depressives. *Biol Psychiatry* 1985;20:576–579.
58. Price WA, Giannini AJ. Antidepressant effects of estrogen. *J Clin Psychiatry* 1985;46:506.
59. Chouinard G, Steinberg S, Steiner W. Estrogen-progesterone combination: Another mood stabilizer? *Am J Psychiatry* 1987;144:826.
60. Field B, Lu C, Hepner GW. Inhibition of hepatic drug metabolism by norethindrone. *Clin Pharmacol Ther* 1979;25:196–198.
61. Bellward GC, Morgan RC, Szombathy VH. The effects of pretreatment of mice with norethindrone on the metabolism of ^{14}C-imipramine by the liver microsomal drug-metabolizing enzymes. *Can J Physiol Pharmacol* 1974;52:28–38.
62. Luscombe DK, John V. Influence of age, cigarette smoking and the oral contraceptive on plasma concentrations of clomipramine. *Postgrad Med J* 1980;56(suppl 1):99–102.
63. Oppenheim G. A case of rapid mood cycling with estrogen: Implications for therapy. *J Clin Psychiatry* 1984;45:34–35.

22

Reserpine Augmentation in Resistant Depression: A Review

Joseph Zohar,[1] Zeev Kaplan,[1] and Jay D. Amsterdam[2]

Preclinical evidence indicates that reserpine depletes biogenic amines from nerve terminals by disrupting the uptake mechanism of intraneuronal amine storage granules (1). Reserpine also increases activity of the rate-limiting enzymes for catecholamine and serotonin biosynthesis, tyrosine hydroxylase (2) and tryptophan hydroxylase (3). The net effect is an enhancement of monoamine concentration in the synaptic cleft for brief periods (4).

Administration of tricyclic antidepressants (TCA) also leads to increased concentration of monoamines in the synaptic cleft by blocking the monoamine reuptake (5). Hence, it seems logical that addition of reserpine to an ongoing TCA treatment regimen might potentiate the effects of the TCAs.

CLINICAL STUDIES

Eight research groups have examined the use of reserpine augmentation of an ongoing TCA treatment regimen in nonresponder depressed patients (6–13).

Poldinger was the first to observe the positive therapeutic potentiation of ongoing imipramine treatment after addition of reserpine (14). He gave 7 to 10 mg reserpine by intramuscular injection for 1 or 2 days on the third and fourth day of imipramine treatment. In a subsequent study, Poldinger (6) treated 7 depressive patients who had been taking desipramine for 3 days with either one or two injections of reserpine 2.5 to 7.5 mg ($n = 4$) or with intravenous or intramuscular injection of tetrabenzine 50 to 100 mg ($n = 3$).

Summing up Poldinger's two clinical observations, 11 of 18 depressed patients had a favorable rapid response to reserpine (or tetrabenzine) added after 4 days of imipramine or desipramine treatment. The response started with an excited state following the injection, which rapidly passed into a marked improvement in the symptoms of depression. The adverse effects included excitation, increased pulse, mydriasis, perspiration, tremor, insomnia, vertigo, and headache. All the adverse effects were short-lived, and hypotension was not a prominent feature.

From our present understanding, it now appears that 4 days of TCA treatment is far too short a period to determine whether a patient is resistant to TCA treatment. Therefore, the relevance of Poldinger's initial observations to the treatment of refractory depression is questionable. However, it raised an interesting possibility that adjunctive reserpine might be beneficial in speeding up the antidepressive response to TCAs or serve as a useful treatment ap-

---

[1]Beer Sheva Mental Health Centre, Ben Gurion University, Beer Sheva, Israel.
[2]Depression Research Unit, Department of Psychiatry, Hospital of the University of Pennsylvania, Philadelphia, PA 19104.

proach for patients with refractory depression.

In this context, Haskovec and Rysanek (7) studied reserpine addition to imipramine-resistant depressive patients under more rigorous research conditions. For example, they evaluated 15 well-characterized patients with endogenous depression diagnosed independently by two psychiatrists. The average duration of imipramine treatment before reserpine augmentation was 92 days (range 21–300 days), and the daily dose of imipramine was gradually increased to 300 mg. All of the patients received a 7.5 to 10 mg daily intramuscular injection of reserpine for 2 successive days. (This dose was based on results from a pilot study they conducted previously, indicating that doses of reserpine less than 7.5 mg for 1 day were not effective.) The clinical condition of the patients before and after reserpine administration was systematically evaluated by two research psychiatrists independently according to Overall's Rating Scale. A 6-month follow-up was carried out.

Fourteen of the 15 patients responded to the combination of imipramine and reserpine. The response was described as a rapid, dramatic stimulation that usually began on the second day of reserpine administration. Although the initial response was only temporary in 8 of the patients, lasting 2 to 17 days before depressive relapse, in the other 6 patients, the improvement lasted throughout the follow-up period of 6 months. Side effects in this study consisted of conspicuous vasodilation, increased intestinal peristalsis, and very slight decrease of blood pressure, pulse, and temperature.

Subsequently, Carney et al. (8) administered reserpine 10 mg/daily for 2 days to 8 patients resistant to at least a 3-week course of imipramine at 225 mg/daily, and they observed a decrease in the mean ($\pm$ SD) Hamilton Depression Rating Scale (HDRS) score from 18 ± 9 to 10 ± 1 ($p < 0.05$). However, changes in the clinical global impression (CGI) scale ratings were less impressive, and none of the patients who were rated as improved demonstrated the previously reported dramatic response. These investigators concluded that "reserpine did not produce a rapid therapeutic response in treatment resistant patients, but it should not, nonetheless, be considered an inactive treatment."

In an attempt to correct some of the methodological deficiencies in these early open-label studies, Hopkinson and Kenny (9) conducted an initial double-blind study specifically examining the therapeutic effects of reserpine augmentation to TCA-nonresponding depressive patients. Only patients with endogenous depression who failed to respond to any TCA (imipramine, trimipramine, and amitryptiline) for a minimum of 3 weeks at 150 mg daily were allowed to participate in the study. Eight patients received injections of 5 mg reserpine on 2 successive days simultaneous with continued administration of their TCA, and 6 patients received saline injections in addition to their TCA. The group was composed only of female patients.

The patients who received reserpine demonstrated a significantly greater drop in depression rating than did the control (saline) group ($p < 0.01$). One reserpine patient had a recurrence of symptoms within 5 days and was given an additional open-label course of reserpine with good response. No serious side effects were observed. However, 3 patients complained of nasal stuffiness, 1 patient experienced facial flushing followed by a transient morbiliform rash that lasted 2 days, and 1 patient complained of mild excitation that lasted a few hours.

More recently, Forsman et al. (10) and Zohar et al. (11) also reported a positive response to reserpine augmentation of TCA in resistant depression. Zohar et al. (11) described 3 patients (2 females and 1 male) who did not respond to at least 1 month of treatment with imipramine or amitryptiline at 300 mg/day. In this trial, patients received open-label intramuscular reserpine 1 mg/day for 2 consecutive days, and all demonstrated a rapid and dramatic euphoric response that was maintained for at least a month.

In contrast to these earlier observations, two recent studies using stringent double-blind, placebo-controlled methods (12,13) have failed to replicate prior reserpine trials. Amsterdam and Berwish (12) randomly assigned 9 patients with DSM-III major depression to a double-blind treatment protocol with either intramuscular reserpine 0.1 mg/kg body weight or nicotinamide 25 mg injections given in two divided doses for 2 consecutive days. Nicotinamide was used as an active placebo to simulate the peripheral autonomic effects of reserpine. All patients had a clear history of nonresponse to prior treatment with at least six antidepressant therapies and currently were refractory to treatment with either desipramine ($n = 8$) or imipramine ($n = 1$) at therapeutic doses and plasma levels for a period of more than 3 weeks duration. Repeated open-label administration of reserpine was made available for patients who failed to respond to the initial double-blind treatment phase, so that a total of 10 active reserpine courses were administered.

Overall, reserpine augmentation showed no statistically significant superiority over placebo, nor did depression ratings decrease from pretreatment after a 1-week assessment period. However, 2 patients did demonstrate a response: 1 patient had a brief partial improvement, and another demonstrated a dramatic and sustained response 3 days after receiving a second open-label course of reserpine. The latter patient had previously failed to respond to 10 other drug treatments as well as a sustained course of electroconvulsive therapy, and the former patient had a transient mild improvement within 3 days of receiving open-label reserpine after showing no response to placebo.

Side effects in this study included nervousness, agitation, flushing, sweating, dizziness, lightheadedness, postural hypotensions (from $118 \pm 18/84 \pm 9$ to $103 \pm 15/71 \pm 11$), tremors, nasal stuffiness, and headache. However, no patient discontinued treatment because of side effects.

Price et al. (13) administered reserpine 5 mg intramuscularly bid over 2 days to 5 psychotic and 3 nonpsychotic depressed patients who had failed to respond to at least 4 weeks of desipramine treatment at 2.5 mg/kg/day, with plasma levels greater than 125 ng/ml. Although augmentation with reserpine had little effect on the group as a whole, 3 patients did demonstrate some response. In particular, 1 patient progressed from intense dysphoria to muteness and catatonia to complete remission of depressive and psychotic symptoms within 48 hours of the last reserpine dose, with the HDRS score decreasing from 32 to 4. The remission sustained for 11 days before relapse. Two other patients experienced transient hypomania lasting 6 hours to 5 days before eventual relapse.

The most frequent adverse effects were orthostatic hypotension (from 116/69 to 110/63), dizziness, agitation, vasomotor flushing, severe insomnia, and subjective sense of warmth.

NEUROBIOLOGICAL CORRELATES

Of the eight investigators who studied reserpine augmentation, only two groups examined the neurobiological changes taking place during a course of combined TCA and reserpine (7,13).

Haskovec and Rysanek (7) assessed 24-hour urine specimens for 5-hydroxyindoleacetic acid (5HIAA) and vanillylmandelic acid (VMA). An association between increased 5HIAA but not VMA excretion during the first day of reserpine and later favorable response was found. This thus suggests a possible link between 5HT activity and the relief of depression by this treatment. However, the lack of a control group and the limited validity of urine measurement of monoamine metabolites as the only indicator for central nervous system activity (15) hampered the interpretation of these observations.

Price et al. (13) measured CSF 3-methoxy-4-hydroxyphenylethyleneglycol (MHPG), 5HIAA, and homovanillic acid (HVA) as indices of central adrenergic, serotonergic, and dopaminergic function, respectively, and plasma as a correlate of central noradrenergic (NE) function. They found a robust reserpine-induced decrease in plasma and CSF MHPG and less marked but substantial increase in CSF HVA and 5HIAA. These findings suggest that decreases in noradrenergic metabolism may play a role in mediating the therapeutic effects of reserpine augmentation. However, the absence of posttreatment CSF data in these patients and the modest antidepressant response observed following reserpine augmentation severely hamper the clinical significance of these biochemical correlations.

CONCLUSION

Reserpine augmentation of TCA treatment in refractory depression appeared to be a safe procedure. Although the overall efficacy of this interesting drug combination is still uncertain, it may be a useful strategy for treating selected patients resistant to more conventional antidepressant approaches.

REFERENCES

1. Shore PA, Giachetti A. Reserpine: Basic and clinical pharmacology. In: Iversen LL, Iversen SD, Snyder SH, eds. *Handbook of psychopharmacology, vol 10. Neuroleptics and schizophrenia.* New York: Plenum, 1978;197–218.
2. Weiner N. Regulation of norepinephrine biosynthesis. *Annu Rev Pharmacol* 1970;10:273–290.
3. Zivkovic B, Guidotti A, Costa E. Increase of tryptophan hydroxylase activity elicited by reserpine. *Brain Res* 1973;57:522–526.
4. Cooper JR, Bloom FE, Roth RH. *The biochemical basis of neuropharmacology,* 3rd ed. New York: Oxford University Press, 1978;213–214.
5. Schildkraut J. The catecholamine hypothesis of affective disorders: A review of supporting evidence. *Am J Psychiatry* 1965;122:509–522.
6. Poldinger W. Discussionsbemerkung an der 129. Verslag der Schweiz Ges. fur psychiatrie. *Schweiz Arch Neurol Psychiatry* 1959;84:327.
7. Haskovec L, Rysanek K. The action of reserpine in imipramine-resistant depressive patients. *Psychopharmalogia* 1967;11:18–30.
8. Carney MWP, Thakurdas H, Sebastian J. Effects of imipramine and reserpine in depression. *Psychopharmacologia* 1969;14:349–350.
9. Hopkinson G, Kenny F. Treatment with reserpine of patients resistant to tricyclic antidepressants. *Psychiatr Clin* 1975;8:109–114.
10. Forsman A, Dahlstrom A, Wahlstrom J, Wendestam C, Akesson HO. Reserpine treatment of certain depressive conditions: Case report, treatment and possible mechanisms of action. *Curr Ther Res* 1983;34:991–998.
11. Zohar J, Moscovich D, Mester R. Addition of reserpine to tricyclic antidepressants in resistant depression. In: Zohar J, Belmaker RH, eds. *Treating resistant depression.* New York: PMA Publishing Corp, 1987.
12. Amsterdam JD, Berwish N. Treatment of refractory depression with combination reserpine and tricyclic antidepressant therapy. *J Clin Psychopharmacol* 1987;7:238–242.
13. Price LH, Charney DS, Heninger GR. Reserpine augmentation of desipramine in refractory depression: Clinical and neurobiological effects. *Psychopharmacology* 1987;92:431–437.
14. Poldinger W. Combined administration of desipramine and reserpine or tetrabenazine in depressive patients. *Psychopharmacologia* 1963;4:308–310.
15. Kopin IJ, Gordon EK, Jimerson DC, Polinsky RJ. Relation between plasma and cerebrospinal fluids of 3-methoxy-4-hydroxyphenyl-glycol. *Science* 1983;219:73–76.

23

Narcotherapy in Resistant Depressive Patients

Rudolf Karazman, Greta Koinig, Gerhard Langer, Georg Schönbeck, Julius Neumark, and Regina Dittrich

Since the introduction of imipramine, extensive research has led to the development of new antidepressant drugs to reach a higher therapeutic efficacy with fewer adverse effects. Nevertheless, a substantial proportion of depressed patients fail to respond to these antidepressant drugs (1), demanding alternative forms of therapy.

The idea to use the anesthestic isoflurane in therapy-resistant depressives, is based on two lines of reasoning. Overactivation (malactivation) of hypothalamic-pituitary function may be a major pathophysiological factor in mediating the psychopathological symptoms of such patients and may, in part, explain their response to a variety of antidepressant modalities (2,3). According to this hypothesis, we suggested that neuroendocrine tests, such as the thyrotropin-releasing hormone (TRH) test, can be applied to assess the activation state of the hypothalamus, a brain region believed to be decisively involved in the functional psychoses. For example, the abnormally low (blunted) thyrotropin (TSH) response to TRH administration may be taken as an indicator of hypothalamic-pituitary activation. In this regard, Langer et al. (3) have found a blunted TSH response to TRH in more than 40% of their depressed patients and a similarly high percentage of blunted TSH responses in patients with other functional psychoses. In that study (3), therapeutic outcome of patients on drug treatment was related to neuroendocrine status. Thus, patients with a blunted TSH response at admission and normalization of TSH response while still in hospital had a significantly higher change of symptomatic recovery than did patients who did not demonstrate normalization of their TSH response pattern during hospitalization. Alternatively, patients whose TSH response remained normal throughout hospitalization (i.e., patients who did not show an initial blunted TSH response or a disblunting in their TSH response after repeat TRH testing) had a smaller chance to recover within this time period.

Based on these findings, we suggested the disactivation hypothesis (2), that is, that psychotherapeutic effects of the major tranquilizers can be achieved by disactivating malactivation states in the brain, and this normalizing effect may be a common therapeutic mechanism of otherwise different psychobiological treatments, including narcotherapy.

Apart from the psychotropic drugs, electroconvulsive therapy (ECT) is a very effective somatic treatment for depressed patients and has been reported to be even more effective than antidepressant drugs (4–7). Thus, ECT may be particularly indicated for patients refractory to antidepressant medication. It has been established that ECT is effective only if a generalized cerebral seizure can be elicited (8). When recorded by electroencephalography (EEG), a seizure is followed by a brief period of no

Department of Psychiatry, University of Vienna, Vienna, Austria.

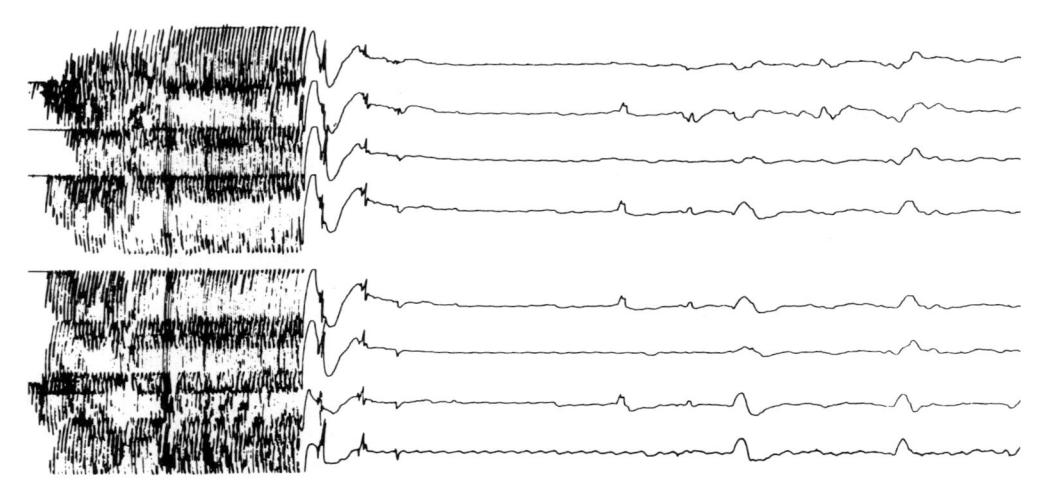

FIG. 1. ECT-induced EEG pattern with postictal electrocerebral silence (ES).

discernible electrical activity (electrocerebral silence or ES) (Fig. 1). We hypothesized that an EEG pattern showing a short period of ES may be indicative of a cerebral disactivation and that this major tranquilizing effect of anesthesia with isoflurane may, in its own right, have therapeutic effects. In essence, we hypothesized that the disactivation hypothesis could bridge the conceptual gap between therapeutic mechanisms believed to be operating in treatment applying the major tranquilizers and ECT.

Based on this reasoning, the aim of our investigations was to evaluate a possible alternative method to ECT that involved dis-

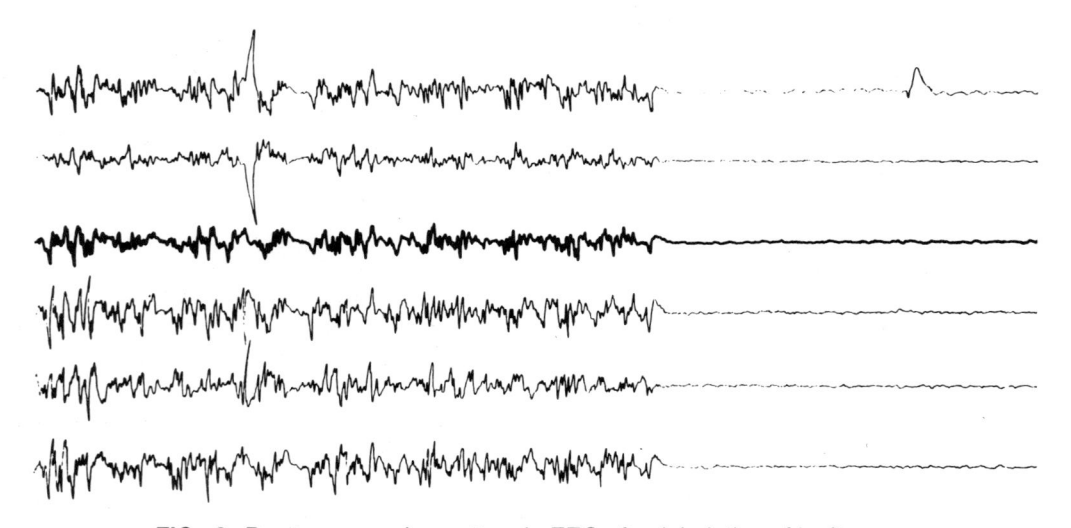

FIG. 2. Burst-suppression pattern in EEG after inhalation of isoflurane.

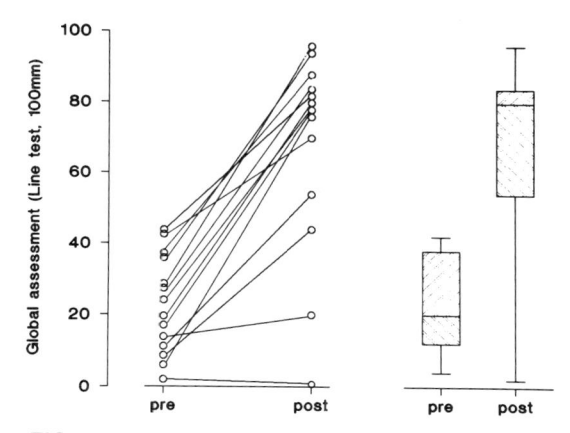

FIG. 3. Rapid psychotherapeutic effects of isoflurane anesthesia evaluated on a 100 mm visual analog scale, self-rated by patients 2 hours before and after the first anesthesia with isoflurane. (From ref. 13.)

activating mechanisms of cerebral functions without producing an organic brain syndrome (4). We suggested that isoflurane possibly could be the drug of choice in the treatment of refractory depressives, who would otherwise be given ECT.

It is known that isoflurane (9) can produce, in nontoxic doses, a transient ES with a flat line in EEG (10,11) (Fig. 2). We, therefore, hypothesized a therapeutic potential for isoflurane narcotherapy (INT). In an earlier study, we demonstrated a rapid antidepressant effect of INT in drug-refractory depressives (11–13) (Fig. 3). This study focuses on subacute therapeutic effects and is based on a prospective open trial of an extended sample of drug-refractory depressed patients.

PATIENTS AND METHODS

Sixteen patients with major depressive disorder (DSM-III) constituted the sample. Fourteen patients were of the melancholic subtype, and 2 had psychotic symptoms.

The first psychiatric episode occurred from 0.5 to 24 years before admission (median 7 years), and the duration of the present episode ranged between 1 and 24 months (median 3 months). The number of admissions before the present hospitalization ranged from 0 to 9 (median 3.5 admissions).

On the first 16 items, the Hamilton Depression Rating Scale (HDRS) score ranged from 12 to 24 (mean 18). All patients had been refractory to adequate antidepressant drug therapy. Six had received ECT in former depressive episodes, although none of them had had ECT in the present episode.

The patients' ages ranged from 20 to 67 years (median 44 years); 14 were women, and 2 were men.

The patients did not receive psychotherapeutic medication except for benzodiazepines on an as-needed basis. Informed consent was obtained after the procedure had been fully explained, and patients had the opportunity to withdraw from the study at any time and to chose an alternative modality. Before anesthesia, the patients' medical status was assessed by an internist for fitness to receive anesthesia.

Psychometric Evaluation

Acute antidepressant effects were rated by the patient 1 hour before and 1 hour after anesthesia using a global assessment rating on a 100 mm visual analog scale (0 = worst, 100 = best).

Possible subacute effects were rated weekly by two psychiatrists on the first 16 items of HDRS. Patients achieving an HDRS score below 9 were defined as recovered.

A close record was maintained of any reported side effects during the course of treatment.

Anesthesia

Patients received the anesthesia treatment two or three times a week, in the morning. The number of anesthesia sessions given to a patient ranged between 1 and 6, and the time of termination of treatment sessions was judged by the progress in clinical status.

The anesthesia was initiated with thiopental (3–6 mg/kg) and succinylcholine (1–1.5 mg/kg), and (after intubation) the patients were maintained with oxygen and nitrous oxide. Controlled ventilation kept the arterial P_{CO_2} between 20 and 25 mm Hg (minute volume 8–11 L/minute).

Isoflurane was administered to establish at 2MAC a burst suppression pattern on EEG. The inspiratory concentration of isoflurane was started with 4% until the first suppression (ES) then reduced to 2.5%. After 2 minutes of a predominant suppression pattern on EEG, inhalation of isoflurane was stopped. It was estimated that thereafter ES persisted for another 3 to 5 minutes.

The anesthesia was monitored by an isoflurane monitor and trend recorder (NORMAC). The cardiovascular conditions were monitored by periodic blood pressure, ECG, peripheral pulsation, and oxygen and carbon dioxide concentrations on a complex multirecorder (CARDIOCAP).

EEG

The EEG monitoring began with a resting EEG before initiation of anesthesia, followed by EEG monitoring throughout anesthesia administration, and was completed with a resting EEG after anesthesia was terminated.

The EEG was obtained by eight paracentral electrodes referred to the contralateral auricle (F3/C3/P3/01 to A2; F4/C4/P4/02 to A1). The sensitivity was fixed at 10 mV/mm of pen deflection, the time was constant at 0.3 seconds, and the high frequency filter was at 30 Hz. ES was followed by a burst suppression pattern. A continuous period of 120 seconds of ES was elected as a criterion to discontinue isoflurane inhalation.

Neuroendocrine Tests

TSH response to TRH stimulation was evaluated weekly at baseline before the first INT session and then at weekly intervals until discharge from hospital (3).

RESULTS

Anesthesia

The total number of anesthesia sessions was 43; 60% of the patients had received 1 or 2 anesthesia treatments. The duration of each anesthesia session ranged between 27 and 72 minutes, and 90% lasted between 32 and 68 minutes. The cumulative period of ES at each session ranged between 9 and 55 minutes, with 90% between 11 and 38 minutes. The average dose of isoflurane for an anesthesia session was 66 mg.

Psychometric Evaluation

Twelve of 16 patients improved clinically, as evaluated by the HDRS score, 3 patients did not improve, and 1 patient's HDRS score increased from 8 to 9[1] (Fig. 4). The mean HDRS score for the sample decreased from 17 to 8 at the end of the treatment period, suggesting significant subacute therapeutic effects of INT (Wilcoxon test: $Z = -3.11$, $p = 0.002$) (Fig. 4). The mean HDRS score by 2 weeks after completion of the anesthesia treatment remained within a stable range when compared to the posttreatment HDRS score (mean 11). This suggested that the therapeutic effect of INT was maintained (Fig. 5).

A detailed analysis of the therapeutic ef-

---

[1]The psychopathological state of this female patient was characterized more by retarded thinking than by depressive mood and behavior. The patient described "a gray curtain" in her head, which disappeared during the isoflurane treatment. In a 1-year follow-up-period, the patient remained free of relapse without any psychopharmacological drug.

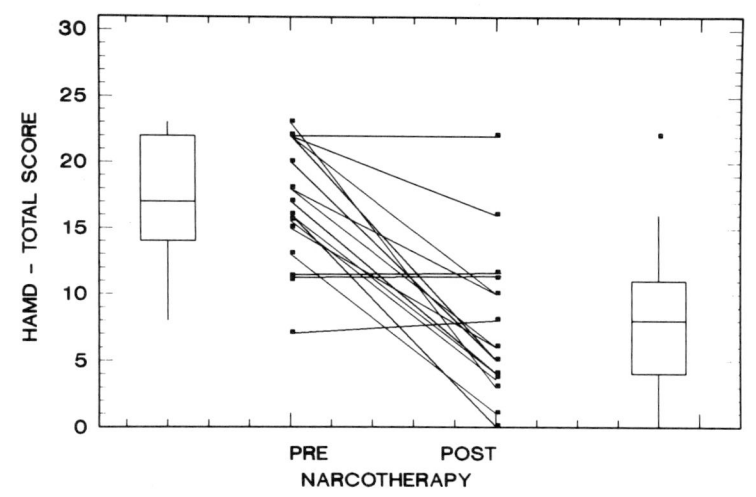

FIG. 4. HDRS (or HAMD) scores and single patient courses pre- and posttreatment. Psychotherapeutic effects after all sessions: pre-/post-score of HAMD (n = 16).

fect on individual items of HDRS indicates that not all symptoms were influenced equally by narcotherapy (Fig. 6). On items 1, 2, 7, and 13 concerning depressed mood, feelings of guilt, reduction of work, and general somatic symptoms, most of the patients improved. A smaller number of patients were therapeutically influenced in such items as psychic and somatic anxiety, agitation, retardation, and genital symptoms (items 8,9,10,11,14). The scores on some of these items increased in a few patients.

Items 4, 5, and 6 concerning sleep disorders were influenced as expected by medication with benzodiazepines.

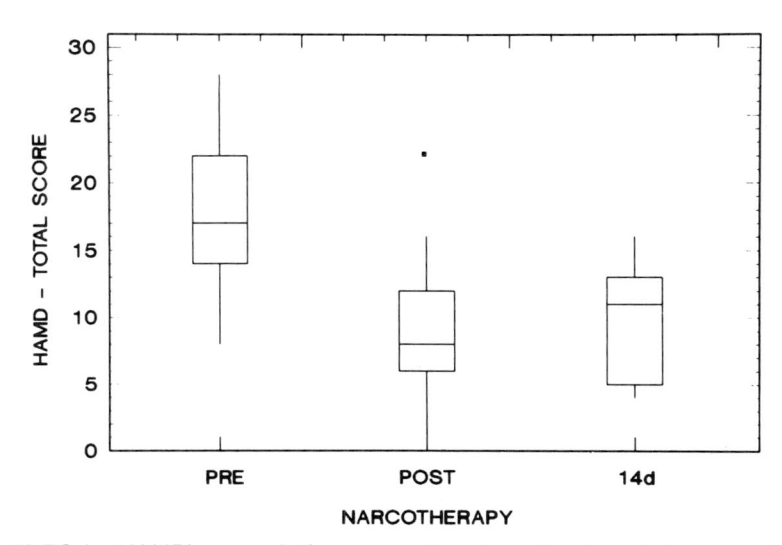

FIG. 5. HDRS (or HAMD) scores before pretreatment, posttreatment, 2 weeks later (14d).

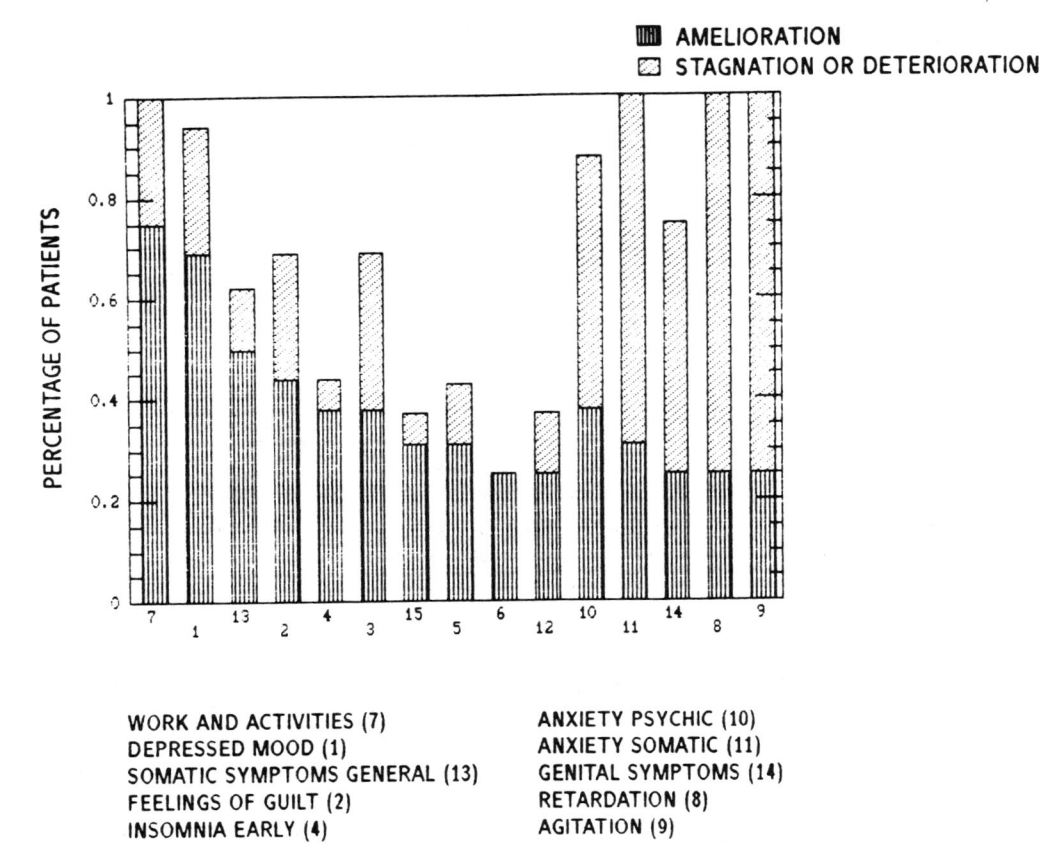

FIG. 6. Single item analysis. The size of the bar represents the percentage of patients with a score more than 0 (i.e., symptom carrier) on this item. The lower part of the bar represents the percentage of amelioration, the upper part the percentage of stagnation or deterioration.

Side Effects of Anesthesia

None of the patients reported the side effects of memory impairment and mental confusion, frequently observed after ECT. It is remarkable that no patient refused to continue the treatment and that none had to be withdrawn because of adverse physical or psychic side effects of the INT.

Neuroendocrine Tests

Nine of the 16 patients had multiple assessments of TSH response to TRH during hospitalization. None of the patients had a long-term clinical outcome and change in TSH response to TRH, which might contradict the malactivation-disactivation hypothesis (2). Patients with a disblunting during or after INT tended to maintain a stable recovery, whereas those with no change in TSH response to TRH challenge over the period of INT treatment had a higher risk for relapse.

Case Reports

Two typical patients courses demonstrated both tendencies. Patient A (Fig. 7), with a blunted TSH response at the begin-

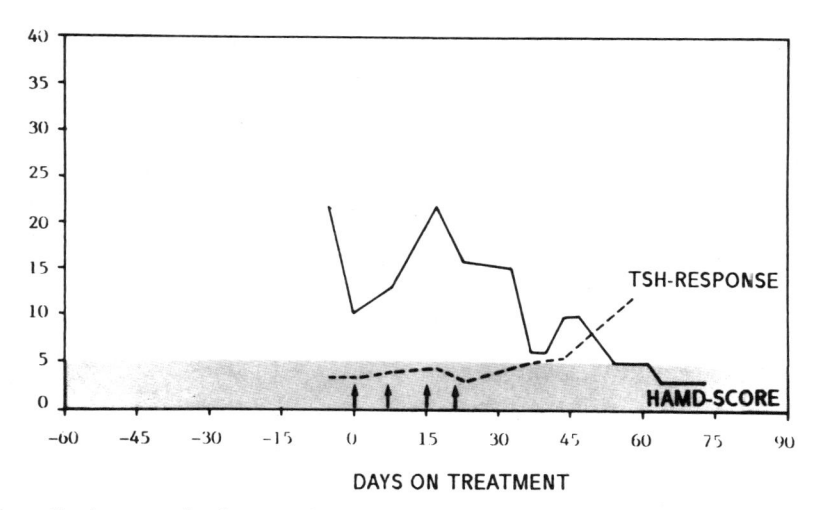

FIG. 7. This patient course is characterized by a disblunting of TSH response to TRH during INT and a stable recovery after INT.

ning, showed normalization of the TSH response and remained normal throughout observation. At the same time, he gradually recovered in symptoms and remained stable over the observation period.

Patient B (Fig. 8) seemed to have a good recovery during a series of narcotherapy, but there was a rapid deterioration of symptoms after the last anesthesia application. This clinical and neuroendocrine course could be interpreted on the basis of the results of Langer et al. (2,3) that the chance for a stable amelioration is smaller if TSH responses to the TRH test remained in a normal range throughout treatment, i.e., if there was no disblunting.

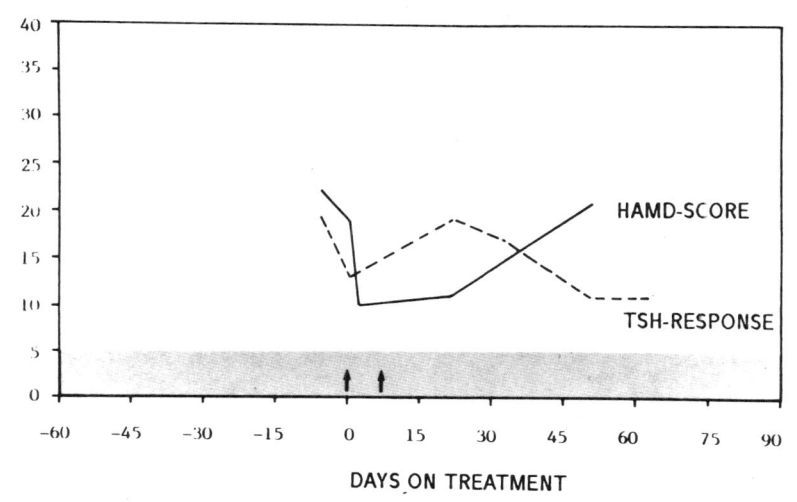

FIG. 8. This patient course is characterized by a normal TSH response throughout treatment; i.e., there was no disblunting. In the psychopathological status, a relapse evaluated by an increasing HDRS score can be seen after finishing isoflurane anesthesia.

CONCLUSION

This study was motivated by the need for an alternative treatment for those patients who manifest therapy-refractory depression.

Although ECT remains as an established treatment for drug-resistant depression, its therapeutic mechanism remains incompletely understood. Among the several physiological changes accompanying ECT, we hypothesized that postictal ES may be indicative of the therapeutic essence of ECT.

Langer et al. postulated that every psychotherapeutic effect by major tranquilizers may involve disactivating mechanisms of the drugs indicated by the TSH response (2,3). We hypothesized that the postictal ES may be interpreted as an intensive disactivation mechanism and that the induction of ES by deep anesthesia might be therapeutic.

Fink et al. demonstrated a positive correlation between postictal slowing of brain electrical activity and the therapeutic effect (12).

Narcotherapy with isoflurane offers an alternative method for inducing ES without a seizure. Isoflurane is an effective drug that produces transient ES in the EEG in nontoxic concentrations. In an initial explorative study, we demonstrated a rapid therapeutic effect to anesthesia therapy in depressives (13–16). However, in a subsequent open study, Greenberg et al. could not demonstrate a significant therapeutic effect of INT in their depressed patients (17). Their sample consisted of 6 patients aged 60 to 82 years. Their patients were considerably older than ours, and two of their patients had to be withdrawn from treatment because of cardiovascular complication. Greenberg et al. gave 21 sessions with an average duration of ES less than 60 seconds, whereas we induced ES intervals lasting 9 to 55 minutes.

Carl et al. (18) compared INT to ECT and demonstrated comparable therapeutic efficacies of both treatments. Likewise, Hoffmann et al. reported that in a double-blind comparison study with ECT, INT was found to be approximately as effective as ECT in depressive patients (19).

Our hypothesis of a possible antidepressive effect of isoflurane-induced ES has been further confirmed by this open prospective trial. In the present explorative study, 80% of drug-refractory depressed patients improved, and a detailed analysis of treatment response suggests a specific therapeutic profile of isoflurane narcotherapy.

To corroborate the findings reported here in an open trial, future research should focus on double-blind comparison of INT versus other somatic antidepressive treatments, extending the indication for INT to patients other than treatment-refractory depressives.

ACKNOWLEDGMENTS

This work was supported in part by Fonds zur Förderung der wissenschaftlichen Forschung, grant 5785.

REFERENCES

1. Sheperd M. Clinical trial of the treatment of depressive illness. *Br Med J* 1965;1:881–886.
2. Langer G, Resch F, Aschauer H, et al. TSH-response patterns to TRH-stimulation may indicate therapeutic mechanisms of antidepressant and neuroleptic drugs. *Neuropsychobiology* 1984;11:213–218.
3. Langer G, Koinig G, Hatzinger R, et al. Response of thyrotropin to thyrotropin-releasing hormone as predictor of treatment outcome. *Arch Gen Psychiatry* 1986;43:861–868.
4. Weiner RD. Does electroconvulsive therapy cause brain damage? *Behav Brain Sci* 1984;7:1–53.
5. Janicack PG, Davis JM, Gibbons RD, Erickson S, Chang S, Gallagher P. Efficacy of ECT: A meta-analysis. *Am J Psychiatry* 1985;142:297–302.
6. Gangadhar BN, Kapur R, Kalyanasundaram S. Comparison of electroconvulsive therapy with imipramine in endogenous depression: A double-blind study. *Br J Psychiatry* 1982;141:367–371.

7. Paul SM, Extein I, Calil HM, Potter WZ, Chodoff P, Goodwin FG. Use of ECT with treatment-resistant depressed patients at the National Institute of Mental Health. *Am J Psychiatry* 1981;138:486–489.
8. Fink M, Johnson L. Monitoring the duration of electroconvulsive therapy seizures. *Arch Gen Psychiatry* 1982;39:1189–1191.
9. Eger EI. Isoflurane: A review. *Anesthesiology* 1981;55:559–576.
10. Eger EI, Stevenson WC, Cromwell TH. The electroencephalogram in men anesthetized with Forane. *Anesthesiology* 1971;35:504–508.
11. Newberg LA, Michenfelder JD. Cerebral protection by isoflurane during hypoxema or ischemia. *Anesthesiology* 1983;59:29–35.
12. Fink M. Convulsive therapy and endogenous depression. *Pharmacopsychiatry* 1980;13:49–54.
13. Langer G, Neumark J, Koinig G, Graf M, Schönbeck G. Rapid psychotherapeutic effects of anesthesia with isoflurane (ES narcotherapy) in treatment-refractory depressed patients. *Neuropsychobiology* 1985;14:118–120.
14. Neumark J, Langer G, Koinig G, Graf M. Isofluran ein psychotrop wirksames Medikament. In: Bergmann H, et al., eds. *Isofluran. Standort und Perspektiven—Beiträge zur Anästhesiologie und Intensivmedizin.* Wien: 1985;256–263.
15. Langer G, Koinig G, Neumark J. "Narcotherapy" with isoflurane anesthesias: Psychotherapeutic profile, "flat line" in EEG and other observations. *Clin Neuropharm* 1986;9(Suppl 4).
16. Koinig G, Langer G, Dittrich R. "Isoflurane narcotherapy" in depression: Methodological issues. In: Lerer B, Gershon S, eds. *New directions in affective disorders.* New York: Springer-Verlag, 1987.
17. Greenberg LB, Gage J, Vitkun S, Fink M. Isoflurane anesthesia therapy: A replacement for ECT in depressive disorders? *Convulsive Ther* 1987;3.
18. Carl C, Engelhardt W, Teichmann G, Fuchs G. Open comparative study with treatment-refractory depressed patients: Electroconvulsive therapy—Anesthetic therapy with isoflurane. *Pharmacopsychiatry* 1988;21:432–433.
19. Hoffmann O, Mebius C, Vinnars E, Johnson L, Stenfors C, Mathe AA. Isoflurane and electroconvulsive treatment in therapy of depression. *Psychiatry today—Accomplishments and promises.* (Abstracts of VIIth World Congress of Psychiatry). 1989;194.

24

The Role of Stereotactic Cingulotomy in the Treatment of Intractable Depression

Anthony J. Bouckoms

Psychosurgery is not a newcomer to psychiatric practice. Since 1936, at least 19 different kinds of brain neurosurgery have been described (1). However, distinctions between the surgical procedures, psychiatric diagnoses, and methods of assessment often are not made, making generalizations about psychosurgery inchoate. For that reason, this review focuses on bilateral stereotactic cingulotomy and major depression.

Bilateral stereotactic cingulotomy is a neurosurgical operation in which two separate 1 cm diameter lesions are made in the fibers of the cingulate bundle. X-ray fluoroscopy and stereotactic instrumentation are used to guide thermistor electrodes through bilateral burr holes in the skull into the anterior cingulum bundle, just above the lateral ventricles and corpus callosum.

Defining the role of cingulotomy as a treatment for major depression is an invective to seven critical questions. Does cingulotomy help patients with intractable depression? How significant are the side effects from cingulotomy? What are the indications and contraindications for cingulotomy in the depressed patient? Does cingulotomy offer benefits to a different subgroup of depressed patients than electroconvulsive therapy (ECT)? How does cingulotomy compare to other current psychosurgical operations for depression, namely, subcaudate tractotomy and capsulotomy? Is there a rational justification for making a lesion in the cingulum? What are the principal ethical issues in the future of limbic surgery?

DOES CINGULOTOMY HELP PATIENTS WITH INTRACTABLE DEPRESSION

The most comprehensive general review of the efficacy of limbic surgery is the compendium of the IVth World Congress of Psychiatric Surgery in Madrid in 1975 (2). The efficacy of the specific operation of cingulotomy for intractable affective disorder has been most extensively studied by Ballantine over the last 28 years (3). Ballantine's study of 120 patients with major affective disorder showed a favorable response at a mean assessment interval of 8.6 years. Nineteen patients were functioning normally without treatment of any kind. Thirty patients were functioning normally on maintenance medication and/or psychotherapy. Twenty-eight patients were considerably improved over the preoperative state, no longer hospitalized, working part time, but still suffering periodic recurrence of disabling symptoms. They still required active continuing psychiatric therapies. Nineteen patients showed slight improvement and improved response to pharmaco/psychotherapy but still required intensive care and were unable to work. Twenty-two patients did not improve or deteriorated

---

Department of Psychiatry, Massachusetts General Hospital, Boston, MA 02114.

over the years. Two patients were lost to follow-up.

Ballantine also determined that the affectively ill subgroup of the total study population were more frequently completely normal after the surgery than the patients with other psychiatric diagnoses. Among these 120 patients, there were 83 unipolar depression, 23 bipolar, and 14 schizoaffective disorder. There was no significant difference in outcome between the depression subtypes in response to cingulotomy. The time course of change after cingulotomy was variable, with optimal improvement beginning between 2 and 24 months after surgery. Only half the patients who eventually benefited from the operation had improved within 2 months. Six months was typical for a plateau of improvement. At the 2-year follow-up, 95% of those who were to improve significantly had done so. The stability of improvement was also notable, with interim follow-ups in 1970 and 1975 showing 78% and 77%, respectively, of the patients had improved significantly. One weakness of this study is that the exact criteria to select cingulotomy patients have been arrived at post hoc over the course of the years.

Changes in the diagnostic criteria from DSM-I to DSM-III has made testing the reliability and validity of specific diagnoses impossible. The remaining literature on cingulotomy is not very helpful in identifying the benefits of cingulotomy per se for major affective disorder (4). The study of Martin et al. is typical in that they had a mixed diagnostic group of patients with anxiety and schizophrenia as well as depression (5). They report good results in 62 psychiatric patients, with 13 having excellent improvement and 7 moderate recovery. The differential outcome of affectively disordered patients is not specified (5). The report of Kelly et al. on combined cingulotomy and subcaudate tractotomy describes improvement in patients with affective components to their psychiatric illness (6). They believed that this multilesion limbic leukotomy was particularly effective for obsessive-compulsive disorder. Critical comparison of these findings with cingulotomy for depression is impossible because standardized diagnostic criteria and follow-up methods were not used (6).

WHAT ARE THE SIDE EFFECTS FROM CINGULOTOMY?

The largest series of cingulotomies studied for safety and efficacy were the 696 procedures performed by Ballantine et al. There were no deaths. There were 2 major complications resulting in 2 hemiplegias. These were caused by laceration of cortical arteries during introduction of ventricular needles. These acute subdural hematomas resulted in 1 transient hemiparesis and 1 persistent hemiparesis (3). A 1972 symposium where seven surgeons reported on 683 cingulotomies showed a total complication rate of 1 death and 2 hemiplegias. The consensus was that these 683 cingulotomies produced good results, with no worsening of behavior or cognition in 70 to 90% of the patients. Long et al. found that 3 patients out of 19 who were treated with bilateral cingulotomy showed a mild generalized decline in neuropsychological functioning after surgery. They thought that although the results of the surgery were good, postoperative impairment in neuropsychological functioning must be considered (7). Kullberg, in a comparison of cingulotomy and anterior capsulotomy, noticed that confusion and affective deficits were less frequent and less severe after cingulotomy (8).

Vilkki has shown that cingulotomy causes a decline in visual imagery (9). This finding gets support from Teuber et al., who found that cingulotomized patients had problems in visual labyrinth tests. However, because the study was retrospective and the authors had not studied the patients before surgery, they could not be sure that the deficit derived from cingulotomy per se.

Riddle and Roberts' study of porteus maze scores in various cingulate lesions concluded that there was initial postoperative decrement in performance after the surgery, and it was not clear if there was complete recovery (10). One comprehensive study of neuropsychological sequelae of cingulotomy is the ongoing study initiated by Teuber and continued by Corkin (11–14). The current test battery consists of 30 standard psychological tests, including 7 for memory, 8 for sensory and motor activity, 3 for personality, 3 for spatial ability, 7 that measure frontal lobe function, and 2 of overall intelligence. A neurological examination also was part of the evaluation.

In general, patients performed less well after cingulotomy compared to preoperatively on some conceptual tests despite clinical improvement. Younger patients (less than 30 years) showed a statistically significant increase in the Hidden Figures Test ability after surgery in contrast to a significant decrease in test performance among older postoperative cases. Cognitively, there appears to be a smaller margin of safety in older patients undergoing cingulotomy. The minimal neurocognitive sequelae are striking given that 40% of Ballantine's patients (also studied by the Teuber/Corkin group) had more than one set of cingulate lesions. Teuber's conclusions concerning neuropsychological sequela of cingulotomy were that (a) there is currently no evidence of lasting neurological behavioral deficits after surgery, (b) a comparison of preoperative and postoperative scores reveals significant gains in the Wechsler IQ ratings, and (c) the only decrement was an irreversible decrease in performance of the Rey-Taylor Complex Figure Test.

Suicide is of considerable concern in patients having cingulotomy and is the subject of a detailed report by the author (in preparation). In his series of 120 patients, Ballantine found 14 of 18 suicides occurred in the affectively disordered group (3). The worrisome association of suicide and cingulotomy requires attention to the following facts. A long period of improved function after the operation was typical for those who eventually killed themselves, making it less likely that a bad result from the surgery could be linked to the suicide. Second, the prevalence of suicide in these intractably ill psychiatric patients is the same or slightly lower than would be predicted from other comparable populations of psychiatrically ill people. Third, case reviews of those patients who had succeeded in suicide showed persistent chaos in their lives, multiplicity of psychiatric diagnoses, and repeated previous suicide attempts and self-destructive behavior. The surprising finding was that most had improved after the operation despite the multiplicity of problems.

The implication of this observation is that cingulotomy does not prevent the recurrence of affective illness or prevent self-destructive behavior. It does, however, alleviate depression, anxiety, and pain, often providing a chance for other interventions to work.

A unique story of a cingulotomy patient was reported by Escobar in a case of bilateral cingulotomy for intractable depression (15). The patient did not improve from her depression after the surgery but did develop affective blunting and somatic delusions for the first time ever. Neuroleptics helped alleviate the symptoms. Escobar noted that cingulate gyrus tumors have been reported to be schizophrenogenic in humans, suggesting the same effect might be possible in some induced lesions of the cingulate gyrus. The authors were cautious in not discarding the possibility that the cingulotomy merely activated an "insidious schizophrenic syndrome that was preexisting" (15).

WHAT ARE THE INDICATIONS AND CONTRAINDICATIONS FOR CINGULOTOMY IN THE DEPRESSED PATIENT?

Depression, anxiety, and pain have been the three symptoms identified as indications for psychosurgery (11,16–20). Lehmann and Ostrow state that patients should have a 2-year plus history of chronic anxiety and depression and a good premorbid personality to be good candidates for surgery. In contrast, psychological tests have proven "very disappointing" as indicators of good response (17). In a literature survey conducted at the request of the National Commission for the Protection of Human Subjects of Biomedical and Behavioral Research (21), Valenstein found that the patients most likely to improve with psychosurgery were those with "severe disturbances of mood and emotion, e.g., the severely depressed, anxious and the obsessive-compulsive neurotic."

The problem is that despite the convergence of opinion that anxiety and depression predict good response to psychosurgery, the definition of terms is not precise. State symptoms, personality traits, personality disorder, primary affective disorder, secondary affective disorder, psychotic and schizophrenic syndromes often are not distinguished. Consequently, precise indications for cingulotomy in affective disorder per se were never exactly defined in the medical literature until 1988 (22). The indications for cingulotomy for affective disorder and pain are a post hoc composite of the accumulated knowledge and current standard of practice at Massachusetts General Hospital. Seven elements constitute the selection criteria for cingulotomy (Table 1).

Diagnosis

The best established psychiatric diagnosis that responds well to cingulotomy is major affective disorder. Many of these patients have comorbidity with anxiety disorder, which by anecdotal experience may increase the chance of success with cingulotomy. A primary anxiety disorder may respond well to cingulotomy, although if this is the exclusive diagnosis, capsulotomy outcome may be as good or better. The presence of pain, usually but not necessarily combined with major affective disorder or anxiety disorder, is an indication for cingulotomy.

Disability

Disability must be significant for at least 12 weeks. Significant disability is defined on DSM-III axis 5 as the highest level of adaptive functioning (range 0–7). Poor (5) to grossly impaired (7) constitute significant disability.

Intractability

Intractability of the affective/anxiety disorder is defined by lack of sustained response to three standard modalities of treatment for these disorders. Pharmacotherapy involving trials of antidepressant medication, stimulants, adjuvant treatment with thyroid, lithium, and neuroleptics must have failed. ECT usually has failed to produce a sustained improvement in the majority of patients. Prior ECT has not been an absolute criterion for the decision to go ahead with cingulotomy. The reasons for not having ECT must be documented, e.g., contraindications, risk factors. Reasons for not treating with ECT would be a patient who has been unable to tolerate a therapeutic course of ECT, a patient who has multiple diagnoses that would predict a poor response to ECT, or a patient with coexisting pain with psychiatric disorder. Psychotherapy, including at least one reasonable trial of psychodynamic exploratory therapy, must have been completed and failed. We have not mandated an absolute standard of particular forms of therapy, since individual needs are so variable. However, we would consider a trial of individual psychodynamic therapy, a trial of either couples, family, or group therapy, and some form of behavioral/cognitive therapy as reasonable. If pharmacotherapy, ECT, and psychotherapy all have failed, the criteria for intractability are met.

TABLE 1. *Selection criteria for limbic surgery*

1. Psychiatric diagnosis	DSM-III/III-R major affective disorder, anxiety disorder
2. Disability	Poor to grossly impaired (DSM-III 5–7)
3. Intractability	Pharmacotherapy
	Electrical stimulation
	Psychotherapy
4. Informed consent	The patient must consent
5. Treating professionals	Tertiary hospital with consensus of neurosurgery, psychiatry, and neurology
6. Evidence	Written past history, family history
7. Exclusion criteria	Delusional psychosis, somatoform disorders, 1° personality disorder, 1° substance abuse, criminality/poor cooperation, compensation neurosis, malingering, unwilling to have psychiatric care

Informed Consent

Informed consent must be obtained from the patient. The nature of the surgery and its risks, benefits, and alternatives must be thoroughly discussed on more than one occasion. The patient's family should be involved in consent discussions but need not agree with the patient. However, the patient may not exclude the family from discussion of the procedure.

Treating Professionals

Cingulotomy is done at a tertiary care center in which the chiefs of neurosurgery, psychiatry, and neurology have approved the evaluating clinicians from each service. Consensus of the treating professionals must be reached about the advisability of cingulotomy. The evidence for the current and past psychiatric history must be complete. It is recommended that screening of applicants and their records should occur well in advance of the initial visit of the patient to the treatment center. Referral to the tertiary care center must be made by a physician or psychologist who has taken responsibility for marshalling all the evidence and synthesizing the indications and history and is willing to follow the patient after the surgery. If this referring doctor is not a psychiatrist, psychiatric follow-up must be arranged and agreed to by the patient.

Evidence

The evidence reviewed should include past records of all treatments and hospitalizations from each significant hospital and physician. Family history corroborated by family members should be checked. Personal interviews with the neurosurgeon, neurologist, and psychiatrist must be completed by the patient to allow for clarification of history and direct examination. A magnetic resonance image (MRI) of the brain, EEG, and neuropsychiatric testing are usual components of the evaluation.

Exclusion Criteria

Criteria that militate against good results are principal diagnoses of personality disorder, primary substance abuse, a history of criminality, or lack of cooperation/reliability with treatment. This includes patients who cannot exercise good judgment for any reason or are unwilling to be maintained on a postsurgical drug regimen and confer regularly with a psychiatrist and another primary physician. The malingerer or patients seeking compensation neurosis would be typical of these kinds of patients who would be excluded. Persistent delusional psychosis unassociated with major affective disorder usually would result in exclusion from surgery. Primary somatoform disorders without depression or anxiety disorders also carry poor prognoses and are a relative contraindication to psychosurgery.

DOES CINGULOTOMY OFFER BENEFITS TO A DIFFERENT PROFILE OF DEPRESSED PATIENTS COMPARED TO OTHER SOMATIC THERAPIES, SUCH AS ELECTROCONVULSIVE THERAPY?

The question is how to choose between somatic therapies for intractable depression. The usual standard of care is that pharmacotherapy and psychotherapy would have failed before the somatic therapies of ECT or cingulotomy would be considered. Table 2 summarizes the indications and contraindications for ECT and cingulotomy.

The indications for ECT have been well defined (23). Intractable melancholic depression, delusional depression, and intractable bipolar disorder are the classic indications for good response to ECT. Some young patients who have schizophrenic-like symptoms but who also exhibit affective symptoms may respond acutely to ECT. Schizophreniform disorder in which the patient has good prognostic features, such as good premorbid social and occupational functioning, the absence of flat affect, confusion at the height of the psychotic episode, and the onset of psychotic symptoms within 4 weeks of the first change of behavior, also can respond well to ECT.

In contrast, cingulotomy is decidedly inferior in these schizophreniform and schizoaffective disorders. Ballantine et al. found that these patients had a generally poor long-term outcome after cingulotomy. Furthermore, patients with delusional psychosis also did not respond well to cingulotomy. Although there may be great variability in outcome to surgery between individual cases, the alleviation of the affective distress with cingulotomy does not necessarily modify the core psychosis. Thus, although delusional psychosis is not an absolute contraindication to cingulotomy, the outcome is quite uncertain.

Bipolar disorder in the depressed and manic phases has been well studied in ECT, where the efficacy is great. There has been no comparable study in cingulotomy so no definitive statement can be made. I do not know of any treatment of an intractable manic patient with cingulotomy. Intractable melancholic depression is a good prognostic indicator for both ECT and cingulotomy and requires ECT as a prerequisite to cingulotomy. The unique indicators for cingu-

TABLE 2. *Electroconvulsive therapy vs cingulotomy: indications and contraindications*

	Electroconvulsive therapy	Cingulotomy
Indications	1. Intractable melancholic depression 2. Delusional depression 3. Intractable bipolar disorder-mania 4. Schizoaffective disorder 5. Schizophreniform (good prognosis)	1. Intractable melancholic depression 2. Anxiety disorders 3. Multiple concurrent axis 1 disorders including depression and anxiety 4. Intractable pain, somatic or neuropathic, combined with depression and anxiety
Contraindications	1. 1° anxiety disorders 2. Somatoform disorder alone 3. Principal diagnosis is Axis 2 or 1° substance abuse 4. Chronic pain	1. Delusional psychosis 2. Somatoform disorder alone 3. Principal diagnosis is Axis 2 or 1° substance abuse

lotomy as opposed to ECT are patients with intractable anxiety disorders. These patients typically have obsessive-compulsive disorder that may include a mixture of generalized anxiety, phobias of various kinds, and secondary depression. In general, patients with DSM-III Axis 1 comorbidity, if it includes depression and anxiety, may respond well to cingulotomy but not as well to ECT. Many of these comorbid conditions are relative contraindications to good response from ECT.

The other unique indication for cingulotomy is intractable pain, either somatic or neuropathic, which along with severe depression and anxiety can improve with cingulotomy. At Massachusetts General Hospital, ECT has not been a standard part of treatment of the intractable pain patient. Although ECT should be considered before proceeding to cingulotomy, there are situations where cingulotomy is preferable.

HOW DOES CINGULOTOMY COMPARE TO OTHER CURRENT PSYCHOSURGICAL OPERATIONS FOR DEPRESSION?

Cingulotomy, capsulotomy, and subcaudate tractotomy constitute the triad of current psychosurgical operations for comparison. The main debate is the differential efficacy of cingulotomy versus anterior capsulotomy for depression versus obsessive anxiety disorder. Kullberg found that cingulotomy was less effective for anxiety disorder than capsulotomy (8). In his series of 55 patients, Laitinen found that cingulotomy was not effective for obsessive-compulsive disorder (24). Mindus et al. (25) contributed the largest series, including more than 300 cases of affective disorder treated with stereotactic interruption of the anterior fibers of the internal capsule (anterior capsulotomy). Their data suggest that capsulotomy is particularly effective in anxiety disorders compared to cingulotomy. However, there may be more cognitive side effects after capsulotomy, with patients showing less initiative than those with operations on other anatomical sites. The rehabilitation from capsulotomy is more prolonged than that from cingulotomy. Data are accumulating that capsulotomy may be preferable for primary anxiety disorders. Complementary data showing a superior efficacy for cingulotomy in depression is not as strong. The main evidence comes from Ballantine's series of 198 patients in which the anxiety disordered patients did less well than those with major depression (3).

Subcaudate tractotomy, wherein lesions are placed in the ventral medial quadrants of the frontal lobes, achieved favorable results compared to the more damaging frontal leukotomy (26). Two thirds of the patients had less depression, and one third to two thirds had significant improvement in anxiety symptoms (27,28). It has been most extensively practiced at the Brook General Hospital in London, England, where it is described as effective for chronic and recurrent depression. Its negative features are sexual disinhibition in 2% of the patients, other side effects in an additional 9% of the patients, and a lengthy rehabilitation period of several months. It is not as effective in the treatment of pain associated with major depression. It is no longer practiced at Massachusetts General Hospital and is rarely done elsewhere.

IS THERE RATIONAL JUSTIFICATION FOR MAKING A LESION IN THE CINGULUM, ASIDE FROM THE OBSERVATION THAT IT WORKS?

The cingulum is a bilateral bundle of white nerve fibers that connect the frontal cortex, thalamic nuclei, and hippocampal formation. It is at the crossroads of the limbic system, and inasmuch as the limbic system is the putative substrate for intractable suffering, there may be a role for surgical interruption of this system. Ascending projections from the midbrain and brainstem arise from the ventral tegmental area and raphe, projecting up to the cingulum, septum, accumbens, amygdala, and thalamus. The raphe projections use serotonin. The ventral tegmental projections are dopaminergic. One demonstration of the importance of these pathways is that stress-induced analgesia can be abolished by lesioning limbic–raphe pathways, whereas hypophysectomy, adrenalectomy, or chemical sympathectomy does not abolish the analgesia.

The neuropsychiatry of affective disorders indicates growing evidence for the possibility that pathophysiology of these diseases may reside in the upper brainstem and limbic system, of which the cingulum is a central part. Neurochemical studies have found increasing evidence for abnormal modulation of several neuropeptides, including somatostatin, cholecystokinin, and calcitonin, in the limbic lobe function in depression. Again, the cingulum is a major anatomical substrate for these peptides.

Monoamine studies of the limbic frontal projections in chronic pain states, psychoses, and affective disorders have implicated dopamine, endorphins, and serotonin as key neuromodulators of these disorders in which the cingulum is an anatomical target of the ascending limbic pathway. The rationale for any kind of limbic surgery is that there is convergent validity to the notion that these limbic–cingulate pathways are the anatomical substrate of pain, mood, and suffering.

WHAT ARE THE PRINCIPAL ETHICAL ISSUES IN THE FUTURE OF LIMBIC SURGERY?

Kleinig has written an erudite treatise on ethical issues in psychosurgery (29). Valenstein's book on the history of psychosurgery describes how important the political and personal processes were in the evolution of psychosurgery (30). The separation of psychiatry from neurological medicine, administrators from clinicians, and media predominating over scientific critique became major problems in the uncontrolled use of psychosurgery. Politics continues to intrude on the decision-making process about psychosurgery. Two recent examples are the incorrect representation of the work of Dr. John Donnelly and T. Corwin Fleming by the US Government Office of Health Technology Assessment (OHTA) and CHAMPUS, respectively. These two organizations use misquotations of their work as information against psychosurgery. These kinds of ethical problems, reviewed by the author in more detail elsewhere, demonstrate that political agendas pose the biggest ethical threat to the use of cingulotomy for the relief of suffering today. The body of experience and written data that document the considerable efficacy and safety of cingulotomy for the treatment of major depression and anxiety disorders should be the deciding factors for its use.

CONCLUSIONS

Twenty-eight years of experience with cingulotomy as a treatment for affective disorder has established it as an effective and safe procedure. The majority of patients with intractable affective disease improve by 6 months after cingulotomy and have improved long-term prospects. Even patients with secondary depression and comorbidity, such as anxiety or pain, may respond to cingulotomy, in contrast to poor results seen with ECT. Cingulotomy does not necessarily prevent relapse of the affective illness or suicidal behavior, and ongoing psychiatric care may be necessary to optimize long-term outcome. Conclusive evidence on the comparative efficacy of cingulotomy versus other limbic surgical procedures is not available, although the data suggest that cingulotomy may be the operation of choice for affective disorders, and capsulotomy may be more effective for anxiety disorders. Future research might focus on the limbic–cingulate mechanisms of depression, the neurochemical effects of cingulate lesions, and the critical anatomical substrate for depression, anxiety, and pain.

Mandates for the future include (a) clinicians interested in limbic system surgery collaborating with basic scientists to focus studies of cerebrospinal fluid monoamines and neuropeptides and imaging studies with PET and MRI, (b) accurate determination of the effects of comorbidity on outcome, critical information in tuning the indications for various limbic interventions, e.g., cingulotomy versus ECT, (c) clinicians continuing to treat the most intractably ill patients with cingulotomy, and (d) physicians holding the position that science preempts politics in decisions regarding limbic surgery and that the intrusion of politics into decisions about medical care is the biggest ethical problem in medical decision making today.

REFERENCES

1. Bouckoms AJ. Psychosurgery. In: Wall P, ed. *Textbook of pain*. Edinburgh: Churchill Livingstone, 1989;868–883.
2. Sweet WH, Obrador S, Martin-Rodrigues JG, eds. *Neurosurgical treatment in psychiatry, pain and epilepsy*. Baltimore: University Park Press, 1977.
3. Ballantine HT, Bouckoms AJ, Thomas EK, Giriunas IE. Treatment of psychiatric illness by stereotactic cingulotomy. *Biol Psychiatry* 1987;22:807–819.
4. Sweet WH. Neurosurgical aspects of primary affective disorders. In: Youmans J, ed. *Neurological surgery: A comprehensive reference guide to diagnosis and management of neurosurgical problems*. Philadelphia: WB Saunders, 1982;3927–3946.
5. Martin WL, McElhaney ML, Meyer GA. Stereotactic cingulotomy: Results of psychological testing and clinical evaluation preoperatively and postoperatively. In: Sweet WH, Obrador S, Martin-Rodrigues JG, eds. *Neurosurgical treatment in psychiatry, pain and epilepsy*. Baltimore: University Park Press, 1977;381–386.
6. Mitchell-Heggs N, Kelly D, Richardson AE. Stereotactic limbic leucotomy: Clinical, psychological and physiological assessment at 16 months. In: Sweet WH, Obrador S, Martin-Rodrigues JG, eds. *Neurosurgical treatment in psychiatry, pain and epilepsy*. Baltimore: University Park Press, 1977;367–379.
7. Long CG, Pueschel K, Hunter SE. Assessment of the effects of cingulate gyrus lesions by neuropsychological techniques. *J Neurosurg* 1978;49:264–271.
8. Kullberg G. Differences in effect of capsulotomy and cingulotomy. In: Sweet WH, Obrador S, Martin-Rodrigues JG, eds. *Neurosurgical treatment in psychiatry, pain and epilepsy*. Baltimore: University Park Press, 1977;301–308.
9. Vilkki J. Late psychological and clinical effects of subrostral cingulotomy and anterior mesoloviotomy in psychiatric illness. In: Sweet WH, Obrador S, Martin-Rodrigues JG, eds. *Neurosurgical treatment in psychiatry, pain and epilepsy*. Baltimore: University Park Press, 1977;253–259.
10. Riddle M, Roberts AH. Psychosurgery and the porteus maze tests: Review and reanalysis of data. *Arch Gen Psychiatry* 1978;35:493–497.
11. Teuber HL, Corkin S, Twitchell TE. A study of cingulotomy in man. Appendix to psychosurgery. Reports prepared for the National Commission for the Protection of Human Subjects of Biomedical and Behavioral Research. US Department of Health, Education and Welfare, publication no (OS) 77-0002, 1977;3:1–115.
12. Teuber HL. Study of cingulotomy in man. In: Sweet WH, Obrador S, Martin-Rodrigues JG, eds. *Neurosurgical treatment in psychiatry, pain and epilepsy*. Baltimore: University Park Press, 1977;355–362.
13. Corkin S. Hidden figures test performance: Lasting unilateral penetrating head injury and transient effects of bilateral cingulotomy. *Neuropsychologia* 1979;17:585–605.
14. Corkin S. A prospective study of cingulotomy. In: Valenstein ES, ed. *The psychosurgery debate*. San Francisco: WH Freeman, 1980;164–204.
15. Escobar JI, Chandel V. Nuclear symptoms of schizophrenia after cingulotomy: A case report by Javier I. Escobar. *Am J Psychiatry* 1977;134:1304–1306.
16. Scoville W. Selective cortical undercutting. *J Neurosurg* 1949;6:65–73.
17. Lehman HE, Ostrow DE. Quizzing the expert: Clinical criteria for psychosurgery. *Hosp Med* 1973;Feb 24–31.
18. Martin-Rodrigues JG, Delgado JMR, Obrador S, Santo-Domingo J, Alonso A. Intractable pain: Dynamics of its psychoneurosurgical approach and brain stimulation. In: Sweet WH, Obrador S, Martin-Rodrigues JG, ed. *Neurosurgical treatment in psychiatry, pain and epilepsy*. Baltimore: University Park Press, 1977;639–649.
19. Mirsky AF, Orzack MH. Final report on psychosurgery pilot study. In: *Psychosurgery appendix of the National Commission for the Protection of Human Subjects of Biomedical and Behavioral Research II-2-168*. Washington DC: US Government Printing, 1976.
20. Office Health Technology Assessment: Stereotactic cingulotomy as a means of psychosurgery. 1985.

21. Valenstein ES. The practice of psychosurgery. A survey of the literature (1971–1976). In: *Appendix to psychosurgery*. New York: US Department of Health, Education, and Welfare publication no (OS) 77-00002, 1977;11–183.
22. Bouckoms AJ. Ethics of psychosurgery. *Acta Neurochir (Suppl)* 1988;44:173–178.
23. Fink M. *Convulsive therapy: Theory and practice*. New York: Raven Press, 1979.
24. Laitinen LV. Stereotactic lesions in the knee of the corpus callosum in the treatment of emotional disorders. *Lancet* 1972;1:472–475.
25. Mindus P, Myerson B. Aspects of personality in patients undergoing psychosurgical interventions. Paper presented at the Eurasian Academy of Neurological Surgery, Brussels, September 1987.
26. Knight GC. Bifrontal stereotactic tractotomy: An atraumatic operation of value in the treatment of intractable psychoneurosis. *Br J Psychiatry* 1969;115:257–266.
27. Strom-Olsen R, Carlisle S. Bifrontal stereotactic tractotomy: A follow-up of its effects on 210 patients. *Br J Psychiatry* 1971;118:141–154.
28. Goktepe EO, Young LB, Bridges PK. A further review of the results of stereotactic subcaudate tractotomy. *Br J Psychiatry* 1975;126:270–280.
29. Kleinig J. *Ethical issues in psychosurgery*. London: George Allen and Unwin, 1985.
30. Valenstein ES. *Great and desperate cures: The rise and decline of psychosurgery and other radical treatments for mental illness*. New York: Basic Books, 1986.

Subject Index

A

A-10 region, 45–46
Absolute resistance, 2
ACTH, 142–143
Adequate antidepressant trial, 3–5
Agranulocytosis, 158
Alcoholism, 195
Alpha-adrenoceptors
 antidepressant mechanisms, 30–34
 and beta-adrenoceptor downregulation, 109–112
Alpha-methyl-*p*-tyrosine, 136
Alprazolam, 4
Amitriptyline
 childhood depression, 53–54
 high plasma level problem, 95
 and MAOIs, combination, 118–120
Amphetamines
 heterogeneity of response, 173
 review of studies, 167–170
Anesthesia treatment, 223–230
Anterior capsulotomy, 239
Anticonvulsant drugs. *See also* Carbamazepine
 in bipolar illness, 194
 as lithium adjuncts, 155–162
Antidepressants. *See also specific drugs*
 adequate trial definition, 3–5
 mechanism of action, 23–37
 receptor effects, 26–35
 selectivity, 93–102
 and signal transduction, 13–19
Aplastic anemia, 158
Apnea, 83–85
Auditory evoked potentials, 76
Autoreceptors, 25–26

B

Baclofen, 34, 161
Behavioral sensitization, 142–144, 202
Beta-adrenoceptors
 antidepressant mechanisms, 30–34

 downregulation, 13–14, 32–33, 109–112
 imipramine/mianserin downregulation, 109–112
 and melatonin secretion, 32
Bipolar disorder. *See also* Rapid cycling
 behavioral sensitization role, 142–144
 and cyclothymia, 135
 electroconvulsive therapy, 161
 hypothalamic-pituitary-adrenal axis, 141–144
 lithium/anticonvulsant combination, 136, 147, 155–162
 lithium resistance, 132–136
 magnetic resonance imaging, 137–138
 novel therapies, 131–149
 pathophysiology, 137–138, 141–144
 phenomenology, 131–149
 stress role, 141–144
 timing of treatment, 161–162
Blood pressure, 126–127
Brief recurrent depression, 100–101
Bromocriptine, 41–42
Bupropion
 adrenergic effects, 31
 in bipolar disorder, 147
 hazards, 147
 unique mechanism, 36

C

Calcium channel blockers, 161
Capsulotomy, 239
Carbamazepine
 and ACTH response, 142
 in acute depression, 155–157, 194
 in affective states, 140, 194
 blood levels, 157
 dosage, 157
 drug combinations, 147
 and kindling, 202
 and lithium, 136, 147, 155–162
 onset of effect, 156, 158
 prophylactic use, 160

Carbamazepine (contd.)
   side effects, 157–160
   and thyroid hormone, 158–159
Carbon dioxide concentrations, 66, 69
Catatonia
   electroconvulsive therapy, 89–90
   lithium response, 135
Catecholamine hypothesis, 23–24, 30
Cerebral blood flow, 65–69
Cerebral disactivation hypothesis, 223–230
Chaotic systems, 196–197, 203–206
Characterological depression, 72
Childhood depression, 53–61
Chlorpromazine, 136
Cholinergic mechanisms, 35
Cingulotomy, 233–241
   ECT comparison, 238–239
   ethics, 240
   indications, 235–239
   side effects, 234–235
Circadian rhythms, 201–202, 205
Clifton Assessment Procedures for the Elderly, 181
Clomipramine
   drug combinations, 146
   efficacy, 99
   in obsessional depression, 100
   and tranylcypromine, hazards, 121
Clonazepam
   antimanic effects, 136–137
   in bipolar disorder, 161
Clonidine
   antidepressant interactions, 32
   in mania, 140
Clorgyline
   in bipolar disorder, 144–146
   dopamine effects, 42
Cognitive sequelae, cingulotomy, 235
Comorbidity, children, 54–55
Compliance, 74
Conditioned tolerance syndrome, 160
Corticotropin-releasing factor, 142
Cortisol hypersecretion
   bipolar disorder, 141–142
   neurotoxocity, 137
Cushing's syndrome, 137
Cyclothymia, 135

D
Daily Sleep Questionnaire, 82
Debrisoquine testing, 95–96
Delta sleep, 84
Delusional depression
   cingulotomy contraindications, 238
   as depression subtype, 99
   electroconvulsive therapy, 89, 100
   lithium, 180
   neuroleptic augmentation, 99–100
Deprenyl, 42
"Depressive core," 139
Desensitization of receptors, 27–28
Desipramine
   beta-adrenoceptor effects, 14–15, 33
   in childhood depression, 56–57
Dexamethasone suppression test
   as predictor, 9–10
   stress pathophysiology, 140–141
Dextroamphetamine, 168–169
Diabetes insipidus, 159
Disactivation hypothesis, 223–230
Dopamine
   antidepressant mechanisms, 34–35
   norepinephrine interactions, 45–46, 48–49
   potentiation of, 41–49
   serotonin interactions, 46–49
Dopamine agonists, 41–42
Dopamine receptors
   antidepressant effects, 42–44
   delusional depression, 100
   noradrenergic interactions, 45–46
Dorsal anterolateral prefrontal cortex, 69
Dosage
   adequacy criteria, 3–4
   and failure to respond, 94–97
Double depression
   definition, 72
   resistance to treatment, 101–102
Downregulation of receptors, 33
Drug dosage. *See* Dosage
DSM-III, 177
Duration of trials, 3–5
Dysphoric mania, 138–141
Dysthymia, 72, 101–102

E

Elderly
  auditory evoked potentials, 76
  cerebral aging, 76
  chronic depression incidence, 70–71
  electroconvulsive therapy, 178–179
  lithium augmentation, 177–182
  management, 178–179
  prognosis, depression, 177–178
  psychostimulant use, 167–174
Electrocerebral silence, 224–230
Electroconvulsive shock
  anticonvulsant effects, 161
  dopamine receptor effects, 43
Electroconvulsive therapy, 87–91
  adequate trial criteria, 4
  in bipolar disorder, 161
  caveats, 91
  cingulotomy comparison, 238–239
  delusional depression, 100
  dopamine effects, 42–44
  efficacy, 89–91
  in elderly, 178–179
  practical considerations, 91
  serotonin receptor density, 27
Estradiol, 212, 214
Estrogen, 209–216
  imipramine combination, 214–215
  monoamine oxidase effects, 210
  and mood, 212–213
  neurobiological effects, 209–211
  receptor effects, 211–212
  and tryptophan, 210–211
Evans ratio, 74–75
Evoked potentials, 76

F

Fenfluramine, 29
Flight of ideas, 135
Fluoxetine
  adequate trial criteria, 4
  drug combinations, dangers, 99, 121, 146
  plasma levels, 96–97
  serotonin receptor effects, 14–15
  tricyclic antidepressant enhancement, 105–107, 147
Fluoxetine enhancement, 105–107, 147

G

G proteins, 16–18
GABA receptors, 34
Geriatric patients. *See* Elderly
Glucocorticoid receptors, 16–19
Glucocorticoids, 13–19
GMS-AGECAT package, 177
Guanine nucleotide regulatory proteins, 16–18

H

Haloperidol, 136
Hamilton Depression Rating Scale, 7–8
HEADTOME, 65–69
5-HIAA (5-Hydroxyindoleacetic acid)
  in chronic depression, CSF, 73–76
  and enlarged ventricles, 75
  reserpine effect, 221–222
  treatment response predictor, 97–89
  tryptophan correlations, 73
  ventricular levels, 73
  visual evoked potential correlation, 76
5-HIAA/HVA ratio, 47–48
Homovanillic acid
  in cerebrospinal fluid, 44–49, 73–76
  evoked potential correlations, 76
  5-HIAA ratio, 47–48
  reserpine effect, 222
  ventricular levels, 73
Hounsfield units, 75
5-Hydroxyindoleacetic acid. *See* 5-HIAA
Hydroxylation, 95
5-Hydroxytryptophan, 29
Hypercortisolism. *See* Cortisol hypersecretion
Hypothalamic-pituitary-adrenal axis, 141–144
Hypothyroidism, 159, 192–193, 203

I

Idazoxam, 34, 147–148
Imipramine
  beta-adrenoceptor downregulation, 109–112
  childhood depression, 53–54, 56–57
  versus ECT, 89
  and estrogen, 214–215
  mianserin combination, 109–112

Imipramine binding
  estrogen effects, 211–212
  and serotonin receptor, 27
Indoleamine hypothesis, 23–24
Insomnia, 82, 84
Inventory of Psychic and Somatic
    Complaints in the Elderly, 171
Iprindole, 180
Iproniazid, 118
Isocarboxazid, 118, 120
Isoflurane, 223–230

K
Kindling
  bipolar disorder model, 143
  and carbamazepine, 160, 202
  and rapid cycling, 202
  timing of effects, 162

L
Late onset depression, 73
Left hemisphere hypoactivity, 67–69
Length of treatment, 94
LIFE assessment, 5
Life chart method, 5, 161–162
Light sensitivity, 202
Limbic surgery, 233–241
Lithium
  adequate trial criteria, 3–4
  anticonvulsant adjuncts, 155–162
  in bipolar disorder, resistance, 132–136
  in childhood depression, 57, 61
  in delusional depression, 180
  drug combinations, hazards, 146
  in elderly, 177–182
  prophylactic use, 132–133
  and rapid cycling, 133–134
  side effects, elderly, 180–181
Lithium augmentation
  adequacy of trial criteria, 4
  efficacy, 98
  in elderly, 177–182
  serotonin receptor effects, 29–30, 35–36

M
Magnetic resonance imaging, 137–138
Mania
  electroconvulsive therapy, 90
  lithium resistance, 134–136
  neuroleptics, 136
  novel therapies, 136–137
  and psychosis, outcome, 135–136
  stress role, 141
Maprotiline, 53–54
McLean Hospital Antidepressant
    Treatment Record, 5–10
Medically ill, 169–170
Medroxyprogesterone, 210, 214
Melatonin, 32–33
Menstrual cycle, 192
Mesolimbic system, 45
Methodology, 1–10
Methylphenidate, 168–169
MHPG levels
  metabolite interrelationships, 49
  as predictor, 9–10, 98
  reserpine effect, 222
Mianserin
  beta-adrenoceptor downregulation, 109–112
  childhood depression, 53–54
  imipramine combination, 109–112
  serotonin receptor density, 27
Mixed affective states, 138–141
Moclobemide, 146
Monoamine oxidase, and estrogen, 210–211
Monoamine oxidase inhibitors
  adequate trial criteria, 4
  bipolar disorder, 144–146
  dopamine receptor effects, 42–43
  drug combinations, 36
  high dosages, 123–128
  and psychostimulants, 169
  side effects, 125–128
  and tricyclics, combination, 115–121
Myoclonus, 84–85

N
Narcotherapy, 223–230
Neuroleptic augmentation
  in delusional depression, 99–100
  lithium, mania, 136
Neuropsychological sequelae,
    cingulotomy, 235
Newcastle cocktail, 98
Nocturnal myoclonus, 84–85

Subject Index

Nomifensine, 35–36
Noncompliance, 94
Noradrenergic mechanisms
   antidepressant action, 30–34
      dopamine interactions, 45–46
      serotonin-glucocorticoid links, 13–19
Norepinephrine uptake inhibitors, 97–98
Norfluoxetine, 96
Nortriptyline
   adequate trial criteria, 4
   childhood depression, 53–54
   high plasma level problem, 95
Norzimelidine, 96

O

Obsessional depression
   cingulotomy indication, 239
   serotonergic drugs, 100
Onset of illness, 72
Oral contraceptives, 215
Ortho-Novum, 215
Orthostatic blood pressure, 126

P

Pain, cingulotomy indication, 239
Parachlorophenylalanine, 29
Parietal cortex, 69
Paroxetine, 99
Pattern visual evoked potentials, 76
Pemoline, 170–173
Perphenazine, 100
Phenelzine
   in childhood depression, 53–54
   and tricyclics, combination, 118–120
Phenylephrine, 32
Phenytoin, 161
Pimozide, 136
Piribedil, 35, 41, 136
Plasma levels, and drug response, 95–96
Pneumoencephalography, 74–75
Polysomnography, 81–85
Postsynaptic receptors
   antidepressant action, 30–31
   neuronal mechanisms, 26
Premarin, 210, 214–215
Presynaptic receptors
   antidepressant action, 30–31
   and neuronal regulation, 25–26
Progabide, 161

Progesterone, 212
Progestins, 215–216
Prognostic index, 8
Prolactin, 28–29, 47
Propranolol, 33
Protein kinases, 16–18
Protooncogenes, 17
Protriptyline, 84
Provera, 210
Psychosis, and mania, lithium, 135–136
Psychostimulants
   combination therapies, 169
   in elderly, 167–174
   review of studies, 167–170
Psychosurgery, 233–241
Psychotic depression, 89
Pulse rate, 126

R

Racing thoughts, 139
Rapid cycling, 191–206
   antidepressants as cause, 192, 194
   chaotic systems, 196–197, 203–206
   circadian rhythms, 201–202
   clinical features, 191–206
   electroconvulsive therapy, 90
   estrogen association, 216
   extreme forms of, 139–140
   gender differences, 192, 197–198
   genetics, 194–195
   kindling, 202
   natural history, 193–194
   prevalence, 192
   resistance to lithium, 133–134
   temporal morphology, 195–197
   theories, 201–203
   thyroid hormones, 159, 192–193, 196–203
   timing of treatment, 162
   treatment, 191–206
Receptor desensitization, 27–28
Receptor downregulation, 33
Receptor sensitivity
   antidepressant action, 26–35
   estrogen effects, 211
Receptor supersensitivity, 27–28
Recurrent brief depression, 100–101
Regional cerebral blood flow, 65–69
Relative resistance, 2

REM latency, 83
Reserpine, 219–222
 beta-adrenoceptor regulation, 14–15
 and imipramine, 219–220
 neurobiology, 221–222
 review, 219–222
 side effects, 220–221
Reward mechanisms, 45–46

S

S-Adenosyl-methionine, 148
SCH-23390, 43
Schizophrenia, 90
Seasonal affective disorder, 201
Selectivity of antidepressants, 93–102
Sensitization. *See* Behavioral
  sensitization; Receptor sensitivity
Serotonergic drugs
 drug combinations, 98–99
 plasma levels, 96
 selectivity, 96–99
Serotonergic syndrome, 146
Serotonin
 dopamine interactions, 46–48
 neuronal mechanisms, 24–25
 norepinephrine-glucocorticoid links, 13–19
Serotonin receptors
 antidepressant effects, 26–30
 behavioral studies, 28
 beta-adrenoceptor interaction, 14–15
 clinical investigations, 28–29
 downregulation, 13–14
 electrophysiology, 27–28
 estrogen effects, 211–212
 lithium augmentation effects, 29–30, 35–36
 signal transduction systems, 16–18
Sex steroids. *See* Estrogen
Sleep apnea, 83–85
Sleep deprivation, 141
Sleep disturbances, 81–85
Sleep efficiency, 83
Sleep onset, 83
Sleep-wake cycle, 201
SPECT, 65–69
Spironolactone, 137
Stereotactic cingulotomy, 233–241

Stimulants. *See* Psychostimulants
Stress
 affective responses, 141
 and beta-adrenoceptor systems, 18
 in chaotic systems, 204–205
Subcaudate tractotomy, 239
Subcortical leukoencephalopathy, 138
Suicide
 and cingulotomy, 235
 in elderly, 178
 electroconvulsive therapy, 90
Superior frontal cortex, 69
Supersensitivity of receptors, 27–28

T

T_3. *See* Triiodothyronine
T_4. *See* Thyroxine
Tardive dyskinesia, 136
Testosterone, 212–213
Thought disorder, 135
Thyroid hormones
 antidepressant potentiation, 159–160, 185–188
 noradrenergic interactions, 203
 lithium-carbamazepine effects, 158–159
 in rapid cyclers, 159–160, 192–193, 198–203
 T_3 and T_4 differential effects, 187–188, 198–201
Thyroid potentiation, 159–160, 185–188
Thyrotropin (TSH), 158–159, 223, 228–229
Thyrotropin-release hormone, 223
Thyroxine (T_4)
 effects on brain, 187
 in rapid cyclers, 198–203
 versus T_3, 187–188, 198–201
Total sleep time, 83
Tranylcypromine
 and chlorimipramine, hazards, 121
 high dosages, 123–128
 side effects, 125–128
 and tricyclics, combination, 118, 121
Trazadone, 146
TRH test, 223, 228–229
Tricyclic antidepressants
 adequate trial definition, 3–5
 in delusional depression, 99–100

Subject Index

dopamine effects, 45
versus ECT, 89
fluoxetine enhancement, 105–107
and MAOIs, combination, 115–121
neuroleptic augmentation, 99–100
and psychostimulants, 169
thyroid hormone augmentation, 185–188
Triiodothyronine (T_3)
antidepressant augmentation, 185–188
and beta-adrenoceptors, 33, 37
effects on brain, 187
in rapid cyclers, 198–203
versus thyroxine, 187–188, 198–201
Trimipramine, 120
Tryptophan
depletion effect, 29
drug combinations, 98–99, 146
estrogen effects, 210–211
hazards, 146
5-HIAA correlations, 73
plasma and brain levels, 75
prolactin response, 28–29
Tryptophan free amino acid drink, 29
Tryptophan pyrrolase, 75

V
Valproic acid
in bipolar disorder, 161
and lithium, 136
Ventricular enlargement
bipolar disorder, 137
cortisol role, 137
monoamine metabolite levels, 73–76
Ventricular skull ratio, 74–75
Verapamil, 161
Visual imagery, cingulotomy, 234

W
Weekly Children's Depression Rating Scale, 57
Women, chronic depression incidence, 72

Y
Yohimbine
and beta-adrenoceptor hypothesis, 33
depressed patients response, 32–33

Z
Zimelidine, 96